Salesforce CRM - The Definitive Admin Handbook

Fourth Edition

Learn how to successfully administer, build, and manage Salesforce CRM and Salesforce mobile solutions using real-world and best practice techniques

Paul Goodey

BIRMINGHAM - MUMBAI

Salesforce CRM - The Definitive Admin Handbook

Fourth Edition

First published: October 2011

Second edition: July 2013

Third edition: January 2015

Fourth edition: December 2016

Production reference: 1141216

Published by Packt Publishing Ltd.

Livery Place
35 Livery Street
Birmingham
B3 2PB, UK.
ISBN 978-1-78646-896-3
www.packtpub.com

Credits

Author

Paul Goodey

Reviewer

Doug Ayers

Commissioning Editor

Aaron Lazar

Acquisition Editor

Denim Pinto

Content Development Editor

Priyanka Mehta

Technical Editor

Prathamesh Gokarn

Copy Editor

Safis Editing

Project Coordinator

Izzat Contractor

Proofreader

Safis Editing

Indexer

Pratik Shirodkar

Graphics

Abhinash Sahu

Production Coordinator

Deepika Naik

About the Author

Paul Goodey is the author of *Salesforce CRM Admin Cookbook*, published by Packt.

He has over 25 year's of experience developing web technology solutions for companies of all sizes across a variety of industries and has been building solutions with Salesforce CRM since 2006.

Paul has enjoyed a variety of roles while working with Salesforce CRM, having worked as a developer, business analyst, solutions architect, and system administrator to provide solutions for both in-house and consultancy-based end users.

Based near London in the UK,his professional qualifications include Salesforce Certified Administrator (ADM-201) and Salesforce Certified Developer (DEV-401). He is a keen and active member of Salesforce's administrator and developer online communities. He can be found on LinkedIn at `http://www.linkedin.com/in/paulgoodey`

In his spare time, Paul is an avid runner, having run several marathons and half marathons.

Acknowledgments

I have enjoyed working on the fourth edition of this book, and I am thankful to the many people who have helped in the creation of this work. First and foremost, I would like to thank you for purchasing this book. I sincerely hope you find it as enjoyable and useful to read as it has been to write. I would like to thank the team at Salesforce for providing me with the Salesforce CRM product. Salesforce products are easy and fun to work with and their solutions constantly innovate both the CRM and cloud computing industries. Next, I would like to thank everyone at Packt who has successfully produced the completed work. During the writing process, the team was thoroughly professional and highly supportive. My family and friends have also been very supportive; it is only with their help, patience, and endless cups of tea that I have been able to complete my part of this endeavor. Finally, I would like to thank everyone who has contributed with useful feedback and suggestions. Instead of trying to name them all and risk not mentioning others, I would like to thank all the Salesforce employees, professionals, and keen enthusiasts who help make the Salesforce community such a productive and collaborative environment. If you haven't participated in Salesforce's online user communities, such as `success.salesforce.com` (where you can post questions or ideas), developer.force.com, LinkedIn `salesforce.com` user groups, and Twitter (look out for hash tags #salesforce and #askforce), I strongly recommend them as they are a truly valuable place to discover and exchange information.

About the Reviewer

Doug Ayers is a multi-certified Salesforce MVP who loves learning and sharing his knowledge with others. Doug is passionate about helping others be successful on the Force.com platform and he does that by leading the Nashville Salesforce Users and Developers groups, answering #askforce questions on Twitter (@DouglasCAyers), contributing to open source projects via `https://github.com/douglascayers`, blogging on his website at `https://douglascayers.com`, and speaking at Dreamforce and other Salesforce conferences. He currently works as a Senior Developer with GearsCRM, a Salesforce Gold Partner.

Doug has served as technical reviewer for other Packt titles including *Salesforce Platform App Builder Certification Handbook* by Siddhesh Kabe.

www.PacktPub.com

For support files and downloads related to your book, please visit www.PacktPub.com.

Did you know that Packt offers eBook versions of every book published, with PDF and ePub files available? You can upgrade to the eBook version at www.PacktPub.com and as a print book customer, you are entitled to a discount on the eBook copy. Get in touch with us at service@packtpub.com for more details.

At www.PacktPub.com, you can also read a collection of free technical articles, sign up for a range of free newsletters and receive exclusive discounts and offers on Packt books and eBooks.

https://www.packtpub.com/mapt

Get the most in-demand software skills with Mapt. Mapt gives you full access to all Packt books and video courses, as well as industry-leading tools to help you plan your personal development and advance your career.

Why subscribe?

- Fully searchable across every book published by Packt
- Copy and paste, print, and bookmark content
- On demand and accessible via a web browser

Table of Contents

Preface

As an industry-leading **Customer Relationship Management (CRM)** application, Salesforce CRM helps enterprises, large and small, improve client relations. It greatly enhances sales performance and provides your business with a robust CRM system. In order to achieve optimum performance from the Salesforce CRM system, there are many areas for you as the Salesforce administrator to tackle. This is the only book that provides a comprehensive guide to the administrative aspects of Salesforce CRM.

This book will give you all the information you need to administer this powerful CRM application. It is the definitive guide for implementing Salesforce CRM. Whether you are looking to enhance the core features, or you have already started customizing your Salesforce CRM system and are looking for guidance on advanced features, this book will show you how to get the maximum benefit from this innovative product.

What this book covers

Chapter 1, *Setting up Salesforce CRM and the Organization Company profile*, shows you how to set up the organization-wide settings that affect the look and feel of the system and provide access to features for all users within the organization.

Chapter 2, *Managing Users and Controlling System Access*, describes how to manage and administer user records and password policies, and describes how profiles and permission sets affect the permissions of individual users.

Chapter 3, *Configuring Objects and Apps*, covers the various methods to configure and tailor the system to suit the way information is used within the organization through the use of objects and fields as well as providing a look at custom field governance.

Chapter 4, *Securing Access to Data Access and Data Validation*, looks in detail at the data access security models in Salesforce CRM and the multiple levels where data access and security can be applied at organization level, object level, field level, and record level.

Chapter 5, *Managing Data in Salesforce CRM*, describes the features for improving data quality through the use of data validation rules and dependent fields and outlines the facilities that are available for importing and exporting data to and from Salesforce CRM.

Chapter 6, *Generating Data Analytics with Reports and Dashboards*, discusses the analytics building blocks that are available within the Salesforce system and details the creation and use of reports and dashboards.

Chapter 7, *Implementing Business Processes in Salesforce CRM*, looks at the features and functionality to automate business workflow and approval mechanisms to automate, improve quality, and generate high-value processes within your organization.

Chapter 8, *Introducing Sales Cloud, Service Cloud, and the Collaborative Features of Salesforce CRM*, describes the core functional areas within Salesforce CRM, that enables Sales teams, Marketing teams, and Service teams to succeed and collaborate.

Chapter 9, *Extending and Enhancing Salesforce CRM*, shows how the standard functionality in the system can be extended and enhanced and describes how advanced customization and additional functionality can be added internally and externally using third-party apps.

Chapter 10, *Administrating the Mobile Features of Salesforce CRM*, looks at how mobile devices, which have become commonplace in both the personal and professional lives of users, can be used in Salesforce CRM and describes the mobile solution offerings provided by Salesforce.

Chapter 11, *Studying for the Certified Administrator Exam*, describes the Salesforce Certified Administrator exam and looks at resources, such as the classroom based training course ADM-201, that are available to prepare for the exam and offers insight into the types of questions and suggested planning for the exam.

What you need for this book

The prerequisite for this book is a computer with an Internet connection and one of these supported browsers: Google Chrome, Mozilla Firefox, Apple Safari, or Microsoft Internet Explorer. You will need either the Enterprise, Unlimited, Performance, or Developer edition of Salesforce CRM along with System Administrator permission.

Who this book is for

This book is for administrators who want to develop and strengthen their Salesforce CRM skills in the areas of configuration and system management. Whether you are a novice or a more experienced admin, this book aims to enhance your knowledge and understanding of the Salesforce CRM platform. By the end of the book, you will be ready to configure and administer Salesforce CRM and Salesforce mobile solutions in a real-world environment that fully supports your business needs.

Conventions

In this book, you will find a number of styles of text that distinguish between different kinds of information. Here are some examples of these styles, and an explanation of their meaning.

Code words in text, database table names, folder names, filenames, file extensions, pathnames, dummy URLs, user input, and Twitter handles are shown as follows:

Salesforce provides a set of standard, prebuilt components, such as `<apex:actionFunction>` and `<apex:actionStatus>`.

A block of code is set as follows:

```
var address =
"{!SUBSTITUTE(JSENCODE(Account.BillingStreet),'\r\n','
')}, " +
"{!Account.BillingCity}, " +
"{!Account.BillingPostalCode}, " +
"{!Account.BillingCountry}";
```

New terms and important words are shown in bold. Words that you see on the screen, in menus or dialog boxes for example, appear in the text like this: Navigate to the **Accounts** tab and select an existing account.

Warnings or important notes appear in a box like this.

 Tips and tricks appear like this.

Reader feedback

Feedback from our readers is always welcome. Let us know what you think about this book—what you liked or may have disliked. Reader feedback is important for us to develop titles that you really get the most out of.

To send us general feedback, simply send an e-mail to feedback@packtpub.com, and mention the book title via the subject of your message.

If there is a topic that you have expertise in and you are interested in either writing or contributing to a book, see our author guide on www.packtpub.com/authors.

Customer support

Now that you are the proud owner of a Packt book, we have a number of things to help you to get the most from your purchase.

Downloading the color images of this book

We also provide you with a PDF file that has color images of the screenshots/diagrams used in this book. The color images will help you better understand the changes in the output. You can download this file from: https://www.packtpub.com/sites/default/files/downloads/SalesforceCRMTheDefinitiveAdminHandbookFourthEdition_ColorImages.pdf

Errata

Although we have taken every care to ensure the accuracy of our content, mistakes do happen. If you find a mistake in one of our books—maybe a mistake in the text or the code—we would be grateful if you would report this to us. By doing so, you can save other readers from frustration and help us improve subsequent versions of this book. If you find any errata, please report them by visiting http://www.packtpub.com/submit-errata, selecting your book, clicking on the errata submission form link, and entering the details of your errata. Once your errata are verified, your submission will be accepted and the errata will be uploaded on our website, or added to any list of existing errata, under the Errata section of that title.

To view the previously submitted errata, go to https://www.packtpub.com/books/content/support and enter the name of the book in the search field. The required information will appear under the Errata section.

Piracy

Piracy of copyright material on the Internet is an ongoing problem across all media. At Packt, we take the protection of our copyright and licenses very seriously. If you come across any illegal copies of our works, in any form, on the Internet, please provide us with the location address or website name immediately so that we can pursue a remedy.

Please contact us at copyright@packtpub.com with a link to the suspected pirated material.

We appreciate your help in protecting our authors, and our ability to bring you valuable content.

Questions

You can contact us at questions@packtpub.com if you are having a problem with any aspect of the book, and we will do our best to address it.

1
Setting up Salesforce CRM and the Company Profile

Application security is always important, and even more so when the application is delivered across a public network, such as the Internet. `Salesforce.com` has developed various mechanisms to secure the platform and reduce the chances of unauthorized people accessing your company data. This chapter describes the way login attempts to the system are controlled and the features available to help you manage your user's access to the Salesforce CRM application.

In this chapter, we will also look at establishing your company profile within Salesforce and how core information, such as the details that are provided when your company first signs up with `Salesforce.com`, can be managed. You will also be shown how to find your way around the Salesforce Setup menu, and will be introduced to the settings available for the organization-wide customization of the application's user interface along with the search facilities offered by the Salesforce CRM application.

Finally, you will be presented with a number of questions about the key features of Salesforce CRM administration in the areas of organization setup and the global user interface, which are covered in this chapter.

Throughout this chapter, notes and tips are provided to offer further guidance within the given areas of functionality; and have been generated from the practical results and experience of the Salesforce CRM system administration.

In this chapter, we will cover:

- The Salesforce setup menu
- User login and authorization
- Company profiles
- User interface
- Search overview and settings
- Questions to test your knowledge

To start with, we will look at the location and the features of the Salesforce Setup menu.

The Salesforce Setup menu

Depending upon your organization's user interface settings, you will access the **Setup** menu from either the drop-down menu under your name or as a top-level setup link, as shown in the following screenshot.

Looking at the top of the Salesforce page you should see the **Setup** link, as shown in the following screenshot:

If you do not see the Setup link at the top of the Salesforce page then click on your name and you will then see the setup option, as shown in the following screenshot:

This setting is controlled by the **Enable Improved Setup User Interface** setting, which is covered later in this chapter.

As a system administrator, you will use the **Setup** menu so frequently that it is recommended that you enable **Improved Setup User Interface**.The **Improved Setup User Interface** setting is activated by default for all new instances. Existing Salesforce instance admins should be aware that this user interface setting determines how everyone in your organization accesses the **Setup** menu.

When describing any setup steps within this book, we will begin the navigation path from **Setup**. For example, to enable the **Improved Setup User Interface**, we will present the navigation path as **Setup** | **Customize** | **User Interface** | **Enable Improved Setup User Interface**.

The **Setup** menu appears on the left side of the page. Clicking the menu option text, (or the drop-down icon to the left of a menu option), expands the menu where you can then select the required menu item link; the following screenshot shows the **Setup** | **Manage Users** | **Users** setup page:

![Screenshot of the Salesforce Setup Manage Users Users page showing the Demo user list with columns for Action, Full Name, Alias, Username, Last Login, Role, Active, Profile, and Manager.]

Clicking the down arrow icon to the left of the expanded menu option collapses the menu option. You can also expand or collapse all the menu options by clicking the **Expand All** or **Collapse All** links as shown in the following screenshot:

To quickly find a **Setup** menu item, type the first few characters of the setup name in the **Quick Find** search box. As you type, any options that match your search term appear in the Setup menu. For example, to find the User Interface page, start to type user interface in the **Quick Find** box as shown in the following screenshot:

We will now look at how user's login requests are verified and authorized by the Salesforce CRM application.

User login and authorization

Organizations have several methods of accessing the Salesforce CRM application. Access can be gained from the user interface (using a web browser), the API (for example, using an integrated client application or the Apex Data Loader), a desktop client (for example, Salesforce for Outlook), or from a mobile client application.

Whenever a login attempt is made to Salesforce using any of these methods, the user's login request is authorized by the system using the following sequence of checks:

- Does the user's profile have any login restrictions?
- Does the user's IP address appear within the organization's trusted IP address list?
- Has the user been activated from this IP address before?
- Does the user's web browser have a valid browser cookie from Salesforce stored?

If the user's login is from neither a trusted IP address nor a browser with a valid Salesforce cookie, the login is denied. To gain access to Salesforce, the user's identity must be confirmed by successfully completing the computer activation process.

Now let's look at each of these login checks in more detail.

Does the user's profile have any login restrictions?

Login hours and IP address restrictions can be set for the user's profile. If these are set and there are login attempts from a user outside the specified hours or from an unknown IP address, access is denied.

Login hour restrictions

If login hour restrictions are set for the user's profile, any login attempt outside the specified hours is denied.

1. To go to the **Profile** menu, navigate to **Setup** | **Manage Users** | **Profiles**. Now choose a profile, select the **Login Hours** link, and then click **Edit**.

Set the days and hours when users with this profile can log in to Salesforce.com.

The login hours that are set are based on the default time zone of the organization, as described later in this chapter.

2. Navigate to **Setup** | **Company Profile** | **Company Information**, click the **Edit** button, and select the required time zone from the **Default Time Zone** picklist.

The login hours that are set apply strictly to that exact time, even if a user has a different personal time zone or if the organization's default time zone is changed.

3. To allow users to log in at any time, click on **Clear times** as shown in the following screenshot:

Profile			

Custom: Sales Profile   Help for this Page ⓘ

🔍 Find Settings... ✖ | Clone Delete Edit Properties

Profile Overview > **Login Hours** ▾

Login Hours   Save Cancel

All times are in (GMT-04:00) Eastern Daylight Time (America/New_York)

Day	Start Time	End Time	
Monday	--None-- ▾	--None-- ▾	Clear times
Tuesday	--None-- ▾	--None-- ▾	Clear times
Wednesday	--None-- ▾	--None-- ▾	Clear times
Thursday	--None-- ▾	--None-- ▾	Clear times
Friday	--None-- ▾	--None-- ▾	Clear times
Saturday	8:00 AM ▾	8:00 AM ▾	Clear times
Sunday	8:00 AM ▾	8:00 AM ▾	Clear times

Clear all times

To prevent users from accessing the system on a specific day, (say, to carry out internal system maintenance), set the Start Time and End Time to the same value. For example, you could set the Start Time to 8:00 AM and End Time to 8:00 AM (as in the Saturday and Sunday example setting in the previous screenshot).

IP address restrictions

If IP address restrictions are defined for the user's profile, any login attempt from an unknown IP address is denied.

To restrict the range of valid IP addresses through the **Profile** menu, navigate to **Setup** | **ManageUsers** | **Profiles**. Now choose a profile, select the **Login IP Ranges** link, and then click **Add IP Ranges**.

Enter a valid IP address in the **Start IP Address** field and a higher IP address in the **End IP Address** field.

The start and end addresses specify the range of IP addresses from which users can log in. To allow a login from a single IP address, enter the same address in both fields.

For example, to allow a login from only `88.110.54.113`, enter `88.110.54.113` as both the start and end IP addresses as shown in the following screenshot:

Does the user's IP address appear within your organization's trusted IP address list?

This check is performed if profile-based IP address restrictions are not set.

If the user's login is from an IP address listed in your organization's trusted IP address list, the login is allowed.

Trusted IP range

To go to the Trusted IP range settings, navigate to **Setup** | **Security Controls** | **Network Access**.

Click on **New** and enter a valid IP address in the **Start IP Address** field and a higher IP address in the **End IP Address** field.

The start and end addresses specify the range of IP addresses from which users can log in. To allow a login from a single IP address, enter the same address in both fields.

For example, to allow a login from only 88.110.54.100, enter 88.110.54.105 as both the start and end addresses as shown in the following screenshot:

Has the user been activated from this IP address before?

Each user has a list of IP addresses from which they've been activated. If the user has previously been activated from this IP address, then this IP address is added to the user's personal list.

To view and remove the login IP addresses that have been recorded by your users, go to **Setup** | **Security Controls** | **Activations**.

To remove an **Activated Login IP**, click the checkbox and then click the **Remove** button, as shown in the following screenshot:

Activated Login IP

Help for this Page

The list below shows login IP addresses representing the device IP addresses that have been activated by a user.

View: All ▾ Create New View

<Previous Page | Next Page>

A B C D E F G H I J K L M N O P Q R S T U V W X Y Z Other **All**

Remove

	Username ↑	Login IP	Created Date	Is Authenticated	Challenge Sent
☐	sales@widgetsxyz.com	81.178.189.173	28.01.2014 17:37	✓	28.01.2014 17:37
☐	sales@widgetsxyz.com	82.12.148.221	28.05.2014 22:21	✓	
☐	sales@widgetsxyz.com	31.100.158.80	11.06.2014 08:18	✓	11.06.2014 08:18
☐	trevor.howard@widgetsxyz.com	80.47.223.92	01.01.2010 11:14	✓	
☐	trevor.howard@widgetsxyz.com	80.47.236.99	18.02.2010 05:44	✓	18.02.2010 05:44
☐	trevor.howard@widgetsxyz.com	88.110.54.113	01.01.2011 12:04	✓	01.01.2011 12:04
☐	trevor.howard@widgetsxyz.com	81.178.188.171	31.01.2011 02:44	✓	31.01.2011 02:44
☐	trevor.howard@widgetsxyz.com	81.178.177.167	23.07.2011 14:15	✓	23.07.2011 14:17
☐	trevor.howard@widgetsxyz.com	81.178.189.7	21.04.2013 21:59	✓	21.04.2013 22:00
☐	trevor.howard@widgetsxyz.com	82.12.148.221	02.07.2014 20:38	✓	02.07.2014 20:38

Activated Client Browsers

Help for this Page

The list below shows Activated Client Browser information, with the browser agent information stored when a user accesses an organization from an activated device IP address.

View: All ▾ Create New View

A B C D E F G H I J K L M N O P Q R S T U V W X Y Z Other **All**

Remove

	Username ↑	User Agent String	Proxy Info	Created Date	Last Update
☐	sales@widgetsxyz.com	Mozilla/5.0 (Windows NT 6.1; WOW64) AppleWebKit/537.36 (KHTML, like Gecko) Chrome/35.0.1916.153 Safari/537.36		28.01.2014 17:38	02.07.2014 20:43
☐	sales@widgetsxyz.com	Mozilla/5.0 (Macintosh; Intel Mac OS X 10_8_5) AppleWebKit/537.36 (KHTML, like Gecko) Chrome/35.0.1916.114 Safari/537.36		11.06.2014 08:21	11.06.2014 08:21
☐	trevor.howard@widgetsxyz.com	Mozilla/5.0 (Windows NT 6.1; WOW64) AppleWebKit/537.36 (KHTML, like Gecko) Chrome/35.0.1916.153 Safari/537.36		02.07.2014 20:43	02.07.2014 20:43

To remove an Activated Login IP, click the checkbox and then click the Remove button, as shown in the screenshot above.

Does the user's web browser have a valid cookie stored from Salesforce?

A cookie is a small file containing a string of characters that is sent to your computer when you visit a website. Whenever you visit the website again, the cookie allows that site to recognize your web browser.

The browser will have the Salesforce cookie if the user has previously used that browser to log in to Salesforce and has not cleared the browser cookies.

So, if the user's login is from a browser that includes a `Salesforce.com` cookie, the login is allowed

Computer activation process

If the user's login is from neither a trusted IP address nor a browser with a Salesforce cookie, the login is denied and becomes blocked, and Salesforce must verify the user's identity.

A trusted, genuine user can access the Salesforce CRM application using the following means:

- User interface (using a web browser)
- API (for example, using an integrated client application or the Apex Data Loader)
- Desktop client (for example, Salesforce for Outlook)

User interface

For access through the user interface for the first time, the user is prompted to select how they would like to receive the verification code. Here, the verification code can be received by either an SMS text message or an e-mail message depending on whether the company-wide SMS-based identity confirmation is enabled.

For new organizations, an SMS text message is the default method for the computer activation process and can only be disabled by a request to Salesforce support. For existing organizations, SMS text message activation can be enabled by you as the system administrator, but once enabled it requires a request to Salesforce support is required to deactivate it.

SMS text message verification code

To receive the SMS text message verification code requires the setting **SMS-Based Identity Confirmation** setting to be enabled (since Spring '2014, it has been enabled by default). This feature enables users to receive a one-time PIN delivered via SMS. This is set by navigating to **Setup | Security Controls | Session Settings** and then enabling **Enable SMS-Based Identity Confirmation**.

Once enabled, users must verify their mobile phone number before taking advantage of this feature, which will present the following screenshot:

Email message verification code

To receive an email verification code, users must have the setting **Email-Based Identity Confirmation Option** enabled on their profile or included as a permission set.

The **Email-Based Identity Confirmation** option is only available to set if the **Enable SMS-Based Identity Confirmation** option is enabled.

Once enabled, and if verification is required, users will automatically receive an activation e-mail to the address specified in the user's Salesforce user record. Users are notified within the Salesforce, and can enter the verification code as shown in the following screenshot:

Verify Your Identity

You're trying to **Log In to Salesforce**. To make sure your Salesforce account is secure, we have to verify your identity.

Enter the verification code we emailed to ·
********@******.com.

Verification Code

[   ]

Verify

☑ Don't ask again

Resend Code

Salesforce sends the verification code e-mail to the e-mail address associated with the user's record in Salesforce. Here, the following screenshot shows an e-mail example:

```
New    Reply  Reply all  Forward   |   Delete  Junk  Sweep ▾  Mark as ▾  Move to ▾   |   🖨 ⟳

Your salesforce.com Activation Email                          Back to messages   ⬇ ⬆

   ⊟ support@salesforce.com   Add to contacts                              07:45  🏳
     To                                                                   Reply ▾
                                                                          ▽

   Dear

   You have requested access to salesforce.com from an unknown device. Use the verification code
   below within 24 hours to activate this device.

   ┌──────────────────────────────────┐
   │ Verification Code: 83295          │
   └──────────────────────────────────┘

   IMPORTANT: If you have not requested to activate a device, or believe you have received this
   message in error, please contact salesforce.com support (support@salesforce.com) immediately.

   What does "activation" mean? Should I activate this computer?

   Activation helps reduce the risk of security issues related to login. Activating this computer
   helps salesforce.com recognize this computer when you use it to access salesforce.com. You
   should activate this computer if it is owned by you or your employer and you are confident it is
   free of malware.
```

The e-mail instructs the user to enter the verification code into the browser window, which activates the device for verified login into the Salesforce CRM platform.

The activation code within the e-mail is valid for up to 24 hours from the time the **E-mail me a verification code** button was clicked. After 24 hours, the activation link will expire and the user must repeat the activation process.

Confusion can occur if your company has remote users that connect to Salesforce away from the company network, such as from home or from public Internet connections. The Remote users are likely to have dynamically assigned IP addresses set as their computer identity. Because of this, whenever they attempt to log in, Salesforce will identify it as an unknown IP address, prompt for verification, and the remote user will have to re-verify the device.

The remote user will then have to access the e-mail associated with their Salesforce user record to retrieve the activation e-mail, and it is here where confusion can occur. If the remote user has to access corporate web e-mail using a **Virtual Private Network (VPN)** connection, the clicking of the activation link may not work because the IP address that is being validated may now no longer be the same IP address used by the browser. This is because the VPN connection may likely be using a web proxy.

 It is recommended that you establish a policy to ensure that the user verifies the login while connected to the VPN, or can access non-VPN-based web mail (if this is permitted in your company) to ensure that the validated IP addresses are the same.

(This is covered in more detail in the *Session settings* section in Chapter 2, *Managing Users and Controlling System Access*.)

API or a desktop client

For access using the API or a desktop client (for example, using the Apex Data Loader), the user must add their security token at the end of the password in order to log in. A security token is an automatically generated key from Salesforce. For example, if a user's password is pa$$word, and their security token is XXXXXX, then the user must enter pa$$wordXXXXXX.

Users can obtain their security token by changing their password, or by resetting their security token via the Salesforce.com user interface by navigating to **Your Name** | **My Settings** | **Personal** | **Reset My Security Token** and then clicking on the **Reset Security Token** button.

When a user changes their password or resets their security token, Salesforce sends a new security token to the e-mail address associated with their Salesforce user record. The security token is valid until a user resets their security token, changes their password, or has their password reset by a system administrator.

 Do not enter a security token within your password when accessing Salesforce from a web browser. It is recommended that you obtain your security token via the Salesforce user interface from a trusted network prior to attempting access from a new IP address. When a user's password is changed, the user's security token is automatically reset. The user will experience a blocked login until they add the security token to the end of their password or enter the new password after you have added their IP address to the organization's trusted IP range.

Establishing your company profile within Salesforce

The company profile contains core information for your organization within Salesforce, some of which is captured during the initial system sign-up, and includes the following:

- Company information and primary contact details
- Default language, locale, and time zone
- License information
- Fiscal year settings
- Currencies and exchange rates

Company information and primary contact details

When your company signs up with Salesforce, the information provided is displayed on the **Company Information** page. This page can be accessed by navigating to **Setup | Company Profile | Company Information**.

From the **Company Information** page, you can edit the company default localization settings and primary contact details as shown in the following screenshot:

Company Information	Help for this Page

WidgetsXYZ

The organization's profile is below.

User Licenses [13] | Permission Set Licenses [1] | Feature Licenses [10]

Organization Detail   [Edit] [Currency Setup]

Organization Name	WidgetsXYZ	Phone	555-123-5678
Primary Contact	Martin Brown	Fax	555-123-5679
Division	ICT	Default Locale	English (United States)
Address	5 East 345th Street New York, NY 55511 US	Default Language	English
Fiscal Year Starts In	January	Default Time Zone	(GMT-04:00) Eastern Daylight Time (America/New_York)
Newsletter	☐	Currency Locale	English (United States)
Admin Newsletter	☐	Used Data Space	842 KB (4%) [View]
Hide Notices About System Maintenance	☐	Used File Space	302 KB (1%) [View]
Hide Notices About System Downtime	☐	API Requests, Last 24 Hours	0 (5,000 max)
		Streaming API Events, Last 24 Hours	0 (10,000 max)
		Restricted Logins, Current Month	0 (0 max)
		Salesforce.com Organization ID	00DA0000000IIs1
Created By	Paul Goodey, 19/12/2009 13:01	Modified By	Paul Goodey, 14/08/2011 11:43

[Edit]

Default language, locale, and time zone

The company information settings for language, locale, and time zone can affect how key data is handled for the organization.

However, individual users can set their own language, locale, and time zone, overriding the organization-wide setting, by navigating to **Your Name** | **My Settings** | **Personal** | **Language & Time Zone** as shown in the following screenshot:

| Home | Chatter | Leads | Accounts | Contacts | Reports | Campaigns | Dashboards | Opportunities | + | ▼ |

Language & Time Zone Help for this Page

My Settings

👤 Personal

Personal Information

Change My Password

Language & Time Zone

Grant Account Login Access

Settings | = Required Information

Time Zone | (GMT-04:00) Eastern Daylight Time (America/New_York) ▼

Locale | English (United States) ▼

Language | English ▼

Email Encoding | General US & Western Europe (ISO-8859-1, ISO-LATIN-1) ▼

Save Cancel

Default language

This is the primary language for the organization. All interface text and online help is displayed in this language. Individual users can, however, set their own language, which will override the organization-wide setting.

For global organizations, it is recommended that you consider how the setting the language impacts the user's ability to access and share information, and whether a common language is preferred to aid reporting and system administration. You can use the feature called **Language Settings** (described later) to restrict the languages that your users can set in their personal information language setting.

Default locale

The default locale setting affects the format of the date, date/time, and number fields.

For example, a given date in the **English (United States)** locale would appear as **07/27/2020**, and in the **English (United Kingdom)** locale as **27/07/2020**.

Time in the **English (United States)** locale is displayed using a twelve-hour clock with AM and PM (for example, **3:00 PM**), whereas in the **English (United Kingdom)** locale, they display using a twenty-four hour clock (for example, **15:00**).

Numbers in the **English (United States)** locale would be displayed as **1,000.00** and in the **German** locale as **1.000,00**.

However, individual users can set their own locale, which will override the organization-wide setting.

Default time zone

This is the primary time zone in which your organization is located, for example, the head-office location. However, individual users can set their own time zone, which will override the organization-wide setting.

The **Company Information** page also displays all of the base licenses, active users, and feature licenses that have been purchased by your organization.

License information

There are four types of licenses:

- **User license**: A user license entitles a user to different functionality within Salesforce and determines the profiles available to the user
- **Feature license**: A feature license entitles a user to an additional Salesforce feature, such as Marketing or Offline User
- **Permission set license**: A permission set license is used to provide a user with access to certain features that are not part of their user licenses
- **Usage-based entitlements**: A usage-based entitlement provides periodic use of a limited resource

 Salesforce bills an organization based on the total number of licenses and not on the number of active users.

Currencies and conversion rates

Currency settings are organization-wide within Salesforce, and can be set using either a single currency option, using the **Currency Locale** setting in **Company Profile**, or as a multiple currencies option where you can add currencies and set conversion rates using the **Manage Currencies** link within the **Company Profile** section.

Multiple currencies can only be enabled by a request to Salesforce customer support. When activated, the **Currency Locale** field and its value are passed to a new field, **Corporate Currency**, also in **Company Profile**.

The corporate currency reflects the currency in which your company reports revenue, and is used as the rate that all other currency conversion rates are based on. This is initially set by `Salesforce.com` when the Salesforce application is activated.

All organizations, whether using single or multiple currencies, are set by default with only one currency in the Company Profile. For single currency instances, this setting is accessed by navigating to **Setup** | **Company Profile** | **Company Information**, and setting the **Currency Locale** field. For multiple currencies, this is set by navigating to **Setup** | **Company Profile** | **Manage Currencies**, and then clicking the **Change Corporate** button.

Single currency

In a single-currency organization, you set the organization-wide currency locale for your company and your Salesforce users cannot set individual currency locales.

Multiple currencies

In a multiple-currency organization, you set the corporate currency instead of the currency locale, and your Salesforce users can also set their individual currency by navigating to **Your Name** | **My Settings** | **Personal** | **Personal Information**.

 Multiple Currencies activation is available by a request to Salesforce customer support.

Your Salesforce user's individual currency is used as the default currency in their own reports, quotas, forecasts, and any records that contain currency amounts, such as opportunities.

 Currency becomes a required field on records where it has been added or was originally defined, and so must be considered when activating the **Multiple Currencies** option and then importing data or a custom object creation.

Users can also create opportunities (and all other data records that contain currency amounts) using any other available active currency.

Only active currencies can be used in currency amount fields.

Active Currencies

The list of active currencies represents the countries or regions in which your company trades. Only an active currency can be set by you, as the system administrator on the organization profile, or by your users on their individual user records or on data records in the currency field.

Manage Currencies

The Manage Currencies section enables you to maintain a list of active currencies and their conversion rates in relation to the corporate currency, and can be accessed by navigating to **Setup** | **Company Profile** | **Manage Currencies**.

The **Manage Currencies** option appears when your organization has enabled **Multiple Currencies**, currently available by request to Salesforce customer support. Changing the conversion rates will update all existing records with the new conversion rates, even the closed opportunities. As a result, you will not be able to measure financial changes due to the effects of currency fluctuations unless you have implemented Advanced Currency Management, which stores dated exchange rates.

If multi-currency has been enabled and the currency is changed on a record using the Data Loader, the currency amounts are converted.

The currency of records can be changed using Data Loader by updating the standard field **Currency ISO Code** and setting the value to the ISO code of the new currency. Here the ISO code is a three-letter alphanumeric such as USD for US Dollars, EUR for Euros, GBP for British Pounds, and so on

If multi-currency has been enabled and the currency is changed on a record using the browser interface, the currency amounts are not converted.

The currency of records can be changed using the browser interface by updating the currency lookup but the currency amount is not converted. Therefore, if you change the currency of an opportunity which has a 450 EUR amount to GBP, the amount remains at 450 and is not converted to 384 GBP (which is 1 EUR = 0,852 GBP at the time of writing).

Dated exchange rates

Dated exchange rates allow you to track conversion rates when an opportunity closes, enabling the accurate reporting of opportunity-converted amounts based on the rate that was set at the opportunity's close date. This is made possible because the historic conversion rates are stored, and rate changes after that close date can be tracked; therefore, reports can include the opportunity amount based on the conversion rate at the close date instead of the rate at the time that the report is run.

Updating currency conversion rates will not change the original opportunity amounts, only the converted amounts. Accounts and their associated contacts must use the same default currency. Account and contact records may be imported using active or inactive currencies. However, importing lead records must use active currencies only.

Dated exchange rates are activated by setting the **Advanced Currency Management** option, and are used for opportunities, opportunity products, opportunity product schedules, campaign opportunity fields, and reports related to these objects and fields.

Dated exchange rates are not currently used in forecasting.

When **Advanced Currency Management** is first enabled, your existing exchange rates automatically become the first set of dated exchange rates.

These exchange rates will be valid until you set another set of exchange rates by navigating to **Setup** | **Company Profile** | **Manage Currencies** | **Manage Dated Exchange Rates**.

If you enable **Advanced Currency Management**, you cannot create roll-up summary fields that calculate the currency on the opportunity object. Any existing currency-related roll-up summary fields on the opportunity object will be disabled and their values will no longer be calculated.

Fiscal year settings

The fiscal year settings in Salesforce can be set by navigating to **Setup** | **Company Profile** | **Fiscal Year**.

Standard fiscal years

Fiscal year settings in Salesforce by default use the Gregorian calendar year (twelve-month structure) starting from January 1 and ending on December 31. If your organization follows the twelve-month structure, you can use a standard fiscal year. Standard fiscal years can start on the first day of any month, and you can specify whether the fiscal year is named for the starting or ending year. For example, if your fiscal year starts in April 2020 and ends in March 2021, your fiscal year setting can be either 2020 or 2021.

Custom fiscal years

Fiscal year is more complicated than this, you can define these periods using custom fiscal years. For example, as part of a custom fiscal year, you can create a 13-week quarter represented by three periods of 4, 4, and 5 weeks, instead of calendar months.

If you use a fiscal year structure, such as a 4-4-5 or a 13-period structure, you can define a fiscal year by specifying a start date and an included template. If your fiscal year structure is not included in the templates, you can modify a template. For example, if you use three fiscal quarters per year (a trimester) instead of four, delete or modify the quarters and periods to meet your needs. These custom fiscal periods can be named based on your standards. For example, a fiscal period could be called **P12** or December.

Fiscal years can be modified any time you need to change their definition. For example, an extra week could be added to synchronize a custom fiscal year with a standard calendar in a leap year. Changes to fiscal year structure take effect immediately upon being saved.

Language settings

The **Language Settings** feature allows you to specify the acceptable languages that can be used within the Salesforce CRM application.

This feature can be set by navigating to **Setup** | **Company Profile** | **Language Settings**.

You then choose the languages that you want to make available to users by selecting them from the **Available Languages** pick list and then clicking on **Add**.

In the following example, we have added**Spanish** and **French** along with **English**, and these appear in the **Displayed Languages** list as shown in the following screenshot:

Language Settings

Help for this Page ?

Language Preferences

☐ Enable End User Languages - Help and Admin Setup are not translated in End User Languages

Spanish (Mexican), Hungarian, Polish, Czech, Turkish, Indonesian, Romanian, Vietnamese, Ukrainian, Hebrew, Greek, Bulgarian, English (UK), Arabic, Norwegian

☐ Enable Platform Only Languages - No default translations are provided for Platform Languages

French (Canadian), Georgian, Serbian (Cyrillic), Serbian (Latin), Slovak, English (Australian), English (Malaysian), English (Indian), English (Phillipines), English (Canadian), Slovene, Romanian (Moldovan), Croatian, Bosnian, Macedonian, Latvian, Lithuanian, Estonian, Albanian, Montenegrin, Maltese, Irish, Basque, Welsh, Icelandic, Portuguese (European), Malay, Tagalog, Luxembourgish, Romansh, Armenian, Hindi, Urdu

Add or remove languages from the Available Language list

Available Languages

German
Italian
Japanese
Swedish
Korean
Chinese (Traditional)
Chinese (Simplified)
Portuguese (Brazilian)
Dutch
Danish
Thai
Finnish
Russian

Add ▶
Remove ◀

Displayed Languages

English
Spanish
French

Top ⊼
Up ▲
Down ▼
Bottom ⊻

Languages that appear in gray are currently used by your company, users, or both. They cannot be deactivated.

Save   Cancel

The languages that appear in the **Displayed Languages** list are now shown as available options in the **Language** picklist section on the user's **Personal Settings** page, as shown in the following screenshot:

User interface and supported browsers

At the time of writing there are three user interface themes. There are two classic themes, namely **Classic 2005** and **Classic 2010**, and there is a new theme called **Lightning Experience**.

Browser support and functionality varies depending on whether Salesforce Classic or Lightning Experience is used, and are described in more detail later on in this section.

User interface

All screenshots and setup details this book shows the Classic 2010 user interface theme.

The difference in the classic themes can be seen in the following screenshot, which appears when you attempt to change from the Classic 2005 to Classic 2010:

Browser Support Warning for the Salesforce Classic 2010 User Interface Theme ⊠

⚠ **Just so you know...**
Enabling the 2010 user interface theme affects the look and feel of Salesforce Classic for all users, but not all browsers can display this interface. **Unsupported browsers display the Salesforce Classic 2005 user interface theme theme, shown on the left below.**

2005 Theme   **2010 Theme**

For a consistent experience in your org, all users should upgrade to the latest version of a supported browser:

- Firefox
- Safari
- Internet Explorer
- Chrome

OK

Not only does the new user interface theme change the look and feel of Salesforce, but it may also position some key links such as **Setup** and **Logout** under the user name for each user in your organization. The Classic 2010 user interface theme is only available for use by users with supported browsers as detailed later in the *Supported browsers* section.

Some newer functional areas, for example **Chatter** (a collaboration application suite), are dependent on the Classic 2010 and Lightning Experience themes and cannot be provided when the Classic 2005 theme is activated. Therefore, to enable Chatter, you must first activate the Classic 2010 theme.

Supported browsers

At the time of writing there are three different user interface themes namely: Salesforce Classic 2005, Salesforce Classic 2010, and Lightning Experience. The Browser support for these themes at the time of writing is as follows.

Salesforce Classic 2005

The following browsers are supported by Salesforce for use with Salesforce Classic 2005:

- Google Chrome, most recent stable version
- Microsoft Internet Explorer versions 9, 10, and 11
- Mozilla Firefox, most recent stable version
- Apple Safari version 8.x on Mac OS X

Salesforce has discontinued browser support for Microsoft Internet Explorer versions 7 and 8 in Salesforce Classic 2005.

Salesforce Classic 2010

The following browsers are supported by Salesforce for use with Salesforce Classic 2010:

- Google Chrome, most recent stable version
- Microsoft Internet Explorer versions 9, 10, and 11
- Mozilla Firefox, most recent stable version
- Apple Safari version 8.x on Mac OS X

Salesforce has discontinued browser support for Microsoft Internet Explorer versions 7 and 8 in Salesforce Classic 2010.

Lightning Experience

The following browsers are supported by Salesforce for use with Lightning Experience:

- Google Chrome, most recent stable version
- Microsoft Edge for Windows 10
- Mozilla Firefox, most recent stable version
- Apple Safari version 8.x and 9.x on Mac OS X

Salesforce will possibly redirect you to Salesforce Classic when using Microsoft Internet Explorer versions 9-11 within Lightning Experience. However, since the Summer '2016 release, Salesforce has stated that users of existing organizations can continue to access Lightning Experience with Microsoft Internet Explorer version 11 (IE11) until December 16, 2017, but users of new organizations created after Summer '2016 will not be able to use IE11 to access Lightning Experience, and will automatically be redirected to Salesforce Classic.

Along with the user interface theme, there are many other aspects of the user interface that can be set up in Salesforce to present the optimum user experience to the users in your organization.

Additional user interface options include **User Interface Settings** (such as collapsible detail page sections and inline field editing), **Sidebar Settings** (Collapsible Sidebar settings and Custom Sidebar Components on All Pages), and **Calendar Settings** (such as Home Page Hover Links for Events and Drag-and-Drop Editing on Calendar Views).

There are also some administrator-specific settings that can improve your users' experience with the application located under the **Setup** settings. It also includes the **Enhanced Page Layout Editor** and **Enhanced Profile List Views Settings**.

Selection of the **User Interface** option can be carried out by navigating to **Setup | Customize | User Interface**.

The **User Interface** option is the final option in the **Customize** section on the left-hand setup sidebar.

The User Interface screen is as shown in the following screenshot:

User Interface   Help for this Page ⓘ

Modify your organization's user interface with the following settings:

User Interface

☑ Enable Collapsible Sections
☑ Show Quick Create
☑ Enable Hover Details
☑ Enable Related List Hover Links
☑ Enable Separate Loading of Related Lists
   ☑ Enable Separate Loading of Related Lists of External Objects ⓘ
☑ Enable Inline Editing
☑ Enable Enhanced Lists
☑ Enable the Salesforce Classic 2010 User Interface Theme

> ⚠ Some features like Chatter require the Salesforce Classic 2010 user interface theme. Disabling this theme automatically disables Chatter in both Salesforce Classic and Lightning Experience.

☑ Enable Tab Bar Organizer
☑ Enable Printable List Views
☑ Enable Customization of Chatter User Profile Pages ⓘ
☑ Enable Salesforce Notification Banner
☑ Disable Lightning Experience IE11 Support Deprecation Notification ⓘ

Sidebar

☐ Enable Collapsible Sidebar
☑ Show Custom Sidebar Components on All Pages

Calendar

☑ Enable Home Page Hover Links for Events
☑ Enable Drag-and-Drop Editing on Calendar Views
   ☐ Enable Click-and-Create Events on Calendar Views
      ☐ Enable Drag-and-Drop Scheduling on List Views
☑ Enable Hover Links for My Tasks list

Name Settings

☐ Enable Middle Names for Person Names
☐ Enable Name Suffixes for Person Names

Setup

☑ Enable Enhanced Page Layout Editor
☑ Enable Enhanced Profile List Views
☐ Enable Enhanced Profile User Interface
☑ Enable Streaming API
☑ Enable Dynamic Streaming Channel Creation
☐ Enable "Set Audit Fields upon Record Creation" and "Update Records with Inactive Owners" User Permissions ⓘ
☐ Enable Custom Object Truncate
☑ Enable Improved Setup User Interface ⓘ
☑ Enable Advanced Setup Search (Beta) ⓘ

Advanced

☑ Activate Extended Mail Merge
☑ Always save Extended Mail Merge documents to the Document tab

[Save] [Cancel]

User Interface settings

In the following sections, we will look through the various User Interface settings one by one.

Enable Collapsible Sections

Collapsible Sections enables your users to collapse or expand sections on record detail pages using the arrow icon next to the section heading. Sections remain expanded or collapsed until the user changes their settings for that section. Salesforce will store a different setting for each record type if the record types have been set up as shown in the following screenshot:

When enabling collapsible sections, you need to ensure that the section headings have been entered on the page layouts.

Clicking on the triangle icon toggles between showing and hiding the section, as shown in the following screenshot:

Opportunity Detail   Edit Delete Clone

Opportunity Owner   <u>Trevor Howard</u> [Change]

Private   ☐

Opportunity Name   Opportunity Y

Account Name   <u>Company X</u>

Type

▶ **Section One**

Show Section - Section One

▼ Section Two

Show Quick Create

The **Show Quick Create** option adds the **Quick Create** fields section to the sidebar on the **Record** tab page to enable users to create a new record using minimal data fields, as shown in the following screenshot:

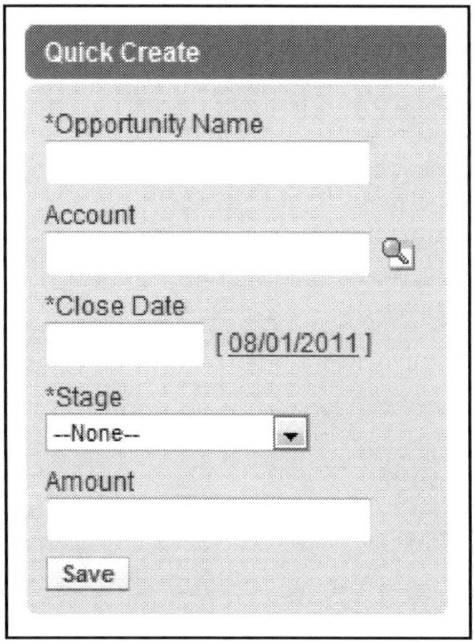

The **Show Quick Create** option also controls whether users can create new records from within the Lookup dialog. With this setting enabled, users see a **New** button in the Lookup dialog screen. The following example shows the creation of a new account within the account **Lookup** dialog while working with an opportunity record:

Clicking on the **New** button reveals the fields that are available for creating the new record.

The option to create new records and displaying the **New** button in the **Lookup** dialog are only available for accounts and contacts. Also, users still need the appropriate **Create record** permission to enter data with **Quick Create**, regardless of whether the entry fields are displayed.

Disable the Quick Create option:
The **Quick Create** option does not allow you to configure the data entry screen, so any custom fields that need to be populated there will not be included. Also, when saving records using the **Quick Create** option any validation rules associated with the record are not triggered. These features allow records to be created that do not conform with your company's business rules and data integrity requirements so it is advisable to disable the **Quick Create** option.

Enable Hover Details

The **Enable Hover Details** option allows users to view interactive information for a record by hovering the mouse pointer over a link to that record in the **Recent Items** list on the sidebar or in a lookup field on the record detail page. The fields displayed in the hover details are determined by the record's mini page layout, which is set at the page layout edit screen.

The **Enable Hover Details** option is selected by default.

In the following screenshot, we are hovering the mouse pointer over a link to a record in the **Recent Items** list on the sidebar:

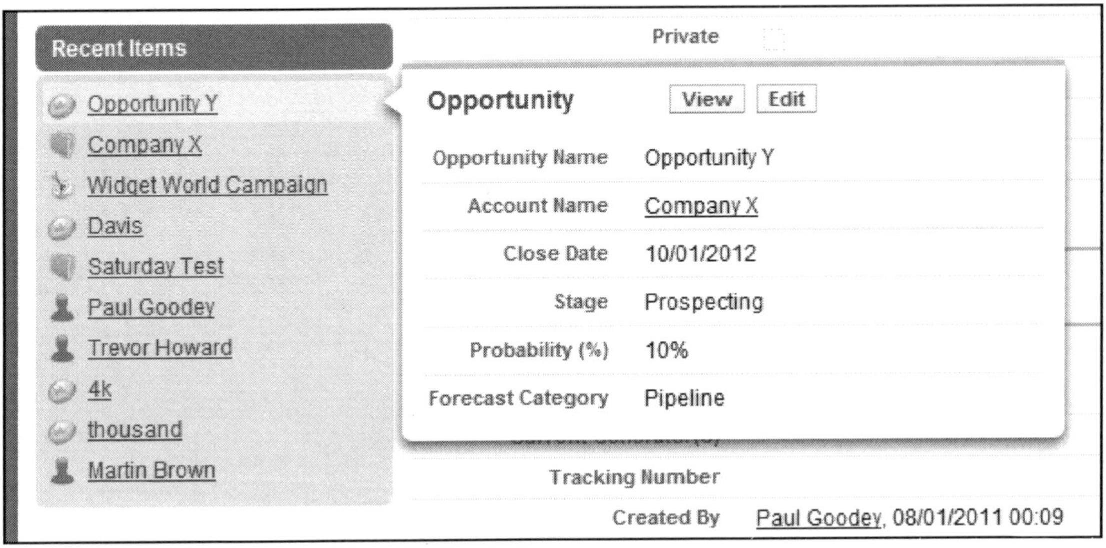

In the following screenshot, we are hovering the mouse pointer over a lookup field on the record detail page:

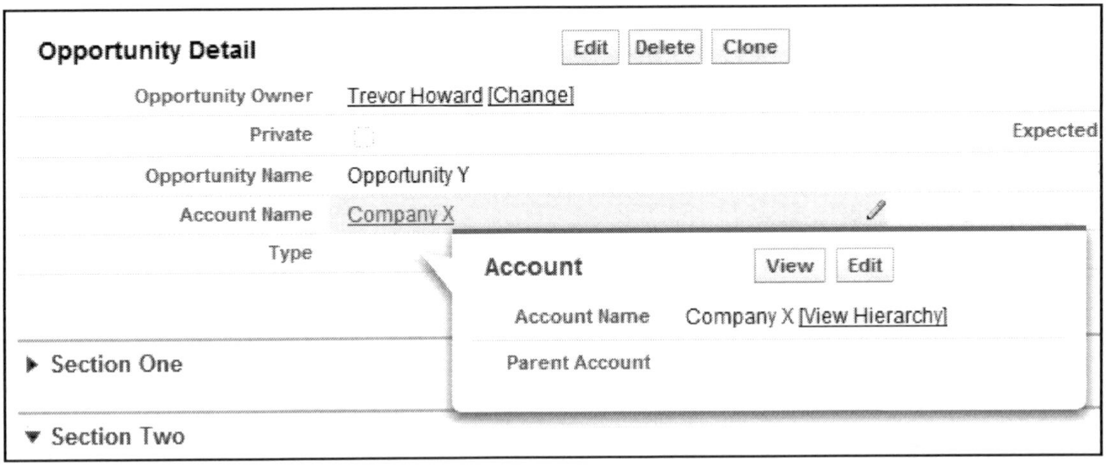

To view the hover details for a record, users require the appropriate sharing access to the record, and field level security to the fields, in the mini page layout, which is set at the page layout edit screen (see `Chapter 3, Configuring Objects and Apps`).

Enable Related List Hover Links

This option enables related list hover links to be displayed at the top of standard and custom object record detail pages. It allows users to view the related list and its records by hovering the mouse pointer over the related list link. Users can also click on the related list hover link to jump down directly to the **Related List** section without having to scroll down the page.

 The **Enable Related List Hover Links** option is selected by default.

Enable Separate Loading of Related Lists

This option enables the separate loading of record detail pages. First, the primary record detail data loads, and then the related list data. This option serves to improve the display performance for organizations with a large number of related lists on record detail pages. When the page is loaded, the record details are displayed immediately; afterwards the related list data loads, during which the users see a progress indicator for the related list.

Account
Edge Communications

« Back to List: Accounts

Contacts [...] | Opportunities [...] | Cases [...] | Open Activities [...] | Activity History [...] | Notes & Attachments [...]

Account Detail   Edit   Delete   Include Offline

Account Owner   Paul Goodey [Change]

Account Name   Edge Communications [View Hierarchy]

You will see that the related list sections are not yet loaded. They appear as **[...]** while the primary record detail (for the account example) is loaded immediately, as shown in the following screenshot:

After the primary record detail has loaded (the account page), the related lists are then loaded. You can see that the number of records for the **Contacts** related list is now displayed as **[2]**.

This option does not apply to pages for which you cannot control the layout (such as user pages or Visualforce pages).

 The **Enable Separate Loading of Related Lists** option is disabled by default.

Enable Separate Loading of Related Lists of External Objects

This option is related to the setting **Enable Separate Loading of Related Lists**, and enables a separate loading of record detail pages and related lists of standard and custom objects.

 External objects are similar to custom objects (described in Chapter 3, *Configuring Objects and Apps*), however the mapped data is not stored inside Salesforce, so there may be delays in loading due to the availability of the external data source and network latency. The **Enable Separate Loading of Related Lists of External Objects** option is enabled by default.

Enable Inline Editing

This option allows users to change field values directly within the record detail page, avoiding the need to load the record edit page first. By double-clicking on the field to be edited within the detail page, the field changes to become editable. The new value can then be entered and saved, or the action can be undone using the **Undo** button.

First, the field is highlighted by hovering over it with the mouse to reveal the pencil icon indicating that the field is editable, as follows:

Industry	
Annual Revenue	$200,000
SF Account Number	SFA-000032

Double-clicking the field causes the field to switch from **View** mode to **Edit** mode to allow a new value to be entered, as follows:

Industry	
Annual Revenue	200,000
SF Account Number	SFA-000032

After a new value has been entered, the value is displayed in orange text and the user has the option of undoing the change using the **Undo** button, as follows:

Industry	
Annual Revenue	350,000
SF Account Number	SFA-000032

The changed value and the detail page can then be saved in the standard way using the Save button, as follows:

Account Detail		Save	Cancel
Account Owner	Paul Goodey [Change]		
Account Name	Company X [View Hierarchy]		
Parent Account			
Account Number			
Account Site			
Type			
Industry			
Annual Revenue	350,000		
SF Account Number	SFA-000032		

To check if inline editing is enabled for your organization, and to discover which value can be edited, you can hover over a value with your mouse and note the result. A field that is editable will have a pencil icon to the far right of the value when the mouse is hovered over it. A field which is non-editable will have a padlock icon to the far right of the value when the mouse is hovered over it.

This option is enabled by default. Certain fields cannot be changed using inline editing, such as **System Fields** (created by, last modified by, and so on), **Calculated Fields** (formula, auto number, roll-up summary, and so on), **Read-Only Fields**, and **Special Fields** (such as owner and record type).

Also, fields on detail pages for documents and forecasts are not currently editable using inline editing.

Enable Enhanced Lists

This option provides the user with the ability to view, customize, and edit list data, which is the resulting data section that is rendered from Views. When enabled along with the **Enable Inline Editing** setting, users can also edit records directly within the list without having to move away from the page, as shown in the following screenshot:

With enhanced lists enabled, users can perform the following actions:

- Create a new view, or edit, delete, or refresh the existing view.
- Navigate through list results by clicking the first, previous, next, and last page links at the bottom of the list. You can jump directly to a specific page by entering a number in the textbox in the lower-right corner. You can also change the width of a column by dragging the right side of the column heading with the mouse. Changes made to column widths apply to that specific list only and are recalled whenever that list is viewed. Please note that, when columns are added or removed from a list, any column width settings for that list is discarded.
- Change the order in which a column is displayed by dragging the entire column heading with your mouse to the desired position. For your users who have permission to edit the list definition, the changes are saved for all who see the list. For your users without permission to edit the list definition, their changes are discarded after leaving the page.
- If inline editing is enabled for your organization, values can be entered directly into the list by double-clicking on individual field values. Users who have been granted the **Mass Edit from Lists** option on their profile can edit up to 200 records at a time.
- The Mass Edit from Lists option only appears on the profile if inline editing is enabled.

A mass edit is performed by first selecting the records to be edited using the checkboxes and then clicking on one of the fields to be edited.

Upon clicking on the field, a new pop-up window is displayed asking whether the change is to be applied to just the selected record or to all records that have been selected. In the following screenshot, we see an example where two account records have been selected, and where one of the record's billing street fields has been clicked.

This feature only allows mass edits; users cannot mass-delete:

Remind users that they cannot mass delete records:
As a system administrator, you may need to remind users that they cannot mass delete records as occasionally users may try to mass delete using the only visible **Delete** link, which is, in fact, the link to delete the **View** as shown in the following screenshot. Communicating this fact will hopefully save you from having to recreate any views that have been deleted in error.

On the **Account**, **Contact**, and **Lead List** views, there is an **Open Calendar** link at the bottom of the page to display a weekly view of a calendar underneath the list. A record can be dragged from the list to a time slot on the calendar to create an event associated with the record.

To perform inline editing on an enhanced list, the **Advanced Filter** options must be turned off in the list view filter criteria. Some standard fields do not support inline editing. For example, **Case Status**, **Opportunity Stage**, and several of the **Task** and **Event** fields can only be edited from the record edit page.

The number of records displayed can be changed per page by setting the view to **10**, **25**, **50**, **100**, or **200** records at a time. When this setting is changed, navigation is set to the first page of the list results, as shown in the following screenshot:

Action	Opportunity Name	Account Name	Amount	Close Date ↓	Stage	Oppo
Edit | Del | ⊕	Test	Westwood	$1,330,000.00	31/07/2014	Proposal/Price Quote	thow
Edit | Del | ⊕	20 Thousand	Company X	$100,000.00	31/07/2014	Prospecting	thow
Edit | Del | ⊕	4k		$100,000,000.00	31/07/2014	Prospecting	thow
Edit | Del | ⊕	Opportunity Y	Company X	$200,000.00	31/07/2014	Proposal/Price Quote	thow
Edit | Del | ⊕	Product 101		$10.00	31/07/2014	Prospecting	thow
Edit | Del | ⊕	500k		$600,000.00	31/07/2014	Qualification	thow
Edit | Del | ✔	Test	Company X	$120,000.00	27/09/2011	Proposal/Price Quote	PGood
Edit | Del | ⊕	Test Move	Contacts First Acco...		31/08/2011	Qualification	PGood
Edit | Del | ⊕	Payment RUS			09/08/2011	Needs Analysis	PGood
Edit | Del | ⊕	MM Test	Six Mile Quarry	$130,000.00	08/08/2011	Id. Decision Makers	PGood

Top of screenshot:
All Opportunities ▼   Edit | Delete | Create New View   List · Feed

New Opportunity

1-10 of 57 ▼   0 Selected ▼   ≪ ◀ Previous Next ▶ ≫   Chat

If users change the number of records to be displayed per page, that setting is applied to all the lists (not just the current list).

Also, if the option of displaying 200 records is selected, a warning message appears, as it can reduce performance, as shown in the following screenshot:

Edit Records Per Page Setting   ✕

⚠ **Your Records Per Page Setting: 200**
Viewing many records at one time may cause lists to load more slowly than usual.
We recommend viewing 100 records or fewer per page. What would you like to do?

◉ Change the number of records displayed per page to [100 ▾]

○ Keep my current setting and don't show me this message again

[Save]   [Cancel]

Enable the Salesforce Classic 2010 user interface theme

At the time of writing there are three different user interface themes, namely Salesforce Classic 2005, Salesforce Classic 2010, and Lightning Experience.

Enabling the Salesforce Classic 2010 user interface theme activates the most recent version of Salesforce Classic, the interface theme that predates Lightning Experience. Disabling this option activates the Salesforce Classic 2005 user interface theme.

There are features, such as Chatter, that require the Salesforce Classic 2010 user interface theme, and disabling this option disables Chatter in Salesforce Classic and also in Lightning Experience.

Enable Tab Bar Organizer

The Tab Bar Organizer automatically arranges user's tabs in the tab bar to control the width of the CRM application pages and prevent horizontal scrolling. It dynamically measures how many application tabs can be displayed, and puts tabs that extend beyond the browser's current width into a drop-down list displayed on the right-hand side of the tab bar, as shown in the following screenshot:

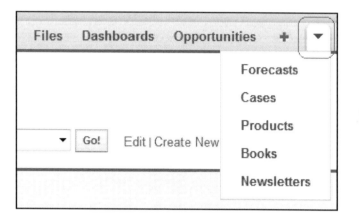

 This setting is only enabled when the **New User Interface Theme** is activated. If your organization is not using the New User Interface Theme, you can enable the feature, but the Tab Bar Organizer will not be activated for your users until the new theme is also enabled.

Enable Printable List Views

This option allows users to easily print list views.

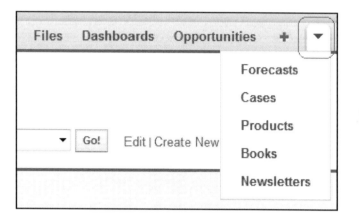

If this is enabled, users can click on the **Printable View** link (the printer logo) located in the top-right corner on any list view to open a new browser window. Within the new window, the current list view is displayed in a print-ready format, as shown in the following screenshot:

This option allows users to click on the **Printable View** link from any list view, which opens a new browser window displaying the current list view in a print-ready format.

Enable Customization of Chatter User Profile Pages

This option allows you to customize the tabs on the Chatter user profile. The way to customize Chatter user profile pages is described in detail later in `Chapter 8`, *Introducing Sales Cloud, Service Cloud, and the Collaborative Features of Salesforce CRM*. In the following example screenshot, we have customized the **Chatter** user profile page tabs and added the **Learning Zone** tab, which results in the following modified page:

| Home | Chatter | Leads | Accounts | Contacts | Reports | Campaigns | Dashboards | Opportunities | Forecasts | Cases |

Chatter › People › **Martin Brown** ⊙

Start Chat   Send a mes

Feed   Overview   Learning Zone

💬 Post   📄 File   🔗 Link   📊 Poll

Share with Martin Brown and your company   **Share**

🔍 | Sort By Post Date ▾

There are no updates

The Winter' 2014 release saw this feature being automatically enabled.

This enables you to add custom tabs or remove default tabs such as the default **Feed** and **Overview** tabs. Custom tabs are available by customizing Subtab Apps, which are described in more detail in Chapter 3, *Configuring Objects and Apps*. If this option is disabled, users only see the default **Feed** and **Overview** tabs.

Enable Salesforce Notification Banner

When this option is selected, an announcement banner appears on certain pages.

 Released as part of the Summer '2014 release, the Salesforce Notification Banner appears on the setup area for your organization and on pages for accounts, contacts, and dashboards.

Your users can prevent the banner from appearing on all pages by clicking the **Close** button, or you can prevent the Salesforce Notification Banner from appearing across your entire organization by disabling this option.

Disable Lightning Experience IE11 Support Deprecation Notification

Since the Summer '2016 release, Salesforce has stated that existing organizations can continue to use Microsoft Internet Explorer version 11 (IE11) to access Lightning Experience until December 16, 2017 (after this date, users will be automatically redirected to Salesforce Classic).

The **Disable Lightning Experience IE11 Support Deprecation Notification** option enables you to prevent screen notifications from appearing when users in your organization access Lightning Experience-activated Salesforce, to cater for your own strategy for transitioning browser use away from IE11. See the Supported browsers section earlier in this chapter for more information.

Sidebar

The following options are available to help users view and edit information on the sidebar, which is presented in the left hand, vertical section of the screen:

- Enable Collapsible Sidebar
- Show Custom Sidebar Components on All Pages

We will now cover the sidebar options in detail.

Enable Collapsible Sidebar

The collapsible sidebar gives users the ability to show or hide the sidebar on every Salesforce page where the sidebar is included. When this option is selected, the collapsible sidebar becomes available to all users in your organization. However, each user can set their own preference for displaying the sidebar. Users can set the sidebar to be permanently displayed or they can collapse the sidebar and show it only when needed.

Show Custom Sidebar Components on All Pages

If you have custom home page layouts that include components in the sidebar, this option displays the sidebar components on all pages in Salesforce and for all users. If only certain profiles are allowed to view sidebar components on all pages, you can assign a **Show Custom Sidebar on All Pages** permission to just those profiles.

 If the **Show Custom Sidebar Components on All Pages** user interface setting is enabled, the **Show Custom Sidebar on All Pages** permission is not available within the profile permissions.

Calendar settings

The following options are available to help users view and edit information on calendar sections and views:

- Enable Home Page Hover Links for Events
- Enable Drag-And-Drop Editing on Calendar Views
- Enable Click-And-Create Events on Calendar Views
- Enable Drag-And-Drop Scheduling on List Views
- Enable Hover Links for My Tasks List

Let us see what they are in detail.

Enable Home Page Hover Links for Events

This option enables hover links in the calendar section of the **Home** tab, and allows users to hover the mouse over the subject of an event to see interactive information for that event.

 This setting controls the **Home** tab only, as hover links are always displayed in other calendar views. Also, this option is enabled by default.

Enable Drag-And-Drop Editing on Calendar Views

This option enables your users to drag and drop existing events around their daily and weekly calendar views to reschedule events without having to navigate from the page to the event creation page. Loading performance of the calendar control may suffer with this option enabled. Drag-and-drop editing is not available for either multi-day events or on console calendar views. Also, this option is enabled by default.

Enable Click-And-Create Events on Calendar Views

This option enables the creation of events on daily and weekly calendar views by double-clicking on a specific time slot and entering the details of the event in an interactive section. The fields presented in the interactive section are set using the mini page layout on the **Event** page layout screen.

 Recurring events and multi-person events cannot be created using the **Enable Click-And-Create Events On Calendar Views** option.

Enable Drag-And-Drop Scheduling on List Views

This option enables users to create events by dragging the record to be linked from the list view onto the weekly calendar view. Upon dropping, an interactive section for the event detail is displayed where the fields available are set using the mini page layout.

 This option is disabled by default.

Enable Hover Links for My Tasks List

This option enables hover links for tasks in the **My Tasks** section of the **Home** tab and on the calendar day view, and allows users to hover the mouse over details of the task in an interactive section.

Name settings

The Name settings feature allows additional fields to be accessed for person objects in Salesforce in order to help avoid confusion when two person records have identical first and last names.

Enable Middle Names for Person Names

This setting adds the middle name field to person objects such as the **Contact**, **Lead**, **Person Account**, and **User** objects.

Enable Name Suffixes for Person Names

This setting adds name suffix fields to person objects such as the **Contact**, **Lead**, **Person Account**, and **User** objects.

Setup settings

There are administrator-specific user interface settings, which that can improve your experience with the application, located under the **Setup** settings. They allow for the following options:

- Enable Enhanced Page Layout Editor
- Enable Enhanced Profile List Views
- Enable Enhanced Profile User Interface
- Enable Streaming API
- Enable Dynamic Streaming Channel Creation
- Enable Set Audit Fields upon Record Creation and Update Records with Inactive Owners User Permissions
- Enable Custom Object Truncate
- Enable Improved Setup User Interface
- Enable Advanced Setup Search

Let's see what they are in detail.

Enable Enhanced Page Layout Editor

This option enables the **Enhanced Page Layout Editor** for editing page layouts with a feature-rich **WYSIWYG** (for **What You See Is What You Get**) editor.

Enable Enhanced Profile List Views

This option enables the enhanced list views and inline editing on the profiles list page, which allows you to manage multiple profiles at once.

To navigate to the **Profile** menu, go to **Setup** | **Manage Users** | **Profiles**. Now select a profile and click on **Create New View**, as shown in the following screenshot:

Profiles

All Profiles ▼		New Profile	

Create New View | Edit | Delete | **Refresh**   A | B | C | D | E | F

	Action	Profile Name ↑	User License
☐	Edit | Clone	Authenticated Website	Platform Portal
☐	Edit | Clone	Chatter Free User	Chatter Free
☐	Edit | Clone	Chatter Moderator User	Chatter Free
☐	Edit | Clone	Contract Manager	Salesforce

The following three steps produce a list of profiles that allow you to modify multiple profile settings at once:

1. Enter View Name.
2. Specify Filter Criteria.
3. Select Columns to Display.

Profiles
Create New View

| Save | Save As | Delete | Cancel |

Step 1. Enter View Name

View Name [My Profile List for Lead Conversion]

Step 2. Specify Filter Criteria

Clear All Rows

Setting		Operator	Value
Convert Leads	🔍	equals ▾	True ▾

Add Row

Examples Modify All Data equals False
Contact: Modify All equals True

Step 3. Select Columns to Display

Specify the columns to show in the list view. To set the columns, you can add profile details, user permissions, and object-level perm

Search All ▾ [   ] Find

Available Settings		Selected Settings	
Created By	▲	Profile Name	
Created By Alias	▤	Convert Leads	
Created Date		Last Modified By	Top
Custom		Last Modified Date	⤒
Description		User License	
	Add		Up

Now that the profile view has been created, we can select multiple profiles to manage all at once, as shown in the following screenshot:

Profiles

My Profile List for Lead Conversion ▾		New Profile

Create New View | Edit | Delete | **Refresh**

☐	Action	Profile Name ↑	Convert Leads
☐	Edit | Clone	Contract Manager	✓
☐	Edit | Del | Clone	Custom: Marketing Profile	✓
☑	Edit | Del | Clone	Custom: Sales Profile	✓
☑	Edit | Del | Clone	Custom: Support Profile	✓
☐	Edit | Clone	Marketing User	✓
☐	Edit | Clone	Partner User	✓
☐	Edit | Clone	Solution Manager	✓
☐	Edit | Clone	Standard User	✓
☐	Edit | Del | Clone	System Admin Custom	✓
☐	Edit | Clone	System Administrator	✓

1-10 of 10 ▾   2 Selected ▾

You can display multiple lists of profiles that can be selected and actioned, as shown in the following screenshot:

Edit Convert Leads ⌧

Change the following setting

☐ Convert Leads

These settings will also be disabled

ⓘ When Convert Leads is disabled, if any of the following permissions are currently enabled, they will be disabled. Don't show this message again

General User Permissions	Administrative Permissions	Object Permissions
Download AppExchange Packages	Author Apex Modify All Data	No Impact

Apply changes to

◯ The record clicked
◉ All 2 selected records

Save Cancel

You can also modify multiple profile selection to apply the setting to all the profiles, as shown in the following screenshot:

Profiles

| My Profile List for Lead Conversion ▼ | New Profile |

Create New View | Edit | Delete | **Refresh**

☐	Action	Profile Name ↑	Convert Leads
☐	Edit | Clone	Contract Manager	✓
☐	Edit | Del | Clone	Custom: Marketing Profile	✓
☐	Edit | Clone	Marketing User	✓
☐	Edit | Clone	Partner User	✓
☐	Edit | Clone	Solution Manager	✓
☐	Edit | Clone	Standard User	✓
☐	Edit | Del | Clone	System Admin Custom	✓
☐	Edit | Clone	System Administrator	✓

1-8 of 8 ▼   0 Selected ▼

The Enable Enhanced Profile User Interface option

The Enable Enhanced Profile User Interface option allows you to enable the **Enhanced Profile User Interface**, which then offers the following features to help you:

- **Find permissions and settings**: Here, you can start typing a specific permission or setting name in the Find Settings box, and then choose from a list of matching results
- **Edit profile properties**: Here, you can change the name or description of a profile
- **Assigned Users**: Find out who belongs to a profile by clicking on the **Assigned Users** button to see a list

- **Browse permissions and settings, for both, app and system properties**:
  Here, app-related system permissions and settings are grouped on individual
  pages, where the profile overview page provides a descriptions and links

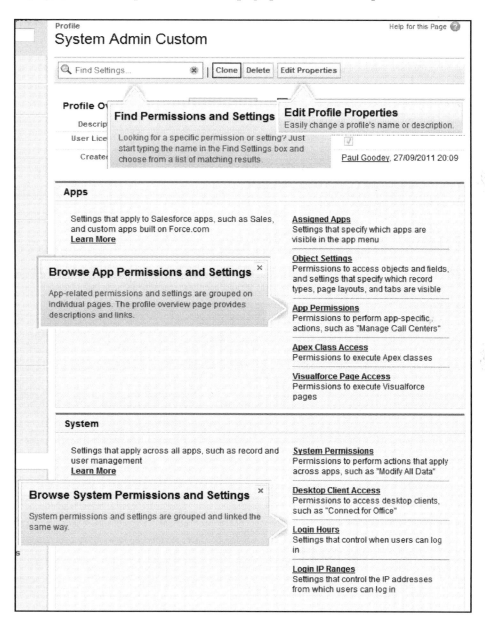

Enable Streaming API

This option enables the use of the Force.com Streaming API in your organization. The Streaming API provides near real-time streams of data from the Force.com platform. You can create topics to which applications can subscribe and receive asynchronous notifications of changes to data in Force.com.

See the Force.com Streaming API Developer's Guide at developer.salesforce.com for more details.

Enable Dynamic Streaming Channel Creation

This option is a feature of the Streaming API; when enabled, it results in the dynamic creation of streaming channels when clients subscribe (if the channel has yet to be created).

This setting is enabled by default.

Enable Set Audit Fields upon Record Creation and Update Records with Inactive Owners User Permissions

This option allows you to set audit fields (such as record creation date) that are read-only by default when records are created using the Salesforce API. you can create records through using tools such as the Data Loader, which is a client application that makes use of the Salesforce API. This setting also allows you to update records that have inactive owners.

Available since the Winter '16 release, this setting makes it easier to migrate historic data to Salesforce and mass-update records not owned by active users. Previously, you needed to contact Salesforce Support to temporarily allow these features. When this option is enabled, it results in two new System Permissions being available in Profiles and Permission Sets that can be assigned to users.

Enable Custom Object Truncate

Select the **Enable Custom Object Truncate** checkbox to activate truncating custom objects, which permanently removes all of the records from a custom object while keeping the object and its metadata intact for future use.

> When this option is enabled, a **Truncate** button appears in the list of edit buttons within the custom object setup page.

Truncating custom objects is a quick way to permanently delete all of the records from a custom object. Take the example of a custom object that has been created and filled with test records. When testing is complete and the test data is no longer required, you can truncate the object to remove the test records, but keep the object ready to be deployed into production. This is much quicker than batch-deleting records and having to recreate the custom object.

> Truncating a custom object permanently removes all of its records, and you cannot recover the records from the **Recycle Bin**. A copy of the truncated object appears in the **Deleted Objects** list for 15 days, during which the object and its records continue to count towards the organization's data limits. The copied object and its records are then permanently deleted after 15 days.

Enable Improved Setup User Interface

When the **Improved Setup User Interface** is enabled in an organization, you might notice several differences from the original user interface.

The Setup menu is accessed from the Setup link in the upper-right corner of any Salesforce page. It is arranged into the following goal-based categories:

- Administer, Build, Deploy, Monitor, and Checkout.
- Personal settings, which all Salesforce users can edit, are available from a separate **My Settings** menu.

> By enabling the **Enable Improved Setup User Interface** option, the Improved Setup User Interface is activated for every user in your organization.

Enable Advanced Setup search

When enabled, this option allows you to search for Setup pages, custom profiles, permission sets, public groups, roles, and users from the sidebar search textbox within the Setup area. When the option is disabled, you can search for Setup pages only.

As you type in the sidebar **Setup** search box, any options that match your search term appear in the **Setup** menu. When you press Enter, you will be presented with a page listing any matching permission sets, custom profiles, public groups, roles, or users.

Advanced settings

Advanced settings provides the activation of two features: activation of **Extended Mail Merge** and the option to **Always save Extended Mail Merge documents to the Documents tab**.

Activate Extended Mail Merge

This option enables the **Mass Mail Merge** link to be available in the **Tools** area on the home pages for accounts, contacts, and leads.

When enabled, this option also sets single mail merges requested from the Activity History-related list on a record to be created with the `Extended Mail Merge` function. The `Extended Mail Merge` function is activated using a wizard comprising the following steps:

1. In the **Tools** area, click **Mass Mail Merge** to start the mass mail merge wizard. Choose a list view from the **View** drop-down list and select the records to include in the mail merge. Selecting the checkbox in the column header will select all records currently displayed on the page.
2. Select the types of Word documents to be generated from the multiple selections of documents, envelopes, and labels. Select the optional **Log an Activity** checkbox to log the creation of these mail merge documents, which adds a completed task to each record.
3. Select the appropriate mail merge templates. For documents, choose whether to create one Word document that includes all output or a separate Word document for each record. Click the optional **Preview Template** button to review the pre-loaded mail merge template.

Although the document preview is editable, do not edit it in Word as the changes will not be saved to your current mail merge request. You have to make a new mail merge template and upload this first.

With **Extended Mail Merge**, the mail merge operation cannot exceed 1,000 records, the selected mail merge template(s) total size cannot be greater than 1 MB, and the number of records multiplied by the combined size of the mail merge templates cannot be greater than 50 MB. Also, **Extended Mail Merge** is available by request from Salesforce customer support.

Always Save Extended Mail Merge Documents to the Documents tab

This option stops the sending of the mail merge documents as e-mail attachments, instead storing them in the user's personal documents folder on the **Documents** tab. Users are still sent e-mails as confirmation when their mail merge requests have completed, and these e-mails contain links to the documents in the **Documents** tab.

These documents count against your organization's storage limits.

Search overview and settings

`Salesforce.com` uses custom algorithms that consider the following within searches:

- The search terms
- Ignored words in search terms (for example, the, to, and for)
- Search term stems (for example, searching for speaking returns items with speak)
- Proximity of search terms in a record
- Record ownership and most recently accessed records

A user might not, therefore, have the same search results as another user performing the same search because searches are configured for the user performing the search. For example, if another user recently viewed a record, the record relevancy increases, and the record moves higher in their search results list. Records that are owned by the user also move higher in their search results. There are currently three types of search, as follows:

- Sidebar search
- Advanced search
- Global search

Let's see what they are, shall we?

Sidebar Search

From the **Sidebar Search** box, users can search a subset of record types and fields.

 If **Global Search** is enabled (described later in this section), **Sidebar Search** is disabled.

Wildcards and filters can be used to help refine the search.

 A wildcard is a special character or token that can be used to substitute for any other character or characters in a string. For example, the asterisk character (*) is used to substitute zero or more characters. More information about wildcard characters can be found using the following link: http://en.wikipedia.org/wiki/Wildcard_character.

Advanced Search

Advanced Search in the sidebar allows searching for a subset of record types in combination and offers more fields including custom fields and long text fields, such as descriptions, notes, tasks, and event comments. Wildcards and filters can be used to help refine the search.

 If **Global Search** is enabled (described later in this section), **Advanced Search** is disabled.

Global Search

From the **Global Search** box, users can search more types of records, including articles, documents, products, solutions, Chatter feeds, and groups. Users can also search more fields, including custom fields and long text fields, such as descriptions, notes, tasks, and event comments. Wildcards and filters can be used to help refine the search.

 To enable **Global Search**, you must enable Chatter. If **Global Search** is enabled, **Sidebar Search** and **Advanced Search** are disabled. Global Search is not supported in **Partner Portal** or **Customer Portal**. Only users with supported browsers can use Global Search, as it has indirect dependencies on the new theme user interface.

Searching in Salesforce.com

Your search term must have two or more characters. Special characters, such as ", ?, *, (, and) are not included in the character count. For example, a search for m* will fail to return any search results.

Search terms are not case-sensitive. For example, a search for martin returns the same results as the search for Martin.

Finding phone numbers can be done by entering part or all of a number. For example, to find (512) 757-6000, enter 5127576000, 757, or 6000. To search for the last seven digits, you must enter the punctuation, such as 757-6000.

In Chinese, Japanese, and Korean, you can find a person by entering the last name before the first name; searching for howard trevor returns any person named Trevor Howard.

 If you're using **Advanced Search** or **Global Search**, refine your search using operators such as **AND**, **OR**, and **AND NOT**. If you're using **Advanced Search** or **Global Search**, search for exact phrases by selecting the **Exact Phrase** checkbox, or by putting quotation marks around multiple keywords; for example, "phone martin brown" returns results with phone martin brown, but not martin brown phoned or phone martina browning.

If you're using **Sidebar Search**, your search string is automatically treated as a phrase search. Search for partially matching terms using wildcards as follows:

Asterisks match one or more characters at the middle or end (not the beginning) of your search term. For example, a search for brown* finds items that start with variations of the term brown, such as browning or brownlow. A search for ma* brown finds items with martin brown or mandy brown. If you're using Sidebar Search, an asterisk (*) is automatically appended at the end of the search string

If you're using Global Search, question marks match only one character in the middle (not the beginning or end) of your search term. For example, a search for ti?a finds items with the term tina or tika, but not tia or tinas. Fields on custom objects are only searched if you have added a custom tab for the object.

If using Sidebar Search or **Advanced Search**, question marks match only one character in the middle or end (not the beginning) of your search term.

Search settings

There are various search options that can be customized to change the way information can be searched by your users in Salesforce. These options either present enhanced search features that are visible as a part of the user interface, or are invisible and used to optimize searching behind the scenes. The **Search settings** can be set by navigating to **Setup** | **Customize** | **Search** | **Search Settings**.

The following screenshot shows the search settings that are available if **Chatter** is not activated in your Salesforce CRM application:

Search Settings

Help for this Page 🔞

Modify your organization's search interface with the following settings:

Search Settings   Save Cancel

☑ Enable "Limit to Items I Own" Search Checkbox
☑ Enable Document Content Search
▢ Enable Search Optimization if your Content is Mostly in Japanese, Chinese, or Korean
☑ Use Recently Viewed User Records for Blank and Auto-Complete Lookups
☑ Enable Drop-Down List for Sidebar Search
☑ Enable Sidebar Search Auto-Complete
▢ Enable Single-Search-Result Shortcut for Sidebar and Advanced Search

Number of Search Results Displayed Per Object

Specify the number of records to display for each object on the Search Results page. The current setting is listed next to each object in parentheses. To make changes, select one or more objects, enter the new number of results per page, and click Save. The new value must be between 5 and 50.

Objects to update:

> Accounts (25)
> Activities (25)
> Activity Tracker (25)
> Assets (25)
> Attachments (25)
> Campaigns (25)
> Case Comments (25)
> Cases (25)
> Contacts (25)
> Contracts (25)

Results per page for selected objects: [   ]

Lookup Settings

Select the objects for which you want to enable the following features and click Save:

- Enhanced lookups provide an updated lookup dialog interface that gives users the ability to filter, sort, and page through results as well as customize columns.
- Lookup auto-completion displays suggestions from the Recent Items list as you type.

Enable	▢ Enhanced Lookups	▢ Lookup Auto-Completion
Accounts	▢	▢

By activating **Chatter**, the **Global Search** setting is automatically enabled and provides the following reduced set of options:

Search Settings

Help for this Page 🔞

Modify your organization's search interface with the following settings:

Search Settings   Save Cancel

☑ Enable "Limit to Items I Own" Search Checkbox
☑ Enable Document Content Search
▢ Enable Search Optimization if your Content is Mostly in Japanese, Chinese, or Korean
☑ Use Recently Viewed User Records for Blank and Auto-Complete Lookups

⚠ You have enabled Global Search and the following search settings no longer apply. To disable Global Search, you must disable Chatter on the Chatter Settings page.

✓ Enable Drop-Down List for Sidebar Search
✓ Enable Sidebar Search Auto-Complete
  Enable Single-Search-Result Shortcut for Sidebar and Advanced Search

In the following sections, you will see how to work with various search settings:

Enable "Limit to Items I Own" Search Checkbox

The **Limit to Items I Own** option allows your users to restrict the search results to find only the records of which they are the record owner when searching in the sidebar.

 The **Limit to Items I Own** checkbox that is available for **Advanced Search** is always displayed, regardless of this option setting.

Enable Document Content Search

This option allows users to perform a full text search of a document. When new documents are uploaded or an existing document is updated, its contents are available as search terms to retrieve the document.

Enable Search Optimization if your content is mostly in Japanese, Chinese, or Korean

This option optimizes searching for Japanese, Chinese, and Korean language sets. It affects **Sidebar Search** and the account search for **Find Duplicates** on a lead record in **Sidebar Search** and **Global Search**.

 This option should not be selected if you expect content and searches to be mostly in other languages.

Use recently viewed user records for Blank and Auto-Complete Lookups

This option causes the list of records returned from a user autocomplete lookup and from a blank user lookup to be generated from the user's recently viewed user records. By not enabling this option, the dialog shows a list of recently accessed user records from across your organization.

Enable drop-down list for Sidebar Search

This option creates a drop-down list in the **Search** section to appears, which allows users to limit searches by the type of record.

Enable English-Only Spell Correction for Knowledge Search

This option is used with the **Articles** and **Article Management** tabs, in the Articles tool in **Case Feed**, and in the **Salesforce Knowledge** sidebar in the Salesforce console.

 This setting applies only to article searches via the API and not to article searches when using the Global Search.

When enabled, any search suggest, and searches for alternate spellings of English search terms.

Enable Sidebar Search Auto-Complete

This option provides the functionality whereby, users start typing search terms, the Sidebar Search displays a matching list of recently viewed records.

 The Global Search feature includes autocomplete as a standard feature and does not require a specific autocomplete option to be set.

Enable Single-Search-Result Shortcut

This option allows users to skip the search results page and navigate directly to the **Record Detail page** if their search produces a single result.

Number of Search Results Displayed Per Object

The **Number of Search Results Displayed Per Object** option allows you to configure the number of items that are returned for each object in the **Search Results** page. The current setting is in brackets next to each object where the new value must be between 5 and 50.

Lookup Settings

The **Lookup Settings** section of the **Search Settings** page allows you to enable enhanced Lookups and lookup auto completion for **Accounts**, **Contacts**, **Users**, and **Custom** objects.

Enhanced lookups

Enhanced Lookups provides an enhanced interface for your users to sort and filter search results by any field that is available in regular search results, as shown in the following screenshot:

With **Enhanced Lookups** enabled, users can hide and reorganize the columns that are displayed in the results window. **Enhanced Lookups** returns all records that match the search criteria, and allow you to page through large sets of search results.

After enabling **Enhanced Lookups**, you must specify which fields users can use to filter lookup search dialog results. This is set by accessing search layouts and choosing the fields from the **Lookup Dialog Fields** layout.

For custom objects, this is done by navigating to **Setup** | **Create** | **Objects**. Choose the object you want to modify, scroll down to the **Search Layouts**-related list, and choose the fields from the **Lookup Dialog Fields**.

For **Accounts**, **Contacts**, or **Users**, this is done by navigating to **Setup** | **Customize**, then going to **Accounts**, **Contacts**, or **Users**, and then **Search Layouts**. Then, choose fields from **Lookup Dialog Fields**, as shown in the following screenshot:

Currently, only **Accounts**, **Contacts**, **Events**, **Users**, **Chatter** objects, and custom objects can use the enhanced lookup settings.

Lookup Auto-Completion

When the**Lookup Auto-Completion** option is enabled, your users are shown a dynamic list of matching, recently used records when they edit a lookup field.

> At the time of writing, this feature is only available for **Accounts**, **Contacts, Events, Chatter, Users**, and custom object lookups.

Questions to test your knowledge

You will now be presented with questions about the key features of Salesforce CRM administration (in the organization setup and global user interface areas) that have been covered in this chapter. The answers can be found at the end of the chapter.

Questions

We present four questions to verify your understanding of the user login and authentication mechanism, company profiles, fiscal years, and the user interface.

Question 1 – user login and authentication

A new field-based salesperson has joined `WidgetsXYZ` and started using Salesforce for the first time. You are the administrator at `WidgetsXYZ`, and the salesperson is telling you that they are always prompted to activate their laptop and always use the same browser. How would you respond? (Select all that apply).

a) Verify that the Trusted IP Ranges for Salesforce have been configured correctly.

b) Verify that Login hour restrictions for Salesforce have been configured.

c) Verify that browser cookies are being stored on the salesperson's laptop correctly.

d) Explain to the salesperson that this is normal behavior and that the laptop is responding as expected.

Question 2 – company profile

Which settings can be modified for individual users? (Select all that apply)

a) Currency

b) Search settings

c) Language

d) Locale

e) User Interface

Question 3 – fiscal years

The `WidgetsXYZ` company has 13-week fiscal quarters made up of 4, 4, and 5 weeks instead of calendar months. What can you do to enable reports to capture activity for the correct quarter? (Select one)

a) Modify the reports to filter dates using these weekly periods.

b) Modify the **Standard Fiscal Year** for these weekly periods.

c) Enable **Custom Fiscal Years** to capture these weekly periods and revert back to **Standard Fiscal Years** if necessary.

d) Enable **Custom Fiscal Years** to capture these weekly periods and be aware that you cannot revert to **Standard Fiscal Years**.

Question 4 – user interface

Which settings can be modified in the Salesforce user interface? (Select all that apply)

a) Language settings.

b) Hover details.

c) Time zone settings.

d) Enhanced list views.

e) Enable Printable List Views.

Answers

Here are the answers to the four questions about user login and authentication mechanism, the company profile, fiscal years, and the user interface.

Answer 1 – user login and authentication

The answer is **a**) Verify that the Trusted IP Ranges for Salesforce have been configured correctly. Salesforce stores a cookie in the browser and activates that device, and prevents the user from being prompted for an activation code when they log in from different IP addresses. If the user has blocked cookies or is deleting them in the browser they would experience this behavior.

Answer 2 – company profile

The answers are **a**) Currency, **c**) language, and **d**) Locale. They can be modified for individual users.

b) User interface and **e**) Search settings cannot be modified for individual users as they are global setting affecting all users.

Default locale, language, and currency are set on the company profile, but these setting can be overridden for users with the values that are set at an individual level.

Answer 3 – fiscal years

The answer is **d**) **Enable Custom Fiscal Years** to capture these weekly periods and be aware that you cannot revert to Standard Fiscal Years.

Enabling custom fiscal years is not reversible and you cannot revert to standard fiscal years. You can, however, set custom fiscal years to mirror the standard fiscal year. Because fiscal quarter is based on weekly periods and not months, Standard Fiscal Years cannot accommodate reporting, which is why Custom Fiscal Years are required.

Answer 4 – user interface

The answers are **c**) **Hover details**, **d**) **Enhanced list views**, and **e**) **Enable Printable List** Views. These are all settings within the user interface and affect all users when set.

a) **Language settings** and **c**) **Time zone settings** are specified on the company profile, where they provide the default values; however, users can override these and set them on their personal settings.

Summary

This chapter looked at the mechanisms in place to help manage login access to the Salesforce CRM application and how organization-wide settings can be set to determine your company-specific information within Salesforce.com.

We also looked at the options to set up and configure the look and feel of the application, along with details of the methods used to search for information in Salesforce.

Notes and tips gained from the experience of Salesforce CRM system administration were outlined to help guide and improve the implementation and understanding of these features.

Finally, we posed some questions to help clarify some of the key features of Salesforce CRM administration in the areas of organization setup and the global user interface.

Having looked at these core customization feature sets, we will now look at how profiles and sharing in Salesforce CRM govern what functionality and access permissions a user has throughout the application.

2
Managing Users and Controlling System Access

In the previous chapter, we looked at user authentication and how user login access is authorized by the Salesforce application. We were introduced to the concept of a user being assigned a profile that could be set to control certain permissions. The user profile login permissions we looked at were restrictions on login hours and IP addresses, which allow you to control when, and from where, users log in to the Salesforce application.

In this chapter, we will look at how users can be managed in more detail and understand how some of the key profile settings are used within the Salesforce CRM application.

We will start to look into the ways in which a user's profile controls both access to objects and also governs what features are available to that user.

Along with profiles, this chapter also begins to look at the concept of record sharing and provides a high-level look at sharing features within Salesforce. It also describes how these features control access to records for users.

Finally, you will be presented with a number of questions about the key features of Salesforce CRM administration in the area of user setup, which is covered in this chapter.

We will now look at the following:

- Introduction to record ownership, profiles, and sharing
- Managing users in Salesforce
- Controlling system access
- Logging in as another user
- Salesforce.com Health Check
- Questions to test your knowledge

Introduction to record ownership, profiles, and sharing

Before looking at the features available to manage users, we start with a brief introduction to the concepts of record owner, profiles, and sharing in Salesforce CRM.

Record owner

The terminology record owner is reflected throughout Salesforce and for each and every data record there can be one, and only one, record owner.

Only users that are active in Salesforce can have records assigned to them.

When a user is marked inactive in Salesforce CRM, he/she no longer has access to the application. However, any records that this inactive user owns remain in the application and continue to show the inactive user as the record owner.

The record owner setting generally determines if access to that record is available to other users within the organization, and is enabled using either profile or sharing settings.

Profiles and sharing

Profiles, sharing, and the optional role hierarchy setting work together and should be considered as a whole when setting up record ownership and data access for users. An overview of the relationship between users, profiles, and the sharing settings can be pictured as follows:

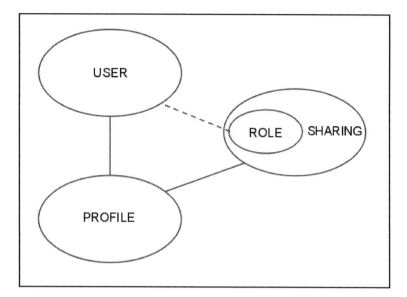

All users in Salesforce must be assigned a profile. The profile is a control mechanism used to determine which functions the user can perform, which types of data they can access, and which operations they can carry out on that data.

All users are associated with sharing mechanisms in Salesforce, which determine the actual records the user can access. Controlling the level of record access can be achieved using options ranging from default sharing, which is set at the organization level, to role hierarchy and beyond using advanced sharing mechanisms. A user does not have to be assigned to a role in Salesforce.

The sharing rules are briefly outlined as follows and covered in far more detail later in this book.

Profiles

Some of the key controls of the profile are to identify the type of license specified for the user, any login hours or IP address restrictions, and control access to objects. If the appropriate object-level permission is not set on the user's profile, the user will be unable to access the records of that object type in the application.

Profiles never override your organization's sharing model or role hierarchy. For example, a profile may be set to allow a user access to create, edit, and delete leads. However, a user with this profile cannot edit or delete other user's leads if your organization's lead sharing model is read-only.

In Chapter 3, *Configuring Objects and Apps*, we will look in detail at the features that the profile controls, which includes tabs, object-level security, field-level security, Apex/Visualforce page accessibility, console layout, application selections, and administrative and general user permissions.

There are two types of profile in Salesforce: standard and custom, with each standard or custom profile belonging to exactly one user license type.

Standard profiles and custom profiles are similar in nature, the difference being that for standard profiles, the following types of settings cannot be applied: administrative permissions, general user permissions, and object-level permissions, plus, notably, the **password never expires** setting, which means you are not required to change your password after a certain amount of time (this is a part of the password policies, which are described later). Hence, you must either create a custom profile or use a permission set, (described later in this chapter), if you want to enable any of those features.

There are a number of standard profile types such as:

- Contract manager
- Marketing user
- Solution manager
- Standard user
- System administrator

Contract manager

The contract manager profile is generally used to manage contracts and override forecasts.

Marketing user

The marketing user profile is generally used to manage campaigns, import leads, and manage public documents. Users with this profile have access to the same functions as standard user profiles.

Solution manager

The solution manager profile is generally used to publish and review solutions. Users with this profile have access to the same functions as standard user profiles.

Standard user

The standard user profile is used to create and edit the main types of records. This profile also allows users to run reports and view the organization's setup. Notably, this profile can view, but not manage, campaigns. This profile can create, but cannot review solutions.

System administrator

The system administrator profile is used to configure and customize the application. Users with this profile has access to all functionality that does not require any additional licenses. For example, system administrators cannot manage campaigns unless they also have a marketing user license.

 Standard profiles have their uses, but it is wise to limit the cloning of them to create custom profiles as it has been known for Salesforce to change the settings for standard profiles when a new release is rolled out, which can result in an undesired outcome for any user assigned with that profile.

Sharing

Sharing settings control the default access for each object across the organization. Sharing rules per object can grant access beyond the default sharing settings; they cannot restrict access. The default sharing settings are as follows:

- **Controlled by Parent**
- **Private**
- **Public Read Only**
- **Public Read/Write**

- **Public Read/Write/Transfer**
- **Public Full Access**
- **Grant Access Using Hierarchies**

When the **Grant Access Using Hierarchies** setting is enabled, the role of the record owner determines visibility throughout the organization. Users in higher roles in the hierarchy will have full access (view/edit/delete) to all records owned by those at a lower level in the role hierarchy.

If Grant Access Using Hierarchies is not enabled, all roles are treated equally regardless of the hierarchy.

Grant Access Using Hierarchies is only applicable for custom objects since they cannot be disabled for standard objects.

Roles

Roles are the principal elements in sharing rules. Users can be grouped into roles based upon their need of access to data, according to how they fit into the role hierarchy. Creating a role for every user's job title is not required.

Roles are accessed throughout the application and are particularly important for reporting. For instance, if you have two departments, Operations and Sales, you can run comparative reports on both roles.

Roles generally report to another role and are used to maintain the role hierarchy. It is a one-to-many hierarchical relationship with the hierarchy, allowing managers to see the data of the users that report to them. Users at any given role level are always able to view, edit, and report on all data owned by, or shared with, users below them in the hierarchy.

You can create up to 500 roles for your organization.

Role hierarchies do not need to specifically match your organization chart. Instead, each role in the hierarchy should represent a level of data access required by users.

Permission Sets

Permission sets allow you to further control access to the system for the users in your organization. They can be considered as a method to fine-tune the permissions for selected individuals and enable access in a similar way to the setting up of profiles.

 Permission Sets allow you to grant further access but not restrict or deny access.

While an individual user can have only one profile, you can assign multiple permissions and permission sets to users. For example, you can create a permission called **Convert Leads** that provides the facility for converting and transferring the leads and assign it to a user who has a profile, which does not provide lead conversion. You can create a permission called **Edit Contacts** and assign it to a user who has a profile that does not provide contact editing. You can also group these permissions into a permission set to create specific profile-like permissions without actually having to create or clone complete profiles, which are often unnecessary.

 You can create up to 1,000 permission sets for your organization.

Permission Sets are an ideal mechanism to apply system access for your users without affecting all other users that have the same profile and without having to create one-off profiles, which sometimes lead to an increase in the amount of maintenance.

A common use for **Permission Sets** is to grant additional permissions in addition to the settings listed in a profile to individuals without changing their profile. For example, to provide more rights than their profile currently allows.

Creating Permission Sets

To create (or clone) **Permission Sets**, navigate to **Setup** | **Manage Users** | **Permission Sets**.

When you clone an existing permission set, the new permission set has the same user license and enabled permissions as the permission set it is cloned from.

To create a new **Permission Sets** click on **New** as shown in the following screenshot:

Permission Sets

Help for this Page

On this page you can create, view, and manage permission sets.

In addition, you can use the SalesforceA mobile app to assign permission sets to a user. Download SalesforceA from the App Store or Google Play: iOS | Android

| All Permission Set ▼ | Edit | Delete | Create New View |

| New | 🔄 | A B C D E F G H I J K L M N O P Q R S T U V W X Y Z Other **All** |

Action	Permission Set Label ↑	Description	License
Del	Clone	Export Reports		Salesforce
Del	Clone	Moderator		Chatter Free
Del	Clone	Moderator Salesforce		Salesforce
Del	Clone	SMS Activation		Salesforce

Now enter a **Label**, **API Name**, and **Description**.

If you plan to assign the permission set to users that all have the same type of user license, a best practice is to associate that user license with the permission set. However, if you plan to assign the permission set to users that currently have different licenses (or may have different licenses in the future), it is probably best to create an organization-wide permission set.

To continue creating the permission set (as outlined previously), either select a **User License** or select the option **None** (to create an organization-wide permission set). Now finally, click on **Save** as shown in the following screenshot:

When you clone an existing permission set, the new permission set has the same user license and enabled permissions as the permission set it is cloned from.

Permission Set
Create

Help for this Page 🕐

| Save | Cancel |

Enter permission set information   ▐ = Required Information

Label |

API Name |
[i]

Description |

Select the type of users who will use this permission set

Who will use this permission set? If you plan to assign this permission set to multiple users with different licenses, choose '--None--'. If only users with one type of license will use this permission set, choose the same license that's associated with them.

User License | --None-- ▼ [i]

| Save | Cancel |

Profile and permission sets summary

Generally, permissions and access settings can be specified for users at profile level and at individual user permission set level. Although certain permissions and access settings can only be specified in profiles. A summary of the permission and settings types that are available in **Profiles** and **Permission Sets** can be seen in the following table:

Permission / Setting Type	Available in Profiles	Available in Permission Sets
Assigned apps	Yes	Yes
Tab settings	Yes	Yes
Record type assignments	Yes	Yes
Page layout assignments	Yes	No
Object permissions	Yes	Yes
Field permissions	Yes	Yes
User permissions (app and system)	Yes	Yes
Apex class access	Yes	Yes
Visualforce page access	Yes	Yes
External data source access	Yes	Yes
Service provider access	Yes	Yes
Custom permissions	Yes	Yes
Desktop client access	Yes	No
Login hours	Yes	No
Login IP ranges	Yes	No

Managing users in Salesforce CRM

All users in your organization with access to Salesforce CRM require a username, an e-mail address, a password, and a profile along with an active user license.

Depending on the features your organization has purchased, you may have user options such as Marketing, Service Cloud, and Mobile, which give particular users the ability to access other features that are only available with a specific user license. A user can be assigned to one or more of these options.

You can also create and manage other types of users outside your organization by applying the appropriate licenses that provide limited access to your Salesforce organization, as detailed later in this chapter.

In association with the user license, you can govern all user's access to data using the options available in either the profile settings or the sharing features.

Profile settings control access to applications and objects while sharing features control access to specific records.

To navigate to the user detail page, go to **Setup** | **Manage Users** | **Users**.

The user detail page shows a list of all the users in your organization as well as any portal users:

Action	Full Name ↑	Alias	Username	Last Login	Role	Active	Profile	Manager
Edit	Brown, Martin	mbrow	martin.brown@widgetsxyz.com		CEO	✓	Custom: Sales Profile	
Edit | Login	Howard, Trevor	thow	trevor.howard@widgetsxyz.com	01/01/2011 12:05	AM, Region B01	✓	Standard Platform User	Goodey, Paul
Edit	One, Platform	POne	p1@widgetsxyz.com		CEO		Standard Platform User	
Edit	Two, Platform	PTwo	p2@widgetsxyz.com		CEO		Standard Platform User	

To show a filtered list of users, select a predefined list from the **View** drop-down list or click on **Create New View** to define your own custom view.

For example, you can create a view with search criteria of **Last Login, less than**, LAST 28 DAYS to show all users that have not logged in for 28 days as shown in the following screenshot:

As the system administrator of Salesforce CRM, you can perform various user management actions such as creating new users, resetting passwords, and even delegating user administration tasks to other users within your organization. The following list of user actions will be covered:

- Creating new users
- Viewing and editing user information
- Password management

- Session management
- Logging in as another user
- Creating custom user fields

Creating new user records

The steps for creating a new user are as following:

1. Click on **New User**.
2. Enter fields in the **General Information** and **Locale Settings** sections.
3. Check the box, **Generate new password and notify user immediately**.
4. Save the new user details.

To create a new user for your organization, navigate to the user detail page. This page displays the list of all the users in your organization. To navigate to the **New User** page, go to **Setup** | **Manage Users** | **Users**. Now click on the **New User** button.

Looking at the top section of the page, you will see the **General Information** section as shown in the following screenshot:

The mandatory user information is shown with a bar and requires the entry of the user's **Last Name**, **Email** address, **Username**, **User License**, and **Profile**.

> The length of user's passwords cannot exceed 16,000 bytes.

The e-mail address automatically becomes the username, but you can change it if you require prior to saving.

> You can restrict the domain names of user's e-mail addresses to a list of values such as xxx@WidgetsXYZ.com, yyy@CompanyXYZ.com, and so on. After which, attempts to set a user's e-mail address to an unlisted domain (such as xxx@MyNonCompanyWebMail.com) will result in an error.

The feature for restricting the domain names of user's e-mail addresses can only be enabled by request to Salesforce customer support. Also, when selecting a user license, note that some further options become unavailable depending on the license type you choose. For example, the **Marketing User** and **Allow Forecasting** options are not available for Force.com user licenses because the **Forecasts and Campaigns** tabs are not available to users with that license.

> You should consider the username that is entered. After the username is saved, it becomes a unique setting throughout the Salesforce.com universe, hence you will not be able to use that same username in any other Salesforce CRM organization.

You can select various checkboxes that give the user additional features or options. The types of additional features are available by selecting one or more of the following example checkboxes:

- **Marketing User**
- **Offline User**
- **Knowledge User**
- **Force.com Flow User**
- **Service Cloud User**
- **Site.com Publisher User**
- **Salesforce CRM Content User**

You will not be able to select these features if they are not supported by your user license type. Also, you will be unable to save the new user record if you do not have any remaining licenses available for these features.

At the bottom of the **New User** edit page, there are further sections, which include the **Locale Settings** section as shown in the following screenshot:

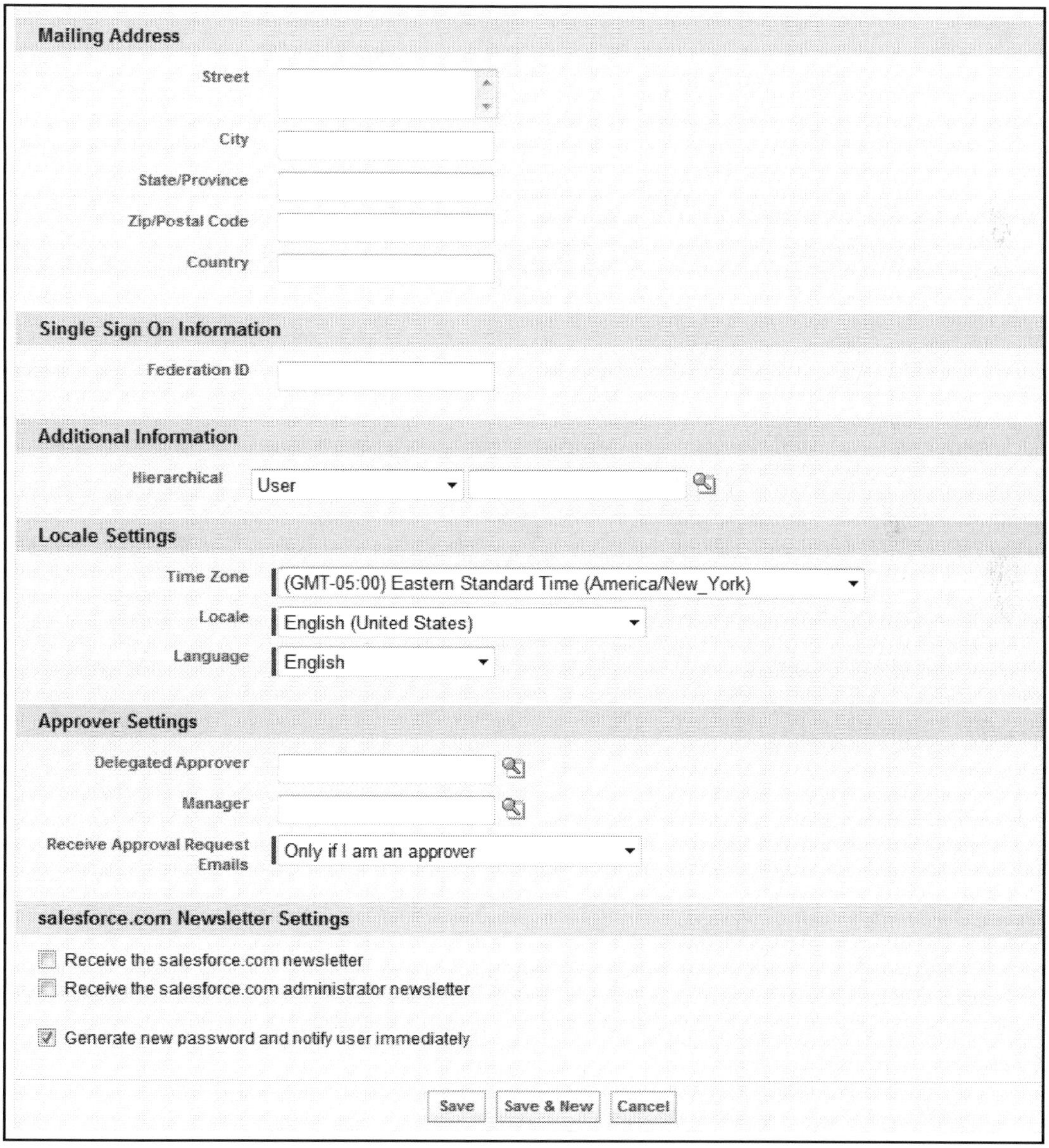

Saving new user records

Complete the required information, which is displayed with a bar, and then check the **Generate new password and notify user immediately** checkbox and save the details by clicking on the **Save** button. Upon saving, the user's login name and a temporary password are e-mailed via `Salesforce.com` to the new user.

Junk e-mail folder
If you have generated the new password to be sent, but the new user cannot see the e-mail notification from `Salesforce.com` in his/her inbox you may need to have the user check his/her junk e-mail folder.

The following table lists the key standard user fields with the required fields shown in bold:

First Name	**Last Name**	**Alias**	**Email**	**Username**
Community Nickname	Title	Company	Department	Division
Role	User License	Profile	Active	Grant Checkout Access
Marketing User	Offline User	Knowledge User	Service Cloud User	Mobile User
Mobile Configuration	Accessibility Mode	Color-Blind Palette on Charts	Salesforce CRM Content User	Receive Salesforce CRM Content Email Alerts
Receive Salesforce CRM Content Alerts as Daily Digest	Allow Forecasting	Call Center	Phone	Extension
Fax	Mobile	Email Encoding	Employee Number	Mailing Address Fields
Time Zone	**Locale**	**Language**	Delegated Approver	Manager
Receive Approval Request Emails	Newsletter	Admin Newsletter	Development Mode	Send Apex Warning Emails

Viewing new user records

After saving the **User Edit** page, you are presented with the details page for the user where you can view the information that was entered as shown in the following screenshot:

User **Trevor Howard**				Edit Layout | Help f
Personal Groups [0] | Public Group Membership [0] | Queue Membership [1] | Managers in the Role Hierarchy [3] | Remote Access [0] | Login History [2+]				
User Detail	Edit	Reset Password	Login	
Name	Trevor Howard		Role	AM, Region B01
Alias	thow		User License	Salesforce
Email	trevor.howard@widgetsxyz.com		Profile	Custom: Sales Profile
Username	trevor.howard@widgetsxyz.com		Active	✓
Community Nickname	th1		Marketing User	
Title			Offline User	
Company	WidgetsXYZ		Knowledge User	

Do not overwrite active or inactive user records with new user data: Salesforce does not recommend overwriting inactive user records with new user data. Doing so prevents you from tracking the history of past users and the records associated with them.

There are also situations where you may feel it appropriate to recycle an active user record, but it is better to deactivate users when they are no longer using Salesforce and create a new record for each new user.

A typical real-world example of recycling a user record, and one to avoid, is sometimes encountered when a sales team is organized into sales territories.

The sales team user records in Salesforce are stamped with a territory indicator and any account records that are located in their particular territory are assigned to the user record (set as the record owner). In this way, the user record simply acts as a container for the territory.

Managing user records in this way results in both audit and maintenance issues. For example, if Tina Fox changes sales territory, her personal information (username, password, e-mail address, phone number, and so on) all has to be transferred to a new user record requiring Tina to reactivate a new password, re-enter both her personal details, and all her personal preferences in the Salesforce application.

The issue worsens if the user record (or territory) that Tina is reassigning to, is held by, say, Timothy Little as he would also need to reset his personal details.

This approach leads to a technically complex method of territory reassignment and a very disappointing user experience for your sales team. Fortunately, Salesforce provides features such as criteria-based sharing rules, sales teams, and territory management to better manage the organization of sales territories.

Adding multiple users

If you have several users to add, you can add more than one at a time.

To add multiple users, navigate to **Setup** | **Manage Users** | **Users**. Now click on the **Add Multiple Users** button.

This is a two-step process: First you select the user license type and then you are presented with multiple sections to add the new user's details. As you can see in the following screenshot, this can be a quick method for creating users, since not all required fields have to be entered in this process:

Users
Add Multiple Users

Number of available Salesforce Platform user licenses: 3
Number of available XOrg Proxy User user licenses: 2
Number of available Chatter Free user licenses: 5000
Number of available Chatter External user licenses: 500

Add Users	Save	Cancel

User License	Salesforce Platform ▼

New Users   ❚ = Required Information

New User	#1
First Name	
Last Name	
Email (User Name)	
Profile	--None-- ▼
Role	<None Specified> ▼

New User	#2
First Name	
Last Name	
Email (User Name)	
Profile	--None-- ▼
Role	<None Specified> ▼

New User	#3
First Name	
Last Name	
Email (User Name)	
Profile	--None-- ▼
Role	<None Specified> ▼

☐ Generate passwords and notify user via email

Save	Cancel

Collapse All   Expand All
- **WidgetsXYZ**
    - Add Role
    - **CEO**
        - Add Role
        - **SVP, Sales & Marketing**
            - Add Role
            - **VP, Global Marketing**
                - Add Role
                - **Marketing Team**
                    - Add Role
            - **VP, International Sales**
                - Add Role
                - **Sales Manager, Region B**
                    - Add Role
                    - **AM, Region B01**
                        - Add Role
            - **VP, North American Sales**
                - Add Role
                - **Sales Manager, Region A**
                    - Add Role
                    - **AM, Region A01**
                        - Add Role

If, however, after the initial saving of multiple user records, you attempt to edit a user record, via the user edit screen, you will be prompted to fill up all mandatory fields.

Delegation of user management

If you have an organization with a large number of users or a complex role hierarchy, you can delegate aspects of user administration to users who are not assigned to the system administrator profile.

This allows you to focus on tasks other than managing users for every department or structure that your company has within Salesforce. This provides further benefits for global organizations that encounter time zone and cultural differences as it allows a user based in that region with local knowledge to create the users, which saves time and results in a better user experience.

For example, you may want to allow the manager of the Asia Pacific Operations team to create and edit users in the Asia Pacific Operations Team Leader role and all subordinate roles.

There are currently two options for providing this delegated user management access:

- Create a profile with the Manage Users permission
- Use delegated administration

Creating a profile with the Manage Users permission

This option is not recommended and should be very carefully considered as it allows a much greater range of system administration functions to be carried out by the user.

In addition to creating and managing users, the **Manage Users** permission also allows the user to perform the following:

- Expire all passwords
- Clone, edit, or delete profiles
- Edit or delete sharing settings
- Edit user login hours

By providing users with the **Manage Users** permission, as you can see, there are many other permissions that are switched on, which introduces security risks.

Using delegated administration

Delegated administration is a more secure method for providing delegated user management access as it allows you to assign limited administrative privileges to the selected non-administrator users in your organization.

Delegated administrators can perform the following tasks:

- Creating and editing users, and resetting passwords for users in specified roles and all subordinate roles
- Assigning users to specified profiles
- Logging in as another user

To create delegated groups, navigate to **Setup** | **Security Controls** | **Delegated Administration**. Now click on the **New** button or select the name of an existing delegated administration group. The following screenshot shows the **Manage Delegated Groups** page:

Manage Delegated Groups   Help for this Page

Below are delegated groups defined for your organization. You can choose to delegate user administration, custom object administration, or both to the delegated administrators of this group.

Delegated Groups   New

Action	Delegated Group Name	Login Access	Created By	Modified By
Edit	User Management	✓	Paul Goodey, 30/01/2011 17:40	Paul Goodey, 31/01/2011 09:03

Here is the screenshot for the existing group that has been named User Management:

The **Delegated Administrators** section allows you to select and add the users that are to be given the delegated administration permission.

The **User Administration** section allows you to select and add roles which the delegated administrators can assign to the users they create and edit. They can assign users for the stated roles and all subordinated roles.

The **Assignable Profiles** section allows you to select and add profiles which the delegated administrators can assign to the users they create and edit.

The **Assignable Permission Sets** section allows you to select and add **Permission Sets** which the delegated administrators can assign to the users they create and edit.

The **Assignable Public Groups** section allows you to select and add **Public Groups** which the delegated administrators can assign to the users they create and edit.

To enforce security, profiles with the Modify All Data permission (such as the System Administrator profile) cannot be assigned by a delegated administrator. See the following example message shown when attempting to allow the delegated administrator to assign the **System Administrator** profile:

Assignable Profiles

Specify the profiles that delegated administrators of this group can assign to the users they create and profile. They can only assign users to these profiles.

| | Save | Save & More | Cancel |

Assignable Profiles

System Administrator 🔍

Error: Profiles with the permission "Modify All Data" cannot be assigned by delegated administrators.

🔍

🔍

🔍

🔍

If a user is a member of more than one delegated administration group, be aware that he/she can assign any of the assignable profiles to any of the users in roles he/she can manage.

Select the **Enable Group for Login Access** option, if you want to allow delegated administrators in this group to log in as users who have granted login access to their administrators and are in the roles selected for the delegated administrator group.

Edit Delegated Group
User Management
Help for this Page

Delegated Group Edit   Save   Cancel

Delegated Group Name | User Management | Enable Group for Login Access   ☑

Save   Cancel

To look at how users can grant login access to their administrators, refer to the section *Logging in as another user* toward the end of this chapter.

Agreement in using active user licenses by delegated user administrators:

If you have established delegated user management in your organization, you will need to have some agreement between yourself and the delegated user administrators about how many of the available licenses can be used for each area of the organization. You cannot automatically limit the number of active users that can be created by users with these permissions.

Viewing and editing user information

To view or edit user information, navigate to **Setup** | **Manage Users** | **Users**. Now, click on **Edit** next to a user's name. Change the necessary information and click on **Save**.

Users can also change, or add to, their own personal information after they log in.

If you change a user's e-mail address and do not select the **Generate new password and notify user immediately** option, a confirmation message will be sent to the new e-mail address that you entered to verify the change of e-mail. The user must click on the link provided in that message for the new e-mail address to take effect.

If you change a user's e-mail and reset the password for a user at the same time, the new password is automatically sent to the user's new e-mail address, and e-mail verification is not required.

Click on **Unlock** to unlock a user that is locked out of Salesforce.

> The **Unlock** button is only available when a user is locked out after they have exceeded the maximum number of incorrect password login attempts.

Searching for users

You can use the search features (described in the previous chapter) to search for any user in your organization, regardless of the user's status. However, when using a lookup dialog from fields within records, the search results return active users only.

Deactivating users

You cannot remove users from the system, but you can deactivate their records so that they can no longer access the application.

To deactivate users, navigate to **Setup** | **Manage Users** | **Users**. Now, click on **Edit** next to a user's name, disable the **Active** checkbox, and then click on **Save**.

If the user is a member of account, sales, or case teams, you are prompted to remove the user from those teams:

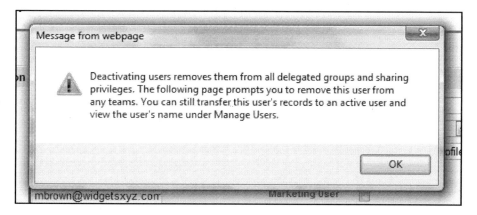

When deactivating users, there are some considerations that ought to be made, such as:

- Deactivating users with **Run as specified user** dependencies set on dashboards causes those dashboards to stop displaying. Each dashboard has a running user, whose security settings determine which data to display in a dashboard. You need to reassign **Run as specified user** to an active user with the appropriate permissions.
- As mentioned in Chapter 1, *Setting up Salesforce CRM and the Company Profile*, in the License information section, Salesforce bills an organization based on the total number of licenses and not on active users.
- If **Chatter** is enabled and a user who has been included in either the **Following** or **Followers** list is deactivated and the user is removed from the list, however, he/she is restored to the lists if he/she is re-activated.

 Deactivating users that have been explicitly included as part of an approval process, which is described in Chapter 7, *Implementing Business Processes in Salesforce CRM*, will cause the approval step to fail.

Freezing user accounts

This feature allows you to freeze user records. Often there are times when you may not want to deactivate a user immediately (such as when a user is part of an approval process) but you must prevent them from logging into your organization (as they have left the company, for example) while you perform the steps to deactivate them.

To freeze a user record, navigate to **Setup** | **Manage Users** | **Users**. Now, click on a user's name to access their user detail page. Now click the **Freeze** button.

Password management

You have the following options for resetting passwords for users in Salesforce CRM:

- Resetting passwords
- Expiring passwords

Resetting passwords

If users have forgotten their password, they can click on the **Forgot your password?** link on the Salesforce CRM login page which presents them with a screen to enter their username, as shown in the following screenshot:

The user will then receive an e-mail from Salesforce that contains a new password link that will require them to answer a previously set security question such as **Where were you born?** before their password is reset and they can log in to Salesforce.

To reset a user's password, navigate to **Setup** | **Manage Users** | **Users**. Now select the checkbox next to the user's name.

Optionally, to change the passwords for all currently displayed users, check the box in the column header to select all rows.

Click on **Reset Password** to have a new password e-mailed to the user(s).

> After you reset user's passwords, some users may need to re-activate their computers to successfully log in to Salesforce (see the previous chapter).

Expiring passwords

You can expire passwords for all users at any time to enforce extra security for your organization. After you expire passwords, users may need to activate their computers to successfully log in to Salesforce (see the previous chapter).

This includes system administrators if they don't have **Password Never Expires** on their profile (or permission set), however, the standard System Administrator profile has the **Password Never Expires** setting activated by default.

To expire passwords for all users, except those with the **Password Never Expires** permission, navigate to **Setup** | **Security Controls** | **Expire All Passwords**. Now, select the **Expire all user passwords** checkbox and then click on **Save**.

The next time each user logs in, he/she will be prompted to reset their password.

After you expire passwords, some users may need to reactivate their computers to successfully log in to Salesforce (see the previous chapter).

Controlling system access

Salesforce provides several features to allow you to control user's access to your instance of Salesforce CRM. Here we are going to look at the key control mechanisms and access policies that are available for you to set.

Password policies

There are several password and login policy features that help you to improve your organization's security. To set these password policies, navigate to **Setup** | **Security Controls** | **Password Policies**. Select the required settings and then click on **Save**.

Let's look at each of the password policies which are shown in the following screenshot:

User passwords expiration period

Password expiration periods for all users in your organization are set by the picklist selection **User passwords expire in**.

This sets the length of time until all user passwords expire and must be changed. Users with the **Password Never Expires** permission are not affected by this setting.

The options are **30 days**, **60 days**, **90 days**, **180 days**, **One Year**, and **Never Expires**.

Enforce password history

This setting is used to remember user's previous passwords so that they must always enter a previously unused password. Password history is not saved until you set this value. You cannot select the **No passwords remembered** option unless you select the **Never expires** option for the **User passwords expire in** field.

The options are either **No passwords remembered** or a number between 1 and 24 passwords remembered.

Minimum password length

This sets the minimum number of characters required for a password. When you set this value, existing users are not affected until the next time they change their passwords.

A numeric value can be set between 5 and 50 characters.

Password complexity requirement

This sets a restriction on which types of characters must be used in a user's password. The following options are available:

- **No Restriction**: This option does not have any requirements to create a password
- **Must mix alpha and numeric**: This option requires at least one alphabetic character and one number

- **Must mix alpha, numeric and special characters**: This option requires at least one alphabetic character, one number, and one of the following characters: ! # $ % – _ = + < >
- **Must mix numbers and uppercase and lowercase letters**: This option requires at least one number, one uppercase letter, and one lowercase letter
- **Must mix numbers, uppercase and lowercase letters, and special characters**: This option requires at least one number, one uppercase letter, and one lowercase letter, and one of the following characters: ! # $ % – _ = + < >

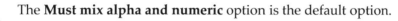

The **Must mix alpha and numeric** option is the default option.

Password question requirement

This setting requires that a user's answer to the password hint question does not contain the password itself.

The options are either **Cannot contain password**, which means that the answer to the password hint question cannot contain the actual password itself; or **None**, which is the default, for no restrictions on the answer.

Maximum invalid login attempts

This sets the number of incorrect login attempts allowed by a user before they become locked out. The options are **No limit**, **3**, **5**, and **10**.

The default number of invalid login attempts is **10**.

Lockout effective period

This sets the duration of the login lockout. The options are **15 minutes**, **30 minutes**, **60 minutes**, and **Forever** (must be reset by admin).

 The default lockout effective period is **15 minutes**.

If a user becomes locked out, he/she can either wait until the lockout effective period expires or you can view the user's information and click on **Unlock**. The **Unlock** button is only displayed when a user is locked out.

Obscure secret answer for password resets

This hides the text as users type the answers to security questions. The default option is unchecked which will display the answer in plain text when users answer a security question, say when resetting their passwords.

Require a minimum one day password lifetime

When selected, this option prevents users from changing their passwords more than once per day. The default option is unchecked which allows users to change their password as often as they like.

Forgot Password or Locked Account Assistance

The following sections discuss the available options:

Message

By setting this message, the text will appear in the lockout e-mail that users receive whenever they need you to reset their password. Your users will also see the message text in the confirm identity screen and e-mail that they receive whenever their password is reset. This is useful to add your contact details and a personal message.

Help link

Setting this link results in the text above this option appearing as a web URL, which when clicked will allow your users to navigate to a separate page such as a custom help page, which you have available.

API only user settings

The following section discusses the available option:

Alternative Home Page

API Only Users will be redirected to this URL after they have confirmed a user management change (such as resetting a password). This would be used as a way of confirming the change since users with the profile or permission set setting of **API Only User** cannot access Salesforce via the user interface and hence receive no visual confirmation.

Session management

There are several session security features that help you improve your organization's security. These features include setting the session expiration timeout, locking sessions to the IP address from which they originated, and other organization-wide session settings. To set these session options, navigate to **Setup** | **Security Controls** | **Session Settings**.

Select the required settings as shown in the following screenshot and then click **Save**.

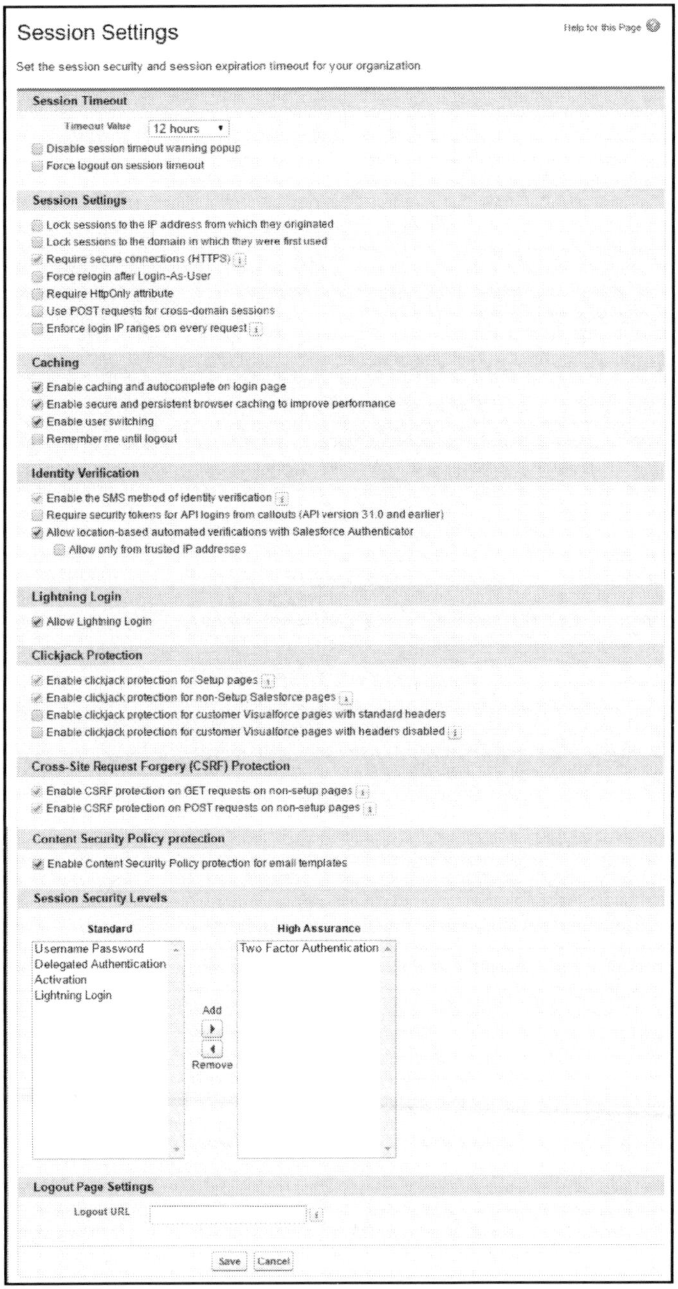

Let's look at each of the session security features.

Session timeout

There are various features for setting the session timeout as per the following sections:

Timeout value

This sets the length of time after which inactive users are automatically logged out of the system.

The options are between **15 minutes** and **12 hours**. As a system administrator you need to balance the requirements for user satisfaction and enforcement of security controls, however it is recommended that you choose as short a timeout period as possible to protect sensitive information and enforce stricter security.

The value of the last active session is not updated until halfway through the timeout period. So if you have a 2-hour timeout, the system does not check for activity until 1 hour has passed. As an example, say you have a 2-hour timeout value. If you update a record after 30 minutes, the last active session value is not updated because there was no activity after 1 hour and hence you will still be logged out in a further 1 hour and 30 minutes because the last active session has not been updated.

Disable session timeout warning popup

This sets whether inactive users are presented with a timeout warning message. Users are warned 30 seconds before the session timeout as set by the **Timeout** value.

Force logout on session timeout

Enabling this option causes inactive users to have their browsers refreshed and set to the Salesforce.com login page when the session times out.

It is recommended that you do not select the **Disable session timeout** warning popup when enabling the **Force logout** on session timeout feature as this can confuse users when they are logged out for no apparent reason.

Session settings

There are various features for setting the session as per the following sections.

Lock sessions to the IP address from which they originated

This option is used to specify if users' sessions are to be locked to the IP address with which they logged in.

> Enabling this option helps to prevent the hijacking of valid user sessions by unauthorized people.

Lock sessions to the domain in which they were first used

This setting associates user's current session with a specific domain to prevent unauthorized use of that session ID in another domain.

> This setting applied to user's logins via the user interface and is enabled by default for new organizations starting from the Spring '15 release.

Require secure connections (HTTPS)

This sets whether HTTPS (instead of the less secure HTTP connection) is required to access Salesforce.

> This option is enabled by default and can only be disabled by request to Salesforce.com support.

Force relogin after Login-As-User

This option, when set, results in you having to log in again to get back into Salesforce after logging out as a logged-in user. When this is not set you are given the original session after logging out as the logged-in user and do not have to re-login.

 This option is enabled by default for new organizations since the Summer '14 release.

Require HttpOnly attribute

Setting this option restricts access to the session ID cookies. The effect of this is that cookies with the **HttpOnly** attribute are not accessible using non-HTTP calls such as JavaScript methods from custom or packaged applications.

 Setting this will result in custom or packaged applications that use JavaScript to call session ID cookies that no longer work as they are denied access to the session cookie.

Use POST requests for cross-domain sessions

This option sets the organization to send session information using a POST request, instead of a GET request, during cross-domain exchanges, such as when calling a Visualforce page which is served on a different URL to the standard Salesforce CRM pages.

 POST requests are more secure than GET requests, in this scenario since the session information in the body of the request.

Enforce login IP ranges on every request

This setting affects users with profiles that have login IP restrictions which allow only IP addresses within the **Login IP Ranges** setting to access Salesforce.

If the setting is not set, login IP ranges are verified only when the user logs into Salesforce. When this setting is enabled, login IP ranges are enforced on each and every page request.

Caching

The feature for setting login page caching and autocomplete which stores, user's login details (just the list of usernames but not the password) is as per the following sections.

Enable caching and autocomplete on login page

Setting this option enables user's browsers to store username text and so, after their initial log in, usernames are automatically set in the **User Name** field on the login page.

 This option is enabled by default.

Enable secure and persistent browser caching to improve performance

This option activates data caching in the browser which is secure and helps to improve page reload performance (by avoiding extra round trips to the server).

 Salesforce recommends setting this option and is enabled by default.

Enable user switching

The user switcher feature allows users that have multiple usernames on the same or different Salesforce instances to switch between their different usernames. By selecting their profile picture, they can view all the available usernames that can be navigated to.

This option hides or shows the user switcher when users select their profile picture. Deselecting this option hides the user switcher and also hides your Salesforce instance from appearing in user switchers in other instances.

 This setting is enabled by default, however it is available in Lightning Experience only. In addition, the **Enable caching and autocomplete on login page** settings must be enabled.

Remember Me until logout

Usernames are cached if a user selects the **Remember Me** checkbox or while a session is active. However, the **Remember Me** checkbox is not available when logging in using **SingleSignOn** (**SSO**). Therefore, when the session expires, the username no longer appears in the login screen or the user switcher.

By enabling this option, the cached usernames are only deleted once the user specifically logs out. Should the session time out, then the username remains on the user switcher, but is set as inactive.

 This option is disabled by default. Salesforce recommends enabling this option as it is helpful for users.

Identity verification

The feature for setting identify confirmation, which allows further mechanisms to extend the standard use of e-mail confirmation, is as per the following sections

Enable the SMS method of identity verification

This option enables users to receive a one-time PIN which they receive via SMS. Once enabled, users must verify their mobile phone number before taking advantage of this feature.

This option is enabled by default and can only be disabled by request to `salesforce.com` support.

Require security tokens for API logins from callouts (API version 31.0 and earlier)

In API version 31.0 and earlier, security tokens for API logins from callouts (such as Apex or AJAX proxy callouts) are required.

In API version 32.0 and later, security tokens for API logins from Apex callouts, AJAX proxy callouts, and so on, are required by default

Allow location-based automated verifications with Salesforce Authenticator

This option allows you to disable the use of location-based automated verifications for users utilizing the *Salesforce Authenticator* mobile app. When enabled users are allowed to verify their identity by automatically approving notifications in *Salesforce Authenticator* (within trusted locations such as a home or office).

This option for automated verification from all locations is enabled by default

Allow only from trusted IP addresses

This option allows you to specify that automated verification from locations using the Salesforce Authenticator mobile app is only permitted from trusted IP addresses.

Lightning Login

Lightning Login is an enhanced security mechanism that moved beyong using passwords. The feature allows users to click their username, tap to approve the notification on their mobile devices, and authenticate with their fingerprint or PIN.

Allow Lightning Login

This option enables or disables the Lightning Login feature for verifying their identity in Salesforce CRM.

 This option is enabled by default and the feature is supported for use in Salesforce Classic as well as Lightning Experience.

Clickjack protection

Clickjacking is a malicious technique that tricks a user into clicking on a button or link to a different page than the one the user intended and often takes the form of embedded code or script that executes without the user's knowledge. There are various features for setting **clickjack** protection as per the following sections

Enable clickjack protection for setup pages

This option adds security to help guard against clickjack attacks on Salesforce setup pages.

 This option is enabled by default and can only be disabled by request to `salesforce.com` support.

Enable clickjack protection for non-setup Salesforce pages

This option adds security to help guard against clickjack attacks on non-setup Salesforce pages.

 This option is enabled by default and can only be disabled by request to `Salesforce.com` support.

Enable clickjack protection for customer Visualforce pages with standard headers

This option protects against clickjack attacks on Visualforce pages with headers enabled.

Enable clickjack protection for customer Visualforce pages with headers disabled

This option protects against clickjack attacks on Visualforce pages with headers disabled (such as the value of `showHeader="false"` on the page tag).

Cross-Site Request Forgery (CSRF) protection

Cross–Site Request Forgery (**CSRF**) is a malicious technique in which unauthorized commands are crafted (by script or a link on a page, for example) to be sent by a user to a website that has been authenticated.

These options protect against **Cross–Site Request Forgery** (**CSRF**) attacks by modifying the non-setup pages to include a random string of characters in the URL parameters or as a hidden embedded field. The system then verifies this string of characters and only executes the command if the value matches the expected value. There are various features for setting protection against CSRF attacks as per the following sections:

Enable CSRF protection on GET requests on non-setup pages

The **Enable CSRF protection on GET requests on non-setup pages** option protects against CSRF attacks on GET requests on non-setup pages.

This option is enabled by default and can only be disabled by request to Salesforce.com support.

Enable CSRF protection on POST requests on non-setup pages

The **Enable CSRF protection on POST requests on non-setup pages** option protects against CSRF attacks on POST requests on non-setup pages.

This option is enabled by default and can only be disabled by request to `Salesforce.com` support.

Content Security Policy protection

Content Security Policy (CSP) is a security standard created to prevent malicious content executing in trusted web content. Setting the option within this section applies the policy to associated e-mail templates within Salesforce.

Session security levels

Session-level security settings are used for connected apps, reports, and dashboards. Here you can restrict access to these areas of functionality based on the level of security associated with the authentication (login) method for the user's current session. You can restrict access to connected apps, reports, and dashboards by setting the level of security associated with the user's current authentication (login) method; each login method has one of two security levels which is either Standard or High Assurance. Different authentication methods are assigned with the following security levels:

- Username Password (Standard)
- Delegated Authentication (Standard)
- Activation (Standard)
- Two-Factor Authentication (High Assurance)
- Authentication Provider (Standard)
- Lightning Login (Standard)

To change the security level associated with a login method navigate to **Setup** | **Security Controls** | **Session Settings**. Locate the **Session Security Levels**, select the login method and then click the **Add** or **Remove** arrow to move it to the required category as shown in the following screenshot:

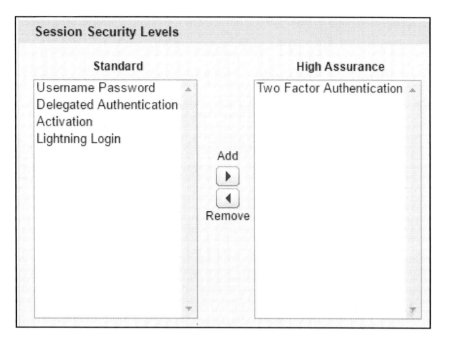

Logout page settings

The Logout URL setting allows you to specify a URL that starts with `http://` or `https://` that users are redirected to after they have logged out of Salesforce. If the Logout URL is not specified, the user is redirected to `https://login.salesforce.com`. If My Domain is enabled and Logout URL is not specified, users are redirected to `https://"my-domain".my.salesforce.com`.

Logging in as another user

To assist other users, you can log in to Salesforce as another user.

To log in as another user, navigate to **Setup** | **Manage Users** | **Users**. Now click on the **Login** link next to the user record as shown in the following screenshot:

	Action	Full Name ↑	Alia
☐	Edit	Brown, Martin	mb
☐	Edit	Goodey, Paul	pgo
☐	Edit | Login	Howard, Trevor	tho
☐	Edit	One, Platform	PO
☐	Edit	Two, Platform	PTv

You can also log in as another user from the **User Detail** page using the **Login** button as shown in the following screenshot:

User
Trevor Howard   Edit Layout | User Profile | Help for this Page

Permission Set Assignments [0] | Permission Set Assignments: Activation Required [0] | Permission Set License Assignments [0] | Personal Groups [0] |
Public Group Membership [0] | Queue Membership [1] | Team [1] | Managers in the Role Hierarchy [3] | OAuth Connected Apps [0] |
Third-Party Account Links [0] | Installed Mobile Apps [0] | Authentication Settings for External Systems [0] | Login History [1+] | User Provisioning Accounts [0]

User Detail   Edit   Sharing   Reset Password   Login   Freeze

Name ˙ Trevor Howard   Role   AM, Region B01
Alias   thow   User License   Salesforce

After you have logged in as another user, you will notice a message at the top-right corner of all Salesforce pages that display the message **You are currently logged in as**.

To return to your administrator account, click on the logged in user's name (the user who has granted you access, Trevor Howard in this example). Then click on the **Logout** option:

Regardless of the login access policy, whenever an administrator logs in as another user, the login and logout events are recorded in the setup audit trail.

Creating a guide to help users grant login access to you

There are many occasions when it is useful for you to log in as one of the users in your organization. This could be, say, to check data access from their role or profile or to check reports or dashboards and so on.

If the **Administrators Can Log in as Any User** feature is disabled, rather than instructing individuals one-by-one, on how to grant you login access you can save time for both yourself and the users in your organization by preparing a how-to guide to help users grant login access to you. The following is a sample how-to guide that lists the steps that they need to take to make the required setting and is shown in the following screenshot:

Step 1: Click "Your Name"
Step 2: Click "Setup"
Step 3: Click "My Personal Information"
Step 4: Click "Grant Login Access"
Step 5: Select the Grant Access To "Your Company's Administrator" and choose a period of either 1 Day, 3 Days, 1 Week, 1 Month or 1 Year
Step 6: Click "Save"

When the **Administrators Can Log in as Any User** feature is enabled, users will no longer have the option to grant login access to administrators, but they can still grant login access to Salesforce.com support.

Where additional apps have been installed, the list of entities that users can select to grant access may increase. For example, if your organization has installed the Non Profit Starter Pack app published by the Salesforce.com Foundation (see http://www.salesforcefounda tion.org/nonprofitstarterpack), you will see the option to grant access to this organization's support team as shown in the following screenshot:

Creating custom user fields

You can create custom fields for users and set custom links that appear on the user detail page. To navigate to the user field's page, go to **Setup** | **Customize** | **Users** | **Fields** and then scroll down to the **User Custom Fields** section:

The `User` object can be considered a special object in Salesforce as there are restrictions on what can be configured. For example, there can be only one record type and page layout for the `User` object.

Salesforce.com Health Check

The Health Check feature enables you to view the key security settings in your organization, such as login access policies, password policies, and so on, and compare these settings to the security standards recommended by Salesforce.

To access the Health Check settings, navigate to **Setup** | **Security Controls** | **Health Check** where you will be presented with a page as shown in the following screenshot:

The **Health Check** page displays actual, and Salesforce recommended, values for the following security controls: **Login Access Policies**; **Network Access**; **Password Policies**; Remote **Site Settings**; **Session Settings**.

Within the page, High-Risk and Medium-Risk settings are shown with details about how they compare against the Salesforce recommended (standard) values. Links are provided within this screen so you can modify any of the given security settings along with a summary health check score that shows how your instance compares to the standard baseline recommended by Salesforce.

Health Check Score

If all the values in your setting groups meet or exceed the standard, your total score is shown as 100% and the settings that meet the standard are listed at the bottom of the page.

If you choose to change security settings, you can then click the **Refresh** button, (shown at the top right of the page), to update your score. Some settings have a higher impact on your score. For example, the **Minimum Password Length** is weighted heavier so a value that does not compare favorably with the standard baseline recommended by Salesforce will reduce the **Health Check Score.**

 The **Health Check score** is a proprietary Salesforce calculation that measures your security settings against the Salesforce Baseline standard. The settings in your organization that are deemed at risk lower your score and the settings that meet or exceed the standard increase the score.

The Salesforce Baseline standard

The following table shows the setting and risk values that meet the Salesforce Baseline standard.

Group	Setting	Standard Value	Medium Risk Value	High Risk Value
Login Access Policies	Administrators Can Log In As Any User	Deselected checkbox	Selected checkbox	Not Applicable
Network Access	Trusted IP Ranges	One or more ranges set	No range set	Not Applicable
Password Policies	User passwords expire in	90 days or less	180 days	One year or Never expires
Enforce password history	3 or more passwords remembered	1 or 2 passwords remembered	No passwords remembered	
Minimum password length	8	6 or 7	5 or less	

Password complexity requirement	Must mix alpha, numeric, and special characters, or more complex	Must mix alpha and numeric characters	No restriction	
Password question requirement	Cannot contain password	None	Not Applicable	
Maximum invalid login attempts	3	5	10 or No Limit	
Lockout effective period	15 minutes or Forever (must be reset by admin)	30 or 60 minutes	Not Applicable	
Obscure secret answer for password resets	Selected checkbox	Deselected checkbox	Not Applicable	
Require a minimum 1 day password lifetime	Selected checkbox	Deselected checkbox	Not Applicable	
Session Settings	Timeout Value	2 hours or less	4, 8, or 12 hours	Not Applicable
Disable session timeout warning popup	Selected checkbox	Selected checkbox	Not Applicable	
Force logout on session timeout	Selected checkbox	Deselected checkbox	Not Applicable	
Lock sessions to the IP address from which they originated	Selected checkbox	Deselected checkbox	Not Applicable	
Lock sessions to the domain in which they were first used	Selected checkbox	Not Applicable	Deselected checkbox	
Force relogin after Login-As-User	Selected checkbox	Not Applicable	Deselected checkbox	
Enforce login IP ranges on every request	Selected checkbox	Deselected checkbox	Not Applicable	
Enable caching and autocomplete on login page	Deselected checkbox	Selected checkbox	Not Applicable	

Enable the SMS method of identity confirmation	Selected checkbox	Not Applicable	Deselected checkbox
Enable clickjack protection for Setup pages	Selected checkbox	Not Applicable	Deselected checkbox
Enable clickjack protection for non-Setup Salesforce pages	Selected checkbox	Not Applicable	Deselected checkbox
Enable clickjack protection for customer Visualforce pages with standard headers	Selected checkbox	Not Applicable	Deselected checkbox
Enable clickjack protection for customer Visualforce pages with headers disabled	Selected checkbox	Not Applicable	Deselected checkbox
Enable CSRF protection on GET requests on non-setup pages	Selected checkbox	Not Applicable	Deselected checkbox
Enable CSRF protection on POST requests on non-setup pages	Selected checkbox	Not Applicable	Deselected checkbox

Questions to test your knowledge

You are now presented with questions about the key features of Salesforce CRM administration in the areas of user setup which have been covered in this chapter. The answers can be found at the end of the chapter.

Questions

We present four questions to verify your understanding of profiles, permission sets, user records, and password policies.

Question 1 – standard profiles

Which of the following is a standard profile? (Select all that apply):

a) Marketing User

b) Solution Manager

c) Sales User

d) Sales Manager

e) Standard User

Question 2 – permission sets

Which of the following does a permission set control? (Select all that apply):

a) Tab settings

b) Field permissions

c) Page layout assignments

d)Record type

e) Login hours

Question 3 – User records

In which situation can user records be deleted from Salesforce? (Select one):

a) Only when the user record has been marked as Inactive

b) Only when the user has not yet logged in

c) Never

d) Anytime

Question 4 – Password Policies

Which of the following password related actions can be carried out by a System Administrator? (Select all that apply):

a) Enforce that passwords containing alpha and numeric characters must be entered by users

b) Set passwords to expire after a certain number of days

c) Assign a given password to multiple users by profile type

d) Prevent users from re-using their last password if it expires

e) Set the password lockout period to forever

Answers

Here are the answers to the four questions about profiles, permission sets, user records, and password policies.

Answer 1 – standard profiles

The answer is **a)** Marketing User, **b)** Solution Manager, and **e)** Standard User.

The choices **c)** Sales User and **d)** Sales Manager are not standard profiles in Salesforce.

Answer 2 – permission sets

The answer is **a)** Tab settings, **b)** Field permissions, and **d)** Record type assignments.

It is possible to set **d)** Record type assignments and **e)** Login hours using profiles but not by using permission sets.

Answer 3 – user records

The answer is **c)** Never.

User records can be deactivated but cannot be deleted in Salesforce.

Answer 4 – password policies

The answer is **a**) Enforce that passwords containing alpha and numeric characters must be entered by users, **b**) Set passwords to expire after a certain number of days, **d**) Prevent users from re-using their last password if it expires, and **e**) Set the password lockout period to forever.

There is no feature that allows the option marked as **c**) Assign a given password to multiple users by profile type.

Summary

In this chapter, we described the features for managing users within Salesforce CRM.

We were introduced to the concepts of record ownership, profiles, and sharing, and discussed how these concepts are used to control the application and record permissions for users in depth.

We looked at how user information can be accessed and the mechanisms for managing user's passwords and the options for setting session security along with the features in the Salesforce **Health Check**.

We discussed other features to help with the administration of users using features such as granting login access to administrators and enabling delegated user administration.

Finally, we posed some questions to help clarify some of the key features of Salesforce CRM administration in the areas of user setup.

In the next chapter, we will look at the mechanisms for controlling access to data and the features that provide data management and record sharing in detail.

3
Configuring Objects and Apps

In Chapter 1, *Setting up Salesforce CRM and the Company Profile* and Chapter 2, *Managing Users and Controlling System Access*, we were introduced to the profile feature in Salesforce, which is a controlling mechanism. Profiles are used to determine the functions users can perform, what types of data they can access, and what operations they can carry out on that data.

In this chapter, we will describe the Salesforce CRM record storage features and customizable user interface in detail, such as objects, fields, and page layouts. In addition, we will see an overview of the relationship that exists between the profile and these customizable features that the profile controls.

This chapter looks at the methods for configuring and tailoring the application to suit the way your company information can be best represented within the Salesforce CRM application. We will look at the mechanisms that allow data to be grouped and presented within the application by looking at apps, tabs, page layouts, record types, related lists, and list views.

Finally, you will be presented with a number of questions about the key features of Salesforce CRM administration in the area of Standard and Custom Objects which are covered in this chapter.

The following topics are being covered in this chapter:

- Objects
- Fields
- Object relationships
- Apps
- Tabs
- Renaming labels for standard tabs, standard objects, and standard fields
- Creating custom objects
- Object limits
- Creating custom object relationships
- Creating custom fields
- Dependent picklists
- Building relationship fields
- Lookup relationship options
- Master-detail relationship options
- Lookup filters
- Building formulas
- Basic formula
- Advanced formula
- Building formulas – best practices
- Building formula text and compiled character size limits
- Custom field governance
- Page layouts
- Feed-based page layouts
- Record types
- Related lists

The relationship between a profile and the features that it controls

The following diagram describes the relationship that exists between a profile and the features that it controls:

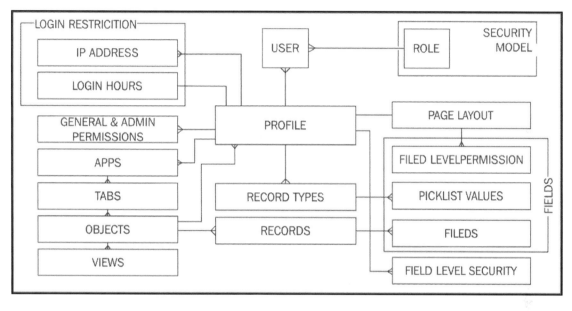

The profile is used to:

- Control access to the type of license specified for the user and any login hours or IP address restrictions that are set. This was covered in detail in Chapter 1, *Setting up Salesforce CRM and the Company profile*.
- Control access to objects and records using the role and sharing model. If the appropriate object-level permission is not set on the user's profile, then the user will be unable to gain access to the records of that object type in the application. This was introduced in Chapter 2, *Managing Users and Controlling System Access*, and will be covered in detail in Chapter 4, *Securing Access to Data and Data Validation*.

In this chapter, we will look at the configurable elements that are set in conjunction with a profile. These are used to control the structure and the user interface for the Salesforce CRM application.

Objects

Objects are a key element in Salesforce CRM as they provide a structure for storing data and are incorporated in the interface, allowing users to interact with the data.

Similar in nature to a database table, objects have properties such as:

- Fields, which are similar in concept to a database column
- Records, which are similar in concept to a database row
- Relationships with other objects
- Optional tabs, which are user-interface components to display the object data

Standard objects

Salesforce provides standard objects in the Salesforce CRM platform by default. Standard objects that are available include **Account**, **Contact**, and **Opportunity**. Standard objects are described in more detail later in this chapter.

In addition to the standard objects, you can create custom objects and custom tabs.

Custom objects

Custom objects are the tables you create to store your data. You can create a custom object to store data specific to your organization. Once you have the custom objects and have created records for these objects, you can also create reports and dashboards based on the record data in your custom object.

Fields

Fields in Salesforce are similar in concept to a database column; they store the data for the object records. An object record is analogous to a row in a database table.

Standard fields

Standard fields are predefined fields that are included as standard within the Salesforce CRM application. Standard fields cannot be deleted but non-required standard fields can be removed from page layouts whenever necessary.

With standard fields, you can customize visual elements that are associated with the field, such as field labels and field-level help, as well as certain data definitions such as picklist values, the formatting of auto-number fields (which are used as unique identifiers for the records), and setting of field history tracking. Some aspects, however, such as the field name, cannot be customized and some standard fields (such as **Opportunity Probability**) do not allow the changing of the field label.

Custom fields

Custom fields are unique to your business needs and can not only be added and amended, but also deleted. Creating custom fields allow you to store the information that is necessary for your organization.

Both standard and custom fields can be customized to include custom help text to help users understand how to use the field:

Object relationships

Object relationships can be set on both standard and custom objects and are used to define how records in one object relate to records in another object. **Accounts**, for example, can have a one-to-many relationship with opportunities; these relationships are presented in the application as related lists.

Apps

An app in Salesforce is a container for all the objects, tabs, processes, and services associated with a business function.

There are standard and custom apps that are accessed using the **App menu** located at the top-right corner of the Salesforce page, as shown in the following screenshot:

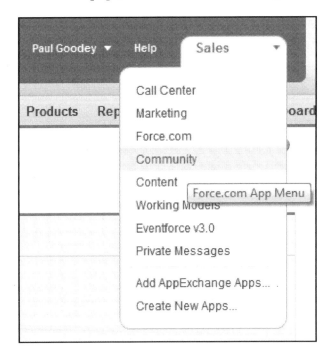

When users select an app from the **App** menu, their screen changes to present the objects associated with that app. For example, when switching from an app that contains the **Campaign** tab to one that does not, the **Campaign** tab no longer appears. This feature is applied to both standard and custom apps.

Standard apps

Salesforce provides standard apps such as **Call Center**, **Community**, **Content**, **Marketing**, **Sales**, **Salesforce Chatter**, and **Site.com**.

Custom apps

A custom app can optionally include a custom logo. Both standard and custom apps consist of a name, a description, and an ordered list of tabs.

Subtab apps

A **Subtab** app is used to specify the tabs that appear on the **Chatter** profile page. **Subtab** apps can include both default and custom tabs. This is described in more detail in the *Salesforce Chatter* section later in `Chapter 8`, *Introducing Sales Cloud, Service Cloud, and Collaborative Features of Salesforce CRM*.

Tabs

A tab is a user-interface element that, when clicked on, displays data or activates custom functionality that you can configure. Standard tabs are provided as an included feature and custom tabs allow you to extend or to build new application functionality. Standard and custom tabs are described in more detail later in this chapter.

Hiding and showing tabs

To customize your personal tab settings, navigate to **Setup** | **My Personal Settings** | **Change My Display** | **Customize My Tabs**. Now, choose the tabs that will display in each of your apps by moving the tab name between the **Available Tabs** and the **Selected Tabs** sections and. Click **Save**. The following screenshot shows the section of tabs for the **Sales** app:

Customize My Tabs   Help for this Page

Choose the tabs that will display in each of your apps.

Custom App:
Sales

Available Tabs   **Selected Tabs**

Action Plan Templates   Home (default)
Activity Tracker   Chatter
App Launcher   Add   Accounts   Up
Books   Campaigns
Console   ▶   Leads   ▲
Content   ◀   Contacts   ▼
Contracts   Remove   Opportunities   Down
Contribute   Reports
Customer Search   Dashboards
Customizable Forecasts   Cases
Data.com

Save   Cancel

To customize the tab settings of your users navigate to **Setup** | **Manage Users** | **Profiles**. Now, select a profile and click on **Edit**. Scroll down to the **Tab Settings** section of the page, and set the tab setting to be either **Default On**, **Default Off**, or **Tab Hidden** as shown in the following screenshot :

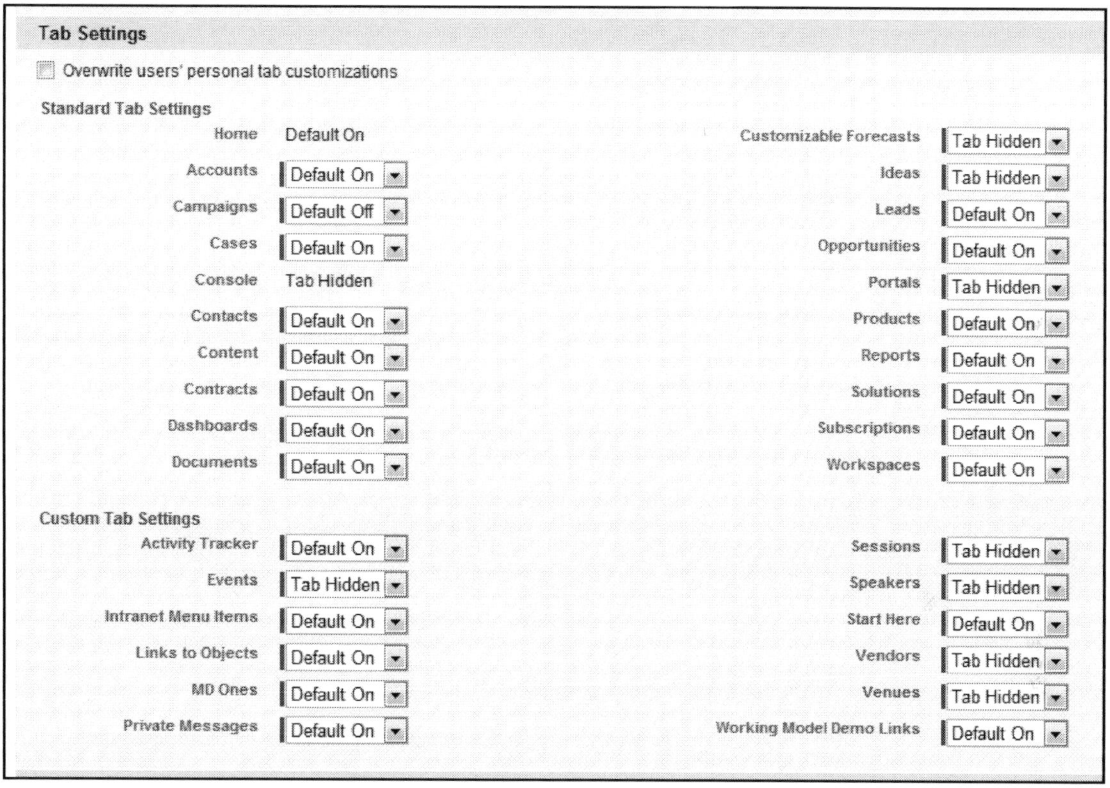

To customize the tab settings of your users when the **Enhanced Profile User Interface option** is enabled, as described in Chapter 1, *Setting up Salesforce CRM and the Company Profile*, navigate to **Setup | Manage Users | Profiles.** Select a profile and click on **Edit.** Now click on **Object Settings** as shown in the following screenshot:

Profile
Custom: Sales Profile

Help for this Page

| Q Find Settings... | ⊗ | | Clone | Delete | Edit Properties |

Profile Overview

Assigned Users

Description			
User License	Salesforce	Custom Profile	✓
Created By	Paul Goodey, 19/12/2009 13:01	Last Modified By	Paul Goodey, 22/07/2016 18:30

Apps

Settings that apply to Salesforce apps, such as Sales, and custom apps built on Force.com
Learn More

Assigned Apps
Settings that specify which apps are visible in the app menu

Assigned Connected Apps
Settings that specify which connected apps are visible in the app menu

Object Settings
Permissions to access objects and fields, and settings that specify which record types, page layouts, and tabs are visible

App Permissions
Permissions to perform app-specific actions, such as "Manage Call Centers"

Apex Class Access
Permissions to execute Apex classes

After accessing the **Object Settings** page for the profile, select the object for which tab setting you want to configure. In this example, we choose the **Account** object as shown in the following screenshot:

Profile				Help for this Page 🌀

Custom: Sales Profile

🔍 Find Settings... ✖ | Clone Delete Edit Properties

Profile Overview > **Object Settings** ▾

All Object Settings

Object Name	Object Permissions	Total Fields	Tab Settings	Page Layouts
About Action Plans	--	--	Tab Hidden	--
Acc Childs	No Access	5	--	Acc Child Layout
Account Last Views	No Access	5	--	Account Last View Layout
Accounts	Read, Create, Edit, Delete	45	Default On	Account (Sales) Layout
Action Plans	No Access	22	--	Action Plan Layout

From within the object profile setup screen click the **Edit** button which allows you to configure the object settings which include **Tab Settings**, **Record Types,** and **Page Layout Assignments**, **Object Permissions**, and so on as shown in the following screenshot:

Profile	Help for this Page 🌀

Custom: Sales Profile

🔍 Find Settings... ✖ | Clone Delete Edit Properties

Profile Overview > Object Settings ▾ **Accounts** ▾

Accounts   Edit

Tab Settings

Default On

Account: Record Types and Page Layout Assignments

Record Types	Page Layout Assignment	Assigned Record Types	Default Record Type
--Master--	Account (Sales) Layout	✓	✓

Object Permissions

Permission Name	Enabled
Read	✓
Create	✓
Edit	✓

From within the object profile settings edit screen, set the **Tab Settings** style to be either **Default On**, **Default Off**, or **Tab Hidden** and finally click the **Save** button as shown in the following screenshot:

Profile
Custom: Sales Profile

| Q Find Settings... | ✖ | | Clone | Delete | Edit Properties |

Profile Overview > Object Settings ▼ **Accounts** ▼

Accounts   Save   Cancel

Tab Settings

Default On ▾
Tab Hidden
A Default Off   d Types and Page Layout Assignments
   Default On

Standard tabs

Salesforce provides tabs for each of the standard objects that are provided in the application when you sign up. For example, there are standard tabs for **Accounts**, **Contacts**, **Opportunities**, and so on:

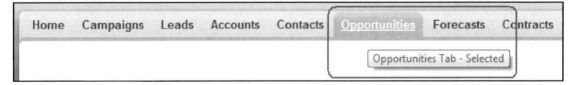

| Home | Campaigns | Leads | Accounts | Contacts | Opportunities | Forecasts | Contracts |

Opportunities Tab - Selected

Visibility of the tab depends on the **Tab Display** setting for the app.

Custom tabs

You can create three different types of custom tabs: Custom Object Tabs, Web Tabs, and Visualforce Tabs.

Custom Object Tabs allow you to create, read, update, and delete the data records in your custom objects. **Web Tabs** display any web URL in a tab within your Salesforce application. **Visualforce Tabs** display custom user-interface pages created using Visualforce.

Creating custom tabs:

- The text displayed on the custom tab is set using the **Plural Label** of the custom object, which is entered when creating the custom object. If the tab text needs to be changed, this can be done by changing the **Plural Label** stored on the custom object.

- Salesforce.com recommends selecting the **Append tab to user's existing personal customizations** checkbox. This benefits your users as they will automatically be presented with the new tab and can immediately access the corresponding functionality without having to first customize their personal settings themselves.

- It is recommended that you do not show tabs (by setting appropriate permissions) so that the users in your organization cannot see any of your changes until you are ready to make them available.

- You can create up to 25 custom tabs in the Enterprise Edition and as many as you require in the Unlimited Edition at the time of writing.

To create custom tabs for a custom object, navigate to **Setup** | **Create** | **Tabs**. Now, select the appropriate tab type and/or object from the available selections, as shown in the following screenshot:

Custom Object Tabs		New	What Is This?		
Action	**Label**		**Tab Style**		**Description**
Edit | Del	Activity Tracker		Hands		
Edit | Del	Events		Big top		
Edit | Del	Intranet Menu Items		Laptop		
Edit | Del	Links to Objects		Guitar		
Edit | Del	MD Ones		Alarm clock		
Edit | Del	Private Messages		Postage		
Edit | Del	Sessions		Presenter		
Edit | Del	Speakers		Microphone		
Edit | Del	Vendors		Desk		
Edit | Del	Venues		Building		

Web Tabs	New	What Is This?
No Web Tabs have been defined		

Visualforce Tabs		New	What Is This?		
Action	**Label**		**Tab Style**		**Description**
Edit | Del	Start Here		Wrench		
Edit | Del	Working Model Demo Links		People		

Renaming labels for standard tabs, standard objects, and standard fields

Labels generally reflect the text that is displayed and presented to your users in the user interface and in reports within the Salesforce application.

You can change the display labels of standard tabs, objects, fields, and other related user interface labels so they reflect your company's terminology and business requirements better. For example, the **Accounts** tab and object could be changed to Clients; similarly, **Opportunities** to Deals, and **Leads** to Prospects. Once changed, the new label is displayed on all user pages.

The **Setup Pages** and **Setup Menu** sections cannot be modified and do not include any renamed labels and continue. Here, the standard tab, object, and field reference continues to use the default, original labels. Also, the standard report names and views continue to use the default labels and are not renamed.

To change standard tab, objects, and field labels, navigate to **Setup** | **Customize** | **Tabs Names** and **Labels** | **Rename Tabs and Labels**. Now, select a language, and then click on **Edit** to modify the tab names and standard field labels:

Rename Tabs and Labels

Help for this Page

Make salesforce.com match your organization's terminology by renaming tab and field labels. Use the lists below to select the tab you want to rename in the language you choose. After renaming any tab or field label, remember to update all custom reports, views, templates and other items you have created containing the original name.

Select Language [English ▼]

Standard Tabs

Standard Tabs Help (?)

Action	Tab Name	Display Label	Renamed	Last Modified
Edit	Accounts	Accounts	☐	
Edit	Activities	Activities	☐	
Edit	Articles	Articles	☐	
Edit	Assets	Assets	☐	
Edit	Campaigns	Campaigns	☐	
Edit	Cases	Cases	☐	

Click on **Edit** to select the tab that you wish to rename.

Although the screen indicates that this is a change for the tab's name, this selection will also allow you to change the labels for the object and fields in addition to the tab name. To change field labels, go through to steps and enter the new field labels.

Here, we are going to rename the **Accounts** tab to `Clients`. Enter the **Singular** and **Plural** names and then click on **Next**:

Step 1. Enter the new tab names	Step 1 of 2

Save | Next | Cancel

Tab	Accounts
Language	English
Singular	Client	Example: Account
Plural	Clients	Example: Accounts
Starts with vowel sound	☐	

Only the following standard tabs and objects can be renamed: **Accounts, Activities, Articles, Assets, Campaigns, Cases, Contacts, Contracts, Documents, Events, Ideas, Leads, Libraries, Opportunities, Opportunity Products, Partners, PriceBooks, Products, Quote Line Items, Quotes, Solutions**, and **Tasks**.

Tabs such as **Home Chatter**, **Forecasts**, **Reports**, and **Dashboards** cannot be renamed.

Step 2. Enter the new field labels			Step 2 of 2

Previous | Save | Cancel

Please review all the auto-populated values below for grammatical accuracy. Edit any <u>standard field labels</u> and <u>other labels</u> for the selected tab and language.

Tab   Accounts

Language   English

Standard Field Labels   <u>Other Labels</u>

	Singular	Plural	Starts with vowel sound
Account Division	Client Division		☐
Account Name	Client Name	Client Names	☐
Account Number	Client Number		☐
Account Owner	Client Owner	Client Owners	☐
Account Site	Client Site	Client Sites	☐
Address	Address		☑
Annual Revenue	Annual Revenue		☑
Billing Address	Billing Address		☐
Billing City	Billing City		☐
Billing Country	Billing Country		☐

Salesforce looks for the **Account** label and displays an auto-populated screen showing where the Account text would be replaced with Client. This auto-population of text is carried out for the standard tab, the standard object, and the standard fields. Review the replaced text, amend as necessary, and then click on **Save**:

Rename Tabs and Labels

Help for this Page ⓘ

Make salesforce.com match your organization's terminology by renaming tab and field labels. Use the lists below to select the tab you want to rename in the language you choose. After renaming any tab or field label, remember to update all custom reports, views, templates and other items you have created containing the original name.

Select Language | English ▾

Standard Tabs

Standard Tabs Help ⓘ

Action	Tab Name	Display Label	Renamed	Last Modified
Edit | Reset	Accounts	Clients	✓	Paul Goodey, 20/02/2011 04:04
Edit	Activities	Activities	☐	
Edit	Articles	Articles	☐	
Edit	Assets	Assets	☐	
Edit	Campaigns	Campaigns	☐	
Edit	Cases	Cases	☐	

After renaming, the new labels are automatically displayed on the tab, in reports, in dashboards, and so on.

 Some standard fields, such as **Created By** and **Last Modified**, are prevented from being renamed because they are audit fields that are used to track system information.

You will, however, need to carry out the following additional steps to ensure consistent renaming throughout the system as these may need manual updates:

- Check all list view names as they do not automatically update and will continue to show the original object name until you change them manually.

- Review standard report names and descriptions for any object that you have renamed.
- Check the titles and descriptions of any e-mail templates that contain the original object or field name, and update them as necessary.
- Review any other items that you have customized with the standard object or field name. For example, custom fields, page layouts, and record types may include the original tab, or field name text that is no longer relevant.

If you have renamed tabs, objects, or fields, you can also replace the Salesforce online help with a different URL. Your users can view this replaced URL whenever they click on any context-sensitive help link on an end-user page or from within their personal setup options.

Challenge the requirement to rename Tabs and Labels.
Consider the benefits of renaming Tabs and labels before doing so. Renaming the labels in particular often results in added complexity and maintenance issues because Salesforce documentation and industry discussion will refer to the default named labels. There should be a compelling reason and a strong business use case to rename standard labels.

Creating custom objects

Custom objects are database tables that allow you to store data specific to your organization, in `Salesforce.com`. You can use custom objects to extend Salesforce functionality or to build new application functionality.

You can create up to 200 custom objects in the Enterprise Edition and 2000 in the Unlimited Edition at the time of writing.

Once you have created a custom object, you can create a custom tab, custom-related lists, reports, and dashboards for users to interact with the custom object data.

To create a custom object, navigate to **Setup** | **Create** | **Objects**. Now click on **New Custom Object**, or click on **Edit** to modify an existing custom object. The following screenshot shows the resulting screen:

On the **Custom Object Information** Edit page, you can enter the following:

- **Label**: This is the visible name that is displayed for the object within the Salesforce CRM user interface and shown on pages, views, and reports, for example.
- **Plural Label**: This is the plural name specified for the object, which is used within the application in places such as reports and on tabs (if you create a tab for the object).
- **Gender** (language dependent): This field appears if your organization-wide default language expects gender. This is used for organizations where the default language settings are, for example, Spanish, French, Italian, German, among many others. Your personal language-preference setting does not affect whether the field appears or not. For example, if your organization's default language is English but your personal language is French, you will not be prompted for gender when creating a custom object.
- **Starts with a vowel sound**: Use of this setting depends on your organization's default language and is a linguistic check to allow you to specify whether your label is to be preceded by an instead of a; for example, resulting in reference to the object as an Order instead of a Order.
- **Object Name**: A unique name used to refer to the object. Here, the **Object Name** field must be unique and can only contain underscores and alphanumeric characters. It must also begin with a letter, not contain spaces, not contain two consecutive underscores, and not end with an underscore.
- **Description**: An optional description of the object. A meaningful description will help to explain the purpose of your custom objects when you are viewing them in a list.
- **Context-Sensitive Help Setting**: Defines what information is displayed when your users click on the **Help** for this page context-sensitive help link from the custom object record home (overview), edit, and detail pages, as well as list views and related lists. The **Help & Training** link at the top of any page is not affected by this setting; it always opens the Salesforce **Help & Training** window.
- **Record Name**: This is the name that is used in areas such as page layouts, search results, key lists, and related lists, as shown next.

- **Data Type**: This sets the type of field for the record name. Here the data type can be either text or auto-number. If the data type is set to be **Text**, then when a record is created, users must enter a text value, which does not need to be unique. If the data type is set to be **Auto Number**, it becomes a read-only field whereby new records are automatically assigned a unique number:

Enter Record Name Label and Format

The Record Name appears in page layouts, key lists, related lists, lookups, and search results. For example, th[e] "Case Number". Note that the Record Name field is always called "Name" when referenced via the API.

Record Name	**Example: Account Name**
Data Type	Auto Number ▾
Display Format	**Example: A-{0000}** What Is This?
Starting Number	

- **Display Format**: As in the preceding example, this option only appears when the **Data Type** field is set to **Auto Number**. It allows you to specify the structure and appearance of the **Auto Number** field. For example: {YYYY}{MM}-{000} is a display format that produces a four-digit year, two-digit month prefix to a number with leading zeros padded to three digits. Example data output would include: 201203-001; 201203-066; 201203-999; 201203-1234. It is worth noting that although you can specify the number three digits, if the number of records created exceeds 999, the record will still be saved but the automatically incremented number becomes 1000, 1001, and so on.

- **Starting Number**: As described, Auto Number fields in Salesforce CRM are automatically incremented for each new record. Here, you must enter the starting number for the incremental count (which does not have to be set to start from one).

- **Allow Reports**: This setting is required if you want to include the record data from the custom object in any report or dashboard analytics. When a custom object has a relationship field associating it to a standard object, a new **Report Type** may appear in the standard report category. The new **Report Type** allows the user to create reports that relate the standard object to the custom object by selecting the standard object for the **Report Type** category instead of the custom object.

A new **Report Type** is created in the standard report category if the custom object is either the lookup object on the standard object or the custom object has a master-detail relationship with the standard object. Lookup relationships and master-detail relationship fields are described in more detail later in this section.

- **Allow Activities**: Allows users to include tasks and events related to the custom object records, which appear as a related list on the custom object page.
- **Track Field History**: Enables the tracking of data-field changes on the custom object records, such as who changed the value of a field and when it was changed. Field history tracking also stores the value of the field before and after the field is edited. This feature is useful for auditing and data-quality measurement and is also available within the reporting tools. The field history data is retained for up to 18 months and you can set field history tracking for a maximum of 20 fields for Enterprise, Unlimited, and Performance Editions.
- **Allow in Chatter Groups**: This setting allows your users to add records of this custom object type to **Chatter** groups. When enabled, records of this object type that are created using the group publisher are associated with the group and also appear in the group record list. When disabled, records of this object type that are created using the group publisher are not associated with the group.
- **Deployment Status**: Indicates whether the custom object is now visible and available for use by other users. This is useful as you can easily set the status to **In Development** until you are happy for users to start working with the new object.
- **Add Notes and Attachments**: This setting allows your users to record notes and attach files to the custom object records. When this is specified, a related list with the **New Note** and **Attach File** buttons automatically appears on the custom object record page where your users can enter notes and attach documents.

 The **Add Notes & Attachments** option is only available when you create a new object.

- **Launch the New Custom Tab Wizard**: Starts the custom tab wizard after you save the custom object. The **New Custom Tab Wizard** option is only available when you create a new object.

If you do not select the **Launch the New Custom Tab Wizard**, you will not be able to create a tab in this step but you can create the tab later as described in the *Custom Tabs* section covered earlier in this chapter. When creating a custom object, a custom tab is not automatically created.

Object Limits

You can access the **Object Limits** page when planning how to customize a particular object, or to monitor the current usage and limits, such as the number of custom fields or rules applied.

Object Limits for standard objects

To access the standard **Object Limits** page, navigate to **Setup** | **Customize**. Click on the name of the desired standard object, and then click on the limits, as shown in the following screenshot (for the `Account` object):

Account Limits

Help for this Page

These limits apply to the setup of this object in your organization. Some limits may vary by object. For a complete list of system limits, see Editions and Limits.

Object Limits

Item	Usage	Limit	% used	Message
Custom Fields	20	500	4%	
Rollup Summary Fields	2	10	20%	
Custom Relationship Fields	0	25	0%	
Active Workflow Rules	0	50	0%	
Total Workflow Rules	0	300	0%	
Approval Processes	0	500	0%	
Active Lookup Filters	0	5	0%	
Active Validation Rules	0	100	0%	
VLOOKUP Functions	0	10	0%	
Sharing Rules (Both Owner- and Criteria-based)	2	300	1%	
Sharing Rules (Criteria-based Only)	1	50	2%	

Here, you can see usage details for the following: **Custom Fields, Rollup Summary Fields, Custom Relationship Fields, Active Workflow Rules, Total Workflow Rules, Approval Processes, Active Lookup Filters, Active Validation Rules, VLOOKUP Functions, Sharing Rules (Both Owner-and Criteria-based)**, and **Sharing Rules (Criteria-based Only)**.

Object Limits for custom objects

To view information about the usage of various fields and rules that have been created on a custom object, you can access the **Object Limits** window displayed on a custom object definitions-related list at the bottom of a custom object definition page.

When an item reaches 75 percent or more of the limit allowed for the object, a warning message appears that identifies what can be done to reduce the amount of usage. The object limit percentages display values that are truncated, and not rounded up. For example, if your organization reaches 79.55 percent of the limit for an item, the limit percentage displays 79 percent.

Creating custom object relationships

Considerations to be observed when creating object relationships are as follows:

- Create the object relationships as a first step before starting to build the custom fields, page layouts, and any related list
- The **Related To** entry cannot be modified after you have saved the object relationship

Each custom object can have up to two master-detail relationships and up to 25 total relationships. Where an object has more than one master-detail relationship, the first master-detail relationship that was created, becomes the primary master-detail relationship. The owner of the record therefore is derived from the first master-detail relationship that was created.

- When planning to create a master-detail relationship on an object, be aware that it can only be created before the object contains record data

Master-detail relationships can be created on an object that contains record data by first creating a lookup relationship field, populating the lookup field, and finally converting the lookup to a master-detail relationship.

- Clicking on **Edit List Layout** allows you to choose columns for the key views and lookups
- The **Standard Name** field is required on all custom object-related lists and also on any page layouts

Creating custom fields

Before you begin to create custom fields, it is worth spending some time to first plan and choose the most appropriate type of field to create. You can create many different custom field types in Salesforce CRM, including text, number, currency, as well as relationship types that enable lookup, master-detail, and hierarchical relationships.

Adding custom fields can be carried out by navigating to the field's area of the appropriate object:

- For standard objects, navigate to **Setup** | **Customize**. Now, select the appropriate object from the **Customize** menu, click on **Fields**, and then click on **New** in the **Custom Fields & Relationships** section of the object page.
- For custom task and event fields, navigate to **Setup** | **Customize** | **Activities** | **Activity Custom Fields**. Now, click on the **New** button.
- For custom objects, navigate to **Setup** | **Create** | **Objects**. Now, select one of the custom objects in the list. Next, click on **New** in the **Custom** field dependencies and field history tracking

Within the field setup pages, you can set field dependencies and field history tracking for the object. Field history tracking captures information for the date, time, nature of the change, and who made the change. A dependent field is a picklist field for which the valid values depend on the value of another field.

Whenever history tracking is set, a separate history data object is created for the object. This history data comprises the record ID and the history-tracked field names whose value has been changed. Here, both the old and the new record values are recorded. This is covered later in this chapter in the *Custom field governance* section.

Field dependencies and field history tracking are not available for task and event fields, and are described in more detail later in this chapter.

Choose a data type for the field to be created. The following screenshot shows the first page (step 1) where a full list of data types (which are described in detail later) are available to choose from:

Room
New Custom Field
Help for this Page ?

Step 1. Choose the field type   **Step 1**

[Next] Cancel

Specify the type of information that the custom field will contain.

Data Type

◉ None Selected	Select one of the data types below.
○ Auto Number	A system-generated sequence number that uses a display format you define. The number is automatically incremented for each new record.
○ Formula	A read-only field that derives its value from a formula expression you define. The formula field is updated when any of the source fields change.
○ Roll-Up Summary [i]	A read-only field that displays the sum, minimum, or maximum value of a field in a related list or the record count of all records listed in a related list.
○ Lookup Relationship	Creates a relationship that links this object to another object. The relationship field allows users to click on a lookup icon to select a value from a popup list. The other object is the

Some data types are only available for certain configurations. For example, the **Master-Detail Relationship** option is available only for custom objects when the custom object does not already have one or more master-detail relationship fields. The **Roll-Up Summary** option is only available for objects defined as Master in master-detail relation and is used to record an aggregate of the child records, using functions such as SUM, MAX, and MIN (these are described in detail later in this chapter).

Field types not listed in custom field types may appear if your organization installed a package from AppExchange that uses those custom field types.

Click on **Next** and enter a **Field Label**. **Field Name** is a mandatory field and must be unique within the Salesforce CRM application. There are also some restrictions on what can be entered and what cannot. Here, you can only enter alphanumeric characters and underscores. In addition, the text must start with a letter; it cannot include spaces, it cannot contain two consecutive underscores, and the final character must not be an underscore.

Step 2. Enter the details	Step 2 of 4

Previous | Next | Cancel

Field Label: [   ] [i]

Default Value: ○ Checked   ◉ Unchecked

Field Name: [   ] [i]

Description: [   ]

Help Text: [   ] [i]

Ensure that the custom field name and label are unique and not the same as any existing standard or custom field for that object. Creating identical values may result in unexpected behavior when you reference that name in a merge field. If a standard field and custom field have matching names or labels, the merge field displays the value of the custom field. If two custom fields have matching names or labels, the merge field may not display the value of the field you expect. For example, if you create a field label called Phone, the field name automatically populates as Phone__c. If you also have a standard field with the label Phone, the merge field may not be able to distinguish between the standard and custom field names. Make the custom field name and label unique by adding a suffix to each, such as Phone_Custom and Phone_Custom__c, respectively.

For relationship fields, choose the object that you want to associate with it:

Room
New Relationship   Help for this Page

Step 2. Choose the related object   Step 2

Previous | Next | Cancel

Select the other object to which this object is related.

Related To   --None--

 The number of custom fields allowed per object is 500 for both Enterprise and Unlimited Editions of Salesforce at the time of writing. Relationship fields count towards these custom-field limits.

Enter any field attributes. In this example, a new checkbox field is set as **Checked** by default:

Step 2. Enter the details   Step 2 of 4

Previous | Next | Cancel

Field Label   Air Conditioned

Default Value   ◉ Checked
             ○ Unchecked

Field Name   Air_Conditioned

Description

Help Text

Object relationship fields allow you to create a lookup filter that can be used to further control the associated returned records and lookup dialog results for the field.

These are available for Lookup, Master-detail, and Hierarchical relationship fields. Here, you can select multiple fields and selection criteria to restrict the results. This is presented in an additional step of the field-creation process and is available at the bottom of the **Lookup Filter** section, available from step 3. Enter the label and name for the lookup field setup page.

Click on **Next** to continue and specify the field's access settings for each profile as shown in the following screenshot:

To set the field-level security, enable the following settings:

The Visible checkbox	The Read-Only checkbox	Result
Checked	Not Checked	Users can view and edit the field
Checked	Checked	Users can view but not edit the field

Click on **Next** and choose the page layouts that you would want to add the new field to as shown in the following screenshot:

Step 4. Add to page layouts	Step 4 of 4

Previous | Save & New | Save | Cancel

Field Label   Air Conditioned

Data Type   Checkbox

Field Name   Air_Conditioned

Description

Select the page layouts that should include this field. The field will be added as the last field in the first 2-column section of these page layouts. The field will not appear on any pages if you do not select a layout.

To change the location of this field on the page, you will need to customize the page layout.

☑ Add Field	Page Layout Name
☑	Room Layout

The new field is automatically positioned on the page layout as the final field in the first two-column section. However, there is an exception for **Text Area (Long)** and **Text Area (Rich)** fields. These fields, due to their double width, are placed as the final field on the first one-column section on the page layout.

For user custom fields, the field is automatically added to the bottom of the user detail page. For universally required fields, you cannot remove the field from page layouts or make it read-only

Click on **Save** to finish, or on **Save & New** to create more custom fields.

For relationship fields, choose whether to create a related list that displays information about the associated records. You can choose to put the related list on any page layout for that object.

To change the label of the custom-related list as it will appear on the page layouts of the associated object, edit the **Related List Label** field. This is covered later in this chapter in the sections on *Page Layouts* and *Related Lists*.

To add the new related list to page layouts that users have already customized, check the **Append-related list to user's existing personal customizations**.

Custom field data types

When creating a custom field, the first step is to select the appropriate type for the field. There are many different field types available in Salesforce that allow the storage of records of various data types, such as numbers, dates, and percentages. The following sections describe the data types that are available:

Auto Number

An **Auto Number** field produces a unique number that is automatically incremented for each saved record. As such, this is a read-only field where the maximum length is 30 characters, of which 20 are reserved for further prefix or suffix text that you can specify.

Checkbox

A Checkbox allows your users to set or unset a value to mark the attribute as either **True** or **False**.

When using a checkbox field in a report, use **True** for values that are checked values and **False** for unchecked values. The import wizards and the weekly export tool use **1** for checked values and **0** for unchecked values.

Currency

Salesforce provides a **Currency** field to specifically capture a monetary value. Here, the Salesforce CRM application applies currency-related codes, which are applied when working with that field record.

Values lose precision after 15 decimal places.

Date

A **Date** field provides a way for your users to either pick a date from a pop-up calendar or to manually enter the date. Your users can also enter the current date by clicking on the date link positioned to the right of the field.

Date/Time

A **Date/Time** field provides a way for your users to either pick a date from a pop-up calendar or to manually enter the date and the time of day. Your users can also enter the current date and time by clicking on the date and time link positioned to the right of the field. Here, the time of day includes the A.M.-P.M. notation.

Email

An **Email** field provides us with the capability to store an individual's e-mail address. The Salesforce CRM application provides a very robust method of verifying the correct format of e-mail addresses before they are allowed to be saved. If this field is specified for contacts or leads, users can choose the address when clicking on **Send an Email**.

You cannot use custom e-mail fields for mass e-mails. Mass e-mail can only be sent to an e-mail address in a standard e-mail field. For e-mail fields, users can enter a maximum length of up to 80 characters.

Formula

A **Formula** field enables a method to automatically calculate a value that is obtained from other fields or values stored within Salesforce CRM. These referenced fields are known as merge fields. Formula fields are very powerful and flexible mechanisms. However, a formula field cannot be set to reference itself within a formula irrespective of whether the reference is made directly or indirectly. Further information concerning formulas is covered later in this chapter under the *Building formulas* section.

Salesforce uses a mechanism for decimal number place calculation in formulas, known as a **round-half up**, **tie-breaking rule**. As an example, a value formulated as *2.345* results in a value of *2.35* and a value formulated as *-2.345* results in a value of *-2.34*.

Geolocation

The geolocation custom field allows you to identify locations by their latitude and longitude, and calculate the distance between locations.

The **Geolocation** field is a compound field that Salesforce stores as three separate custom fields: one for latitude, one for longitude, and one for internal use. Three fields are therefore added to the custom field limit count, for the object, when creating a geolocation field.

You can then use the geolocation field with the DISTANCE and GEOLOCATION formula functions to calculate distance between locations. For example, you can calculate the distance between two geolocation fields (such as between the warehouse and an account-shipping address), or between a geolocation field and any fixed latitude-longitude coordinate.

The geolocation field is currently in beta release and so has the following limitations:

- History tracking is not available on geolocation fields
- Geolocation fields cannot be used on custom settings
- Geolocation fields cannot be included in reports, dashboards, validation rules, Visual workflow, workflow, or approvals
- Geolocation fields cannot be searched
- Geolocation fields cannot be accessed within the Schema Builder

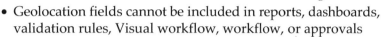DISTANCE and GEOLOCATION formula functions are available only when creating formula fields or using them in Visual Workflow

Lookup relationship

The lookup relationship field is used to relate two records. Relationships can be set up between two records of the same object type or different object types. For example, opportunities can be related by a lookup so an opportunity hierarchy can be shown, or cases have a lookup relationship with contacts that enable you to associate a specific contact with a case.

A lookup relationship creates a field that allows users to click on a lookup icon which opens up a pop-up window and allows the user to select a record to get the relationship. On the associated record, you can display a related list to show all of the records that are linked to it, and you can create lookup relationship fields that link to the following: users, and custom or standard objects. See the *Building relationship fields* section, later in this chapter for further options.

Master-detail relationship

This field creates a parent-child type relationship between records, where the master record controls certain behaviors, such as security and record deletion, of the detail record.

Master-detail relationship fields can only be created on custom objects that relate to a standard object and not the other way around. If the master record is deleted, then all detail records are also deleted. You can create up to two master-detail relationship fields per custom object. Ownership and access to the child record are determined by the parent and the parent relationship field on the child record is not optional.

See the *Building relationship fields* section for further options, discussed later in this chapter.

As a best practice, Salesforce.com recommends that you do not exceed 10,000 child records for a master-detail relationship.

External lookup relationship

An external lookup field creates a relationship that links the object to an external object that contains data that is housed outside your Salesforce CRM organization.

As this typically requires the setup of a non-Salesforce CRM external data source, detailed discussion of this relationship is beyond the scope of this book.

Hierarchical relationship

This field type forms a hierarchical lookup relationship between relevant objects. For the user hierarchical relationship, users can use a lookup field to associate one user with another. For example, you can create a custom hierarchical relationship field to store each user's direct manager. See the *Building relationship fields* section for further options, discussed later in this chapter.

This type of lookup relationship is available only for the user object.

Number

The **Number** field can be used to enter any number, with or without a decimal place (the number of decimal places can be specified), and saved as a real number with any leading zeros removed.

Percent

A **Percent** field in Salesforce CRM, is similar to a number field entered as a decimal which results in a percentage sign automatically appended to the entered value.

 The value of a **Percent** field loses precision after 15 decimal places. A runtime error is generated if users attempt to enter a value that contains a decimal taken to more than 15 decimal places.

Phone

The **Phone** field allows the users in your organization to enter any telephone number. While saving the record, the Salesforce CRM application will attempt to format it into a known phone format.

When your users enter phone numbers in **Phone** fields, Salesforce keeps the phone number format that has been entered. However, if the **Locale** field is set to **English (United States)** or **English (Canada)**, ten-digit phone numbers and 11-digit numbers that start with one are automatically formatted as (800) 555-1234 when you save the record. If you do not want this formatting for a 10- or 11-digit number, you can enter a + before the number, for example, +44 117 123 4567.

 For phone numbers, users can enter a maximum length of up to 40 characters.

Picklist

The **Picklist** field allows users to choose a value from a set of predefined text values. The maximum length of the text values is 255 characters.

Picklist (Multi-select)

The **Picklist (Multi-select)** field allows users to choose more than one picklist value from a set of predefined text values. The maximum length of the text values is 255 characters. When saving and viewing, the data is stored as text along with semi-colons, which are used to separate the individual picklist values.

Roll-up summary

A **Roll-up Summary** field, which is sometimes abbreviated to **RUS** in online forums or discussion groups, is used to automatically display the summarized values of the related records. This can be a record count of related records or a calculation of the sum, minimum, or maximum value of the related records.

 The records must be directly related to the selected record and on the detail side of a custom master-detail relationship with the object that contains the roll-up summary field. For example, a custom account field called **Total Number of Branches** displays the number of branches the custom object records in the branch-related list for **Accounts.**

Text

The **Text** field allows users to enter any combination of alphanumeric characters or symbols. The maximum length of the text value is 255 characters.

Text (Encrypted)

The **Text (Encrypted)** field allows users to enter any combination of alphanumeric characters or symbols. The text is then stored in an encrypted form. As an example, you can create a credit card number field named `Credit Card Number` with a mask type of `Credit Card Number` and a mask character of `X`. When users enter data in this field, it is encrypted and stored in the database. When users without the **View Encrypted Data** permission view the field, Salesforce displays the mask (e.g., `XXXX-XXXX-XXX-1234`) instead of the value that was originally entered.

 For encrypted text, you can set a maximum length of up to 175 characters.

Encrypted fields are encrypted with 128-bit master keys and use the **Advanced Encryption Standard (AES)** algorithm.

 Your master encryption key can be archived, deleted, and imported using the Master Encryption Key Management feature, which is made available by sending a request to Salesforce customer support.

Text Area

The **Text Area** field allows users to enter alphanumeric characters on separate lines. The maximum length of the text value is 255 characters and a warning is displayed when the number is about to be reached (as shown previously).

Text Area (Long)

The **Text Area (Long)** field provides for the storage of up to 131,072 characters that display on separate lines, similar to a **Text Area** field. However, you can specify a lower maximum length of this field type, between 256 and 131,072 characters.

Every time you press *Enter* within a long text area field, a line break and a return character are added to the text. These two characters count towards the 131,072 character limit. This data type is not available for activities or products, on opportunities. In a report, only the first 254 characters of a long-text area field are shown.

Text Area (Rich)

Using the **Text Area (Rich)** data type, your users are provided with a text field with an embedded toolbar. This toolbar allows simple formatting of the text and provides for the adding of images and URL web links.

The maximum size for uploaded images is 1 MB and only GIF, JPEG, and PNG file types are currently supported.

The toolbar offers the ability to undo, redo, bolden, italicize, underline, strike-out, and modify the alignment of text. Users can also embed a hyperlink, upload, or create a link to an image, and add a list which can be numbered or non-numbered.

The maximum field size is 131,072 characters, which is inclusive of any formatting or HTML tags and in reports, only the first 254 characters of a Rich-Text area are shown.

URL

The **URL** field allows users to enter a web link.

The URL field can store up to 255 characters. However, only the first 50 characters are displayed on the record detail pages.

When the web link is clicked, the Salesforce CRM application opens a new browser window to show the web page.

 Whenever your users enter values into either a currency amount or a number field, they can use the shortcuts k, m, or b, to indicate thousands, millions, or billions. For example, when you enter *7k*, it is displayed as 7,000.

Dependent picklists

Dependent picklists are picklists (including multi-select picklists) in which the values available in the picklist depend on the value of another field, which is called the controlling field.

 Controlling fields can be any picklist or checkbox field within the same record.

Controlling fields that are picklists are fields with at least one and fewer than 300 values. These are used to help with efficient, accurate data entry and help to achieve consistent data.

- To define a dependent picklist, navigate to the field's area of the appropriate object.
- For standard objects, this is carried out by navigating to **Setup** | **Customize** | (select the appropriate standard object) | **Fields**. Click on **Field Dependencies**.
- For custom objects, navigate to **Setup** | **Create** | **Objects** | (select the appropriate custom object). Click on **Field Dependencies**.

Now click on **New**, choose a controlling field and dependent field, and then click on **Continue**.

Use the field-dependency matrix to specify the dependent picklist values that are available when a user selects each controlling field value, as shown in the following screenshot:

Edit Field Dependency

Help for this Page ⊘

| Save | Cancel | Preview |

Controlling Field   Stage

Dependent Field   Reason Lost

▼ **Instructions**

- Double click on a cell to toggle its visibility for the Controlling Field value shown in the column heading.
- To change multiple cells at once, select multiple cells and then click the Include Values or Exclude Values button to change the visibility of all selected cells at once.
- Use SHIFT + click to select a range of adjacent cells. Use CTRL + click to select multiple cells that are not adjacent.
- Use the Preview button to test the results.

Legend
Excluded Value
Included Value

Click button to include or exclude selected values from the dependent picklist:

| Include Values | Exclude Values |

Showing Columns: 6 - 10 (of 10) < Previous | Next >   View All   ▶ Go to

Stage:	Perception Analysis	Proposal/Price Quote	Negotiation/Review	Closed Won	Closed Lost
Reason Lost:	*No Budget*	*No Budget*	*No Budget*	*No Budget*	**No Budget**
	Missing Product Features	*Missing Product Features*	*Missing Product Features*	*Missing Product Features*	**Missing Product Features**
	Better Price	*Better Price*	*Better Price*	*Better Price*	**Better Price**
	Cost / Value	*Cost / Value*	*Cost / Value*	*Cost / Value*	**Cost / Value**

Showing Columns: 6 - 10 (of 10) < Previous | Next >   View All

Click button to include or exclude selected values from the dependent picklist:

| Include Values | Exclude Values |

| Save | Cancel | Preview |

Finally, click on **Save**.

Please note the following points:

- Checkbox fields can be controlling fields but not dependent fields
- You can set default values for controlling fields but not for dependent picklists
- Multi-select picklists can be dependent picklists but not controlling fields

- Standard picklist fields can be controlling fields but not dependent fields
- Custom picklist fields can be either controlling or dependent fields
- The maximum number of values allowed in a controlling field is 300

Building relationship fields

When building lookup and master-detail relationship fields, there are various options and settings that you can set, which will enforce data integrity. These options and settings are covered in the next section.

Lookup relationship options

When you create a lookup field on an object, you can choose whether the lookup field is required or optional. If it is set as optional, you can choose one of the following three actions to take place if the lookup record is deleted:

- **Clear the value of this field:**

  This is a default option and is a good choice when the field does not have to contain a value from the associated lookup record.

- **Don't allow deletion of the lookup record that's part of a lookup relationship**

  This option prevents the lookup record from being deleted and is a good choice for restricting deletions if you have dependencies, such as workflow rules, based on the lookup relationship.

- **Delete this record also**

  This option works similar to the master-detail relationship and deletes the record whenever the lookup record is deleted. However, such a deletion on a lookup relationship is known as a cascade-delete and bypasses security and sharing settings. As a result, users can delete records when the lookup record is deleted even if they do not have access to the related records.

 The cascade-delete feature is disabled by default and is available only by sending a request to Salesforce support.

  This option is a good choice when the lookup field and its associated record are highly coupled and you need to delete related data whenever the lookup data is removed.

 This option is only available within custom objects and is not available for standard objects. However, the lookup field object can be either a standard or custom object.

Master-detail relationship options

When you create a master-detail field on an object, you can choose the **Allow reparenting** option.

Allow reparenting option

By default, records in master-detail relationships cannot be reparented. However, you can allow child records in a master-detail relationship to be reparented to a different parent by selecting **Allow reparenting** option in the master-detail relationship definition.

Lookup filters

Lookup filters are used to restrict the values and lookup dialog results for Lookup, Master-detail, and Hierarchical relationship fields.

You can specify the restrictions by configuring filter criteria that compare fields and values based on:

- The current record
- The related object (via the Lookup, Master-detail, or Hierarchical field)
- The current user's record, permissions, and role
- The records directly associated to the related object

As an example, you can:

- Restrict the **Contact Name** field on an Account record to allow only those contacts that have a custom status of active, filtering out inactive contacts
- Restrict the **Contact Name** field on a case record to allow only those contacts that are associated with the Account record specified in the **Account Name** field on the Case record
- Restrict the **Account Name** field on an Opportunity record to allow only those users who have an International profile to create or edit Opportunity records, for accounts outside the United States

You can optionally click on **Insert Suggested Criteria** to choose from a list of lookup filter criteria that the Salesforce CRM system suggests based on the defined relationships between the objects in your organization.

You can make lookup filters either required or optional.

For fields with required lookup filters, only values that match the lookup filter criteria appear in the lookup dialog. For non-valid values that are manually entered into the field, you can set a custom error message which is presented to the user as the record is prevented from saving.

For fields with optional lookup filters, only values that match the lookup filter criteria appear in the lookup dialog initially. However, users can click on the **Show all results** link in the lookup dialog to remove the filter and view all search result values for the lookup field. Optional lookup filters also allow users to save values that do not match the lookup filter criteria.

Building formulas

Custom formula fields require additional settings as specified by the Salesforce CRM application, which are carried out using the following actions and steps:

1. Create the Formula field.
2. Choose the data type for the field, based on the output of the calculation.
3. Enter the number of decimal places for currency, number, or percent data types.

The setting for the number of decimal places is ignored for currency fields in multi-currency organizations. Instead, the decimal places for your currency setting apply. Salesforce uses the round-half up, tie-breaking rule for numbers in formula fields. For example, *12.345* becomes *12.35* and *−12.345* becomes *−12.34*.

4. Click on **Next** to display the formula creation screen.

Basic formula

To create a basic formula that passes specific Salesforce data, select the **Simple Formula** tab, choose the field type in the **Select Field Type** drop-down list, and choose one of the fields listed in the **Insert Field** drop-down list.

To insert an operator, choose the appropriate operator icon from the **Insert Operator** drop-down list. Here, you can select from the following operators: **+ Add, − Subtract, * Multiply, / Divide, ^ Exponentiation, ((open parenthesis character),) (close parenthesis character), & Concatenate, = Equal, <> Not Equal, < Less Than, > Greater Than, <= Less Than or Equal, >= Greater Than or Equal, && And**, and **|| Or**.

Advanced formula

The basic formula feature is quite restricted and you will likely seek to create more complicated formulas which can be performed by selecting the **Advanced Formula** tab.

Within this tab, click on **Insert Field**, choose a field, and then click on **Insert**.

You can now include merge fields along with advanced operators as well as functions, which are prebuilt Salesforce CRM formulas that you can invoke and pass your input values to by performing following steps :

Function description and example usage:
Select a function and click on **Help** to view a description and examples of formulas using that function.

1. Click on **Check Syntax** to check your formula for errors.
2. Enter a description of the formula in the **Description** box (this is optional).
3. For formulas that result in either a number, a currency, or a percentage field, you can decide how to display blank fields. To display blank fields as a zero value, select the option **Treat blank fields as zeros**. To display these fields as blank values, select the **Treat blank fields as blanks** option.
4. Click on **Next** to continue.
5. To set the field visibility for user's profiles, set the field level security and then click on **Next**.
6. Now choose which page layouts are to display the field. In this step, the field is added to the specified page layout and appears as the last field in the first two-column section detail page.

Formula fields are automatically calculated. Therefore, they are not visible on edit pages and are read-only on record detail pages. Formula fields do not update last-modified date fields. Technically, formula fields are computed at the point in time a user or system queries the record and retrieves the field to view it. Hence the field is not altered as such and the record is not updated due to the formula value calculation change therefore means workflow rules, validation rules, and so on are not triggered by a change of formula field calculation.

7. Click on **Save** to finish, or on **Save & New** to create more custom fields.

Formula fields have character and byte size limits and cannot contain more than 3,900 characters.

Building formulas – best practices

Some best practices and methods to improve the creation and maintenance of formula fields are as follows:

- Formatting with carriage returns and spacing
- Commenting

Formatting with carriage returns and spacing

Consider the following formula:

```
Sales Tax (Percent) =
IF(TEXT(Account.Market__c) = "US", IF(TEXT(Account.State__c) =
"California", 0.0925, IF(TEXT(Account.State__c) = "Nevada", 0.081,
IF(TEXT(Account.State__c) = "Utah", 0.0835, 0) )) , 0)
```

To improve the readability of formula fields, you can add spacing and carriage returns. The preceding formula can be made far easier to understand, simply by adding spaces and carriage returns, as in the following snippet:

```
Sales Tax (Percent) =
IF( TEXT(Account.Market__c) = "US",
IF(TEXT(Account.State__c) = "California", 0.0925,
IF(TEXT(Account.State__c) = "Nevada", 0.081,
IF(TEXT(Account.State__c) = "Utah", 0.0835, 0) ))
, 0)
```

Commenting

Salesforce CRM allows you to put comments in your formulas. These are sections of text that are not run as part of the formula and are typically used to make notes about the formula code, especially if it is particularly complicated. Comments must start with a forward slash followed by an asterisk (/*), and finish with an asterisk followed by a forward slash (*/).

Comments are useful for explaining specific parts of a formula to other system administrators viewing the formula definition. Look at the following code block as an example:

```
Sales Tax (Percent) =
/* value only set for US opportunities */
IF( TEXT(Account.Market__c) = "US",
/* Check for the US State of the Account record and set accordingly */
IF(TEXT(Account.State__c) = "California", 0.0925,
IF(TEXT(Account.State__c) = "Nevada", 0.081,
IF(TEXT(Account.State__c) = "Utah", 0.0835, 0) ))
)
, 0)
```

Carefully using comments to prevent parts of the formula from being activated allows you to test and verify the syntax as you construct and iron out bugs in the formula. However, if you try to comment out the entire formula as syntax, an error is shown. Also, you will experience a syntax error if you try to place comments within other comments because this is not supported in the Salesforce CRM application:

```
/* /* comment */ */
```

> Including comments and formatting with carriage returns and spacing adds to the number of characters used and therefore counts against the character and byte size limits.

Building formula text and compiled character size limits

There is a text character and byte size limit of 3,900 characters, and a limit of 5,000 characters for the compiled characters for formulas.

When this limit is reached, you will be unable to save the formula field and will be presented with the following error:

```
Compiled formula is too big to execute (7,085 characters). Maximum size is
5,000 characters.
```

It is common to encounter these limits when building complicated formula field calculations and particularly so when building formulas that reference other formula fields. While there is no way to increase this limit, there are some methods to help avoid and workaround these limitations, listed as follows:

- Use the CASE function for branch conditions
- Use algebra

For formulas that use multiple branch conditions to derive the values, as in the preceding example formula, check if the market is US and the state is California, Nevada, or Utah. You can replace the nested IF statements and instead use the CASE statement.

Nested IF statements often result in larger compiled sizes where the IF function is used multiple times, as in our example:

```
IF(TEXT(Account.State__c) = "California", 0.0925,
IF(TEXT(Account.State__c) = "Nevada", 0.081,
IF(TEXT(Account.State__c) = "Utah", 0.0835, 0) ))
```

Using the CASE statement can provide better logic and often results in a smaller compiled size for the formula:

```
IF( TEXT(Account.Market__c) = "US",
CASE(Account.State__c,
"California", 0.0925,
""Nevada", 0.0685,
"Utah", 0.0475, 0) ,
0)
```

Using algebra

The compiled size of formula fields increases as you increase the number of fields that are referenced. This is compounded when you are referencing fields that are themselves formula fields. A way to reduce the overall size is to use algebra to avoid the need to reference fields, wherever possible. The following example shows how the Item_Price__c and Support_Price__c fields are used multiple times:

```
Total Price =
(Item_Price__c + (Item_Price__c * Sales_Tax__c)) +
(Support_Price__c + (Support_Price__c * Sales_Tax__c))
```

To reduce the compiled size, use simple algebra to avoid multiple uses of the Item_Price__c and Support_Price__c fields, as in the following example:

```
Total Price =
(Item_Price__c * (1 + Sales_Tax__c)) +
(Support_Price__c * (1 + Sales_Tax__c))
```

Formula field size limit workarounds

There may be situations where the logic that is required for a formula is simply too complex for the current size limitations in formula fields. The proven methods to overcome this are to implement a solution using either of the following:

- Workflow field updates
- Apex trigger updates
- Process Builder field updates

There are two ways in which workflow field updates can help to provide the formula logic workaround. Firstly, larger and more complex formulas can be saved using the formula-building function within the workflow mechanism. Secondly, large formula logic can be decomposed into smaller functions of resulting data. For example, you could create simple formulas that get the data fed from fields that have been updated by multiple workflow field updates.

Workflows are covered in detail later in this book. However, the general approach for implementing a workflow field update to provide a solution to the formula field limit is to:

- Create a non-formula field on the object, such as a currency or number field, in place of the desired formula field. Administrators often identify this field with a suffix to indicate it is a workflow field-for example, **Total Price (workflow)**. This field is then set as read-only on page layouts as the field can be considered a system field (as it should not be available for manual updating).
- Create a workflow rule that will always fire.
- Create a field update with an appropriate formula to update the workflow field-**Total Price (workflow)** in our preceding example.

Any subsequent formulas can reference the populated field. The disadvantages to this workaround are that creating many workflows can add to the complexity of the application and may eventually introduce performance issues. Also, whenever an object has multiple complex workflows assigned, the order in which the workflows are evaluated cannot always be guaranteed, which if not properly maintained can lead to subtle data discrepancies.

Custom field governance

Controlling the creation of fields is necessary to avoid adding unnecessary new fields in Salesforce. Without appropriate field creation governance, there is a risk of producing an application with a complex data structure that provides a poor user experience.

This issue can often be observed due to the ease of creating new custom fields. However, there are other causes such as:

- Configuring spontaneous responses to end-user field creation requests without gathering full requirements

- Lack of specification or understanding of reporting requirements for field usage
- Creation of fields that are too specific for common uses, thus driving the need to create ever more fields
- Lack of knowledge or awareness of existing fields that could be used rather than creating new ones

As the number of unnecessary fields increases, users will find it ever more difficult to enter the correct data into the correct fields. Therefore, the amount of entered data is reduced along with user's satisfaction because the application requires less effort to work with. It is all too easy for your users to become dissatisfied and this can lead to less overall usage and hence poor data quality due to lack of user participation.

Addressing the issue

Create new fields with care because as each new custom field is added, your application structure increases in complexity. As a system administrator, you are responsible for knowing which fields are used, where they appear on Page Layouts, and which fields are required for reporting.

If the benefits and long-term use for a new field cannot be easily understood, it is unlikely to be of much use. One method to help determine its use is to consider where and how the proposed new field would be used. If it is never going to be reported, it may be worth querying its purpose and value. The following considerations can be made when creating new fields.

More generic field names

Try to make your field names more generic so that they can serve multiple purposes. In some situations, different business units share objects but track different information. Although they may have different requirements, they can often share fields. Here you need to be proactive, forward-thinking, and reach out to the business and propose fields that can be used across multiple business units.

Field history tracking

Often there are unnecessary date fields that are used to track milestones or data-processing dates. With native field history tracking, these milestones can be tracked and reported without the need to always create new fields.

Field history tracking can be applied on certain custom and standard fields for custom objects and the following core standard objects: **Accounts**, **Cases**, **Contacts**, **Contracts**, **Leads**, and **Opportunities** using the **Set History Tracking** button, as shown in the following screenshot:

Account Fields

Help for this Page ?

This page allows you to specify the fields that can appear on the Account page. You can create up to 500 Account custom fields.

Note that deleting a custom field will delete any filters that use the custom field. It may also change the result of Assignment or Escalation Rules that rely on the custom field data.

> Set History Tracking

Account Standard Fields

Account Standard Fields Help ?

Action	Field Label	Field Name	Data Type	Controlling Field
	Account Name	Name	Name	

Upon clicking on the **Set History Tracking** button, a page appears, displaying the activation of field history tracking and selection of the fields to be tracked, as shown in the following screenshot:

Account Field History

Help for this Page

☑ Enable Account History

This page allows you to select the fields you want to track on the Account History related list. Whenever a user modifies any of the fields selected below, the old and new field values are added to the History related list as well as the date, time, nature of the change, and user making the change. Note that multi-select picklist and large text field values are tracked as edited; their old and new field values are not recorded.

| Save | Cancel |

Deselect all fields

Track old and new values

Account Name	☐		Account Number	☐
Account Owner	☐		Account Site	☐
Account Source	☐		Active	☐
Annual Revenue	☐		Billing Address	☐
Customer	☐		Data.com Key	☐

Changes to fields that have been set up for field history tracking will see a new entry to the object's history-related list whenever changes are made to records (where that field is modified). All entries include the date, time, details of the change, and the name of the user that made the change as shown here.

Not all field types can have their history tracked. Changes to field types greater than 255 characters are tracked as edited; their old and new values are not recorded.

There is a maximum of 20 fields per object that can be set to be tracked.

 Field history data does not count against your organization's storage limit, however, at the time of publication, `Salesforce.com` are planning to move toward a policy of deleting field history data that is older than 18 months. Here, they recommend establishing your own field history retention policy such as extracting the data from the system.

Custom objects to store dated information

You can create custom objects to store dated information and related lists to avoid hard-coding date fields on a record. For example, avoid creating fields to track dated historical financial information within an object. Here, you may have to create redundant fields for each year. For example, 2011 Budgets, 2012 Budgets, and so on. Instead, create a `Financials` object with one set of fields and a corresponding date field where you can create a new record each year. This can result in fewer fields and far better display and reporting.

Chatter

Consider the use of **Chatter** to eliminate unnecessary fields. Often, text-area boxes are used to track conversation flows such as support comments and internal review. These text messages can often be better facilitated with the use of **Chatter** posts. **Chatter** is covered later in `Chapter 8`, *Introducing Sales Cloud, Service Cloud, and the Collaborative Features of Salesforce CRM*.

Page layouts

Page layouts are used to organize the display of fields, buttons, custom links, inline Visualforce pages, Report charts, and related lists on an object detail or edit page. They are used to establish unique layouts for different business scenarios.

The displayed fields within a related list are controlled by the page layout; the name of the related list is determined by the lookup/master-detail relationship on the related object.

Page layouts are comprised of sections containing the buttons, fields, related lists, and customer links which can be edited using the enhanced page layout editor as shown in the following screenshot. Here, we are showing how we can edit the properties of the **Account Site** field.

Within the field sections, the user interface can be used to make a field **Required** or **Read-only**, as shown in the following screenshot:

The enhanced page-layout editor showing read-only settings, as indicated with the padlock icons, is shown in the following screenshot:

In the corresponding **Account Edit** page, the required field for the **Account Site** is displayed with a *red* bar as shown:

Account Edit						Help for this Page
Edge Communications						

Account Edit	Save	Save & New	Cancel		
Account Information					**| = Required Information**
Account Owner	Paul Goodey		Active	Yes ▼	
Account Name	Edge Communications		Upsell Opportunity	Maybe ▼	
Parent Account		🔍	Type	Customer ▼	
Account Number	CD451796		Rating	Hot ▼	
Account Site			Phone	(512) 757-6000	
Industry	Electronics ▼		Fax	(512) 757-9000	
SIC Code	6576		Website	http://edgecomm.com	

You can combine page layouts and field-level security to make the lowest possible permission setting. For example, a hidden field (field-level permission) will never be displayed regardless of page layout. Likewise, a field marked as **Always** requires a value in this field to save a record will always be required on the page layout.

Page layouts allow you to create and organize sections on a page and to show or hide fields within sections.

Hidden fields may still be accessible elsewhere in the application. Use field-level security to restrict all possible means of accessing a field.

Creating and modifying a page layout

To create or modify a page layout, navigate to **Setup** | **Customize**. Select the appropriate object and click on **Page Layouts**. In the **Page Layouts** page, you can either click on the **New** button or choose the existing page layout to modify and click on **Edit**, as shown in the following screenshot:

Account Page Layout

This page allows you to create different page layouts to display Account data.
After creating page layouts, click the Page Layout Assignment button to control which page layout

Account Page Layouts   [New]   [Page Layout Assignment]

Action	Page Layout Name	Created By
Edit | Del	Account (Marketing) Layout	Paul Goodey, 19/12/2009 13:01
Edit | Del	Account (Sales) Layout	Paul Goodey, 19/12/2009 13:01
Edit | Del	Account (Support) Layout	Paul Goodey, 19/12/2009 13:01
Edit | Del	Account Layout	Paul Goodey, 19/12/2009 13:01

When clicking on the **New** button, you can optionally choose an existing layout to copy.

Creating a page layout based on an existing page layout:
In the enhanced page-layout editor, select an existing page layout from the list of page layouts, and then click on **Save As** to create a copy of the layout. In the original page-layout editor, select an existing page layout from the list of page layouts, and then click on the **Clone** button.

Enter a name for the new page layout and finally, click on **Save**.

You can set different page layouts for profiles and different page layouts for record types.

Feed-based page layouts

Feed-based page layouts offer a two tabbed page that allows users to switch between a **Chatter** feed and a detail page for the record. The tabs are marked **Feed** and **Details** as shown in the following screenshot:

A prerequisite for feed-based layouts, is the enabling of feed tracking for the object that you wish to create a feed-based layout. **Feed tracking** allows users to follow records which then lets them see feed updates when those fields are changed.

Feed Tracking

To enable **Feed Tracking**, navigate to **Setup** I **Customize** I **Chatter** I **Feed Tracking**. Here you are presented with a screen containing two panes. The left pane shows the object selection and the right pane shows the field selection as shown in the following screenshot:

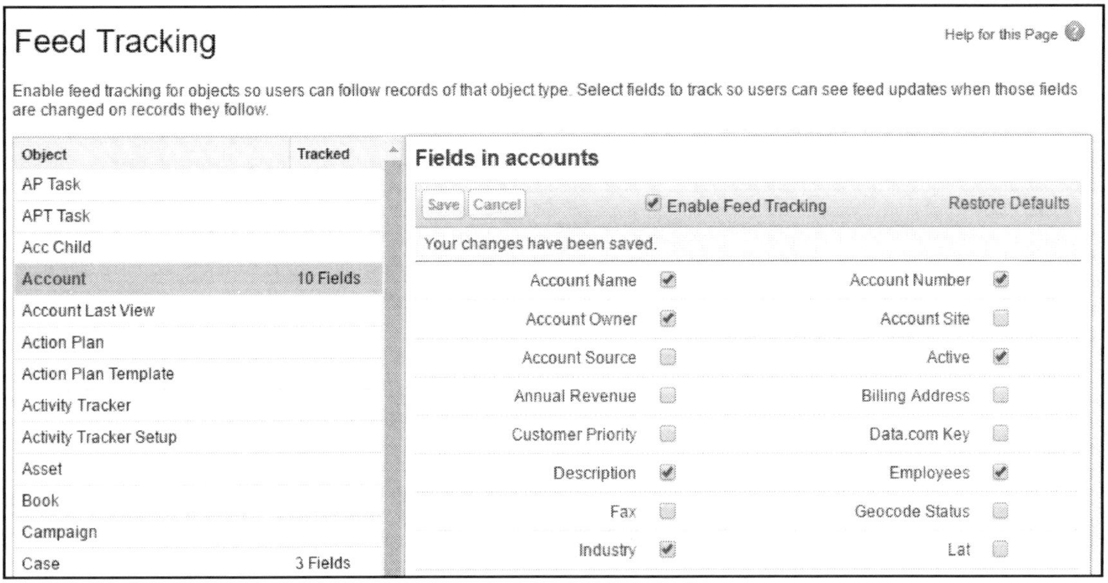

To enable feed tracking, select an object in the left pane, enable the **Enable Feed Tracking** checkbox in the right pane, select the desired fields, and then click the **Save** button.

Up to 20 fields can be selected for feed tracking.

Creating feed-based page layouts

To create a feed-based page layout you must have first set the associated object as one that is feed tracked (see *Feed Tracking* section in this chapter).

To create the feed-based page layout navigate to **Setup | Customize**. Select the appropriate object, click on **Page Layouts**, and then click on the **New** button.

In the **Create New Page Layout** page optionally select an existing layout to clone, enter a **Page Layout Name**, enable the **Feed-based Layout** checkbox, and finally click the **Save** button as shown in the following screenshot:

Create New Page Layout — Help for this Page

As an option, you may select an existing layout to clone. If you create a page layout without cloning, your page layout will not include the standard sections whose names are translated for your international users.

Existing Page Layout: --None--
Page Layout Name:
Feed-Based Layout: ☑

Save Cancel

On the main page layout editor page, you can customize **Quick Actions in the Salesforce Classic Publisher** to include actions you want to make available to users, and also add any custom buttons or links as shown in the following screenshot:

To customize the way the feed page appears, click the **Feed View** link in the page layout editor header as shown in the following screenshot:

Within the **Feed View** setup page, you are presented with a number of options to control the way the **Feed View** page appears to users when clicking on a record. These options are shown in the following screenshot:

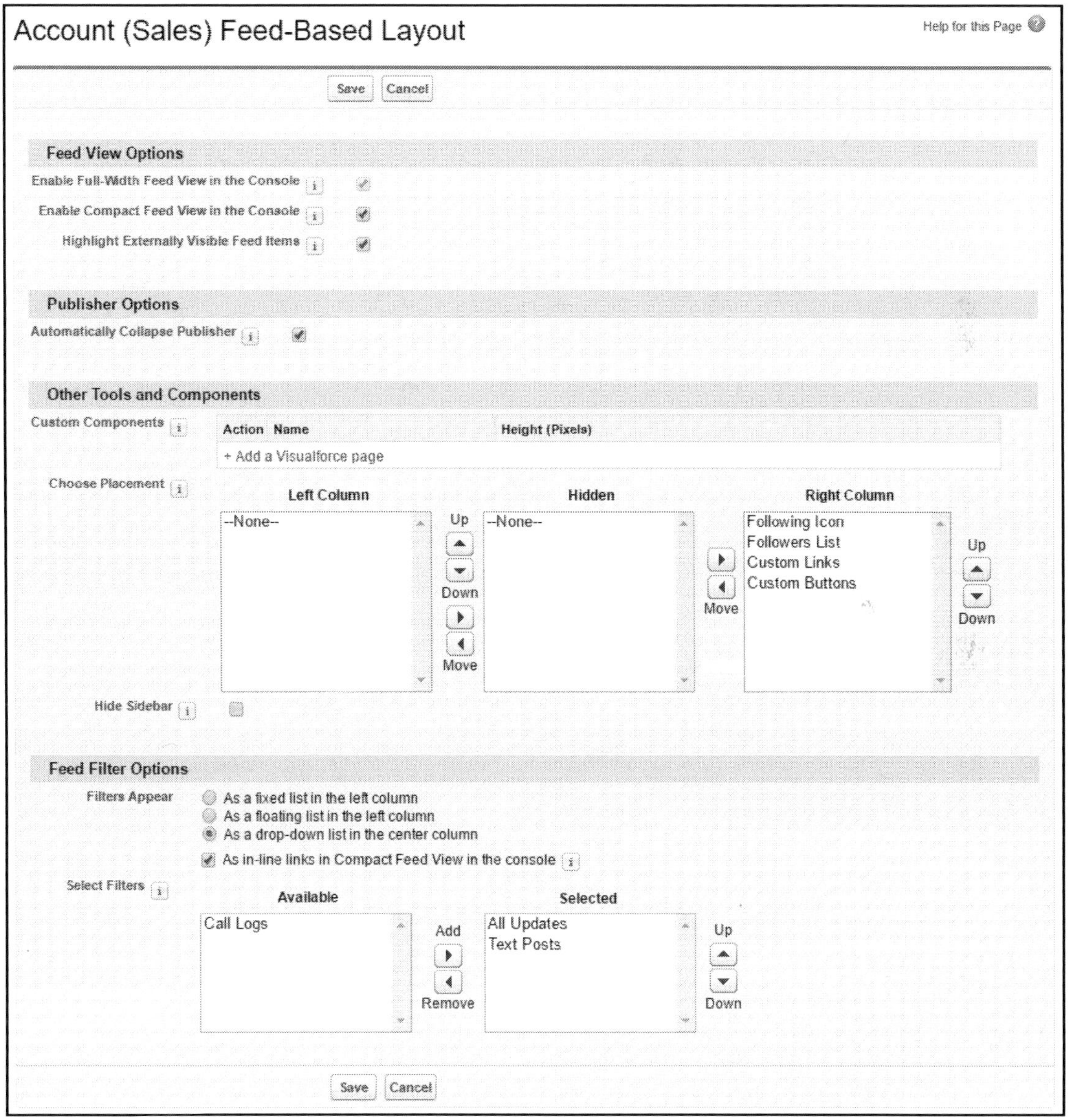

Feed View Options

The following **Feed View** options can be configured:

Enable Full-Width Feed View in the Console

Selecting this option makes the feed expand horizontally to take up the full available width of the page in console tabs or subtabs.

 To use this option, **Actions** in the **Publisher** must have been enabled.

Enable Compact Feed View in the Console

Selecting this option shows a compact view of actions and feed items to give users a more streamlined view of the feed in console tabs or subtabs.

 To use this option, **Actions** in the **Publisher** must have been enabled.

Highlight Externally Visible Feed Items

Selecting this option uses a gray user icon along with orange shading to mark the feed items that are visible to external users.

 To use this option, the **Compact Feed View** must have been enabled.

Publisher options – Automatically Collapse Publisher

Selecting this option automatically collapses the publisher when it is not in use, allowing users to view more of the page content below it.

Other Tools and Components

In this section you can configure the page to carry out the following:

Custom Components

Adding custom components using the **Custom Components** option. Here you select up to 10 Visualforce pages to use as custom components. These Visualforce pages must use a standard controller for the object.

Choose Placement

This option allows you to choose where the items set in the **Other Tools and Components** appear on the page.

Hide Sidebar

This option allows you to choose if the page is displayed with the sidebar removed from the page.

Feed Filter Options

This set of options allow you to choose which feed filters are available, and where they appear. Here you can set the filters to appear as a fixed list in the left column, as a floating list in the left column, or as a drop-down list in the center column.

You can also set the feed filter to appear as in-line links in **Compact Feed View** in the console. When **Compact Feed** is enabled, this option overrides the list selection used for standard feed layouts.

To configure feed-based layouts you need to use the enhanced page layout editor; you cannot configure feed-based layouts with the original page layout editor.

One you have selected the option for the feed-based page layout, you can then assign the page layout to appropriate user profiles as required.

You cannot change existing standard page layouts to feed-based. Only newly created page layouts can be set to be feed-based. Currently, feed-based page layouts can only created for Account, Contact, Leads, Opportunity, Case, Asset, and Custom Objects.

Record types

Record types are a feature of Salesforce CRM that allow you to provide different sets of object picklists, different page layouts, and custom business processes to specific users, based on their profile or assigned permission set. Record types can be used in various ways, for example:

- Create record types for opportunities to differentiate your internal sales deals from your field sales deals and show different fields and picklist values
- Create record types for leads to display different page layouts for your tele-sales leads versus your internal sales prospecting functions

Creating a record type

The record type, `Master`, is always set for every object and contains all the picklist and process options. It is not, however, listed under the record types list and it can be assigned as a record type for a profile, provided it is the only assigned as a record type for that profile.

Since each record type is assigned to one page-layout type per profile, the numbers of page assignments can easily increase. This means that if you have two custom record types for an account and five profiles, you will have 15 page assignments (5*2 for each custom record type, and five for the `Master` record type).

Selectable record types are assigned per profile and field-level security is configured separately for each record type. Consider the following when creating a record type:

- Which record types are associated with the current profile?
- If more than one record type is associated with the current profile, prompt the user for record-type selection
- If only one, select that record type without prompting (this would be set as default)
- Based upon record type and profile, assign the appropriate page layout

- Based upon record type, assign the appropriate process and picklist values
- By associating different record types to different page layouts, fields, and picklist values, you can formulate a set of object-specific processes. In Salesforce CRM, the following are available:
  - The `Lead` process using the `Lead` object, which is governed by the `Status` field (which is configured to be **Open**, **Closed**, and so on)
  - The `Sales` process, which uses the `Opportunity` object and the `Stage` field (set to be **WON**, **LOST**, and so on), plus the `Amount` and `Probability` fields
  - The `Support` process, which uses the `Case` object and is controlled by the `CaseStatus` field (which may be set to **Open**, **Closed**, and so on)
  - The `Solutions` process, which uses the `Solution` object and the fields `Status` (which are set to be **Draft**, **Deployed**, and so on)

For example, your sales team creates an opportunity that represents a sales deal. Your sales support team then upsells on this deal. You can then create two sales processes with two different record types and two different page layouts: **Sales and Support**.

You would want to create a lookup relationship from opportunity to opportunity, and only require or display this relationship for the support team profile.

You would also be able to configure the sharing rules so that they could not modify each other's opportunities. This is covered in detail in `Chapter 4`, *Securing Access to Data and Data Validation*.

 You can assign custom **Record Types** in **Permission Sets** as well as in **Profiles**.

Related lists

Related lists display on the lower portion of the object detail page to display the related record details. Related lists show the object records that are associated with that record.

From a related list, you can:

- Click on the object record name to view detailed information
- Click on **Edit** or **Del** to edit or delete the object record
- Click on **New** to create a new object record that is associated with the record you are viewing

To define if an object can be related to another type of record, you would use either a master-detail or a lookup relationship.

Here, we show how editing a page layout for the account object enables the arrangement and configuration of any related list:

The following screenshot shows the results of changing the related lists in the page-layout editor screen when navigating to the **Account detail** page:

List views

When you click on a tab, the **Accounts** tab for instance, you will be shown the **My Accounts** field in that view. This is termed as a list view and can be seen as shown in the following screenshot:

Other list views can be selected from the picklist:

You can modify existing views and define which columns and buttons (including standard and custom buttons) are to be displayed. You can click on **New** to create new views:

Accounts
Create New View

Save Cancel

Step 1. Enter View Name

View Name:

View Unique Name:

Step 2. Specify Filter Criteria

Filter By Owner:
- All Accounts
- My Accounts

Filter By Additional Fields (Optional):

Field	Operator	Value
--None--	--None--	
--None--	--None--	
--None--	--None--	
--None--	--None--	
--None--	--None--	

Add Filter Logic...

Step 3. Select Fields to Display

Available Fields

Billing Street
Billing City

Selected Fields

Account Name
Account Site

Top

The following points apply to list views:

- Every object in Salesforce CRM that is associated with a tab automatically has at least one list view. If there is no tab set up for the object, then there would be no corresponding list view.

- List views can be modified by assigning filter criteria to control which records are returned for the affected object.
- List views can be set up to be seen and accessed only by you, or you can set it to be accessed by certain roles and groups of individuals.
- List view has a print feature that can be used by you and your users. To print from a list view, click on the printable view button located in the top-right corner of the page, as shown in the following screenshot:

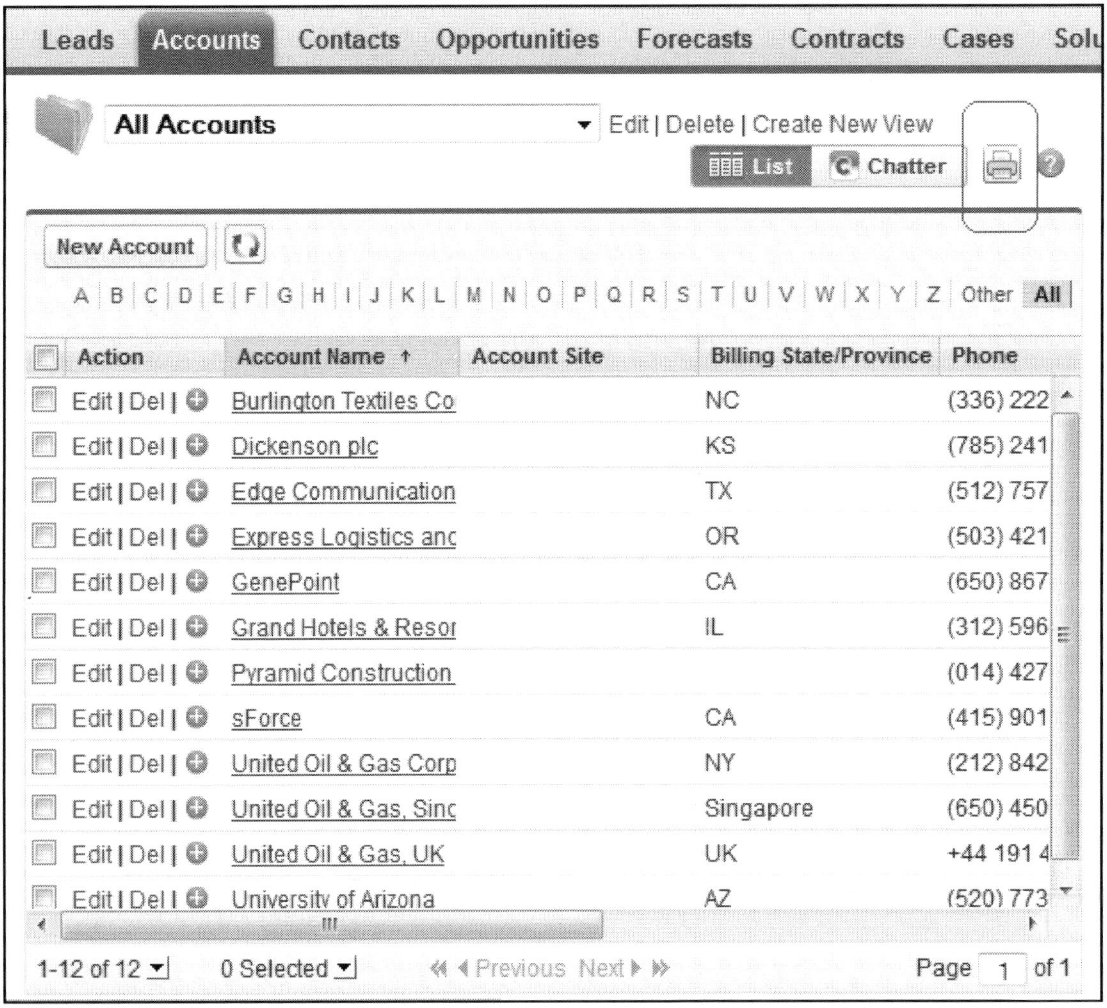

Printable list views need to be enabled organization-wide for the print feature to be available. See user interface settings in `Chapter 1`, *Setting up Salesforce CRM and the Company Profile.*

Force.com Quick Access Menu

Whenever you want to view or configure object or app-related setup information, use the Force.com **Quick Access** Menu to navigate directly to the relevant customization option.

The Force.com **Quick Access** Menu is available from object list view pages and record detail pages, and provides shortcuts to the configuration features within Salesforce CRM.

The menu can be accessed by clicking on the arrow located on the right margin of the screen, as shown in the following screenshot:

You can then use the links to navigate directly to the desired setup page or you can remove the menu by clicking on **Turn off menu** (this will remove the option from all list views and record pages), as shown in the following screenshot:

You can restore the menu by navigating to **Setup** | **My Personal Information** | **Personal Information**. Now, click on **Edit** on the user detail page, select **Force.com Quick Access Menu**, and then finally click on **Save**.

Questions to test your knowledge

You are now presented with questions about the key features of Salesforce CRM administration in the areas of **Standard and Custom Objects** which have been covered in this chapter. The answers can be found at the end of the chapter.

Questions

We present seven questions to verify your understanding of apps, tabs, objects, and fields.

Question 1 – Standard apps

Which of the following are standard Salesforce apps? (Select all that apply)

a) Site.com

b) Campaigns

c) Collaboration Community

d) Call Center

e) Service Cloud

Question 2 – Custom App Permission

What can a system administrator use to provide a group of users with access to a custom app? (Select all that apply)

a) Public groups

b) Profiles

c) Sharing rules

d) Page layouts

Question 3 – Custom tabs

When a custom object is created, a custom tab is created in which of the following scenarios? (Select one)

a) Always (tabs are automatically created)

b) Never (tabs cannot be created during the creation of an object)

c) If desired (tabs can be optionally created during the creation of an object)

Question 4 – Relationship fields

A Roll-up Summary field can be created when which relationship field is already in place? (Select one)

a) Lookup relationship

b) Hierarchical relationship

c) Master-detail relationship

d) Any of the above

Question 5 – Master-detail relationship fields

Which of the following is true about Master-detail relationship fields on custom objects? (Select two)

a) Ownership and access to the child record are determined by the parent

b) The child record can be optionally deleted when the parent record is deleted

c) Up to two master-detail relationship fields can be created on a custom object

d) The parent relationship field on the child record is optional

Question 6 – Dependent fields

Which of the following field type variations cannot be a controlling field for dependent fields? (Select one)

a) Custom Picklist

b) Standard Checkbox

c) Custom Multi-select Picklist

d) Standard Picklist

e) Custom Checkbox

Question 7 – Formula fields

When are the values in a formula field re-calculated? (Select one)

a) Every 3 minutes

b) After the record has been saved

c) Automatically

d) Nightly at 00:00 based on the Salesforce CRM timezone

Answers

Here are the answers to the seven questions about apps, tabs, objects, and fields.

Answer 1 – Standard Apps

The answer is **a**) Site.com and **d**) Call Center

The choices **b**) Campaigns, **c**) Collaboration Community, and **e**) Service Cloud are not standard Salesforce apps.

Answer 2 – Custom App Permission

The answer is **b**) Profiles

The choices **a**) Public Groups, **c**) Sharing Rules, and **d**) Page Layouts cannot be used to provide a group of users with access to a custom app.

Answer 3 – Custom Tabs

The answer is **c**) If desired. Custom tabs can be optionally created during the creation of an object by selecting the **Launch the New Custom Tab Wizard** checkbox.

The choices **a**) Always (tabs are automatically created) and **b**) Never (tabs cannot be created during the creation of an object) are not correct.

Answer 4 – Relationship fields

The answer is **c**) Master-detail relationship

The choices **a**) Lookup relationship and **b**) Hierarchical relationship do not allow a Roll-up Summary field to be created.

Answer 5 – Master-detail relationship fields

The answer is **a**) Ownership and access to the child record are determined by the parent and **c**) Up to two master-detail relationship field can be created on a custom object

The choices **b**) The child record can be optionally deleted when the parent record is deleted and **d**) The parent relationship field on the child record is optional are incorrect.

Answer 6 – Dependent fields

The answer is **c**) Custom Multi-select Picklist

The choices **a**) Custom Picklist, **b**) Standard Checkbox, **d**) Standard Picklist, and **e**) Custom Checkbox can't be a controlling field for dependent fields.

Answer 7 – Formula fields

The answer is **c**) Automatically

The choices **a**) Every 3 minutes, **b**) After the record has been saved, and **d**) Nightly at 00:00 based on the Salesforce CRM timezone are not measures for when a formula field is re-calculated.

Summary

In this chapter, we described the ways in which the data structure and user-interface features can be configured within Salesforce CRM.

We looked at how object and records information can be accessed. We also looked at the mechanisms for managing the methods that users use to view this information using views and page layouts.

We were shown how these record structures and user interfaces are controlled by the profile and the wider picture for the way configuration of these concepts are applied for users.

We discussed some techniques to help govern the way the configuration and creation of fields can be carried out and some common pitfalls to avoid.

Finally, we posed some questions to help clarify some of the key features of Salesforce CRM administration in the areas of Standard and Custom Objects.

In the next chapter, we will look in detail at the mechanisms for controlling access to data records and the features that provide data management and record sharing.

4
Securing Access to Data and Data Validation

In the previous chapters, we have looked at how Salesforce controls access to information using the user profile mechanism. We have seen how the appropriate object level permissions, such as create, read, update, and delete have to be set on the user's profile to allow the user corresponding permissions to the records of that object type.

In this chapter, we will look at organization-wide sharing defaults, roles, and other sharing settings which compliment and extend the assigning of access permissions to users within the Salesforce CRM application.

This chapter also looks in detail at some of the mechanisms for controlling record updates and features that allow you to govern and control the quality of data entered into Salesforce CRM.

Finally, you will be presented with a number of questions about the key features of Salesforce CRM administration in the area of security and access which are covered in this chapter.

The following topics are being covered in this chapter:

- Levels of data access and security
- Data access security model
- Organization-Wide Defaults
- Granting access using hierarchies
- Granting users additional access
- Permission sets
- Role hierarchy

- Organization-wide defaults and sharing rules
- Sharing rules
- Groups
- Public groups
- Personal groups
- Effects of adding or modifying sharing rules
- Criteria-based sharing
- Manual sharing
- Queues

Levels of data access and security

There are various features within Salesforce CRM that provide data access and security that can be configured by system administrators and these can be applied at different levels in the platform. We will now look at the multiple levels that allow you to apply data access and security control to the information in your Salesforce org.

Organization

The first and highest level of data access and security is at the organization level. This allows for controlled access to Salesforce by authorized users where you can configure rules such as password policies and login access rules. These settings are covered in `Chapter 2`, *Managing Users and Controlling System Access*.

Objects and fields

The second and third level of data access and security is at object and field level respectively. Data access and security at object level provides the most basic category of controlling which data users have access to. Objects can have permissions applied to allow or prevent users from creating, reading, updating, or deleting data records for that particular object. The third level is at field level. Here, you can use field-level security to control access to specific fields. You can restrict access to a particular field and prevent a user from accessing it even if they have full access to the associated object. These features are covered in `Chapter 3`, *Configuring Objects and Apps*.

Records

The lowest level of data access and security enables you to control access at record level. The mechanisms for record level access allow for control at the most precise level where you can allow particular users to view object and fields, but then restrict the actual records associated with that object. For example, record-level access can be set to allow a user to view and edit their own records, without exposing these records to other users in the system. This level of access is made possible in Salesforce CRM with the in-built data access security model.

The data access security model

There are several flexible options for you to control how records are accessed within your organization.

In the previous chapter, we looked at the broadest way that you can control data by setting properties for the objects that a user can view, edit, and create through the configuration and assignment of profiles.

We also looked at the creation of fields and field-level security which is set at profile level and is applied to records at the database level. Returning to the diagram, we will now look at the security model shown at the top-right corner of the following diagram:

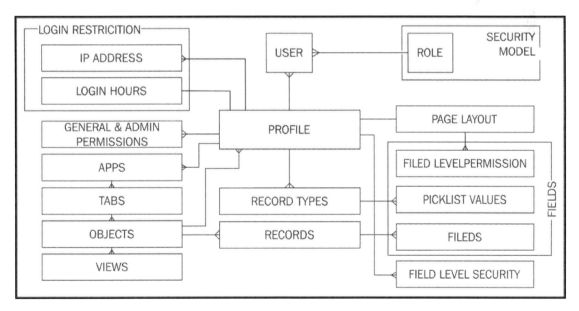

The data access security model is the lowest level of data access and security, and enables you to control access at record level using the following four features:

- Organization-Wide Defaults (OWDs)
- Role hierarchy
- Sharing rules
- Manual sharing

The following diagram shows how, with the addition of each extra feature shown, the scope of provided access to records widens:

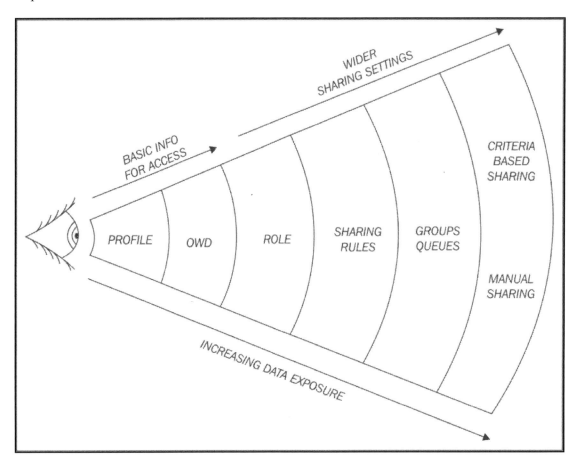

We will now look at mechanisms to control access at record level using the following features: **Organization-Wide Defaults (OWDs)**; Role hierarchy; Sharing rules; and Manual sharing. We will begin by describing the OWDs.

Organization-Wide Defaults

OWDs sharing settings are used to define the default sharing settings for an organization. For most objects, sharing settings can be set to **Private**, **Public Read Only**, or **Public Read/Write**.

OWDs sharing settings, specify the default level of access to records and can be set separately for most of the objects in Salesforce such as accounts, contacts, and activities.

When setting up the OWDs, you can set the access level for internal users using the **Default Internal Access** settings and set a different default access level for external users using the **Default External Access** settings. Here, external users are part of the Community Management feature which is provided by Salesforce at additional cost and is used to collaborate with individuals associated with your company's ecosystem such as suppliers, vendors or any other third-party venture.

As shown in the preceding diagram, along with the user's profile, the OWD defines the baseline level of access to data records that users do not own. The diagram represents the visibility or data access which is increasing as the other features are incorporated to provide wider sharing settings.

To customize your OWD settings, navigate to **Setup** | **Security Controls** | **Sharing Settings**. Now click on **Edit** in the Organization-Wide Defaults area and then for each object, select the **Default Internal Access** you want as shown in the following screenshot:

OWDs access level actions

The OWDs access levels allow the following actions to be applied to object records:

Access Level	Action
Public Full Access (Option for setting the **Campaign** object only)	Change ownership of record
	Search records
	Report on records
	Add related records
	Edit details of record
	Delete record
Public Read/Write/Transfer (Option for setting the Lead and Case objects only)	Change ownership of record
	Search records

	Report on records
	Add related records
	Edit details of record
Public Read/Write	Search records
	Report on records
	Add related records
	Edit details of record
Public Read Only	Search records
	Report on records
	Add related records
Private	No searching
	No reporting

Public Full Access (Campaigns only)

Access levels for the Campaign OWDs can be set to **Private**, **Public Read Only**, **Public Read/Write**, or **Public Full Access**. When **Campaign** is set to **Public Full Access**, all users can view, edit, transfer, delete, and report on all Campaign records.

For example, in the scenario where John is the owner of a Campaign, all other users in the application can view, edit, transfer, or delete that Campaign.

 The **Public Full Access** option is available only for the **Campaign** object.

Public Read/Write/Transfer (Cases Or Leads Only)

Access levels for **Case** or **Lead** OWDs can be set to **Private**, **Public Read Only**, **Public Read/Write**, or **Public Read/Write/Transfer**. When **Case** or **Lead** are set to **PublicRead/Write/Transfer**, all users can view, edit, transfer, and report on all Case or Lead records.

For example, if Lucy is the owner of WidgetX case number 101, all other users can view, edit, transfer ownership, and report on that case. But only Lucy can delete or change the sharing on case number 101 (see *Manual sharing rules* later in this chapter).

 The Public Read/Write/Transfer option is available only for Case or Lead.

Public Read/Write

All users can view, edit, and report on all records.

For example, if Mike is the owner of the Emerald Inc. Account record, all other users can view, edit, and report on the Emerald Inc. account. However, only Mike has the ability to delete the Emerald Inc. account record or alter the sharing settings.

Public Read Only

All users can view and report on records but they cannot edit them. Here, only the record owner and if the Grant Access Using Hierarchies checkbox is enabled (see earlier Organization-Wide Sharing Defaults Edit screen screenshot) users above that user's role in the role hierarchy can edit the records.

 The **Grant Access Using Hierarchies** checkbox is enabled by default for standard objects and cannot be disabled. The Grant Access Using Hierarchies checkbox can be enabled or disabled for custom objects.

For example, Nicole is the owner of the EuroCorp Inc. Account record and Nicole works in the International Sales department, reporting to Julia, who is the VP of International Sales. In this scenario, both Nicole and Julia have full read/write access to EuroCorp Inc.

Now, say Mike also works in International Sales; however, with the Public Read Only setting he can view and report on the EuroCorp Inc. account record, but cannot edit or delete it.

Private

Only the record owner and if the Grant Access Using Hierarchies checkbox is enabled (see earlier Organization-Wide Sharing Defaults Edit screen screenshot) users above that role in the hierarchy can view, edit, and report on those records. For example, if Mike is the owner of an Account record, and he is assigned to the role of International Sales, reporting to Julia, who is the VP of International Sales, then Julia can also view, edit, and report on Mike's accounts.

No Access, View Only, or Use (Price Book only)

Access levels for the **Price Book** OWDs can be set to either, **No Access**, **View Only**, or **Use**. Use is the default access level and allows all users to access the Price Book information as well as using the Price Book configuration for opportunities with products. View Only allows users to access Price Book information but not to use that Price Book detail in opportunities with products. No Access restricts users from accessing information for Price Books and Prices.

 The **No Access**, **View Only**, or **Use choice of** options is available only for Price Books which is covered in Chapter 8, *Introducing Sales Cloud, Service Cloud, and Collaborative Features of Salesforce CRM.*

Granting Access using Hierarchies

By default, Salesforce uses hierarchies, such as the role or territory hierarchy, to automatically grant record access to users above the record owner in the hierarchy.

This automatic granting of access to user's data to other users higher up in the Salesforce CRM hierarchy can be disabled for custom objects using the **Grant Access Using Hierarchies** checkbox. When this checkbox is not selected, only the record owner and users granted access by the Organization-Wide Defaults gain access to the records. For standard objects the **Grant Access Using Hierarchies** checkbox is set by default and cannot be unchecked.

Here we see the options available for an example custom object where, for the custom object **Country**, we have set the default access to **Public Read/Write** and the **Grant Access Using Hierarchies** setting is checked as shown in the following screenshot:

Object	Default Access	Grant Access Using Hierarchies
Lead	Public Read/Write/Transfer	☑
Account, Contract and Asset	Public Read/Write	☑
Contact	Controlled by Parent	☑
Opportunity	Public Read/Write	☑
Case	Public Read/Write/Transfer	☑
Campaign	Public Full Access	☑
Activity	Private	☑
Calendar	Hide Details and Add Events	☑
Price Book	Use	☑
Activity Tracker Setup	Public Read/Write	☑
Country	Public Read Only	☑
Currency	Public Read Only	☑

Controlled by Parent

When **Controlled by Parent** is set on an object, as a result of the object being the detail side of a master-detail relationship, a user can perform an action (such as view, edit, or delete) on the record based on whether they can perform that same action on the parent record associated with it. For example, if a Contact record is associated with the WidgetX account using **Controlled by Parent**, then a user can only edit that contact if they can also only edit the WidgetX account record.

Allow users to update each other's activities:
Tasks and **Events** are by default set to Private (via the **Activity** setting as shown in the preceding screenshot). To allow users to update each other's activities (for example, to permit a user to set a task that they do not own to complete), you will need to set the **Activity** setting to be **Controlled by Parent** and ensure that the object that is related to the activity is also accessible to that user.

When a custom object is on the detail side of a master-detail relationship with a standard object, its OWDs is automatically set to **Controlled by Parent** and it is not editable, as shown in the following screenshot for the custom object **Book**:

Default Sharing Settings			
Organization-Wide Defaults Edit			Organization-Wide Defaults Help (?)
Object	**Default Internal Access**	**Default External Access**	**Grant Access Using Hierarchies**
Lead	Private	Private	✓
Account, Contract, Order and Asset	Private	Private	✓
Contact	Controlled by Parent	Controlled by Parent	✓
Opportunity	Private	Private	✓
Quote	Controlled by Parent	Controlled by Parent	✓
Case	Private	Private	✓
Campaign	Private	Private	✓
User	Public Read Only	Private	✓
Activity	Private	Private	✓
Calendar	Hide Details and Add Events	Hide Details and Add Events	✓
Price Book	Use	Use	✓
Quick Text	Public Read Only	Public Read Only	✓
Service Contract	Private	Private	✓
abc	Public Read/Write	Public Read/Write	✓
Book	Controlled by Parent	Controlled by Parent	
File Attachment	Controlled by Parent	Controlled by Parent	
Add Recipient	Controlled by Parent	Controlled by Parent	

Although Grant Access Using Hierarchies can be deselected to prevent users that are higher in the role or territory hierarchy having automatic access, users with the **View All** and **Modify All** object permissions and the **View All Data** and **Modify All Data** profile permissions can still access records they do not own.

OWDs need to be defined separately for any custom objects that are created in the Salesforce CRM application.

For some standard objects, you cannot actually change the **Organization-Wide Sharing Default** setting.

For example, the OWDs for the Solution object in Salesforce is preset to Public Read/Write which cannot be changed.

You can use OWDs to set the default level of record access for the following standard objects where the default organization-wide sharing settings are:

Object	Default Access
Accounts	**Public Read/Write**
Activities	**Private**
Assets	**Public Read/Write**
Calendar	**Hide Details and Add Events**
Campaigns	**Public Full Access**
Cases	**Public Read/Write/Transfer**
Contacts	**Controlled by Parent**
Contracts	**Public Read/Write**
Custom Objects	**Public Read/Write**
Leads	**Public Read/Write/Transfer**
Opportunities	**Public Read Only**
Price Books	**Use**
Service Contracts	**Contracts Private**
Users	**Public Read Only** **Private for external users**

Activities behave differently to other objects and in spite of the Private setting for the **Organization-Wide Sharing Default**, users with read access to the parent record to which the activity is associated can view all the activities regardless of who owns the activity. Therefore if you share an account record to a user or set of users all the activities on that record become visible to the user or set of users.

External OWDs for sharing

Organization-Wide Defaults often referred to in Salesforce CRM as OWDs, specify the default level of access to records and can be set separately for most of the objects in Salesforce such as accounts, contacts, and activities.

External OWDs allow you to apply a different default access level for external users such as Chatter external users, Community users, Customer Portal users, and so on.

Using External OWDs allows you to simplify the sharing model for your organization. For example, without External OWDs, if you want **Public Read Only** or **Public Read/Write** access for internal users but Private for external users, you would have to set the default access to **Private** and create a sharing rule to share records with all internal users. With separate OWDs, one for internal and one for external users, you can achieve similar behavior by setting the default internal access to **Public Read Only** or **Public Read/Write** and the default external access to **Private**.

 External organization-wide defaults can be used to set sharing for **Accounts** (and their associated contracts and assets), **Cases**, **Contacts**, **Opportunities**, **Users**, and **Custom Objects**.

Having separate OWDs, one for internal and one for external users also speeds up performance for reports, list views, and searches.

 External users include: Authenticated website users, Chatter external users, Community users, Customer Portal users, Guest users, High-volume portal users, Partner Portal users, and Service Cloud Portal users.

To activate External OWD settings, navigate to **Setup** | **Security Controls** | **Sharing Settings**. Now click on the **Enable External Sharing Model** button as shown in the following screenshot:

Effects of Modifying Default Access Type

When you change the default access type, say from **Private** to **Public Read/Write**, the organization record sharing for that object is re-calculated and you may be presented with a warning confirmation dialog message, as shown in the following screenshot, notifying that an e-mail will be received when the OWDs update finishes:

Sharing Settings

Criteria-Based Sharing Rules Video Tutorial | Help for this Page

This page displays your organization's sharing settings. These settings specify the level of access your users have to each others' data.

> ⚠ Paul Goodey initiated a organization-wide default update on 19/07/2019 12:19. You can't submit any changes until the operation finishes. Paul Goodey will receive an email when the organization-wide default update finishes.

Manage sharing settings for: All Objects ▾

Enable External Sharing Model

Default Sharing Settings

Organization-Wide Defaults	Edit	Organization-Wide Defaults Help

Object	Default Access	Grant Access Using Hierarchies
Lead	Public Read/Write/Transfer	✓
Account, Contract and Asset	Public Read/Write	✓

Granting users additional access

Where the OWDs setting for an object is **Private** or **Public Read Only**, you can grant users additional access to records with the use of permission sets, role hierarchies, and sharing rules.

Sharing rules and permission sets can only be used to grant additional access and cannot be used to restrict access to records from what was originally specified with the OWDs

Permission sets

Permission sets allow you to further control access to the system for the users in your organization. They can be considered as a method to fine-tune the permissions for selected individuals and enable access in a similar way to the setting up of profiles.

While an individual user can have only one profile, you can assign multiple permissions and permission sets to users. For example, you can create a permission set called **Convert Leads**, say, that provides the facility for converting and transfer of **Leads**, using the App Permissions and assign it to a user who has a profile that does not provide Lead Conversion. You can create a permission set called Export Reports, say, that uses the System Permissions Export Reports to allow specific users to export data from reports. You can also create a permission set called Access Widget, using an **Object Settings** permission, which is associated to a custom object called Widget that is set in the OWDs as **Private**. Here, you can assign it to a user who has a profile that does not include the ability to access Widgets through their profile settings.

It is a two-step process to set up permission sets for users which includes:

1. Creating the permission set from the **Permission Set** edit page.
2. Assigning the user to the permission set from the **User** edit page.

Creating the permission set from the Permission Set edit page

To view and manage your organization's permission set, navigate to **Setup** | **Manage Users** | **Permission Sets**. For a new permission set, click on the **New** button, and complete the sections permission set information and Select the type of users who will use this permission set. Now edit the **Object Permissions** and **Field Permissions** and choose the required object.

The following screenshot shows the creation of a permission set that allows users to access the widgets object (which is set to Private in the Organization-Wide Default access model):

Assigning the user to the permission set from the User edit page

To view and manage which of your users are assigned to permission sets, navigate to **Setup** | **Manage Users** | **Users**. Now choose a user by clicking on their **Username**.

Click on **Permission Set Assignments** and then **Edit Assignment** to view and select from the list of available permissions. The following screenshot shows the resulting section:

User
Sales Person

Edit Layout | Help for this Page

| Permission Set Assignments [1] | Personal Groups [0] | Public Group Membership [0] | Queue Membership [0] |

Permission Set Assignments   [Edit Assignments]   Permission Set Assignments Help (?)

Action	Permission Set Label	Date Assigned
Del	Widget Access	25/09/2011

You can create up to 1,000 permission sets for your organization.

You can group multiple permissions into a permission set to create specific profile-like permissions without actually having to create or clone complete profiles which are often unnecessary and time-consuming.

Role hierarchy

Once the Organization-Wide Defaults have been established, you can use a role hierarchy to ensure that managers can view and edit the same records as their line reports (or subordinates). Users at any given role level are always able to view, edit, and report on all data owned by or shared with users below them in the hierarchy, unless the OWD settings specify to ignore the hierarchies.

To view and manage your organization's role hierarchy, navigate to **Setup | Manage Users | Roles** as shown in the following screenshot:

Creating the Role Hierarchy

Help for this Page

You can build on the existing role hierarchy shown on this page. To insert a new role, click **Add Role**.

Your Organization's Role Hierarchy

Show in tree view ▼

Collapse All Expand All

Show in tree view
Show in sorted list view
Show in list view

⊟ **WidgetsXYZ**
    Add Role
    ⊟ **CEO** Edit | Del | Assign
      Add Role
      ⊟ **SVP, Sales & Marketing** Edit | Del | Assign
        Add Role
        ⊟ **VP, Global Marketing** Edit | Del | Assign
          Add Role
          ⊟ **Marketing Team** Edit | Del | Assign
            Add Role
        ⊟ **VP, International Sales** Edit | Del | Assign
          Add Role
          ⊟ **Sales Manager, Region B** Edit | Del | Assign
            Add Role
            ⊟ **AM, Region B01** Edit | Del | Assign

Here you can choose to view the hierarchy in one of the following options:

Show in tree view

This view displays a visual representation of the parent-child relationships between your roles. Click on **Expand All** to see all roles or **Collapse All** to see only top-level roles. To expand or collapse an individual role node, you may click on the plus [+] or minus [–] icon as shown in the preceding screenshot.

Show in sorted list view

This view displays the roles as a list that you can sort alphabetically by role name, parent role (Reports to), or report display name. If your organization has a large number of roles, this view provides a far easier way to navigate the hierarchy as shown in the following screenshot:

Roles

Help for this Page

Below is a list of the roles for your organization. You can view more information by clicking the role link.

	Show in sorted list view ▾
	Show in tree view
	Show in sorted list view
	Show in list view

View: All ▾ Edit | Create New View

A | B | C | D | E | F | G | H | I | J | K | L | M | N | O | P | Q | R | S | T | U | V | W

New Role

Action	Role ↑	Reports to	Report Display Name
Edit	Del	Assign	AM, Region A01	Sales Manager, Region A	AM, Region A01
Edit	Del	Assign	AM, Region B01	Sales Manager, Region B	AM, Region B01
Edit	Del	Assign	CEO		CEO
Edit	Del	Assign	Marketing Team	VP, Global Marketing	Marketing Team
Edit	Del	Assign	Sales Manager, Region A	VP, North American Sales	Sales Manager, Region A
Edit	Del	Assign	Sales Manager, Region B	VP, International Sales	Sales Manager, Region B
Edit	Del	Assign	SVP, Sales & Marketing	CEO	SVP, Sales & Marketing
Edit	Del	Assign	VP, Global Marketing	SVP, Sales & Marketing	VP, Global Marketing
Edit	Del	Assign	VP, International Sales	SVP, Sales & Marketing	VP, International Sales

To show a filtered list of roles, select a predefined list from the **View** drop-down list, or click on **Create New View** to define your own custom view of roles. To edit or delete any view you have created, select it from the **View** drop-down list and click on the **Edit** link. Once in the **Edit View** page you can click on the **Delete** button to delete the list view.

The columns that are shown in **Show in sorted list view** screen are **Action, Role, Reports to**, and **Report Display Name** and the columns can be sorted

Show in List View

This view displays the roles as an indented list of roles and their child nodes, grouped alphabetically by the name of the top-level role as follows:

Roles

Help for this Page

Below is a list of the roles for your organization. You can view more information by clicking the role link.

New Role

Show in list view ▼

Show in tree view
Show in sorted list view
Show in list view

Action	Role	Reports To	
Edit | Del | Assign	CEO		
Edit | Del | Assign	SVP, Sales & Marketing	CEO	SVP, Sales & Marketing
Edit | Del | Assign	VP, Global Marketing	SVP, Sales & Marketing	VP, Global Marketing
Edit | Del | Assign	Marketing Team	VP, Global Marketing	Marketing Team
Edit | Del | Assign	VP, International Sales	SVP, Sales & Marketing	VP, International Sales
Edit | Del | Assign	Sales Manager, Region B	VP, International Sales	Sales Manager, Region B
Edit | Del | Assign	AM, Region B01	Sales Manager, Region B	AM, Region B01
Edit | Del | Assign	VP, North American Sales	SVP, Sales & Marketing	VP, North American Sales
Edit | Del | Assign	Sales Manager, Region A	VP, North American	Sales Manager, Region

The columns that are shown in Show in list view screen are role, reports to, and report display name and the columns cannot be sorted.

To create a role, click on **New Role** or **Add Role**, depending on whether your view of roles is using the list view or tree view, and enter the role fields as needed.

You can create up to 500 roles for your organization at the time of writing.

To edit a role, click on **Edit** next to a role name, then update the role fields as needed. You can delete a role, by clicking on **Del** next to the role name.

To assign other users to a role, click on **Assign** next to the role name and to view detailed information about a role, click on the role name.

If your organization uses territory management, forecasts are based on the territory hierarchy instead of the role hierarchy.

Role hierarchies do not need to represent your company's organization chart and instead, each role in the hierarchy should be considered as a level of data access that your users or groups in Salesforce require.

Depending on your sharing settings, roles can control the level of visibility that users have into your organizations data. Users at a particular role level can view, edit, and report on all data that is owned by, or has been shared with, users below them in the hierarchy. This is assuming your organization's sharing mechanism for that object type does not specify otherwise.

Specifically, in the Organization-wide defaults related list, if the Grant Access Using Hierarchies option is disabled for a custom object, say, then only the record owner and users granted access by the organization-wide defaults can access that custom object's records.

Although, it is possible to create a user record without a role, users would need to be assigned to a role, so that their records will appear in opportunity reports, forecast roll-ups, and any other display based on roles.

When an account owner is not assigned a role, the sharing access for related contacts is **Read/Write**, provided the Organization-wide default for contacts is not **Controlled by Parent**. Sharing access on related opportunities and cases is **No Access**.

Users that are to have access to all records in Salesforce CRM should be set at the top-most position of the role hierarchy.

When you change a user's role, any relevant sharing rules are re-evaluated to add or remove access to records as necessary.

 It is not necessary to create individual roles for each and every job title within your company. Instead, aim to define a hierarchy of roles that will help to control the access of information entered by users in lower level roles.

To view detailed information about a role, navigate to **Setup** | **Manage Users** | **Roles**. Clicking on the role name will present the role details page as shown in the following screenshot:

Role   Help for this Page ?

VP, International Sales

Below is the list of users assigned to this role. Click Edit to modify the role name. Click Assign Users to Role to assign existing users to this role. Click New User to create a user for this role.

Hierarchy: WidgetsXYZ » CEO » SVP, Sales & Marketing » VP, International Sales
Siblings: VP, North American Sales, VP, Global Marketing

Users in VP, International Sales Role [1]

Role Detail   [Edit] [Delete]

Role Name	VP, International Sales	Role Name as displayed on reports	VP, International Sales
This role reports to	SVP, Sales & Marketing	Sharing Groups	Role, Role and Subordinates
Modified By	Paul Goodey, 19/12/2009 13:01		
Customer Portal Role			

Users in VP, International Sales Role   [Assign Users to Role] [New User]   Users in VP, International Sales Role Help ?

Action	Full Name	Alias	Username	Last Login	Active
Edit	Trevor Howard	thow	trevor.howard@widgetsxyz.com	31/01/2011 02:45	✓

To view the **Role Detail** page for a parent or sibling role, click the **Role Name** in the hierarchy or siblings list.

To edit the role details, click on **Edit**.

To remove the role from the hierarchy, click on **Delete**.

Within the Users in Role related list you have the following options:

- Assign a user to the role by clicking on **Assign Users to Role**
- Add a user to your organization by clicking on **New User**
- Modify user information by clicking on **Edit** next to a user's name
- View a user's details by clicking on the user's **Full Name**, **Alias**, or **Username**

When you edit roles, sharing rules are usually automatically re-evaluated to add or remove access to records as required. If these changes result in too many records changing at once, a message appears warning that the sharing rules will not be automatically re-evaluated, and that you have to manually recalculate them (as shown further). Sharing rules should be used when a user or group of users need access to records not already granted to them with either the role hierarchy setup or the organization-wide default settings. When you modify users in a role, any sharing rules are also re-evaluated to add or remove access as necessary.

Organization-wide defaults and sharing rules

A user's level of access to records will never be more restrictive with the use of sharing rules than the options chosen in the OWDs. The OWDs are a minimum level of access for all users.

Sharing rules

With sharing rules, you are in effect setting automatic extensions to your **Organization-Wide Sharing Defaults** settings for particular sets of users. As shown in the following screenshot, this can be considered as opening up visibility and access to records for those users.

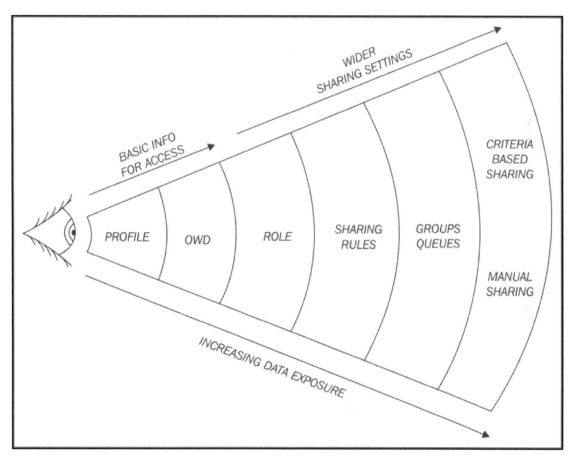

Sharing rules apply to:

- All new and existing records owned by the specified role or group members
- Both active and inactive users

Sharing rules extend the access specified by OWDs and the role hierarchy.

Sharing rules can never be stricter than your OWDs settings and allow wider data access for the included users or groups of users. To define sharing rules, navigate to **Setup** | **Security Controls** | **Sharing Settings**. Now scroll down to the lower part of the page to reveal the **Sharing Rules** sections.

The following screenshot shows the **Sharing Rules** page where there are sections to set the sharing rules for the various standard objects within the application, such as **Lead**, **Account**, and **Contact**, as well as any custom objects in your organization:

Sharing Rules

Lead Sharing Rules | New | Recalculate | Lead Sharing Rules Help (?)

No sharing rules specified.

Account Sharing Rules | New | Recalculate | Account Sharing Rules Help (?)

Action	Criteria	Shared With	Account, Contract and Asset	Opportunity	Case
Edit | Del	Account: Market EQUALS US	Role: VP, North American Sales	Read Only	Read Only	Read Only
Edit | Del	Owner in All Internal Users	Role and Subordinates: VP, Global Marketing	Read Only	Read Only	Read/Write

Contact Sharing Rules | New | Recalculate | Contact Sharing Rules Help (?)

No sharing rules specified.

Opportunity Sharing Rules | New | Recalculate | Opportunity Sharing Rules Help (?)

Action	Criteria	Shared With	Opportunity
Edit | Del	Owner in Role and Subordinates: Sales Manager, Region A	Role: Sales Manager, Region B	Read Only
Edit | Del	Owner in Role and Subordinates: Sales Manager, Region B	Role: Sales Manager, Region A	Read Only

Case Sharing Rules | New | Recalculate | Case Sharing Rules Help (?)

Within the **Sharing Rules** setup section, the following object sharing rules can be applied:

Account sharing rules

These rules are based on the account owner or other criteria, including account record types or field values, and set the default sharing access for accounts and their associated **Contract**, **Asset**, **Opportunity**, **Case**, and (optionally) **Contact** records.

Account territory sharing rules

These rules are based on territory assignment and set the default sharing access for **Account** and their associated **Case**, **Contact**, **Contract**, and **Opportunity** records.

Campaign sharing rules

These rules are based on Campaign owner and set the default sharing access for the individual Campaign records.

Case sharing rules

These rules are based on the Case owner or other criteria, including case record types or field values and set the default sharing access for the individual case and associated account records.

Contact sharing rules

These rules are based on the Contact owner or other criteria, including contact record types or field values and set the default sharing access for the individual contact and associated account records.

Lead sharing rules

These rules are based on the Lead owner and set the default sharing access for the individual lead records.

Opportunity sharing rules

These rules are based on the Opportunity owner or other criteria, including opportunity record types or field values and set the default sharing access for the individual opportunity and their associated account records.

User sharing rules

These rules are based on Group membership (described later in this chapter) or other criteria and set the default sharing access for the individual user records.

Custom object sharing rules

These rules are based on the custom object record owner or other criteria, including custom object record types or field values and set default sharing access for individual custom object records.

Groups

Groups allow you to simplify the setting up of OWD sharing access via a sharing rule for sets of users or for individual users to selectively share their records with other users.

Public groups

Public groups are sets of users that only administrators are permitted to create and edit. However, when created, public groups can be used by everyone in the organization.

Public groups may contain individual users, users in a particular role or territory, users in a specified role along with all the users below that role in the role hierarchy, or other public groups.

Personal groups

Personal groups are sets of users that everyone can create and edit for their personal use.

Personal groups may contain individual users, public groups, the users in a particular role or territory, or the users in a particular role along with all the users below that role or in the hierarchy.

Effects of adding or modifying sharing rules

When you add a new sharing rule, the access levels for the sharing rule are calculated and you are provided with a warning confirmation dialog message, as shown in the following screenshot, indicating that this operation could take a significant time:

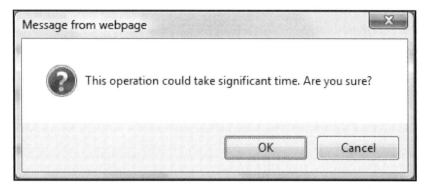

The effects of changing or deleting sharing rules, as well as the transferring of records between users, cause re-evaluation of appropriate record access for the impacted users.

 If these changes affect too many records at once, a message appears warning that the sharing rules will not be automatically re-evaluated, and you must manually recalculate them.

The following list outlines what changes can be done to **Sharing Rules** and the consequence of applying these changes:

- When you change the access levels for a sharing rule, all existing records are automatically updated to reflect the new access levels
- When you delete a sharing rule, the sharing access created by that rule is automatically removed
- When you transfer records from one user to another, the sharing rules are re-evaluated to add or remove access to the transferred records as necessary
- When you modify which users are in a group or role, any sharing rules are re-evaluated to add or remove access to these users as necessary
- Users higher in the role hierarchy are automatically granted the same access that users below them in the hierarchy have from a sharing rule

When you edit groups, roles, and territories, sharing rules are usually automatically re-evaluated to add or remove access as needed. Manually recalculating sharing rules can be performed at any time.

To manually recalculate sharing rules, navigate to **Setup** | **Security Controls** | **Sharing Settings**. Now scroll down to the lower part of the page to reveal the **Sharing Rules** sections and in the **Sharing Rules** related list for the object you want, click on **Recalculate** as shown in the following screenshot:

Sharing Rules

Lead Sharing Rules [New] [Recalculate]   Lead Sharing Rules Help (?)

No sharing rules specified.

Account Sharing Rules [New] [Recalculate]   Account Sharing Rules Help (?)

Action	Criteria	Shared With	Account, Contract and Asset	Opportunity	Case
Edit | Del	Account: Market EQUALS US	Role: VP, North American Sales	Read Only	Read Only	Read Only
Edit | Del	Owner in All Internal Users	Role and Subordinates: VP, Global Marketing	Read Only	Read Only	Read/Write

Contact Sharing Rules [New] [Recalculate]   Contact Sharing Rules Help (?)

No sharing rules specified.

Opportunity Sharing Rules [New] [Recalculate]   Opportunity Sharing Rules Help (?)

Action	Criteria	Shared With	Opportunity
Edit | Del	Owner in Role and Subordinates: Sales Manager, Region A	Role: Sales Manager, Region B	Read Only
Edit | Del	Owner in Role and Subordinates: Sales Manager, Region B	Role: Sales Manager, Region A	Read Only

Case Sharing Rules [New] [Recalculate]   Case Sharing Rules Help (?)

Criteria-based sharing

Criteria-based sharing rules are used to control which users have access to records based on specified field values on the records. For example, the account object has a custom picklist field named **Market**. You can create a criteria-based sharing rule that shares all accounts in which the **Market** field is set to **US** with, say, a **North American Sales** team in your organization as shown in the following screenshot:

Although criteria-based sharing rules are based on values in the records and not the record owners, a role or territory hierarchy still allows users higher in the hierarchy to access the records.

You can create criteria-based sharing rules for **Account**, **Opportunity**, **Case**, **Contact**, and **Custom** object.

For example, a custom object has been created for Newsletter. You can create a criteria-based sharing rule that shares all newsletters in which the name is set to **International** with the **International Sales** team in your organization as follows:

Setup   Help for this Page ❓

Newsletter Sharing Rule

Use sharing rules to make automatic exceptions to your organization-wide sharing settings for defined sets of users.

Note: "Roles and subordinates" includes all users in a role, and the roles below that role. This includes portal roles that may give access to users outside the organization.

You can use sharing rules only to grant wider access to data, not to restrict access.

Label	International in Name			
Rule Name	International_in_Name ⓘ			
Criteria	**Field**	**Operator**	**Value**	
	Newsletter Name ▼	contains ▼	International,international	AND
	--None-- ▼	--None-- ▼		AND
	--None-- ▼	--None-- ▼		AND
	--None-- ▼	--None-- ▼		AND
	--None-- ▼	--None-- ▼		
	Add Filter Logic...			
Share with	Role, Internal and Portal Subordinates: VP, International Sales			
Access Level	Read Only ▼			
Created By	Paul Goodey, 28/03/2011 05:23	**Modified By**	Paul Goodey, 28/03/2011 05:23	

Save   Cancel

Text and text area fields must be specified exactly, as they are case sensitive. For example, a criteria-based sharing rule that specifies `International` in a text field would not share records with `International` in the field.

Criteria-based sharing rule with text fields
To create a criteria-based sharing rule that matches with several cases of a word, enter each value separated by a comma. For example, `International, international`, and use the **contains** operator.

There is a restriction on the type of field that can be used for sharing as part of the Criteria-based sharing. Along with record types, the following list of fields can be set as criteria for sharing:

Auto Number, Checkbox, Date, Date/Time, E-mail, Number, Percent, Phone, Picklist, Text, Text Area, URL, and **Lookup Relationship** (to either User or Queue).

Up to 50 criteria-based sharing rules can be created per object.

Manual sharing rules

Users can manually share certain types of records with other users within the Salesforce CRM application. Some objects that are shared automatically include access to all other associated records. For example, if a user shares one of their account records, then the granted user will also have access to all the opportunities and cases connected to that account.

Manual sharing rules are generally used either on a one-off basis to share a record or whenever there is difficulty trying to determine a consistent set of users, groups, and the associated rules that would be involved as a part of an Organization-Wide Sharing setting. To be able to grant sharing access for a record, the user must either be the record owner, a system administrator, a user in a role above the owner in the hierarchy, or any user that has been granted full access; or the Organization-Wide settings for that object must allow access through hierarchies.

Users grant access simply by clicking on the **Sharing** button found on the **Record Detail** page as shown in the following screenshot:

Account
Company X

↯ Show Feed

« Back to List: Documents
Action Plans [1] | Contacts [0] | Opportunities [4] | Cases [4]

Account Detail   Edit | Delete | Sharing

Account Owner   ☺ Paul Goodey [Change]
Account Name   Company X [View Hierarchy]

The **Sharing** button does not appear if the object's **Organization-Wide Sharing Defaults** are set to **Public Read/Write**.

Manual Sharing for user records

You can specify whether the **Sharing** button, used to grant others access to the user's own user record, is displayed on user detail pages.

To hide or display the user **Sharing** button for all users, navigate to **Setup** | **Security Controls** | **Sharing Settings**. Now click **Edit** in the **Organization-Wide Defaults** area and scroll to the bottom of the page.

To hide or display the **Sharing** button on user detail pages select the **Manual User Record Sharing** checkbox, as shown in the following screenshot, and then click **Save**.

User Visibility Settings

Portal User Visibility ☑ i
Standard Report Visibility ☑ i   Manual User Record Sharing ☑
                                      i

Save | Cancel

Queues

Queues allow groups of users to manage shared records.

A Queue is a location where records can be routed to await processing by a group member. The records remain in the queue until a user accepts them for processing or they are transferred to another queue.

When creating a new queue, you must specify the set of objects that are stored. Permitted objects for queues are leads, cases, service contracts, and custom objects. You must also specify the set of users that are allowed to retrieve records from the queue.

Records can be added to a queue either manually or through an automatic case or lead assignment rules upon which the owner of the record is changed to that of the queue.

Once records are added to a queue they remain there until they are either assigned to a user or retrieved by one of the queue members. Then the owner of the record is changed to the respective queue member user. Here, any queue member or any user located above a queue member in the role hierarchy can take ownership of records in a queue.

Sharing access diagram

Many security options work together to determine whether users can view or edit a record. First, Salesforce checks whether the user's profile has object level permission to access that object. Then, Salesforce checks whether the user's profile has any administrative permissions, such as **View All Data** or **Modify All Data**.

 The View All Data profile or permission set assignment allows the user to read all records and the **Modify All Data** profile or permission set assignment allows the user to update and delete records regardless of the data access security model of that object type.

Finally, Salesforce will check the ownership of the record. Here, the OWDs, role-level access, and any sharing rules will be checked to see if there are any rules that give the user access to that record.

The following flow diagram shows how users are affected by the different security options associated with record ownership and sharing models and rules that can be set:

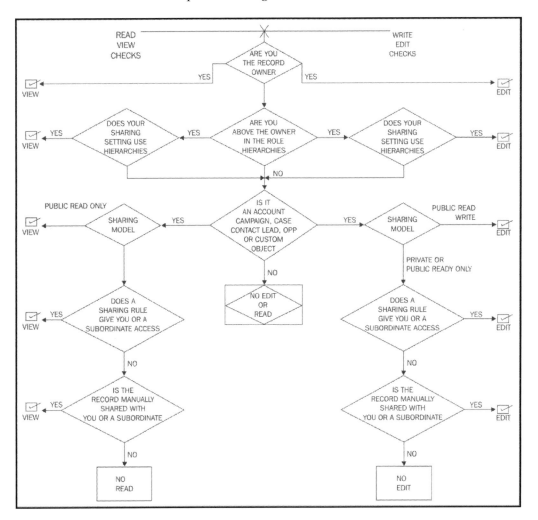

In addition to the check to determine whether a user can view a record, shown in the previous screenshot, their profile (or permission set) must be set with the view permission for the relevant object.

In addition to the check to determine whether a user can edit a record, shown in the previous screenshot, their profile (or permission set) must be set with the edit permission for the relevant object.

Questions to test your knowledge

You are now presented with questions about the key features of Salesforce CRM administration in the areas of Security and Access which have been covered in this chapter. The answers can be found at the end of the chapter.

Questions

We present five questions to verify your understanding of data access levels, OWDs, and data access security model exceptions.

Question 1 – Field-level access

Which of the following can be used to control field-level access to give viewing rights to a user's profile? (Select one)

a) Profile

b) Role Hierarchy

c) Field Level Security

d) Permission Set

Question 2 – Data access levels

For which of the following levels can data access be configured? (Select all that apply) except:

a) Organization-level

b) Object-level

c) Profile-level

d) Page Layout-level

e) Record-level

Question 3 – Record-level access

Which of the following can be used to control record-level access? (Select all that apply)

a) Permission Sets

b) Role Hierarchy

c) Profile

d) Sharing Rules

e) Organization-Wide Defaults

Question 4 – Organization-Wide Defaults

An object has an Organization-Wide Default set to Public Read/Write. Which feature(s) can be used to restrict access to that object? (Select all that apply)

a) Page Layout

b) Record Type

c) Role Hierarchy

d) Profile

e) None of the above

Question 5 – Role Hierarchy

Which statements(s) are correct for the Role Hierarchy in Salesforce CRM? (Select all that apply)

a) Roles control the level of visibility that users have of an organization's data

b) Users at a role level can view all data that is owned by users below them in the hierarchy

c) Users can be assigned to multiple roles

d) Users must be associated to a single role

Question 6 – Data Access Security Model Exception

Which of the following profile permissions allows the user to update any record of that object type, regardless of the data access security model? (Select one)

a) Session Settings

b) Password Policies

c) Modify All Data

d) View All Data

e) None of the Above

Answers

Here are the answers to the six questions about about the features of Salesforce CRM administration in the areas of Security and Access.

Answer 1- Field-level access

The answer is **c**) Field Level Security.

Answer 2 – Data Access Levels

The answer is **a**) Organization-level, **b**) Object-level, and **e**) Record-level.

Answer 3 – Record-level access

The answer is **b**) Role Hierarchy, **d**) Sharing Rules, and **e**) Organization-Wide Defaults

The choices **a**) Permission Sets and **c**) Profiles allow you set security at object level and not at record level.

Answer 4 – Organization-Wide Defaults

The answer is **d**) Profile.

Answer 5 – Role Hierarchy

The answer is **a**) Roles control the level of visibility that users have into an organization's data and **b**) Users at a role level can view all data that is owned by users below them in the hierarchy.

c) Users can be assigned to multiple roles and **d**) Users must be associated to a single role are not correct. Users may optionally be assigned to a role.

Answer 6 – Data Access Security Model Exception

The answer is **c**) Modify All Data.

Summary

In this chapter, we described the features that provide data access and security configuration for system administrators and their levels of data access. **Organization-Wide Sharing Defaults**, **Roles**, and other sharing settings were described.

We looked at how the access to records could be further widened through the use of Permission Sets, Sharing Rules, criteria-based sharing, and also manual sharing.

Finally, we posed some questions to help clarify some of the key features of Salesforce CRM administration in the areas of Security and Access.

In the next chapter, we will be looking at ways of loading and extracting data from Salesforce CRM, where we will look at the utilities available for importing and exporting data to and from Salesforce. Included in the next chapter is a look at Data Loader and the data import wizards.

5
Managing Data in Salesforce CRM

In the previous chapter, we looked at the features that provide data access and security configuration by system administrators and discussed the four main levels where data access and security can be applied, namely: organization level, object level, field level, and finally, at the record level.

In this chapter, we will discuss the options for improving data quality using data validation rules and dependent fields. We will also outline the features and tools available within Salesforce CRM that allow you to import and export data into and out of the Salesforce system.

Finally, we will address a number of questions about the key features of Salesforce CRM administration in the area of data management.

The following topics will be covered in this chapter:

- Data quality
- Data validation rules
- Dependent picklists
- Data import and export utilities
- Data Import Wizard
- Individual import wizards
- Data Loader

- Data Loader and import wizards compared
- Best practice for mass data updating
- Export backup data
- Recycle Bin
- Data storage utilization

Now let's begin by looking at the key features available for you to help control the data that users enter into the Salesforce CRM system.

Data quality

In Chapter 3, *Configuring Objects and Apps*, we looked at how we can set the required field and auto number field properties on custom fields to help improve the quality and maintain the data integrity of records in the system.

Salesforce also provides other data quality mechanisms, such as:

- Data validation rules
- Dependent picklists

Data validation rules

Data validation rules can be applied to both custom and standard fields and are used to verify that the data entered in a record meets the criteria you have specified before the record can be saved.

Validation rules contain a formula or expression that evaluates the data in one or more fields and returns a value of either true or false.

The logic that is used for validation rules is to seek an error condition, upon which a pre-configured error message is shown to the user whenever the formula or expression returns a value of true.

When validation rules are defined for a field or set of fields, the following actions are fired when the user creates a new record, or edits an existing record and then clicks on the **Save** button:

- Salesforce executes the validation rules and if all data is valid, the record is saved
- For any invalid data, Salesforce displays the associated error message without saving the record

You can specify the error message to display when a validation rule gets fired, along with the option to either show the error message inline next to a field or at the top of the page. For example, your error message could be The close date must occur after today's date. As stated you can choose to display the error message at the top of the page or near a field which you can select; this can be the field that is causing the validation rule to fire, which is typical, or you can choose a different field. Like all other Salesforce error messages, validation rule errors are displayed in red text and are preceded by the word Error.

Validation rules apply to all new and updated records for an object. If your organization has multiple page layouts for the object on which you create a validation rule, you should verify that the validation rule operates as expected on each layout. Also, if you have any data integrations that affect the object, then you should also verify that the validation rule operates as intended.

Even if the fields referenced in the validation rule are not visible on the page layout, the validation rules still apply and will result in an error message if the rule criteria are met.

To begin using validation rules, navigate to **Setup | Customize**. For standard objects, go to the appropriate activity, standard object, or user's link from the menu, and click on **Validation Rules**.

For custom objects, navigate to **Setup | Create | Objects**. Now go to the custom object.

Validation rules are listed in the **Validation Rules** list.

To begin adding a new validation rule, click on the **New** button in the **Validation Rules** section, as shown in the following screenshot:

Opportunity Validation Rules

Help for this Page ⓘ

Validation rules help improve data quality by preventing users from saving incorrect data. You can define one or more validation rules that consist of an error condition and corresponding error message. Validation rules are executed at record save time. If an error condition is met, the save is aborted and an error message displayed.

Quick Tips

- Getting Started
- Resources on CRM Community
- Useful Sample Validation Rules

Example uses:

- Make fields conditionally required, depending on the value of another field
- Ensure that numbers are within a specified range, such as discount is less than 30%
- Enforce that date fields are the correct chronological sequence, such as start date is before end date

Validation Rules   [New]   Validation Rules Help ⓘ

No validation rules defined.

Now enter the properties of your validation rule, which should include the properties detailed in the following section:

Field description section

Add a **Rule Name**, which is a unique identifier of up to 80 characters, with no spaces or special characters (such as extended characters).

The **Active** checkbox, which is used to set the rule, is enabled.

Fill in the **Description field**, which is an optional 255 characters (or fewer) textbox that you can set to describe the purpose of the validation rule.

Error condition formula section

The formula that is entered here forms the expression used to validate the field.

Error message section

The **Error Message** field is the text to be displayed to the user when a record update fails the validation rule.

The **Error Location** is used to determine where on the page the error is displayed to the user. Options available are as follows:

- Top of Page
- Field

The **Top of Page** option sets the error message to be displayed at the top of the page. To display the error next to a field, choose the **Field** option and then select the appropriate field.

If the error location is a field, the validation rule is also listed on the **Detail** page of that field.

You can click on **Check Syntax** to check your formula for errors. Finally, click on Save to finish or **Save & New** to create additional validation rules.

As an example, the following formula text shows an opportunity validation rule to ensure that users cannot enter a date in the past into the **Close Date** field:

The formula would be: `CloseDate < TODAY()`

 If the error location is set to a field that is later deleted, or a field that is read-only or not visible on the page layout, Salesforce automatically changes the error location to **Top of Page**.

An example error message for this validation rule is **Close Date Must Be a Future Date**, as shown in the following screenshot:

Opportunity Validation Rule

Help for this Page

Define a validation rule by specifying an error condition and a corresponding error message. The error condition is written as a Boolean formula expression that returns true or false. When the formula expression returns true, the save will be aborted and the error message will be displayed. The user can correct the error and try again.

Validation Rule Edit   Save   Save & New   Cancel

Rule Name	Opportunity_Close_Date_Not_in_the_Past
Active	☑
Description	Ensure Close dates are not entered that are in the past

Quick Tips
- Operators & Functions

Error Condition Formula

| = Required Information

Example: Discount_Percent__c>0.30   More Examples...

Display an error if Discount is more than 30%

If this formula expression is **true**, display the text defined in the Error Message area

Insert Field   Insert Operator ▼

```
CloseDate < TODAY()
```

Check Syntax

Functions
-- All Function Categories -- ▼

ABS
AND
BEGINS
BLANKVALUE
BR
CASE

Insert Selected Function

ABS(number)
Returns the absolute value of a number, a number without its sign

Help on this function

Error Message

Example: Discount percent cannot exceed 30%

This message will appear when Error Condition formula is **true**

Error Message	Close Date Must Be a Future Date

This error message can either appear at the top of the page or below a specific field on the page

Error Location | ○ Top of Page ● Field Close Date ▼ i

Save   Save & New   Cancel

The validation rule will be fired when the preceding formula is true and will present the error message as per the preceding example, as shown in the following screenshot:

Opportunity Detail　　　Save　Cancel

Error: Invalid Data.
Review all error messages below to correct your data.

Opportunity Owner	⊙ Trevor Howard [Change]	Amount	$200,000.00
Private	☐	Expected Revenue	$150,000.00
Opportunity Name	Opportunity Y	Close Date	14/07/2016 ↩
			Error: Close Date Must Be a Future Date
Account Name	Company X	Next Step	

Dependent picklists

Dependent picklists help to make data more accurate and consistent by applying filters.

A dependent field works in conjunction with a controlling field to filter its values. The value chosen in the controlling field affects the values in the dependent field.

In the following screenshot, we see the **Speaker Status** field being controlled by the **Speaker Event Status** field:

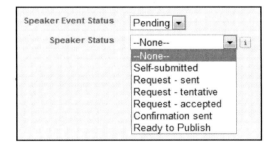

Dependent and controlling picklists

Dependent and controlling picklists work in conjunction where the value chosen in the controlling picklist dynamically changes the values available in the dependent picklist.

Both controlling and dependent picklists are indicated on the edit pages by an icon. By hovering the mouse over these icons, users can see the name of the controlling or dependent picklist.

To define a dependent picklist, navigate to the **Fields** area of the appropriate object.

For standard objects, navigate to **Setup | Customize**. Now select the appropriate object from the **Customize** menu and click on **Fields**.

For custom objects, navigate to **Setup | Create | Objects**. Now select one of the custom objects in the list.

For custom task and event fields, navigate to **Setup | Customize | Activities | Activity Custom Fields**.

Now click on the **Field Dependencies** in the **Custom Fields & Relationships** section, as shown in the following screenshot:

Custom Object
Speaker

Standard Fields [4] | Custom Fields & Relationships [21] | Validation Rules [0] | Page Layou
Custom Buttons and Links [0] | Record Types [0] | Apex Sharing Reas

Custom Object Definition Detail   Edit   Delete

Singular Label	Speaker
Plural Label	Speakers
Object Name	Speaker
API Name	Speaker__c

Created By   Paul Goodey, 27/11/2010 18:44

Standard Fields

Action	Field Label	Field Name	Data Type
	Created By	CreatedBy	Lookup(User)
	Last Modified By	LastModifiedBy	Lookup(User)
Edit	Owner	Owner	Lookup(User,Queue)
Edit	Speaker Name	Name	Auto Number

Custom Fields & Relationships   New   Field Dependencies   Set History Tra

Action	Field Label	API Name	Data

Now click on New to navigate to the **New Field Dependency** screen and then choose a **Controlling Field** and a **Dependent Field**, as shown in the following screenshot:

New Field Dependency

Create a dependent relationship that causes the values in a picklist or multi-select picklist to be dynamically filtered based on the value selected by the user in another field.
 • The field that drives filtering is called the "controlling field." Standard and custom checkboxes and picklists with at least one and less than 300 values can be controlling fields.
 • The field that has its values filtered is called the "dependent field." Custom picklists and multi-select picklists can be dependent fields.

Step 1. Select a controlling field and a dependent field. Click Continue when finished.

Step 2. On the following page, edit the filter rules that control the values that appear in the dependent field for each value in the controlling field.

[Continue] [Cancel]

| Controlling Field | Speaker Event Status ▾ |
| Dependent Field | Speaker Status ▾ |

[Continue] [Cancel]

Click on **Continue** to display the next screen, where you are presented with the field dependency matrix to specify the dependent picklist values that are available when a user selects each controlling field value.

The field dependency matrix lets you specify which dependent picklist values will be available when a user selects each controlling field value. The top row of the matrix shows the controlling field values, while the columns show the dependent field values.

Using this matrix, you can include or exclude values. Included values are available in the dependent picklist when a value in the controlling field is selected and excluded fields are not available.

Here you can include or exclude values by performing the following steps:

1. Double-click values to include them. Included values are then highlighted(double-clicking again on any highlighted values will exclude it).

2. To work with more than one value, you should press and hold the *Shift* key and click on each value to select the required range of values, as shown in the following screenshot:

After selecting the values, click on **Include Values** to make the values available, or click on **Exclude Values** to remove them from the list of available values.

You can also press and hold the *Ctrl* key and click on the individual values to select multiple values. Again, clicking on **Include Values** makes the values available, and clicking on **Exclude Values** removes them from the list of available values. By clicking a column header, you can select all the values in that column, as follows:

Edit Field Dependency

Help for this Page

Save   Cancel   Preview

Controlling Field   Speaker Event Status
Dependent Field   Speaker Status

▶ **Instructions**

Click button to include or exclude selected values from the dependent picklist:

Include Values   Exclude Values

Showing Columns: 1 - 3 (of 3) < Previous | Next >   View All   ▶ Go to

Speaker Event Status: Speaker Status:	New	Pending	Closed
	Nominated	*Nominated*	*Nominated*
	Self-submitted	**Self-submitted**	*Self-submitted*
	Not a good fit	*Not a good fit*	**Not a good fit**
	Request - sent	**Request - sent**	*Request - sent*
	Request - tentative	**Request - tentative**	*Request - tentative*
	Request - accepted	**Request - accepted**	*Request - accepted*
	Request - declined	*Request - declined*	**Request - declined**
	Speaker Approved	*Speaker Approved*	**Speaker Approved**
	Confirmation sent	**Confirmation sent**	*Confirmation sent*
	No comp pass	*No comp pass*	**No comp pass**
	Canceled	*Canceled*	**Canceled**
	Duplicate	*Duplicate*	**Duplicate**
	Ready to Publish	**Ready to Publish**	*Ready to Publish*

Showing Columns: 1 - 3 (of 3) < Previous | Next >   View All

Click button to include or exclude selected values from the dependent picklist:

Include Values   Exclude Values

Save   Cancel   Preview

To change the values in your view, you can do the following:

- Click on **View All** to view all available values at once
- Click on **Go To** and choose a controlling value to view all the dependent values in that column
- Click on **Previous** or **Next** to view the values in columns that are on the previous or next page
- Click on **View sets of 5** to view five columns at a time
- Optionally, click on **Preview** to test your selections before clicking **Save**

Controlling picklist restrictions and limitations

There are various restrictions and limitations associated with the creation and configuration of dependent and controlling Picklist fields.

Controlling fields restrictions and limitations

There are various nuances associated with the creation and configuration of dependent and controlling fields. The following restrictions and limitations exist for controlling fields:

- Standard Picklist fields can be controlling fields
- Checklist fields can be controlling fields
- Default values can be set for controlling fields
- Multi-select Picklist fields cannot be controlling fields
- There is a maximum of 300 values allowed in a controlling field

Dependent fields restrictions and limitations

The following restrictions exist for dependent fields:

- Standard Picklist fields cannot be dependent fields
- Checkboxes cannot be dependent fields
- Default values cannot be set for dependent fields
- Multi-select Picklist fields can be dependent picklists

Converting fields

When converting existing fields to dependent picklists or controlling fields, this can be done without affecting the existing values in records. Only for changes going forward are the dependency rules applied to the updates to existing records or new records.

Page layouts

For best practice and improved user visibility, make sure the dependent picklist is lower on the page layout than its controlling field.

If a dependent picklist is required and no values are available for it based on the controlling field value, users can save the record without entering a value. In this scenario, the record is saved with no value for that field.

 Make sure controlling fields are added to any page layouts that contain their associated dependent picklists. If the controlling field is not on the same page layout, the dependent picklist shows no available values.

Record types

The values in controlling fields are determined by the pre-selected record type and the values in dependent picklists are determined by both the record type and the selected controlling field value.

The values available in dependent picklists are, therefore, an intersection of the pre-selected record type and subsequent controlling field selection.

Importing data

The data import utilities do not consider field dependencies unless the picklist value has the **Strictly enforce picklist values** option enabled.

Therefore, any value can be imported into a dependent picklist field, regardless of the value imported for a controlling field.

 The **Strictly enforce picklist values** setting within the setup screen for a picklist field prevents the field from allowing values that are not specified in the picklist options, even if the field is updated through the API. See Chapter 3, *Configuring Objects and Apps*, for more details about field types.

An overview of data import and export utilities

Salesforce provides data utilities, which are available to import and export data to and from Salesforce. There is also a wide variety of third-party tools that allow data to be imported to and exported from Salesforce and use the publicly available Salesforce APIs to provide the data integration.

The third-party data import and export tools are not provided by Salesforce; therefore, we will not be covering these in this book. However, you can locate and find information about these tools via the AppExchange, a website provided by Salesforce that enables organizations to select additional apps to extend Salesforce CRM. The AppExchange is covered in detail in Chapter 9, *Extending and Enhancing Salesforce CRM*, and can be accessed at the web URL: https://appexchange.salesforce.com.

Looking at the available Salesforce-provided facilities for importing and exporting data, we have the following specific options:

- Data Import Wizard
- Individual import wizards
- Import Accounts/Contacts
- Import Leads
- Import Solutions
- Import Custom Objects
- Data Loader

 At the time of writing, Salesforce has announced that the individual import wizards are to be retired in February 2017. Salesforce recommends users to use the **Data Import Wizard** instead as the individual import wizards will no longer be available starting from the Spring '17 release.

Data Import Wizard

Data Import Wizard opens in a full browser window and provides a unified interface that lets you import data for a number of standard Salesforce objects, including **Account**, **Contact**, **Leads**, **CustomObject**, and **Solution**.

To access **Data Import Wizard**, navigate to **Setup | Data Management | Data Import Wizard**. Now click on the **Launch Wizard** button, as shown in the following screenshot:

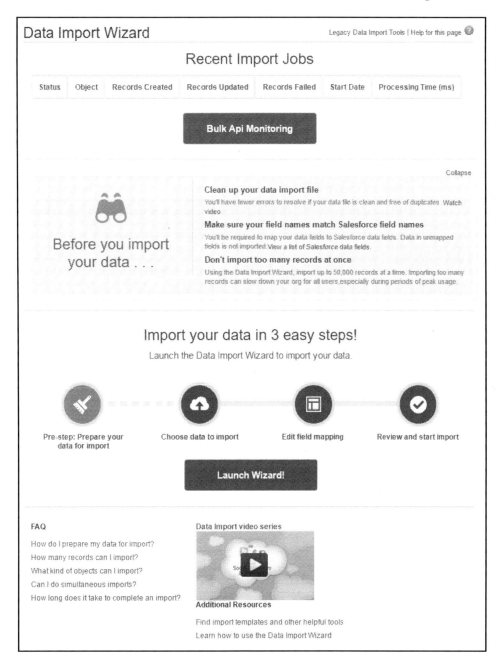

Individual import wizards

Salesforce individual import wizards open in a small pop-up window and present an easy-to-use multi-step wizard for importing new **Account (Person and Business Accounts)**, **Contact**, **Leads**, **Custom Object**, or **Solution** Object records into Salesforce.

 At the time of writing, Salesforce has announced that the individual import wizards are to be retired in February 2017. Salesforce recommends users to use the **Data Import Wizard** instead as the individual import wizards will no longer be available starting from the Spring '17 release.

To access the individual import wizards, click on the tab for the required object and locate the **Tools** section at the bottom of the page. As an example, the Leads import wizard is located as shown in the following screenshot:

The wizard can also be used for **Account (Person and Business Accounts)**, **Contact**, **Leads**, **Custom Object**, or **Solution** updates based on a matching identifier.

 Contact and **Leads** can be updated by matching the e-mail address, and **Custom Object** or **Solution** may be updated based on custom object names, solution titles, Salesforce ID, or an external ID.

A **comma-separated value (CSV)** file format is required when using the import wizard where imports are limited to 50,000 records per session.

 Account and **Contact** import wizards have a built-in de-duplicating functionality. Account can be matched using the account name and account site. For Contact, de-duplicating matching can be carried out using first name, last name, or e-mail address.

Data Loader

Data Loader is a client application available from Salesforce, which provides the facilities to bulk import and export data. Using **Data Loader**, you can create, edit, and delete Salesforce records for both standard and custom objects. **Data Loader** is supported for Windows XP, Windows 7, and Mac OS X.

The **Data Loader** client application must first be installed onto your local machine. The installation files can be obtained by navigating to **Setup | Data Management | Data Loader**.

Within the **Data Loader** installation files download screen, you can choose the appropriate installation download link for your operating system using either Download **Data Loader** for Windows or Download **Data Loader** for Mac, as shown in the following screenshot:

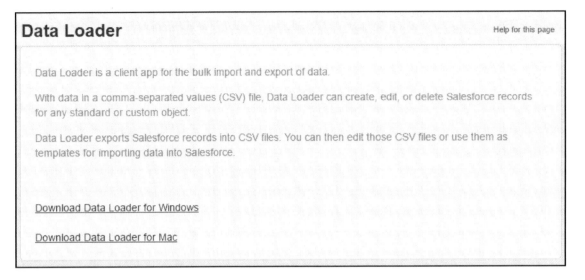

Data Loader can create, edit, or delete records for both standard and custom objects in Salesforce CRM. When importing data, **Data Loader** loads data from (CSV) files (or from a database connection). When exporting data, **Data Loader** exports records into CSV files. The CSV files can then be edited or used as data-key templates for data imports into Salesforce.

 Commas are commonly used to separate field values; however, since commas are used in certain locales as a way of formatting currency or numeric values, the comma delimiter may not be appropriate for every locale. In this scenario, users can specify delimiters such as tab, colon, or any other character delimiter.

The **Data Loader** client application provides the following features:

- A simple-to-use interactive wizard interface providing drag-and-drop field mapping between the source and destination data fields
- Support for importing and exporting large data files with anything upto five million records
- Support for all Salesforce objects, which includes both standard and custom objects

- Post-processing log files showing error and success results in CSV format, along with a built-in CSV file reader
- For the Windows operating system only, a command-line interface to enable automated importing and exporting of Salesforce data

 Data Loader does not support the export of attachments. Instead, Salesforce recommends using the weekly export feature described later in this chapter to export attachments.

Data Loader and import wizards compared

With **Data Loader**, you can perform operations such as insert, delete, update, extract, or upsert. You can move data into or out of any Salesforce object. There is less validation when adding data.

The import wizards are more limited as they only support **Account**, **Contact**, **Leads**, **Solution**, and **Custom** object. However, they have built-in de-duplication logic.

As a general guide, use **Data Loader** when:

- You need to load 50,000 or more records, up to the maximum of five million records
- You need to load into an object that is not yet supported by web-based import wizards
- You want to schedule regular data loads, such as nightly imports
- You want to save mappings for later use
- You want to export your data for backup purposes

 Add your IP address in the list of trusted IP ranges:
When logging into **Data Loader**, you must add a security token as described in Chapter 3, *Configuring Objects and Apps*. However, by adding your IP address as an entry in the list of trusted IP ranges, you can log in with only your Salesforce username and password.

As a general guide, use web-based import wizards when:

- You are loading fewer than 50,000 records
- The object you need to import is an **Account**, **Contact**, **Leads**, **Solution**, or **Custom object**
- You want to prevent duplicates by uploading records according to account name and site, contact e-mail address, or lead e-mail address

> Should you need to load more than five million records, Salesforce recommends that you work with a Salesforce partner, either directly or by visiting the AppExchange (covered in `Chapter 9`, *Extending and Enhancing Salesforce CRM*), where you will find a number of suitable products.

Best practices for mass data updating

When carrying out any kind of mass data update or deletion in Salesforce CRM, you should ensure that the data to be changed is correct, but you should also consider applying the following best practices.

Back up data

Back up your data before performing a mass update, or delete it by either requesting a data export or exporting your own report of the data.

Test batch

Create a test file containing a few records first to ensure that your source data has been correctly prepared.

> **Mass deleting data:**
> Consider including both the Date/Time Stamp and Created by Alias criteria in your mass delete to ensure that you are only deleting your imports and no other data.

Export backup data

Your organization can sign up to receive backup files of your data. Here, you can export all your organization's data into a set of CSV files.

With the data export feature, you can generate backup files manually once every six days or schedule them to generate automatically at weekly or monthly intervals.

 The weekly export service is available in Enterprise Edition and Unlimited Edition. The Developer Edition provides a monthly export service. When the export is ready, you will receive an e-mail with a link; navigate to the link provided.

To schedule a weekly or monthly export (as governed by the edition of Salesforce CRM that you are using), navigate to **Setup | Data Management | Data Export**. Then click on either the **Export Now** or **Schedule Export** buttons, as shown in the following screenshot:

Monthly Export Service

Help for this Page

Data Export lets you prepare a copy of all your data in salesforce.com. From this page you can start the export process manually or schedule it to run automatically. When an export is ready for download you will receive an email containing a link that allows you to download the file(s). The export files are also available on this page for 48 hours, after which time they are deleted.

Next scheduled export:
None

Export Now   Schedule Export

The data export can be set to run immediately or scheduled to run in the future, as discussed in the following subsections.

Export Now

The **Export Now** option prepares your files for immediate export. This option is only available if a week has passed since your last export and presents the options shown in the following screenshot:

Monthly Export Service

Help for this Page

Export File Encoding	ISO-8859-1 (General US & Western European, ISO-LATIN-1) ▼
Include images, documents, and attachments	☐ ⓘ
Include Salesforce Files and Salesforce CRM Content document versions	☐ ⓘ
Replace carriage returns with spaces	☑

Start Export | Cancel

Exported Data

Select what type of information you would like to include in the export. The data types listed below use the Apex API names. If you are not familiar with these names, select Include all data for your export.

☑ Include all data

| ☐ Contract | ☐ Approval | ☐ ContractContactRole |
| ☐ RecordType | ☐ BusinessProcess | ☐ EntityHistory |

Schedule Export

The **Schedule Export** option allows you to schedule the export process for weekly or monthly intervals and presents the options shown in the following screenshot:

Schedule Data Export

Help for this Page ⓘ

Schedule Data Export   [Save] [Cancel]

Export File Encoding	ISO-8859-1 (General US & Western European, ISO-LATIN-1) ▾
Include images, documents, and attachments	☐ ⓘ
Include Salesforce Files and Salesforce CRM Content document versions	☐ ⓘ
Replace carriage returns with spaces	☑

Schedule Data Export

Frequency
- ◉ On day [1 ▾] of every month
- ◯ On [the 1st ▾] [Sunday ▾] of every month

Start	16/08/2020	[16/08/2016]
End	16/09/2020	[16/08/2016]
Preferred Start Time	--None-- ▾	

Exact start time will depend on job queue activity.

[Save] [Cancel]

Exported Data

Select what type of information you would like to include in the export. The data types listed below use the Apex API names. If you are not familiar with these names, select Include all data for your export.

☑ Include all data

| ☐ Contract | ☐ Approval | ☐ ContractContactRole |
| ☐ RecordType | ☐ BusinessProcess | ☐ EntityHistory |

If new objects are created in the org after the Data Export has been scheduled you must then reschedule the data export to include the newly created objects if you want them to be included in the data export.

Recycle Bin

The **Recycle Bin** can be accessed from the **Home** tab by clicking on the link in the sidebar as shown in the following screenshot:

The **Recycle Bin** is where deleted data is stored. It can be accessed for 15 days, after which the data becomes permanently deleted and is no longer recoverable.

Clicking on **Recycle Bin** allows you to view both your deleted items and your organization's deleted items, as shown in the following screenshot:

You can use the **Empty your recycle bin** button to permanently remove deleted items prior to the 15-day expiration.

Records in the **Recycle Bin** do not count against your organizations storage limits.

To calculate the number of records that your **Recycle Bin** can store, Salesforce uses the following formula: 25 multiplied by the number of Megabytes (MB) in your storage.

For example, if your organization has 1 GB, which equates to 1000 MB (a 1000 MB storage unit is used here and not 1028 MB), your limit is 25 multiplied by 1000 MB, which equals 25,000 records.

When your organization reaches the **Recycle Bin** limit, the Salesforce CRM application automatically removes the oldest records (if they have been in the Recycle Bin for at least two hours).

Data storage utilization

Salesforce CRM has two categories of storage, namely, data, which is used to store records (for example, Opportunity, Account, or Custom object data records), and file storage, which is used to store file attachments (for example, presentations, spreadsheets, images, PDFs, and so on).

Salesforce CRM (Enterprise Edition) provides, as a minimum, 1 GB for data storage and 11 GB for file storage. In total, this 12 GB storage amount (1 GB for data plus 11 GB for files) is the minimum total storage allocated for a Salesforce CRM organization. However, the storage amount increases as more active users are added, since there is also a 20-MB-per-user for data and 2-GB-per-user for files storage factor.

As an example, an organization with 500 active users sees the storage amount for data increase to 10 GB. This is calculated as 500 (users) multiplied by 20 MB, which equals 10,000 MB or 10 GB. The storage amount for files is increased to 1,000 GB (500 users multiplied by 2 GB).

To view your organization's used data space and used file space, navigate to **Setup | Data Management | Storage Usage**. Here, you can view the limits and used amounts for data and file storage, the amounts in use per record type, and the current file-storage usage. You can also view the top users of data and file storage. To see exactly what is being stored by a listed user, you can click that user's name.

Questions to test your knowledge

You are now presented with questions about the key features of Salesforce CRM administration in the areas of data management which have been covered in this chapter. The answers can be found at the end of the chapter.

Questions

We present six questions to verify your understanding of data validation, dependent picklists, data importing and exporting facilities, and **Recycle Bin** storage.

Question 1 – Data validation rules

A validation rule has been created to ensure that users do not set the Close Date of an opportunity to a date in the past. What will happen if a user attempts to save an opportunity record that has a Close Date from last year? (Select one):

a) The error message defined within the validation rule is displayed on the record after the record is saved

b) The error message defined within the validation rule is sent by e-mail to the user after the record is saved

c) The error message defined within the validation rule is displayed on the record and the record is not saved

d) The error message defined within the validation rule is displayed on the record and the user is shown a confirmation screen to either continue or cancel the saving of the record

Question 2 – Dependent fields

Which of the following statements (if any) are true about dependent picklists? (Select all that apply):

a) Multi-select picklists can be dependent picklists

b) Checkboxes can be dependent fields

c) Standard picklist fields can be dependent fields

d) Custom picklist fields can be dependent fields

Question 3 – Data Import Wizard

Which of the following object types cannot be imported using the Data Import Wizard? (Select one):

a) Account

b) Leads

c) Opportunity

d) Solution

Question 4 – Data Import Wizard features

The Data Import Wizard provides which benefits for importing data into Salesforce CRM? (Select two):

a) Ability to import data for all standard and custom objects

b) Prevents duplicate records from being imported

c) Ability to import more than 50,000 records

d) Prevents workflow rules from firing as records are loaded into the system

Question 5 – Data Loader and import wizards compared

Which data import facility can be used to import 25,000 case records into Salesforce? (Select all that apply):

a) Data Import Wizard

b) Data Loader

c) Individual import wizard for the Case object

d) None of the above

Question 6 – Recycle Bin

How many days will the Recycle Bin store deleted data? (Select one):

a) 5

b) 10

c) 15

d) 30

Answers

Here are the answers to the six questions about data validation, dependent picklists, data importing and exporting facilities, and **Recycle Bin** storage.

Answer 1 – Data Validation rules

The answer is **a)** Data Validation rules allows you to specify your own business-specific criteria to prevent users from saving invalid data in one or more fields. In this scenario, if a user enters an invalid **Close Date** (one in the past), the error message defined within the validation rule is displayed on the record and the record is not saved.

Answer 2 – Dependent fields

The answer is **a)** Multi-select picklists can be dependent picklists, and **d)** Custom picklist fields can be dependent fields. Multi-select picklists can be dependent picklists but cannot be controlling fields. Checkbox fields can be controlling fields but cannot be dependent fields. Standard picklist fields can be controlling fields but cannot be a dependent field. Custom picklist fields can be used as either a controlling field or a dependent field.

Answer 3 – Data Import Wizard

The answer is **c)** Opportunity is the object type in the list that cannot be imported using the Data Import Wizard.

Answer 4 – Data Import Wizard features

The answer is **b**) Prevent duplicate records from being imported, and **d**) Prevent workflow rules from firing as records are loaded into the system. The **Data Import Wizard** can be used to import accounts, contacts, leads, solutions, and custom object records; prevent duplicate records from being imported; import up to 50,000 records; choose whether to allow workflow rules to fire during the loading of data.

Answer 5 – Data Loader and import wizards compared

The answer is **b**) Data Loader. Neither the **Data Import Wizard** nor the Individual Import Wizard supports the importing of Case records.

Answer 6 – Recycle Bin

The answer is **c**) Deleted data is stored in the Recycle Bin, where it can be accessed for 15 days, after which the data becomes permanently deleted and is no longer recoverable.

Summary

In this chapter, we described the features that offer improvements to data quality through the use of data validation rules and dependent fields.

We also looked at the options and facilities available within Salesforce CRM for importing and exporting data into and out of the system. We briefly outlined the data storage feature in Salesforce, along with texporting backup data and the **Recycle Bin**.

Finally, we posed some questions to help clarify some of the key features of Salesforce CRM administration in the area of data management.

In the following chapter, we will be covering data analytics, where we will see how we can report on the data in Salesforce.

Included in the next chapter is the setting up of reports, dashboards, custom reports, and a discussion of how to use the Report Builder.

6
Generating Data Analytics with Reports and Dashboards

In the previous chapter, we looked at the various mechanisms in Salesforce CRM that help manage the quality and integrity of data. The previous chapter also outlined the features and tools that are available for importing and exporting data to and from Salesforce CRM.

In this chapter, We will continue to look at the subject of data, but from the viewpoint of reporting, We will describe the analytics building blocks within Salesforce CRM.

These analytics tools allow you and your users to customize and manage the reporting and visual representation of data. For example, the sales team can produce reports that show the sales pipeline, the marketing team can report on the progress of campaigns, and you can create reports that display the number of active users in your Salesforce organization. The features available to report data are described in detail, including details on how to create, customize, and export purpose-built report data. Reports can also be used to improve the quality of data. You can, for example, create a report that lists all accounts with missing annual revenue fields.

We will also look in detail at how these analytical elements can be used to provide sophisticated dashboard charting and graphics.

Salesforce CRM analytics consist of the basic mechanisms of reports, dashboards, and folders:

- **Reports**: Reports are the key building blocks for analytics in Salesforce CRM, where a resulting set of records are displayed in rows and columns to match the specified criteria. Report results may be further filtered and grouped, and may also be displayed as graphical summaries.
- **Dashboards**: Dashboards are visual Components generated from data in reports. These Components can include the following five types: charts, gauges, tables, metrics, and Visualforce pages.
- **Folders**: Folders are used to store the reports and dashboards and can be set to either read-only or read/write. To configure which of your users have access to a folder, you can set it to be accessible by all users, hidden from all users, or accessible only by certain users. When restricting to certain users, options exist to restrict by Public Groups, Roles, and Roles and Subordinates.

Reports

Within Salesforce CRM, reports are accessed from the **Reports** tab (as shown in the following screenshot). There is a large variety of predefined reports that are automatically provided when your organization is first set up by Salesforce. These predefined reports are known as standard reports and are located in pre-prepared report folders known as standard report folders. For example, standard reports provide information about accounts and contacts; details about opportunities, forecasts, products, and sales pipelines; information about your organizations leads; details about forecast reports for customizable forecasting, and so on.

In this section on reports, we will outline the available standard reports and describe some of the key reports for system administrators in particular.

The predefined reports are suitable for existing objects and fields. They would not be suitable for reporting on any new objects that you have created. For this, we will look at how to extend the existing reports and how to create completely new types of reports, which are known as custom report types in Salesforce CRM.

Texisting objects and fields. They would are not be suitable for reporting on any new objects that you have created. For this, we will look at how to extend the existing reports and how to create completely new types of reports, known in Salesforce CRM as custom report types.

When building reports from either standard or custom report types, Salesforce provides a full-featured drag-and-drop editor to simplify the setup and layout of reports.

We will first look at how to use report folders, which can help organize and control users access to reports within Salesforce CRM. When we click on the **Reports** tab, the **Reports and Dashboards** home page presents the following features:

1. This represents the **New Report** and **New Dashboard** buttons.
2. This represents the **Folders** search box, which allows users to search for specific report and dashboard folders.
3. This represents the **New Report Folder** and **Create New Dashboard Folder** selections.
4. This represents the **Report** search box, which allows users to search for specific reports and dashboards.
5. This represents the **Reports and Dashboards Folder** pane with different icons to show whether the folder is a report or a dashboard.
6. This represents the **Main Reports and Dashboards List** View section. This allows filtering of Recent Reports tabs, displays appropriate reports, and allows the creation of new reports.

These features can be identified by their respective number, as shown in the following screenshot:

Report and Dashboard Folders

The **Report and Dashboards Folders** section allows you and your users to select the reports and dashboards that are stored in that specific folder.

In Salesforce CRM, you cannot save reports to the standard report folders. You can save reports to the `My Personal Custom Reports` folder, the `Unfiled Public Reports` folder, or any custom report folder where you have the appropriate read/write access.

 Standard reports may not be deleted or removed, but the folder and the standard report type, described further on in this chapter, can be hidden.

Creating new report and dashboard folders

Using the create folder icon and associated options allows you to create new report and dashboard folders for custom reports and dashboards, as shown in the following screenshot:

The option to create new folders is not available to all users. The user permission required to access the **Create New Folder** option is **Manage Public Reports**.

> It is good practice to create new folders to help manage the structure of reports for your organization.

You cannot mix standard and custom reports in the same folder.

Keep favorite report folders in view

The reports and dashboards folder pane may contain many report and dashboard folders, which means your users have to scroll up and down the list to find the required folder. To help users keep their favorite folders at the top of the list, they can pin report and dashboard folders to the top of the folder list. This can be done by clicking to the right of the folder name and selecting the **Pin to top** option, as shown in the following screenshot:

Unlike many IT systems, creating reports in Salesforce CRM is very simple; users can create reports themselves. Since it is so easy for users to create reports, without careful control and an organized approach to report creation, it is easy for the number of reports to rapidly increase and become difficult to manage. You should, for example, create report folders that only certain users have access to. This could be restricted to certain departments or geographical regions. For example, reports could be restricted to Global Marketing or to the North American Sales Team.

To create new report folders, click on the **New Report Folder** option, where the **New Report Folder** page is presented, as shown in the following screenshot:

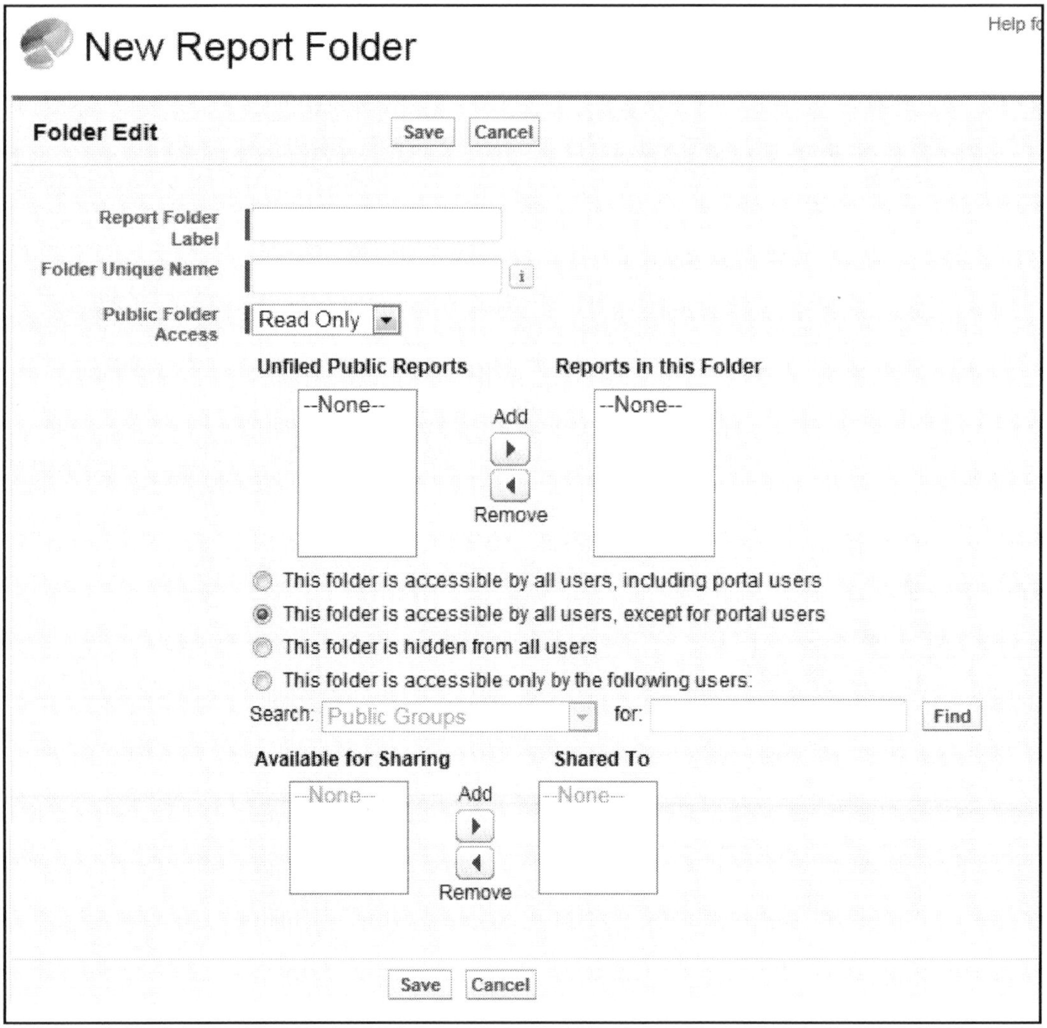

Here, you provide the name of the report folder and decide whether the public folder access is set to be read-only or read/write. You can optionally move reports from the Unfiled `Public Reports` folder. You must specify the accessibility to users. You can select either the accessible by all users, hidden from all users, or accessible by certain users options. These options are available in the following: **Public Groups**, **Roles**, and **Roles and Subordinates**.

Only users with the **Manage Public Reports** user permission are able to delete reports from the report folders. This is true even if the user has read/write access and has created the report themselves.

Enhanced sharing for reports and dashboards

This setting lets users share reports and dashboards with other users, roles, or public user groups. When it is activated, Salesforce converts the existing public report folder access levels described previously, whereupon access to folders is then derived from the combination of folder access and user permissions.

The enhanced access levels grants all users as a **Viewer** (by default) to the report and dashboard folders that are shared with them.

To activate enhanced sharing for reports and dashboards, navigate to **Setup** | **Reports & Dashboards** | **Customize** | **Folder Sharing**. Select the **Enable access levels for sharing report and dashboard folders** checkbox and then click **Save**.

Users are then able to share the reports and dashboards folders by clicking to the right of the folder in the folders pane and selecting the **Share** option, as shown in the following screenshot:

When users click the **Share** option, they are presented with a new screen that allows them to set the sharing access for other users. The options are **Viewer**, **Editor**, or **Manager**, as shown in the following screenshot:

Viewer access

The Viewer access setting allows users to view, refresh, and run reports and dashboards.

Editor access

The Editor access setting provides the same access as Viewer plus the ability to edit, move, save, and delete reports and dashboards.

Manager access

The Manager access setting provides the same access as Editor plus the ability to share and rename the folder.

Creating reports

The basic steps for creating new reports are as follows:

1. From the **Reports** tab, click on the **New Report**… button.
2. Select the report type for the report and click on the **Create button**.
3. Customize your report, enter a report name, and then save or run it.

Report name on two lines:
It is possible to format the report name to be split onto two lines to help make it easier to show the name. This can be done by entering the colon (:) character. Simply enter the report name with a colon character, for example, A01 North America: April Sales and the report name will be shown on two lines when viewing the report.
Caution: this is a non-documented feature so may not be supported by Salesforce.

Selecting the appropriate report type is one of the most important steps in creating a report. Report types set the rules for which records can be shown in reports. They allow predefined sets of records and fields to be available within a report based on the relationship between a primary object and any related objects.

Best practices for reports:
Establish a report naming convention, for example, A01 NA April Sales, B02 INT April Sales, and so on, as this can make it easier to refer to reports using the coding scheme (there is an upper limit of 40 characters). Use the Description field to describe exactly what the report is intended for (there is an upper limit of 255 characters). Consider creating reports that are only needed for dashboards in separate report folders, called something like Dashboard Reports Sales, for example. Perform regular spring cleans where you delete unwanted reports. You can also create temporary reports that are hidden from all users and save these reports there while you figure out if they are required.

In the Salesforce CRM application, there are standard report types, and you, as system administrator, can set up custom report types.

Terminology check:
Custom Report Type is different from Custom Report in Salesforce CRM. When users create a new report using the **New Report** button on the **Reports** home page, this is sometimes known as a custom report. Custom Report Type is a report template that only system administrators can create. It provides a custom set of associated objects and fields to produce predefined report templates from which any users custom report can be created.

Standard report types

Salesforce provides a large range of predefined standard report types along with standard report folders accessible from the **Reports** tab, as shown in the following table:

Standard report type	Standard report folder	Description
	Unfiled Public Reports	Shared custom reports created by system administrators, but not moved into a custom report folder
	My Personal Custom Reports	Customized reports that users have saved by clicking on Save As or Save within a report
Account & Contacts	Account and Contact Reports	Information about accounts and contacts
Activities	Activity Reports	Information about calendar events and tasks
Administrative Reports	Administrative Reports	Information about your Salesforce users, documents, and reports
Call Center Reports	Call Center Reports	Information about phone calls that were handled with Salesforce CRM call center
Campaigns	Campaign Reports	Information about marketing campaigns
CRM File and Content Reports	File and Content Reports	Information about files and Salesforce CRM Content
Forecasts	Forecast Reports	Details about forecast reports for customizable forecasting
Leads	Lead Reports	Information about leads

| Opportunities | Opportunity and Forecast Reports | Details about opportunities, forecasts, products, and sales pipelines |
| Price Books, Products, and Assets | Price Books, Products and Asset Reports | Information about products, price books, and assets |

From the **Create New Report** screen, the creation of standard reports in Salesforce CRM begins with the selection of an appropriate report type, as shown in the following screenshot:

By default, the standard report folders are set to read-only and are accessible by all users.

Administrative reports

One of the most useful standard reports for system administrators is the administrator report, which can be found in the `Administrative Reports` folder, and can be used to analyze your Salesforce users documents, reports, and login locations. For example, you can run reports on the active Salesforce users and see who has been logging in. The following administrative reports are available:

Report	Description
All Active Users	Lists the active users in your organization and when they last logged in
Users Logged in This Week	Lists all users who have logged in to Salesforce in the past seven days
Documents	Lists the documents within each document folder
New Login Locations	List of users, IP addresses, and login dates

Creating a custom report to list your organizations reports:
You can create a custom report that lists the reports within your organization and the last time each report was used. Choose **Administrative Reports** and then select **Reports** as the report type.

Hiding standard report types

There is a large number of standard report types provided by Salesforce and presented in the **Create New Report** page. Some of the report types may not be of any value in your organization and only serve to clutter up the list of useful report types. You can hide unwanted standard report types from users by enabling the Select Report Types to Hide checkbox to reveal a check mark or cross mark against each of the report types.

The green check mark next to a report type means it is visible. Clicking the check mark to change it to an cross mark means it is hidden, as shown in the following screenshot:

Create New Report

☑ **Select Report Types to Hide** ⓘ

Select Report Type

🔍 Quick Find

⊟ 📁 Accounts & Contacts
    ✔ Accounts
    ✔ Contacts & Accounts
    ✔ Accounts with Partners
    ✔ Account with Account Teams
    ✔ Accounts with Contact Roles
    ✘ Accounts with Assets
    ✘ Contacts with Assets
    ✔ Accounts with Activity Tracker

 Hidden report types do not show up when using the search box on the **Create New Report** page, and if you hide all the report types in a folder, the folder becomes hidden too.

Custom report types

In addition to the standard report types, you can also create custom report types. Custom report types extend the types of reports from which all users in your organization can create or update custom reports.

Creating custom report types

Custom report types are set up using the following steps:

1. Define a custom report type by name, description, primary object, development status, and the category of report to store it.

2. Choose the related objects for the custom report type.
3. Specify the layout for the resulting standard and custom fields that a report can display when created using the custom report type.
4. Create a report from the **Custom Report Type** template to verify that all of the objects and field definitions are correct.

Once you have created a custom report type, you can later update or delete it, as required.

When a **Custom Report Type** template is deleted, any reports that have been created from it are also deleted. Furthermore, any dashboard Components that have been created from a report that was created from a deleted `Custom Report Type` template will show an error message when viewed.

Defining custom report types

To navigate to the **Custom Report Types** page, navigate to **Setup** | **Create** | **Report Types**. Then click on **New Custom Report Type**:

New Custom Report Type   Help for this Page

Step 1. Define the Custom Report Type   **Step 1 of 2**

                                                                    Next   Cancel

Report Type Focus | = Required Information

Specify what type of records (rows) will be the focus of reports generated by this report type.

Example: If reporting on "Contacts with Opportunities with Partners," select "Contacts" as the primary object.

Primary Object   --Select--   ▼

Identification

Report Type Label   [   ]

Report Type Name   [   ] i

            Note: Description will be visible to users who create reports.

Description   [   ]

Store in Category   --Select--   ▼

Deployment

A report type with deployed status is available for use in the report wizard. While in development, report types are visible only to authorized administrators and their delegates.

Deployment Status   ◉ In Development

                    ○ Deployed

                                                                    Next   Cancel

---

Step 1 – Defining the Custom Report Type template

From the **Primary Object** drop-down list, select the primary object from which you want to build your custom report type.

The primary object you choose determines the views available to users creating or running reports from your custom report type. For example, if you select accounts as the primary object for your custom report type, users can view their report results by **All Accounts** or **My Accounts** from the report builders **Show** drop-down list.

If you select **opportunities**, when users create reports based on that report type, they can view their report results by **My opportunities**, **My teams opportunities**, or by **All opportunities**, as shown in the following screenshot:

![Screenshot of the Salesforce report builder showing the Report Type: Opportunities with Activities, an Unsaved Report, with Save, Save As, Close, Report Properties, and Run Report buttons. The Fields panel has a Quick Find box and Opportunities fields. The Filters panel shows a Show drop-down with My opportunities, My team's opportunities, and All opportunities options.]

When a `Custom Report Type` template is saved, the primary object associated with it cannot be changed. So, if you later want to change the primary object, you have to define a new custom report type.

Now enter the **Report Type Label** and the **Report Type Name** fields, and enter a description for the custom report type. The description will be visible to users who create reports and is used to help explain the purpose for the `Custom Report Type` template.

The **Report Type Label** field can be up to 50 characters and the description can be up to 255 characters.

Select the category to store the custom report type in. Then, select a development status. Here, you can select **In Development** when you first create the custom report type to hide it from users while you define it. This will hide the **Custom Report Type** template and prevent users from creating and running reports from the report type. Choose **Deployed** when you have finished defining it and want to let users create and run reports using that **Custom Report Type** template.

Now click on **Next** and choose the object relationships a report can display when run from a custom report type.

Step 2 – Defining report records set

After the initial definition of the **Custom Report Type** template, the object relationships for it can be selected. These object relationships determine the objects and fields available for display on reports. Using diagrams, they help to understand the object relationships formed within **Custom Report Type**, which will display the data fields whenever reports are created from the **Custom Report Type** template:

In this **Custom Report Type** example, called **Events with or without Sessions**, we have object relationships for a custom primary object **Event** which has relationships with **Sessions** and **Speakers**.

To add an object that is associated with another object to the report type, click on the rectangle section **(Click to relate another object)**. Then, select the object from the picklist.

The objects available for you to choose from are based on the primary object's relationships to other objects.

For example, our custom object, Event, is set as the primary object for the **Custom Report Type** template, so only standard and custom objects associated with Events can be chosen, such as Sessions. This also applies to additional objects added to the **Custom Report Type** template. In our example, with Events selected as the primary object and Sessions selected as the secondary object, only the objects associated with Sessions can be selected as the third object on the **Custom Report Type** template, which is our custom object, Speakers.

 Although up to four object levels can be set up for **Custom Report Type** templates, some of the object combinations may not be able to reach that limit. For example, if you add contacts as the primary object, opportunities as the secondary object, and activities as the third object, then you cannot add any additional objects because activities do not have any child object relationships.

Within the diagram, there is the option of setting the first relationship to the primary object with either **"A" records may or may not have related "B" records** or **Each "A" record must have at least one related "B" record**.

The following paragraph describes the effects of selecting may or may not options.

All subsequent objects automatically include the may-or-may-not association on the custom report type. For example, if accounts are the primary objects and opportunities are the secondary objects, and you choose that accounts may or may not have opportunities, then any third and fourth level objects included on the CustomReportType template default to may-or-may-not associations.

Blank fields display on report results for object B when object A does not have object B. For example, if a user runs a report on accounts with or without opportunities, then opportunity fields display as blank for accounts without opportunities.

Edit layout

After clicking on **Save**, the **Custom Report Type** definition and the object relationships are set as shown in the following screenshot:

Now the layout can be edited to specify which standard and custom fields a report can display when created or run from the template.

Clicking on **Preview Layout** shows which fields will display on the **Select Columns** page of a report based on this report type.

To start configuring the layout, select fields from the right-hand box and drag them to a section on the left, as shown in the following screenshot:

You can view a specific objects fields by selecting an object from the View drop-down list and arrange fields within sections as they should appear to users.

Fields not dragged onto a section will not be visible to users when they create reports using this report type.

You can add up to 1,000 fields to each `Custom Report Type` **template**.

To rename or set which fields are selected by default for users, select one or more fields and click on **Edit Properties**, as shown in the following screenshot:

  Any new fields that are created on the referenced object(s) are not automatically added to the custom report type. If you want the new fields to be available in the custom report type for users to select the you must edit the custom report type and manually configure the fields.

Click on the **Checked by Default** checkbox next to the field you want selected by default. Change the text in the **Display** As field next to the field you want to rename. To rename the sections, click on **Edit** next to an existing section or create a new section by clicking on **Create New Section**. Then click on **Save**.

Running reports

The **Reports** tab presents the reports home page, on which users can search for reports and select or create a folder for reports:

The list of folders (represented by the folder icon) displays all the report folders that the user has permission to access. Within this section, you can view, edit, and manage all of your organization's public report folders. By clicking on the **Reorder Folders** option, you can change the order in which folders appear on the sub-tab.

The section on the right displays the selected report folder and allows users to click on the **Actions** drop-down, which appears as the first column. Here, the options are **Edit**, **Delete**, and **Export**.

Choosing the **Delete** option will remove the report for all users and move it to the Recycle Bin. Here, you are prompted with a warning before the deletion is carried out.

Before doing so, you need to check that the report is no longer required, as it will be removed for all users you are able to recover it from the Recycle Bin for 15 days (if necessary), though.

> You cannot delete reports that are being used by dashboards. To delete these reports, you must first delete the calling dashboard component.

Users with appropriate permissions can click on **Export** to export a report directly to an Excel spreadsheet or CSV file, which is described next.

Printing and exporting reports

To print a report, users can perform the following steps:

1. Click on the **Printable View** button to open (or save) the report as a printed view, as shown in the following screenshot:

2. Click on the print icon.

To export a report, users with the system permission of **Export Reports**, (either within their profile or via a permission set), can perform the following steps:

1. Click on **Export Details**.

2. Set the appropriate file encoding option for the language. The default option is **ISO-8859-1 (General US & Western European, ISO-LATIN-1)**, as shown in the following screenshot:

3. Set the **Export File Format** field to either **Excel** or **CSV.**
4. Click on **Export**.

In the browser's **File Download dialog**, users can then choose where to save the file to on their local or network disk.

Up to 256 columns and 65,536 rows of data can be exported from a report.

Report considerations

There are various issues to consider when running reports, whether in Salesforce CRM or on any other information system. There are typical limits to the volume of data that can be processed, or restrictions to the types of changes that can be made to existing reports. Both the method of controlling the amount of data that is returned in Salesforce and the effects of changing aspects of existing reports are described next.

Running large reports

If your report returns more than 2,000 records, only the first 2,000 records are displayed. To see a complete view of your report results, click on **Export Details**.

 Reports that take longer than ten minutes to complete will be cancelled by the Salesforce system.

Report timeout warning

The report timeout warning analyzes reports that are invoked from the **Run Reports** page. The standard timeout for reports is ten minutes. If the report is identified to be highly complex and is likely to time out, a warning is displayed.

The report timeout warning analyzes reports that are activated manually and ignores reports run via dashboards or scheduled reports.

 You can have the timeout period for reports extended from the default ten minutes by sending a request to Salesforce customer support.

If your organization has extended the limit to, say, 20 minutes, the report timeout warning might be less likely to appear. However, bear in mind that highly complex reports may still time out in the future.

 Salesforce recommends that you follow the steps outlined in their online help section, *Tips for Improving Report Performance*, to simplify the report.

You can disable the report timeout warning by navigating to **Setup | Customize | Reports & Dashboards | User Interface** Settings. Uncheck the **Enable Report Timeout Warning** checkbox and then click on **Save**.

Exporting reports to the background

Exporting reports to the background enables you to run reports in the background so that you can continue working in Salesforce without waiting for report results to be displayed. Exporting reports to the background is very useful when creating large reports that would otherwise time out due to the volume of resulting report data.

When the report has finished running and the results are ready for viewing, an e-mail notification is sent by Salesforce. The email contains a link that, when clicked, enables the viewing of the report information. From this page, you can then download the report results in CSV format.

 The feature for exporting reports to the background can only be enabled by sending a request to Salesforce customer support.

User verification test

For security purposes, user verification can be set up to require users to be tested before exporting data from the Salesforce CRM application. This text data-entry test prevents automated programs from attempting to access the data from within Salesforce. This feature is available on request from Salesforce customer support.

To pass the test, users must type the two words displayed into a textbox field and submit. Note that the words entered into the textbox field must be separated by a space.

Salesforce uses **CAPTCHA** technology provided by **reCAPTCHA** for user-verification testing.

CAPTCHA is an acronym that stands for **Completely Automated Public Turing Test To Tell Computers and Humans Apart**. It is a computer data-entry verification that ensures the entry is being carried out by a person. The verification requests the user to complete a small test, which the computer creates first, and then checks the result. Because only humans are able to solve the test, whenever the correct solution is returned, the computer accepts that it is a request by a person and not an automated computer program.

Mass Deleting Reports

You can delete reports individually or use the **Mass Delete Reports** page to search and select multiple reports to be deleted. This can be used to help declutter the list of reports on the Reports tab and remove multiple reports that are no longer in use.

To mass delete reports, navigate to **Setup** | **Data Management** | **Mass Delete Records** and then click the **Mass Delete Reports** link. Specify the criteria that the selected reports to be deleted must match, for example, **Report Name contains activity**, and then click **Search**. The list of any matching reports will then be presented. You can then select and click **Delete**, as shown in the following screenshot:

Mass delete reports

Help for this Page

Personal reports of other users, reports used in dashboards or analytic snapshots are not deletable through mass delete.

Report Name ▼	contains ▼	activity	AND
--None-- ▼	--None-- ▼		AND
--None-- ▼	--None-- ▼		AND
--None-- ▼	--None-- ▼		AND
--None-- ▼	--None-- ▼		

Search

Delete

☑	Report Name	Description	Folder	Name
☑	Accounts with Activity Tracker Report		Working Models	Goodey, Paul
☑	Activity Tracker		Working Models	Goodey, Paul

Delete

You cannot mass delete other users personal reports, reports within dashboards, or analytic snapshots.

Report builder

The report builder in Salesforce CRM is a visual editor to enable the creation and modification of reports. The report builder interface uses drag-and-drop functionality to configure reports, and the interface consists of the following three sections, known as panes:

- The **Fields** pane
- The **Filters** pane
- The **Preview** pane

The following screenshot shows the report builder page, which is presented as a full-screen window in order to maximize the display of the **Fields**, **Filters**, and **Preview** panes:

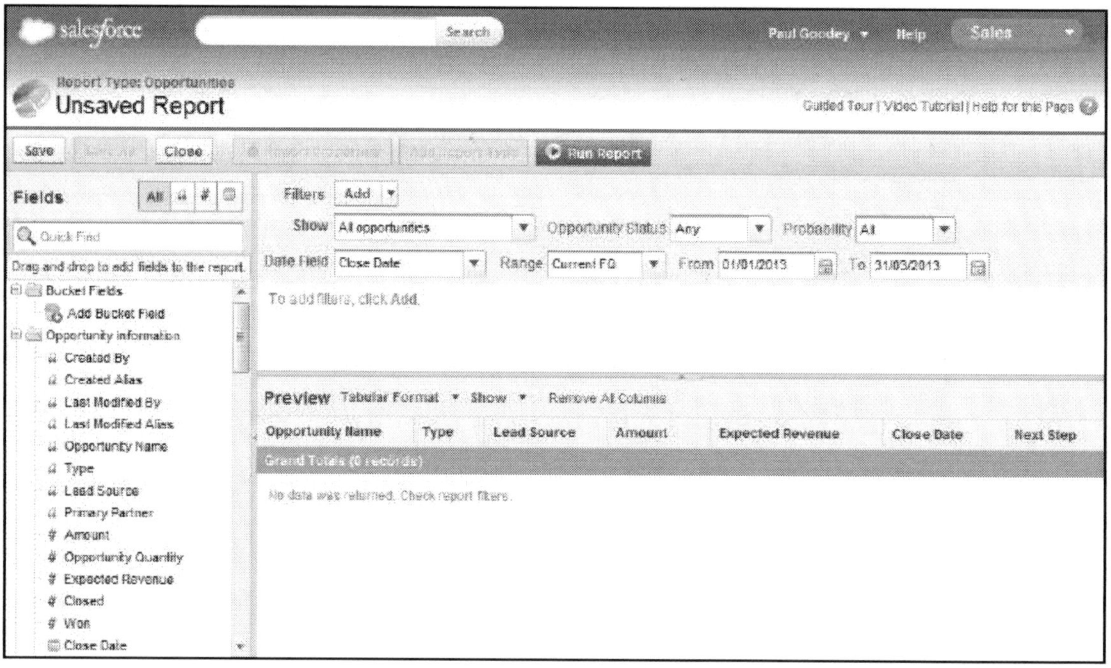

To exit the report builder editor page, click on the **Close** button located in the top-left corner of the page, where you will be prompted to save any changes.

You can also click on the Salesforce logo in the top-left corner of the page. However, you will not be prompted to save any changes. We will now look at each of the panes in detail, beginning with the **Fields** pane.

The Fields pane

The **Fields** pane is shown on the left-hand side of the report builder page and, as the name suggests, lists all the accessible fields in the selected report type. The list of fields is organized by the sections that were set in the page layout of the associated report type. Here, fields can easily be identified by using the **Quick Find** search box at the top of the pane. You can also limit the number of fields shown by using the field type filters. In this pane, the fields can be dragged into the **Preview** pane to add them to the report. Additional calculated fields can be created just for the specific report. These are known as **custom summary formulas and buckets**.

The Filters pane

To limit the number of rows of data results that are returned when you run a report, you can either limit your report results by clicking on the **Hide Details** button at the top of the report, or you can add custom filters. To restore the full set of returned data, click on the **Show Details** button.

For Tabular reports (only), you can set the maximum number of records to be displayed by clicking on **Add Row Limit** in the report builder accessed from the **Add** button in the **Filters** pane.

The **Filters** pane is displayed in the top-right part of the report builder page, and is used to configure the view, the time period, and also any custom filters to limit the data that is actually displayed as part of the report.

Within the Filters pane, you click on the **Add** box to add report filters, as shown here:

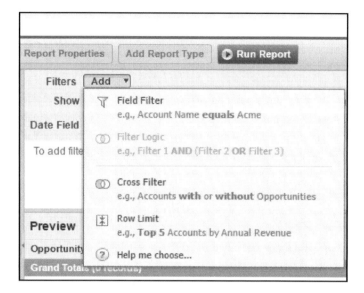

Report filters set the criteria for the data in a report according to the following:

Report filter	Description	Notes
Field Filter	**Field Filter** allows you to set the field, the operator, and the value.	For example, **Account Name equals Acme**.
Filter Logic	**Filter Logic** adds Boolean conditions to control how field filters are evaluated.	For example, **Filter 1 and (Filter 2 OR Filter 3)**. You must add at least one field filter before applying filter logic.
Cross Filter	**Cross Filter** allows you to link fields on related objects using a with or without sub-filter.	For example, a cross filter on **Accounts with Opportunities** allows you to show only Accounts that have Closed Won Opportunities.
Row Limit	With a **Row Limit**, you set the maximum number of rows to be displayed; choose a field to sort by and the sort order.	Only available for Tabular reports. Tabular reports that have a limited row count can be used in dashboards.

The Preview pane

The **Preview pane** is where the report can be customized. You and your users can add, rearrange, and remove columns, summary fields, formulas, and field groupings. When you enter the report builder for the first time, the **Preview pane** shows an initial result to provide a starting point from which the crafting and fine tuning of the report results can be done. In the **Preview** pane, you can also set the required report format, which can be either **Tabular**, **Summary**, or **Matrix**.

The preview shows only a limited number of result records. You need to actually run the report in order to see all the results.

You can drag-and-drop report columns to change the order in which they are displayed. By clicking on the data-column header, you can sort your report using that column. Sorting can also be performed by clicking on the **column** menu and then choosing either the **Sort Ascending** or the **Sort Descending** option from the drop-down list.

Sort is disabled when **Show Details** has not been selected.

If a field has been added to the preview pane and is not required, it can be removed by grabbing its column header and dragging it back to the **Fields** pane. You can also click on the column menu and choose **Remove Column**, or click on **Remove All Columns** to clear the **Preview** pane of all the fields.

While **Show Details** is disabled, you can only add summary fields.

Setting the Date Range option to All Time:

When first creating a report involving dates, the date range may not initially be set appropriately. So, there will be no obvious results returned. By setting the date range to **All Time**, you will most probably see some data returned, which can be useful as a quick check to see whether the report is working as intended.

Report formats

The following four report formats are available in Salesforce CRM: **Tabular**, **Summary**, **Matrix**, and **Joined**. The features and benefits of each format are outlined next.

The Tabular report format

Tabular reports are the easiest and quickest way to report data. They can be likened to a spreadsheet, where they comprise a set of records listed in rows and fields (ordered in columns). Tabular reports are best suited for creating lists of records or a list with a single grand total, as they cannot be used to group data.

 Tabular reports cannot be used in dashboards unless the number of rows that are returned are limited.

The Summary report format

Summary reports are similar to tabular reports except that they allow the grouping of rows of data. They can be used for reports to show subtotals based on the value of a field. Summary reports with no groupings are simply displayed as tabular reports.

 Summary reports can be used as the source report for dashboard Components.

The Matrix report format

Matrix reports are similar to summary reports, but they also allow the grouping and summarizing of data by both rows and columns and can be used for comparing related totals.

Matrix reports are useful for summarizing large amounts of data to compare values in several different fields or for analyzing data by date or by product, person, region, and so on.

 Matrix reports can be used as the source report for dashboard Components.

The Joined report format

Joined reports are reports that can store and group multiple reports together and allow you to build a single report that contains data from multiple report types.

A joined report can have up to five report blocks that can be added from either standard or custom report types, but can only be included if they share a common object relationship. For example, if you have a joined report that contains the Opportunities report type, you can then add the Contacts report type, since both Opportunity and Contact objects have a relationship with the Accounts object.

For joined reports with multiple report types, any field that is shared by all report types is known as a common field. Common fields appear in the **Common Fields** area in the **Fields** pane and can be used to group together the separate report blocks.

 Joined reports can be used as the source report for dashboard Components if the joined report includes a **report chart by configuring the dashboard** component with the Use chart as defined in the source report setting. The following features are not available in joined reports: **Bucket** fields, **Cross** filters, The **Rows to Display** filters, and **Conditional Highlighting**.

Groupings

Groupings can be added to summary, matrix, and joined reports to group together sections of report data. For example, you might want to group accounts by the number of employees that the account has.

To add a summary field, follow these steps:

1. Drag a field from within the **Fields** pane.
2. Drag the field into the grouping section of the **Preview** pane.

3. Wait for the loading dialog to complete.

4. Observe what the field is showing on the grouping section:

This will produce a report showing the grouped sections, as shown in the following screenshot:

	Account Owner	Account Name	Type	Rati
☐	**Employees: 100,000 (1 record)**			
	Paul Goodey	United Oil & Gas Corp.	Customer	Hot
☐	**Employees: 39,000 (1 record)**			
	Paul Goodey	University of Arizona	Customer	Warn
☐	**Employees: 24,000 (2 records)**			
	Paul Goodey	Express Logistics and Transport	Customer - Channel	Cold
	Paul Goodey	United Oil & Gas, UK	Customer	-
☐	**Employees: 5,000 (2 records)**			
	Paul Goodey	Burlington Textiles Corp of America	Customer	Warn
	Paul Goodey	Grand Hotels & Resorts Ltd	Customer	Warn
☐	**Employees: 3,000 (1 record)**			
	Paul Goodey	United Oil & Gas, Singapore	Customer	-
☐	**Employees: 1,000 (4 records)**			
	Paul Goodey	Pyramid Construction Inc.	Customer - Channel	-
	Paul Goodey	Edge Communications	Customer	Hot
	Paul Goodey	Company X	-	-
	Paul Goodey	Carr	-	-

Summary reports can have up to three grouping levels.

Matrix reports can have two row and two column groupings. You cannot use the same field for both the row and the column groupings.

Joined reports can have up to three grouping levels.

Summary fields

A summary field is the SUM, AVERAGE, MIN, or MAX for a number or a currency field. Summary fields are displayed at all grouping levels, including the grand total level for reports that have been created using the summary and matrix report formats.

To add a summary field, click on a column drop-down menu section (shown in the following screenshot) for a field in the report and choose **Summarize this Field**. You can also use this method to add a grouping by choosing **Group by this Field**, as shown in the following screenshot:

Clicking on the **Summarize this Field** button gives you the following options:

This will produce a report result, as shown in the following screenshot:

	Account Owner	Account Name	Type	Rating	Annual Revenue	La
☐	**Employees: 100,000 (1 record)**					
					avg $5,600,000,000	
	Paul Goodey	United Oil & Gas Corp.	Customer	Hot	$5,600,000,000	
☐	**Employees: 39,000 (1 record)**					
					avg $0	
	Paul Goodey	University of Arizona	Customer	Warm	-	
☐	**Employees: 24,000 (2 records)**					
					avg $475,000,000	
	Paul Goodey	Express Logistics and Transport	Customer - Channel	Cold	$950,000,000	
	Paul Goodey	United Oil & Gas, UK	Customer	-	-	
☐	**Employees: 5,000 (2 records)**					
					avg $425,000,000	
	Paul Goodey	Burlington Textiles Corp of America	Customer	Warm	$350,000,000	
	Paul Goodey	Grand Hotels & Resorts Ltd	Customer	Warm	$500,000,000	
☐	**Employees: 3,000 (1 record)**					
					avg $0	
	Paul Goodey	United Oil & Gas, Singapore	Customer	-	-	
☐	**Employees: 1,000 (4 records)**					
					avg $272,300,000	
	Paul Goodey	Pyramid Construction Inc.	Customer - Channel	-	$950,000,000	
	Paul Goodey	Edge Communications	Customer	Hot	$139,000,000	
	Paul Goodey	Company X	-	-	$200,000	
	Paul Goodey	Carr	-	-		

Toolbar: Run Report ▼ | Hide Details | Customize | Save As | Printable View | Export Details

Conditional highlighting

Conditional highlighting is a very powerful way to show, at a glance, whether the values in reports are within acceptable limits. By setting up **Conditional highlighting**, you can specify different colors for different ranges of values in your reports. It is relatively easy to set up and it offers great visual benefits, and yet it is a feature that seems to be underused by users within Salesforce CRM.

To enable **Conditional highlighting**, your report must contain at least one summary field or custom summary formula, which at the time of writing is available for Summary or Matrix reports.

To set up **Conditional highlighting**, click on **Show** and then on **Conditional Highlighting**, as shown from within the **Preview** pane on the report builder page:

You then have the option to set colors according to whether the value falls below a low breakpoint threshold, above a high breakpoint threshold, or a value that sits between the range of values. The following screenshot shows an example of how the thresholds might be set:

The following table aims to show given settings and the table helps clarify the thresholds and mentions the colors that would are be seen, given the settings above.

The color to show data that is below the Low Breakpoint value.	The threshold value between the Low Color and the Mid Color values.	The color to show data that is between the Low Breakpoint and High Breakpoint values.	The threshold value between the Mid Color and the High Color values.	The color to show data that is above the High Breakpoint value.
In this example: Red	In this example, 60,000 Values that are exactly the same as the Low Breakpoint value are shown as Mid Color.	In this example: Amber	In this example, 95,000 Values that are exactly the same as the High Breakpoint value are shown as High Color.	In this example: Green

When running the report, the result appears as shown in the following screenshot:

Filtered By: Edit
Stage equals **Needs Analysis,Perception Analysis,Proposal/Price Quote** Clear

Opportunity Name	Expected Revenue	Opportunity Owner	Account Name ↓	Avg Expected Revenue
Stage: Needs Analysis (3 records)				$52,066.67
United Oil Plant Standby Generators	$135,000.00	Paul Goodey	United Oil & Gas Corp.	
Starr Toolset	$1,200.00	Paul Goodey	Starr Hardware Wholesalers	
Toolset Q1	$20,000.00	Paul Goodey	Drews	
Stage: Perception Analysis (1 record)				$84,000.00
Express Logistics SLA	$84,000.00	Paul Goodey	Express Logistics and Transport	
Stage: Proposal/Price Quote (3 records)				$95,500.00
University of AZ Installations	$75,000.00	Paul Goodey	University of Arizona	
United Oil Refinery Generators	$202,500.00	Paul Goodey	United Oil & Gas Corp.	
Steane	$9,000.00	Paul Goodey	Steane & Co	
Grand Totals (7 records)				$75,242.86

Custom summary formulas

Custom summary formulas allow you to calculate values based on the numeric fields available in the report type. This means you do not have to create custom formula fields for calculated results if they are only relevant in reports.

Formulas must be 3,900 characters or fewer. Up to five formulas can be created per report. Fields available for custom summary formulas are **Number**, **Percent**, and **Currency**. To add a new formula to a summary or matrix report, navigate to the **Fields** pane, where at the top, you will see the formulas folder icon. By double-clicking on the **Add Formula** option, you can define it and then click on **OK**. After you have defined a new formula on the report, it automatically gets added to the preview pane as a column for summary reports and as a summary field for matrix reports. The following screenshot shows the formula called **Opportunity Average Expected Revenue** in the top-left section of the **Fields** pane and how it automatically appears in the preview pane as a column (on the far right) for the example summary report:

To define a formula field, follow these steps:

1. Click on **Add Formula** in the **Fields** pane:

Custom Summary Formula   Help for this Page ❓ ✕

Column Name: | Avg Expected Revenue

Description: |

Format: | Currency ▼   Decimal Places: | 2 ▼

      Number

Where will this formula b   Percent   ation will be displayed in the report at the level you select.

    Currency

  ◉ All summary levels
  ○ Grand summary only
  ○ Grouping 1: Stage

Formula   **Functions**   **Tips**

Summary Fields ▼ Operators ▼ | Check Syntax | All ▼ | ABS ▼

EXP_AMOUNT:AVG

ABS(number)

Returns the absolute value of a number, a number without its sign

< Insert   Help on this function

OK Cancel

2. Enter a column name for the formula. This will be displayed within the report.
3. Optionally, enter a description.
4. Select the data type from the **Format** picklist.
5. Select the number of decimal places from the **Decimal Places** picklist.
6. Set the option where this formula is to be displayed.
7. The formula calculation will be displayed in the report at the level that is selected.
8. Build the formula by selecting one of the fields listed in the **Summary Fields** picklist and then select the summary type:

Summary type	Description
Sum	The sum of data in a field or grouping of fields
Largest Value	The largest value of data in a field or grouping of fields
Smallest Value	The smallest value of data in a field or grouping of fields
Average	The average of data in a field or grouping of fields

9. Click on **Operators** to add operators to the formula. Select the function category, choose the function you want to use in your formula, and click on **Insert**.

10. Click on **Check Syntax** to check that the formula contains no errors, and then click on **OK**.

Hiding details when building new reports:
Often when building new reports, you will not necessarily know just how many records are actually going to be returned. This can be the reason for the report in the first place. You may also be experimenting with the report format to see which data is being returned. In these cases, you should set the **Hide Details** option to prevent the detailed data being returned and show just the skeleton of the report this shows the number of rows that will be returned. Limiting rows on a Tabular report allows you to use it as a source report for dashboard table and chart Components. However, if you change the report format, the **Row Limit** setting is automatically removed.

Bucket fields

Bucket fields allow you to categorize values based on fields available in the report type. This means you do not have to create custom formula fields for categories or segmentation of values if they are only relevant in reports. For example, sales managers can bucket or group opportunities by size based on amount, support managers can age cases based on days opened, and sales reps can group accounts into strategic accounts.

Fields available as Bucket fields are **Number**, **Percent**, **Currency**, **Picklist**, and **text** fields.

Changing the Report format

Sometimes it is necessary to change the report format for the existing reports. The effects of changing the report format are as follows:

Report format change	Effects of the change
Change from Tabular to either Summary or Matrix	The Rows to Display filter is not applicable for Summary or Matrix reports, and is therefore removed.
Change from Summary, Matrix, or Joined to Tabular reports	Groupings are not applicable for Tabular reports and are removed from the report. The fields used for grouping are removed and not converted to columns in the Tabular report.
Change from Summary report to Matrix report	The Summary first grouping is used as the first Matrix row grouping. The second Summary grouping is used as the first column grouping. The third Summary grouping is used as the second row grouping. Note: When using the report wizard, the third Summary grouping is automatically removed.
Change from Matrix report to Summary report	The Matrix first row grouping becomes the first Summary grouping. The second row grouping becomes the third Summary grouping. The first column grouping becomes the second Summary grouping. The Matrix second column grouping is removed. Note: When using the report wizard, both the second row grouping and second column grouping are removed.
Change from Tabular, Summary, or Matrix to Joined	The Matrix first row grouping becomes the first Summary grouping. The second row grouping becomes the third Summary grouping. The first column grouping becomes the second summary grouping. The Matrix second column grouping is removed. Note: When using the report wizard, both the second row grouping and second column grouping are removed.

Dashboards

Dashboards are visual information snapshots that are generated from the data in associated reports and are presented as graphical elements. These graphical elements are known as dashboard Components, which can be categorized into five types.

Chart

Chart component types may be used to show data graphically, where the following variety of chart types can be selected: horizontal and vertical bar charts, line charts, pie charts, donut charts, funnel charts, and scatter charts.

Gauge

Gauge component types may be used to show a single value that is to be shown as a part of a range of custom set values. Here, the ranges that can be set can represent, say, low, medium, and high values, and the value from the report is plotted accordingly.

Metric

Metric component types may be used to show a single value to display.

Table

Table component types may be used to show a set of report data in column form.

Visualforce page

In addition to the standard types, Visualforce page component types may be used to create a custom component type and present information in a way not available in the standard dashboard component types.

Dashboards can have up to 20 Components, and you can control users access to dashboards by storing them in folders with appropriate permissions, where folders can be public, hidden, or restricted to groups or roles.

Dashboards can be further configured to run with the concept of a running user, which means that the named users security settings determine which data to display. Here, all dashboard viewers see data according to the security settings of that user who has been set as the running user, irrespective of the dashboard viewers own personal security settings.

A more flexible and dynamic approach, however, allows you to set the running user to be the logged-in user, so that each user is presented with the dashboard according to their own data access level. This is known as dynamic dashboards.

Dashboard component types

In Salesforce CRM, the following dashboard component types are available:

- Horizontal Bar Chart
- Vertical Bar Chart
- Line Chart
- Pie Chart
- Donut Chart
- Funnel Chart
- Scatter Chart
- Gauge
- Metric
- Table

The logos to access these dashboard component types are shown in the following screenshot:

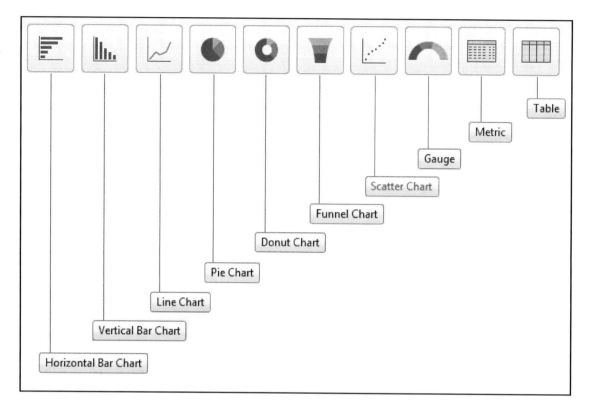

Creating dashboards

Before creating dashboards, you need to have pre-prepared source reports containing the data you wish to display.

 These source reports must be stored in folders that your intended dashboard viewers have access to or they will not be able to view the information.

To create a dashboard, click on the **Reports** tab. This then presents the common reports and dashboards main page with the heading **Reports & Dashboards**. On this page, click on the **New Dashboard** button, as shown in the following screenshot:

| Home | Chatter | Leads | Accounts | Contacts | Reports | Files | Dashboards | Opportunities | Forecasts | Cases | + | ▼ |

Reports & Dashboards   [New Report...] [New Dashboard...]   Guided Tour | Help for this Page

Folders   All Folders

🔍 Find a folder .

All Folders
- Unfiled Public Reports
- My Personal Custom Re...
- My Personal Dashboards
- Incident Dashboards
- Incident Reports
- Working Models
- Account and Contact R...
- Opportunity Reports
- Sales Reports
- Lead Reports
- Support Reports
- Campaign Reports
- Self-Service Reports
- Administrative Reports
- Activity Reports

🔍 Find reports and dashboards...   Recently Viewed ▼   All Types ▼

Action	Name		Folder	Created By
▼ ⊕	Incident Metrics / Support Metrics		Incident Dashboards	Goodey, Paul
▼ ✓	Company Performance Dashboard		My Personal Dashbo...	Goodey, Paul
▼	Efforts per incident		Incident Reports	Goodey, Paul
▼	All Open Incidents		Incident Reports	Goodey, Paul
▼	All Incidents grouped by Status and Appl		Incident Reports	Goodey, Paul
▼	All Incidents Till Date		Incident Reports	Goodey, Paul
▼	Contacts		My Personal Custom...	Goodey, Paul
▼ ⊕	Dashboard Component Types		My Personal Dashbo...	Goodey, Paul
▼	Parent Account		My Personal Custom...	Goodey, Paul

1-25 of 40 ▼   ≪ ◀ Previous Next ▶ ≫   Page 1 of 2

Dynamic dashboards

A dynamic dashboard runs using the security settings of the user viewing the dashboard. Each user sees the dashboard according to his or her own access level. This approach helps you to share one common set of dashboard Components to users with different levels of access. A single dynamic dashboard can display a standard set of metrics across all levels of your organization.

> Salesforce CRM limits at the time of writing permit organizations to have up to five dynamic dashboards for Enterprise Edition and up to ten for Unlimited Edition.

Setting up dynamic dashboards

Before setting up dynamic dashboards, you should create folders, accessible to all dashboard viewers, in which to store dynamic dashboards and corresponding component source reports.

To create dynamic dashboards, follow the steps given here:

1. From the **Dashboards** tab, create a new dashboard by following the steps discussed in the section *Dashboards* in this chapter.
2. Click on the drop-down arrow button to the right of the **View dashboard as field option**.
3. Select the **Run as logged-in user** option.
4. Optionally, check the **Let authorized users change running user checkbox** to enable those with permission to change the running user on the dashboard view page.
5. Click on **OK**.
6. Finally, click **Save** on the main dashboard.

Customizing dashboards

The Salesforce dashboard builder is a drag-and-drop interface for creating and modifying dashboards. To customize an existing dashboard, display it and then click on **Edit**. The dashboard builder main page presents options to set the properties for the dashboard and also to change how the dashboard is viewed by selecting the appropriate running user option.

Clicking on **Dashboard Properties** allows you to set the title, a unique name, and the dashboard folder:

Setting the running user

To view or set the running user for the dashboard, select from the **View** dashboard as option located in the top right of the page:

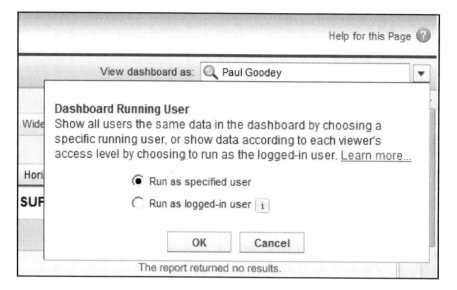

You can add a description to the dashboard by clicking on the text **Click to enter a dashboard description** at the top of the dashboard.

Changes are lost if you close or navigate away from the dashboard builder without saving it first.

Column – level controls

Within the main dashboards editing page, you are able to add the specific dashboard Components:

- Click on + to add a new column. Dashboards can have up to three columns.
- Click on x on a column to delete it. Before removing a column, move the dashboard components to another column if you want them to remain visible.

Dashboards must have at least two columns.

- To set the width for the column, you can select either **Narrow**, **Medium**, or **Wide** in the column-width drop-down list, as shown in the following screenshot:

If the component is a pie or donut chart with **Show Values** or Show **Percentages** enabled and **Legend Position** set to **Right**, the dashboard column width must be **Wide** for the values and percentages to be shown on the dashboard.

Component – level controls

You can add Components by dragging a component type onto a column and then dropping a data source (which is a source report) or a **Visualforce** page onto it.

You can also drop the data source first and then drop a component type onto it. To change the type or source after you have created it, you can drop a different one onto the component. Each component must have a type and a data source.

 Each folder can display up to 200 data sources. However, if there are more than 200, you can use the **Quick Find** option or set filters to reduce the displayed list.

The following screenshot shows the drag-and-drop feature using a report from the **Data Sources** tab:

Dashboard
Company Performance Dashboard

| Save | Save As | Close | ⚙ Dashboard Properties |

| Components | **Data Sources** |

Click to enter a dashboard description.

Narrow ▼ ✕

| Recent | My | All |

🔍 Quick Find

⊟ **Reports**
  ⊟ 📁 My Personal Custom Report
    Opportunity Average Expec
    Sample Report: Closed Sale
    Sample Report: Closed Sale

Gauge   ☑ Opportunity Average Expected Revenue

KEY METRICS

Closed Sales to Date

Wide ▼

ource

Edit Hea

To drag-and-drop a line chart from the **Components** tab, you simply select, hold, and drag the icon onto the source, as shown here:

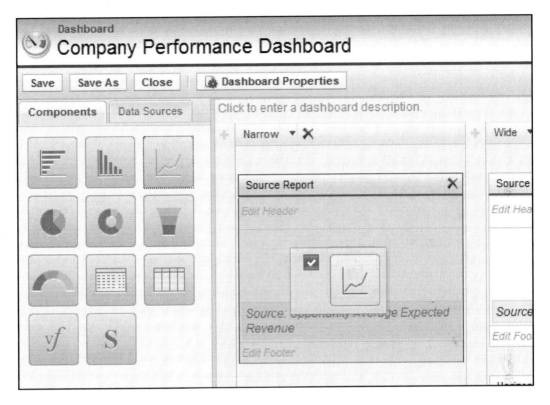

The following screenshot shows the graph displayed after we drag and drop the icon:

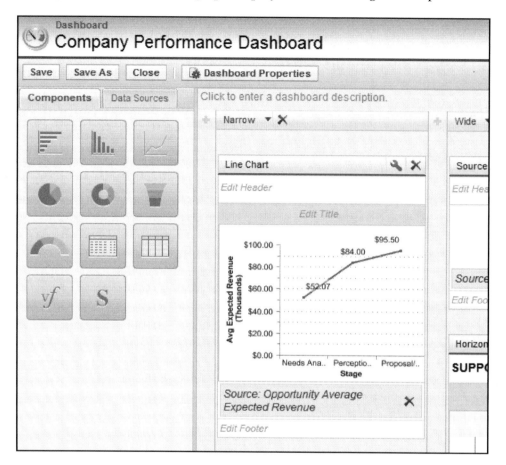

Again, using the drag and drop feature, it is possible to rearrange Components. Start by grabbing Components by the header bar and then dragging them to the right-hand side of the dashboard.

As shown in the preceding screenshot, you can edit or delete the dashboard component and also edit the header, title, and footer.

Here, you can also delete the data source associated with the dashboard component.

Dashboard Metric Components that are positioned above and below each other in a dashboard column are presented together as a single component.

Setting dashboard properties

To set dashboard properties, follow these steps:

1. Edit a dashboard and click on **DashboardProperties**.
2. Enter a title for the dashboard.
3. Select a folder to store the dashboard.
4. Under **ComponentSettings**, select the title color and size, text color, and background fade. If you don't want a gradient, choose the same color for both **StartingColor** and **EndingColor**.
5. Click on **Save**.

Deleting dashboards

Deleting a dashboard also deletes the Components within it, although the custom reports used by the Components are not deleted. Deleted dashboards are moved to the Recycle Bin.

To delete a dashboard, follow these steps:

1. Click on the **Dashboards** tab.
2. Click on **Go To Dashboards List**.
3. Choose the folder where the dashboard is stored.
4. Click on **Del** next to the name of the dashboard.

Printing dashboards

Dashboards can be printed using the web browsers **Print** option. Set the paper orientation to print in landscape format so that it is wide enough for all three columns of dashboard components.

Some dashboards may not print as expected due to browser issues. Here, you can try resizing the dashboard columns and removing the browser-imposed headers and footers. Also, setting the paper orientation to print in landscape format can help ensure that the printed output is wide enough for all three columns that contain the dashboard Components.

Questions to test your knowledge

You are now presented with questions about the key features of Salesforce CRM administration in the areas of **Reports and Dashboards** that have been covered in this chapter. The answers can be found at the end of the chapter.

Questions

We present five questions about report formats, report groupings, Conditional highlighting, dashboard components, and dynamic dashboards to verify your understanding of reports and dashboards.

Question 1 – Report formats

You have been asked to generate a list of contacts for use as a marketing mailing list. Which report type would be the most suitable for this purpose? (Select one):

a) Custom

b) Joined

c) Matrix

d) Tabular

e) Summary

Question 2 – Groupings

You have been asked to generate a report of accounts grouped by the number of employees that the account has. Which report type would be the most suitable for this purpose? (Select one):

a) Tabular

b) Joined

c) Summary

d) Matrix

Question 3 – Conditional Highlighting

Which report type(s) can contain Conditional Highlighting? (Select all that apply):

a) Tabular

b) Summary

c) Matrix

d) Joined

Question 4 – Dashboard Components

What is the maximum number of Components that can be made available on a dashboard? (Select one):

a) 9

b) 12

c) 20

d) 30

Question 5 – Dynamic dashboards

What features or experiences are presented when you set up a dynamic dashboard? (Select all that apply):

a) Dynamic dashboards run using the security settings of the named running user.

b) Dynamic dashboards show blank graphs if the viewing user is a non-active user.

c) Dynamic dashboards run using the security settings of the user viewing the dashboard.

d) Dynamic dashboards refresh automatically when the underlying data changes.

Answers

Here are the answers to the five questions about report formats, report groupings, Conditional highlighting, dashboard components, and dynamic dashboards.

Answer 1 – Report formats

The answer is **d**) Reports generated using the Tabular Report Format are the easiest and quickest way to report data and are most suited for creating lists of records.

Answer 2 – Groupings

The answer is **c**) Summary. Although **b**) Joined and d) Matrix can also be used to create grouped reports, the most suitable (and simplest) report type is Summary. Option **a**) Tabular does not allow the grouping of report data fields.

Answer 3 – Conditional Highlighting

The answer is **b**) Summary, and **c**) Matrix. Conditional Highlighting is used in reports that contain at least one summary field, so Tabular reports cannot be used. Although Joined reports can have grouping, they cannot have Conditional Highlighting.

Answer 4 – Dashboard Components

The answer is **c**). The maximum number of Components that can be made available on a dashboard is 20.

Answer 5 – Dynamic dashboards

The answer is **c**) Dynamic dashboards run using the security settings of the user viewing the dashboard.

Summary

In this chapter, we looked at data analytics, where it was shown how data can be reported and presented within Salesforce CRM. We looked at setting up reports and dashboards, and how to use the report builder.

We covered the use of the building reports from standard and custom report types and looked at the mechanisms for sharing, hiding, and mass deleting reports.

Finally, we posed some questions to help clarify some of the key features of Salesforce reports and dashboards.

In the coming chapter, we will look at the methods for automating business tasks and activities to align them with business rules. The mechanisms that are available to help manage business processes will also be covered in detail, where we will look at the way approvals can be configured.

7
Implementing Business Processes in Salesforce CRM

In the previous chapter, we looked at data analytics, where we covered reports and dashboards.

In this chapter, we will cover in detail how you can automate and streamline the key business processes for your organization with the use of the workflow rules and approval process features within the Salesforce CRM application.

This chapter will focus on how you can configure actions for workflow rules and approval processes to automate, improve quality, and generate high-value processes within your organization.

Finally, you will be presented with a number of questions about the key features of Salesforce CRM administration in the area of Workflow Automation covered in this chapter.

The following topics will be covered:

- Workflow rules
- Approval process
- Workflow actions
- Workflow queue
- Approval wizard
- Approvals in Chatter
- Process visualizer
- Visual Workflow

- Flow Designer
- Introduction to Lightning Process Builder
- Comparison of Workflow Automation Tools

Workflow rules and approval processes

The workflow rules and approval process features within the Salesforce CRM application allow you to automate and streamline key business processes for your organization.

Workflow rules can be used to capture key business processes and events to generate automated actions. They allow you to configure various types of actions to fire based on the field or fields of the record, meeting predefined conditions. In essence, a workflow rule sets workflow actions into motion when its predefined conditions are met. You can configure workflow actions to execute immediately whenever a record meets the conditions specified in the workflow rule, or you can set time-dependent features that execute the workflow actions on a specific day.

Approval processes are a structured set of steps used to facilitate formal sign-off on data records. They can range from simple, single steps to complex, sophisticated routing to provide automated processing that your organization can use to approve records in Salesforce CRM. Along with the steps that must be taken, the approval process also specifies who must approve these steps. Approval steps can either be specified for all records included in the process or restricted to records that have certain attributes. Approval processes also specify the actions that are to be taken when a record is first submitted, approved, rejected, or recalled.

Workflow rules and approval processes provide benefits such as improving the quality and consistency of data, increasing data integrity, improving efficiency and productivity, lowering costs, and reducing risks.

Workflow rules and approval processes allow you to automate the following types of actions: e-mail alerts, tasks, field updates, and outbound messages.

E-mail alerts can be sent to one or more recipients. For example, e-mail alert actions can be used to automatically send an account owner an e-mail whenever updates are made to one of their accounts by another user.

Tasks can be assigned to users or record owners. For example, task actions can be used to automatically assign follow-up tasks to a marketing executive whenever a new lead is entered in the system.

Field updates can be used to modify the value of a field on a record. For example, a field update action can be used to automatically update an opportunity field called **Next Step** when it reaches a certain sales stage.

Outbound messages can be used to send a secure configurable API message (in XML format) to a designated listener. For example, outbound messages can be used to automatically invoke a new account creation process. This could be, say, whenever a new account is entered in the Salesforce CRM application by triggering an outbound API message to an external financial system.

Workflow rules in Salesforce CRM can be combined to help manage an entire process. For example, when a lead is entered through your website using the Web to lead (covered later), workflow rules can be used to automatically send a responding e-mail to the lead contact and also to someone within your organization. Here, a workflow rule can be set to create a task for one of your salespersons to telephone the lead contact along with a reminder e-mail alert, to be sent a specified number of days after the lead record has been entered.

If the salesperson changes the lead status, then a date field could be updated automatically with the date that the lead was contacted.

Up until now, we have looked at the similarity of workflow rules and approval processes. However, there are some key differences. Workflow rules consist of a single step and a single result, whereas approval processes consist of multiple steps and different results depending upon whether the record is approved or rejected. Workflow rules trigger automatically and the rules, when triggered, are not visible to the user. Approval processes, on the other hand, contain multiple steps, each requiring a specific I approve or reject user action by the specified approver(s).

In practice, the first step in creating workflow rules and approval processes is to define and map out the process and, for each step in the process, detail the objects, the criteria, the users, and the actions required.

Workflow and approval actions

Workflow and approval actions consist of e-mail alerts, tasks, field updates, and outbound messages that can be triggered either by a workflow rule or by an approval process:

- **Email alert**: An e-mail alert is an action that can be generated by both workflow and approval actions using an e-mail template that is sent to specified recipients, who can be either Salesforce CRM application users or external e-mail recipients.
- **Field update**: A field update is an action that can be activated by use of both workflow and approval actions, and which specifies the field for update and the new value for it. The field's update action depends on the data type of the field, where you can choose to apply a specific value, clear the field, or calculate a value according to a criterion or a derived formula you can specify.
- **Task**: Tasks are workflow and approval actions that are triggered by workflow rules or approval processes, and they allow the assignment of tasks to a user who you can specify. You would also specify the **Subject**, **Status**, **Priority**, and **Due Date** of the task. Tasks appear on the user's calendar, and can be accessed by the **My Tasks** section of the **Home** tab or on the specific day for the task within the **Day View** section on the user's calendar. Tasks can be assigned on their own, but you can also combine them with an e-mail alert to inform the user.
- **Outbound message**: An outbound message in Salesforce CRM is an action that can be activated by both workflows and approvals, and which sends information to a web URL endpoint, all of which can specify. The outbound message contains the data in specified fields, in what is known as a SOAP message to the endpoint. As this requires development of a receiving web-service, this action is not covered in this book.

Configuring e-mail alerts for workflow rules and approval processes

To configure e-mail alerts, follow the path**Setup** | **Create** | **Workflow**| **Email Alerts**, and then click on the **New Email Alert** button.

Within the **Email Alert Edit** page, the following settings are presented:

approvals, or entitlement processes associated with it.

Email Alert Edit   Save   Save & New   Cancel

Edit Email Alert

Description	Notify Close Date
Unique Name	Notify_Close_Date [i]
Object	Opportunity
Email Template	Notify_Close_Date 🔍
Protected Component	☐
Recipient Type	Search: Case Team ▼ for: Find

Recipients

Availab   Account Owner   **cipients**

  --N Case Team odey
      Creator
      Email Field
      Owner
      Public Groups
      Related Contact
      Related Lead or Contact Owner
      Related User
      Role
      Role and Subordinates
      User

You can enter up to five (5) email addresses to be notified.

Additional Emails	

From Email Address	Current User's email address ▼
	☐ Make this address the default From email address for this object's email alerts. [i]

To set the details for the e-mail alert, carry out the following steps:

1. Enter a description for the e-mail alert.
2. Enter a unique name for the e-mail alert.

The unique name for the e-mail alert is required and used by the API and managed packages. The name is auto-populated when you enter the preceding field, called Description. There are restrictions for permitted characters whereby the unique name must begin with a letter and use only alphanumeric characters and underscores. Also, the unique name cannot end with an underscore nor have two consecutive underscores.

3. Choose an e-mail template.

The **Protected Component** checkbox is used to mark the alert as protected. This option can be ignored as it is a setting used by developers who are building applications with the managed release package functionality. If you install a managed package, there are restrictions on what can be edited by non-developers. Managed Packages in Salesforce are discussed in `Chapter 9`, *Extending and Enhancing Salesforce CRM*.

4. Now select who should receive this e-mail alert from the available options:

Recipients	Description
Account Owner	If the **Account Owner** is selected, then the e-mail alert is sent to the user in Salesforce CRM who is set as the account owner of either the account record or the account that is related to the record. Since this option requires an account relationship to be present, it is only valid on accounts, opportunities, contacts, and custom objects that are children of the account object.
Account Team	Choose from the list of users that are assigned to a particular accounts team role. Note that e-mail alerts are only sent when the rule is associated with the account object or any of its direct child objects.
Case Team	Choose from the list of users assigned to a particular case team role.
Creator	This is the user listed as the record creator, and is the user who is set in the **Created By** field.
Customer Portal User	Choose from the list of users that are associated with a Customer Portal.
Email Field	An e-mail address field on the selected object, such as the **Email Field** on contact records or a custom e-mail field.
Owner	The record owner.
Partner User	Choose from the list of users that are associated with a partner portal.

Portal Role	Choose from the list of users that are assigned to a particular portal role.
Portal Role and Subordinates	Choose from the list of users assigned to a particular portal role, plus all users in roles below that role.
Public Groups	Choose from the list of users in a particular public group.
Related Contact	An associated contact on the record. For example, you may have created a custom contact on the opportunity object called **Key Decision Maker**.
Related Lead or Contact Owner	This is a related user lookup to the owner fields set on either the lead or contact record that is associated to the record. As an example, for opportunities, this field could be set to a contact role field linking to a contact.
Related User	A Related User is a user lookup field that is associated to the record. As an example, this field may be set to the **Last Modified By** field.
Role	Choose from the list of users assigned a particular role.
Role and Internal Subordinates	Choose from the list of users in a particular role, plus all users in roles below that role, excluding partner portal and customer portal users.
Role and Subordinates	Choose from the list of users in a particular role, plus all users in roles below that role.
User	Choose from the list of available users in Salesforce CRM.
Opportunity Team	Once you have set up sales opportunity teams, this option allows you to choose from the list of users associated to an opportunity team.

Select the recipients who should receive this e-mail alert in the **Available Recipients** list and click on **Add**.

 If you change the object after selecting the recipients, the **Selected Recipients** list will be automatically cleared.

Optionally, enter to and from e-mail addresses, and then click on **Save**.

Here, you can do the following:

- Enter up to five additional recipient e-mail addresses (which may or may not be users in Salesforce)
- Set the **From Email Address** to either the current user's e-mail address or to the default workflow user's e-mail address
- Finally, to begin using the e-mail alert, associate it with either a workflow rule or an approval process

Set the From Email Address:
Setting the **From Email Address** also allows you to use a standard global e-mail address for your organization, such as `Customer_Services@WidgetXYZ.com`, instead of the default **From** field, which is the e-mail address of the user who updates the record. Only verified, organization-wide e-mail addresses will appear in the **From Email Address** picklist options.

There is a daily limit of 1,000 e-mail alerts per standard Salesforce license for workflows and approvals.

There is also an overall daily limit of 2 million e-mail alerts for your entire organization and when the daily limits are reached, a warning e-mail is sent out by the Salesforce CRM application to the default workflow user where one is set. If there is no default workflow user set, then the warning e-mail goes out to a system administrator.

Organization-wide e-mail addresses

By setting up organization-wide e-mail addresses, your users can share a set of common e-mail aliases. Here, you can define a list of organization-wide e-mail addresses for each user profile.

When sending e-mails from Salesforce, users with these profiles can then choose a different From address than the e-mail address that they have defined on their user record, and any e-mail responses are then returned to the organization-wide address.

To set up the list of organization-wide e-mail addresses, follow the path **Setup** | **Email Administration** | **Organization-Wide Addresses**.

From **Organization-Wide Addresses**, you can set the display name, the e-mail address, and the profiles that are permitted to use that address, as shown in the following screenshot:

Edit Organization-Wide Email Addresses

Help for this Page ❓

An organization-wide email address associates a single email address to a user profile. Each user in the profile can send email using this address. Users will share the same display name and email address.

| Save | Save and New | Cancel |

Organization-Wide Email Address

❚ = Required Information

Display Name ❚ Cust_Srv WidgetsXYZ

Email Address ❚ vices@WidgetXYZ.com

○ Allow All Profiles to Use this From Address
◉ Allow Only Selected Profiles to Use the From Address

Profiles
```
Standard Platform User
Partner User
Customer Portal Manager
Authenticated Website
High Volume Customer Portal
System Admin Custom
System Administrator
Solution Manager
Read Only
Custom: Sales Profile
```

| Save | Save and New | Cancel |

When the organization-wide e-mail address is saved or changed, Salesforce will send an e-mail to the address specified in the e-mail address field to verify that the e-mail address is valid, as shown in the following screenshot:

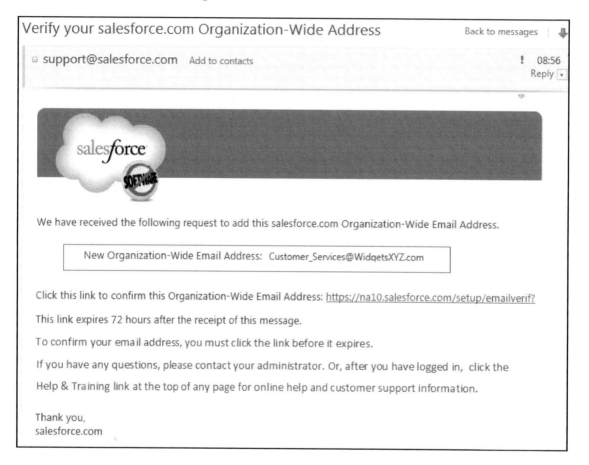

Now, the verified organization-wide e-mail addresses will appear in the **From Email Address** picklist options when configuring e-mail alerts, as shown in the following screenshot:

From Email Address	Default Workflow User's email address ▾	
	Current User's email address	ess for this object's email alerts. [i]
	Default Workflow User's email address	
	"Cust_Srv WidgetsXYZ"	
	Save Save & New Cancel	

Configuring tasks for workflow rules and approval processes

To configure tasks, follow the path **Setup** | **Create** | **Workflow** | **Tasks**, and then click on the **New Task** button.

From the **Step 1: Select Object** page, select the object type for the record from the **Select Object** picklist and click on **Next**.

 When creating tasks for custom objects, only custom objects that have been set with activities are available for selection in the picklist.

Within the **Step 2: Configure Task** page, the following settings are presented:

Step 2 : Configure Task		Step 2 of 2

Step 2 : Configure Task   **Step 2 of 2**

Previous | Save | Cancel

Create a task to associate with one or more workflow rules, approval processes, or entitlement processes. When changing a task, any modifications will apply to all rules, approvals, or entitlement processes associated with it.

Edit Task | = Required Information

Object	Opportunity	Status	Not Started
Assigned To	[ ]	Priority	Normal
Subject	[ ]		
Unique Name	[ ]		
Due Date	--None--	plus	days
Notify Assignee	☐		
Protected Component	☐		

Description Information

| Comments | [ ] |

To set the details for the task, carry out the following steps:

1. You must select an individual or individuals for whom you want to can set the required **Assigned To** field. Here, the options when you click on the lookup dialog for the. **Assigned To** setting allow for the selection of either **User**, **Role**, or **Record Owner**.

 If the assignee of a workflow task is a role, and that particular role has multiple users, the record owner is then assigned the task. This is done regardless of the type of role that the record owner has, which can cause some confusion. This is because tasks cannot be assigned to more than one user, and hence best practice dictates that you do not assign tasks to roles, even though the option exists.

2. Enter a subject and a unique name for the task.

The unique name for the task is required and used by the API and any managed packages. The name is auto-populated when you move from the preceding field, called **Subject**. There are restrictions for permitted characters, whereby the unique name must begin with a letter and use only alphanumeric characters and underscores. Also, the unique name cannot end with an underscore nor have two consecutive underscores.

3. Choose a due date, status, and priority, where due dates appear in the time zone of the assignee.

4. Set the **Notify Assignee** checkbox to also send an e-mail notification when the task is assigned.

The **Protected Component** checkbox is used to mark the alert as protected. This is used by developers who are building managed package applications for the AppExchange marketplace (AppExchange is covered in `Chapter 9`, *Extending and Enhancing Salesforce CRM*).

5. Finally, to set the task into action, associate it with the required workflow rule or approval process.

6. Optionally, enter any comments for the description information that is included with the task and then click on **Save**.

When the task is assigned, it will include a **Created By** field that contains the name of the person who saved the record that triggered the rule to assign the task.

Configuring field updates for workflow rules and approval processes

To configure field updates, follow the path **Setup** | **Create** | **Workflow** | **Field Updates**, and then click on the **New Field Update** button.

Within the **Field Update Edit** page, perform the following:

1. Enter a name and a unique name for the field update.

Both the name and a unique name for the field update are required. The unique name is used by the API and managed packages. The name is auto-populated when you exit the preceding **Name** field. There are restrictions for permitted characters in that the unique name must begin with a letter and use only alphanumeric characters and underscores. Also, the unique name cannot end with an underscore or have two consecutive underscores.

2. Now, optionally, enter a description for the field to update and then choose the object type to present the field to be updated, as shown here for the **Opportunity** object:

Field Update Edit | Save | Save & New | Cancel |

Identification ❘ = Required Information

Name	New Deal Close Date
Unique Name	New_Deal_Close_Date ⓘ
Description	This automatically sets the Close date to be 60 days in advance for new opportunities
Object	Opportunity ▾
Field to Update	Close Date ▾
Field Data Type	Date

Specify New Field Value

Date Options

◉ Use a formula to set the new value
Show Formula Editor

Today() + 60

Use formula syntax: e.g., Text in double quotes: "hello", Number: 25, Percent as decimal: 0.10, Date expression: Today() + 7

| Save | Save & New | Cancel |

Upon choosing the object and field to update, a new section called **Specify New Field Value** appears where you can set the logic of the desired field update. Here, the available options depend on the type of field you are updating, with the following options.

Checkboxes

For checkboxes, choose **True** to select the checkbox and **False** to deselect it, as shown in the following screenshot:

This is useful for automating the setting of status flags for records whenever a certain business process is completed. In the previous example, the field update of the field **Publish to Web?** allows the automatic setting of the checkbox option to **True**, say, so that the record can be published.

Record owners

For record owners, choose the user to whom the record should be assigned, as shown in the following screenshot:

Object	Opportunity ▾
Field to Update	Opportunity Owner ▾
Field Data Type	Lookup

Specify New Field Value

Opportunity Owner	User ▾	🔍
Notify Assignee	☐	

Save   Save & New   Cancel

This is useful for automating the changing of the record owner for records whenever a certain business process is complete. For example, you could automate the field update of the record owner from, say, a marketing executive to an account manager, if a lead matches certain criteria. When selecting the user for the record owner field update, you must use the user lookup icon and select a specific active user. You cannot, therefore, automatically derive the new owner from any given criteria.

Selecting **Notify Assignee** allows the automatic sending of an e-mail to the new record owner whenever the field update fires.

Picklists

For picklist fields, you can either select a specific value from the picklist or you can select the value above or below the current value as shown in the following screenshot. The options **The value above the current one** and **The value below the current one** selection is based on the sorting order that is set in the **Picklist** field definition:

Other data types

For all other data types, you can set the following **Text Options** as shown here:

Follow these steps to finish the field update configuration:

1. Choose **A blank value (null)** if you want to remove any existing value and leave the field blank.

> This option is not available for required fields, checkboxes, and some other types of fields.

2. Choose **Use a formula to set the new value** to calculate the value based on the formula logic.
3. Now click on **Save** to complete the configuration of the field update.
4. Finally, to set the field update into action, associate it with the required workflow rule or approval process.

Configuring outbound message notifications for workflow rules and approval processes

An outbound message in Salesforce CRM is an action – that can be activated by both workflows and approvals – that sends information to a web-URL endpoint you specify.

The outbound message contains the data using the specified fields in what is known as a SOAP message to the endpoint URL. Once the endpoint receives the message data, it consumes the information from the message and processes it.

> The **Simple Object Access Protocol** (**SOAP**) is an industry-standard protocol that defines a uniform way of passing data encoded in the XML format. **Extensible Markup Language** (**XML**) is an industry-standard markup language that enables the sharing and transportation of structured data.

As this requires the development of a receiving web-service endpoint, setting up this action is beyond the scope of this book.

Configuring workflow rules

You can configure your organization's workflow by creating workflow rules. Each workflow rule consists of the following:

- Criteria that cause the Salesforce CRM application to trigger the workflow rule
- Actions that execute immediately when a record matches the criteria
- Time-dependent actions that the Salesforce CRM application processes when a record matches the criteria, and executes according to the specified time triggers

The following table is an overview of the key aspects of configuring workflow rules in Salesforce CRM:

Rules		>Actions		Users
Object	Criteria	E-mail alerts	Immediate	People
			Time-dependent	
		Tasks	Immediate	
			Time-dependent	
		Field updates	Immediate	System
			Time-dependent	
		Outbound messages	Immediate	
			Time-dependent	
>Example workflow rule				
Opportunity	Whenever an opportunity record is updated	E-mail Alert	Immediate	Account Owner

 Create workflow actions ahead of workflow rules. Create actions and any associated e-mail templates before starting to configure workflow rules.

The following outlines the steps required to create a workflow rule:

1. Create the workflow rule and select the object.
2. Configure the settings and criteria for the workflow rule.
3. Specify the workflow actions.
4. Activate the workflow rule.

To create a workflow rule, follow the path **Setup | Create | Workflow & Approvals | Workflow Rules**.

The **Workflow Rules** detail page shows a list of the current workflow rules, along with various properties such as the associated object and whether the rule is active. On this page, you can create views to help filter and manage the list of rules as the numbers increase. The following screen shows the list of all the workflow rules in our organization using the **All Workflow Rules** view:

All Workflow Rules

Help for this Page

Configure your organization's workflow by creating workflow rules. Each workflow rule consists of:

- Criteria that cause salesforce.com to apply the workflow rule.
- Immediate actions that execute when a record matches the criteria. For example, salesforce.com can automatically send an email that notifies the account team when a new high-value opportunity is created.
- Time-dependent actions that salesforce.com queues when a record matches the criteria, and executes according to time triggers. For example, salesforce.com can automatically send an email reminder to the account team if a high-value opportunity is still open ten days before the close date.

Quick Tips

- Getting Started
- Resources on CRM Community
- Useful Sample Workflow Rules
- Video Tutorial (English Only)

View: All Workflow Rules | Edit | Create New View

A | B | C | D | E | F | G | H | I | J | K | L | M | N | O | P | Q | R | S | T | U | V | W | X | Y | Z | Other | **All**

New Rule

Action	Rule Name ↑	Description	Object	Active
Edit	Del	Deactivate	Test		MD One	✓
Edit	Deactivate	Timer		MD One	✓

A | B | C | D | E | F | G | H | I | J | K | L | M | N | O | P | Q | R | S | T | U | V | W | X | Y | Z | Other | **All**

From the **Workflow Rules list** page, you can click on the **New Rule** button and then select an object (either a custom or standard object) on which you want to apply your new workflow rule. In the **Step 1: Select object** screen shown as follows, the standard object, **Opportunity,** has been selected:

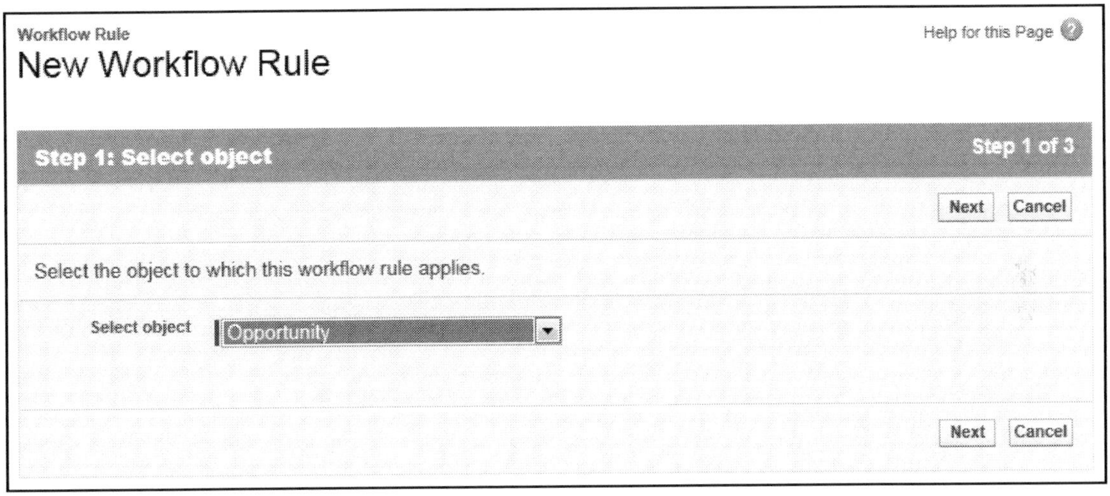

Workflow Rule

New Workflow Rule

| Step 1: Select object | Step 1 of 3 |

Next Cancel

Select the object to which this workflow rule applies.

Select object [Opportunity ▼]

Next Cancel

Help for this Page ②

Now, click on **Next** to navigate and display the **Step 2: Configure Workflow Rule** page to allow the rule settings and criteria to be specified, as shown in the following screenshot:

Configuring rule settings and criteria

In the **Edit Rule** section, you must enter a rule name and, optionally, you may enter a description for the rule.

Evaluation Criteria

In the **Evaluation Criteria** section, you choose the appropriate criteria that causes the Salesforce CRM application to trigger the workflow rule.

The criteria can be selected from the following three options:

- **created**: Choose this option to ignore any subsequent updates to existing records, as the rule will only ever run once: when the record is inserted.
- **created, and every time it's edited**: Choose this option to include new record inserts and updates to existing records. These actions cause repeated triggering of the rule as long as the record meets the criteria.

 You cannot add time-dependent actions to a rule if you choose the created, and every time it's edited option.

- **created, and any time it's edited to subsequently meet criteria**: Choose this option to include new records and updates to existing records.

 The rule is not re-triggered on record updates that do not affect the specified rule criteria.

For example, if the updating of an opportunity record's probability to 90 percent causes the rule to run, with this option, the rule will only get triggered again if the probability changes and then changes back to 90 percent, regardless of how many times the record is itself updated.

Rule Criteria

In the **Rule Criteria** section, there are two ways of formulating the logic used to trigger the workflow rule. They are as follows:

- Run this rule if the following criteria are met
- Run this rule if the following formula evaluates to true

Run this rule if the following criteria are met

This option is displayed by default and allows you to select the filter criteria a record must meet to trigger the rule.

As an example, the filter has been set to one of the following:

- **Opportunity: Close Date equals NEXT 7 DAYS AND**
- **Opportunity: Closed not equal to True**

These criteria would allow us to construct a workflow rule to notify a salesperson that they have an open opportunity with a close date that will be reached within a week:

Clicking on the **Add Filter Logic** link presents additional options for adding rows and advanced filter conditions, as shown in the following screenshot:

Rule Criteria

Run this rule if the following | criteria are met ▾ | :

	Field		Operator		Value	
1.	Opportunity: Close Date	▾	equals	▾	NEXT 7 DAYS	
2.	Opportunity: Closed	▾	not equal to	▾	True	🔍
3.	--None--	▾	--None--	▾		
4.	--None--	▾	--None--	▾		
5.	--None--	▾	--None--	▾		

Add Row Remove Row

Clear Filter Logic
Filter Logic:

| 1 AND 2 | Tips ? |

Example: If you wanted to filter to key deals for your company, where key deals are deals over $1,000,000 that are closing in the next 45 days, or deals owned by a VP, you would set up your filters as follows

Advanced Filters:

	Field	Operator	Value
1.	Amount	greater than	1 000000
2.	Closed Date	equals	NEXT 45 DAYS
3.	Owner Role	starts with	VP
4.	--None--	equa	

Advanced Filter Conditions:
(1 AND 2) OR 3

ALL OPPORTUNITIES

Amount > $1M

Close Date = next 45 days

Deals owned by a VP

1 and 2   3

RESULT

Save   Cancel

The **Add Row** link allows you to add more criteria options, where up to a maximum of 25 can be added.

The **Filter Logic** section allows you to use Boolean expressions to set the criteria. These expressions are known as **Advanced Filters**.

For example, **(1 AND 2)** results in an expression that requires both of the first two filter lines to be valid.

Run this rule if the following formula evaluates to true option

This option allows you to enter a formula that returns a value of True or False. The Salesforce CRM application triggers the rule if the formula returns True.

Workflow formulas can be used to capture complicated logic, as in the following use-case example.

Whenever an opportunity is set as lost, where the sales stage was previously **Negotiation/Review** and the amount is greater than $50,000, send an e-mail or task to be sent to Sales Management for follow-up:

Rule Criteria

Run this rule if the following [formula evaluates to true ▼] :

Example: [OwnerId <> LastModifiedById] evaluates to true when the person who last modified the record is not the record owner. More Examples ...

[Insert Field]   [Insert Operator ▼]   Functions
                                                                        [-- All Function Categories -- ▼]

```
AND
(
  ISCHANGED(StageName),
  ISPICKVAL(PRIORVALUE(StageName), "Negotiation/Review"),
  ISPICKVAL(StageName,"Closed Lost"),
  Amount > 50000
)
```
ABS
AND
BEGINS
BLANKVALUE
BR
CASE

[Insert Selected Function]

[Check Syntax] No errors found

[Previous] [Save & Next] [Cancel]

 Some functions are not available in workflow rule formulas; you cannot create a formula in which a custom object references fields on a parent object.

In addition to the functions shown on the right-hand side of the **Rule Criteria** section, you can also use merge fields for directly related objects in workflow-rule formulas. The **formula evaluates to true** rule can be useful wherever it is needed to trigger some actions, if the value of a particular field is being changed. As for all formula-merge fields that allow you to reference fields on related objects across multiple relationships, the field name is prefixed by the name of the relationship. For standard relationships, the name of the relationship is the master object. For example, you can reference the account name merge field from an opportunity using `Account.Name`.

Click on the **Check Syntax** button to validate that the formula contains no error before progressing beyond this page.

Now click on **Save & Next** to proceed to the **Step 3: Specify Workflow Actions** page, which allows you to configure the workflow actions.

Specifying the workflow actions

The **Specify Workflow Actions** page allows you to add both immediate and time-dependent actions to the workflow rule, as shown in the following screenshot:

Immediate workflow actions

Immediate actions trigger as soon as the evaluation criteria are met. As shown in the preceding example, the Salesforce CRM application can immediately send an e-mail to the salesperson if an opportunity is created or edited and is still open seven days before the specified close date.

Time-dependent workflow actions

Time-dependent actions specify when Salesforce CRM is to execute the workflow action. As shown in the preceding example, the Salesforce CRM application can automatically send an e-mail reminder to the salesperson three days later if an opportunity is created or edited and is still open seven days before the specified close date.

Time-dependent actions and time triggers are complex features with several considerations Workflow rules that have time-dependent actions should be specified with a default workflow user to ensure they fire for future actions. This is in case the user who activated the workflow later leaves the organization and is set as an inactive user.

Adding immediate workflow actions

To add an immediate workflow action, click on the **Add Workflow Action** drop-down selection in the **Immediate Workflow Actions** section and choose either **New Task**, **New Email Alert**, **New Field Update**, **New Outbound Message**, or **Select Existing Action** to select an existing action to associate with the rule:

- **New Task** to create a task to associate with the rule
- **New Email** to create an e-mail alert to associate with the rule
- **New Field Update** to define a field update to associate with the rule
- **New Outbound Message** to define an outbound message to associate with the rule
- **Existing Action** to select an existing action to associate with the rule

Adding time-dependent workflow actions

To add a time-dependent workflow action, click on **Add Time Trigger** in the **Time-Dependent Workflow Actions** section. Then, specify the number of days or hours before or after a date relevant to the record, such as the date the record was created or modified, or even for an opportunity close date, as shown in the following screenshot:

The **Add Time Trigger** button is not displayed and the option to create a time trigger is unavailable under the following workflow rule scenarios:

- The workflow rule criteria has been configured to fire using the option, **created, and any time it's edited to subsequently meet criteria**
- The workflow rule is already active (here, you must temporarily deactivate it in order to apply the action)
- The workflow rule is not active, but there are pending actions which are yet to be processed in the workflow queue

Additional, immediate, or time-dependent actions can now be configured. Finally, click on the **Done** button in the top-right corner of the screen.

Activating the workflow rule

The Salesforce CRM application will not trigger a workflow rule until you have manually activated it.

To activate a workflow rule, click on **Activate** on the workflow rule detail page. Click on **Deactivate** to stop a rule from triggering (or if you want to edit the time-dependent actions and time triggers associated with the rule):

Action	Rule Name ↑	Description	Object	Active
Edit | Del | Activate	Close Date Within 7 Days	Any Open Opportunities are due to be closed within 7 days	Opportunity	
Edit | Del | Activate	Lost Negotiation 50k		Opportunity	
Edit | Del | Deactivate	Test		MD One	✓
Edit | Deactivate	Timer		MD One	✓

View: All Workflow Rules ▾ Edit | Create New View

A | B | C | D | E | F | G | H | I | J | K | L | M | N | O | P | Q | R | S | T | U | V | W | X | Y | Z | Other | **All**

New Rule

Workflow rule considerations

Consider the following when configuring workflow rules:

- You can deactivate a workflow rule at any time. However, if you deactivate a rule that has pending actions, Salesforce.com completes those actions as long as the record that triggered the rule is not updated.
- You cannot add time-dependent workflow actions to active workflow rules. You must deactivate the workflow rule first, add the time-dependent workflow action, and then re-activate the rule.
- Workflow rules on custom objects are automatically deleted if the custom object is deleted.
- You cannot create e-mail alerts for workflow rules on activity records.
- Creating new records or updating existing records can trigger more than one rule.
- Time-dependent field updates can retrigger the re-evaluation of workflow rules.
- The order in which actions are executed is not guaranteed. Field update actions are executed first, followed by other actions.

For custom, and some standard, objects, you can create workflow actions where a change to a detail record updates a field on the related master record.

For example, in a custom publishing application, you may create a workflow rule that sets the status of a book (the master object) to **In Process – Author** when a chapter (the detail object) is being reviewed by the editor.

Cross-object field updates work for custom-to-custom master-detail relationships, custom-to-standard master-detail relationships, and a few standard-to-standard master-detail relationships. They are displayed in the following way:

Identification				= R
Name	Update Book Status			
Unique Name	Update_Book_Status [i]			
Description	Update the Status of the book title whenever a chapter status is being set			
Object	Chapter			
Field to Update	Book ▼	Status ▼		
Field Data Type	Picklist			

Specify New Field Value

Picklist Options
- The value above the current one
- The value below the current one
- ⦿ A specific value In Process - Author ▼

 If you require cross-object actions for standard objects such as updating a field on each **Opportunity Product** record when a certain field on the **Opportunity** changes, or further complex updating such as automatic record creation or deletion actions, you would need to use Process Builder, Visual Workflow or develop **Apex triggers** instead of workflow rules.

Monitoring the workflow queue

You can use the time-based workflow queue to monitor any outstanding workflow rule that has time-dependent actions. Here you can view pending actions and cancel them if necessary.

To access the **Time-Based Workflow** queue, follow the path **Setup** | **Monitoring** | **Time-Based Workflow**, where the following page is presented:

Click on **Search** to view all the pending actions for any active time-based workflow rules, or set the filter criteria and click on **Search** to view only the pending actions that match the criteria. Set the checkbox for any listed workflow rule(s) you wish to cancel and then click on **Delete** to terminate the selected queued workflow rule(s).

In summary, workflow rules allow one or more actions to fire based on fields on the record (or its parent) meeting certain conditions. Workflow rules are a little more complex than validation rules, and take a bit more familiarity with Salesforce.com to properly execute. However, they can offer powerful business automation and can be implemented without any custom code or the work of a developer.

Approval process

An approval process in Salesforce CRM is an automated mechanism that you can set up to process the approval of records within your organization.

Working with approval processes involves the creation of a structured set of steps to enable the sign-off of specified records that must be approved, along with specifying which users must be set to approve it at each of the steps. Here, each step can apply to all the records within the process or specified records that have certain field values. The building of approval processes also requires the setting of the required actions to be taken after the record is either first submitted, approved, rejected, or recalled for approval.

Approval processes are similar to workflow rules in the sense that they can invoke the same key actions; however, there are significant differences between workflow rules and approval processes, such as:

- Workflow rules are activated when a record is saved, whereas approval processes are manually triggered by explicitly clicking on the **Submit for Approval** button.
- Workflow rules consist of a single step and a single action. Approval processes consist of multiple steps, where a different action is taken based upon whether the record is approved or rejected.
- Workflows can be modified or deleted. In approvals, some attributes cannot be modified, and approval processes must be deactivated before outstanding approvals can be deleted.
- Approval processes result in the approval history being automatically tracked, which is not applied to workflow rules.
- When an approval is initiated, the record is locked down and cannot be changed by someone, other than the approver or system administrator, until the record has completed the approval process.

Approval processes require a good understanding of your business rules and processes in order to be successfully implemented.

They must, therefore, be implemented correctly, so that records are locked down only when necessary to avoid hindering Salesforce users that are attempting to update records.

Approval processes can, however, be a powerful mechanism to control an internal process that must be completed as part of a business process.

Example uses for approval processes are obtaining management sign-off before quotes or contracts are sent to customers or prospects for certain deals, or getting authorization before users are set up in the Salesforce CRM application itself. In this example, the user activation request could be approved by the sales management team and individuals from other departments, such as finance, before the user license is obtained and the user record created.

In the same way as workflow actions, approval actions consist of e-mail alerts, tasks, field updates, and outbound messages that can be triggered by the approval process.

The following outlines the work items required to configure approval processes:

- Providing the name of the process
- Specifying the entry criteria for the records
- Specifying who is going to approve
- Specifying the e-mail template
- Determining the fields to be displayed on the approver page
- Specifying who is going to send the approval mail

Approval process checklist

It is useful to plan Salesforce CRM approval processes carefully to help ensure a successful and smooth implementation. The following checklist specifies the required information and prerequisites needed before starting to configure your approval process:

- Determine the steps and how many levels your process has. It is often useful to map out the process using a charting tool such as Microsoft Visio.
- Decide if users can approve requests by e-mail and set up this feature accordingly.
- Create an approval-request e-mail template.
- Determine the approval-request sender.
- Determine the assigned approver.
- Determine the delegated approver, if necessary.
- Decide if your approval process needs a filter.
- Design initial submission actions.

- Determine if users can edit records that are awaiting approval.
- Decide if records should be auto-approved or rejected.
- Determine the actions when an approval request is approved or rejected.

Salesforce recommends that you educate users about each approval process and the entry criteria for the approval process. This is because users have no visibility of which approval processes are fired when the **Submit for Approval** button is pressed. Furthermore, Salesforce shows an error if the user is not an allowed submitter for the approval process or the record does not meet the entry criteria.

Approvals in Chatter

If your organization has both Approvals and Chatter enabled, you can activate Approvals in Chatter, which enables users to receive approval requests in their Chatter feeds. To enable **Approvals in Chatter**, navigate to **Setup | Customize | Chatter | Chatter Settings**. Click the **Edit** button and check the **Allow Approvals** checkbox, as shown in the following screenshot:

Approval Posts

Allow users to receive approval requests as posts.

Allow Approvals ☑

The approval request appears as a Chatter post, which you can customize by creating unique post templates and associating them with the approval processes.

Approvals in Chatter checklist

To ensure that your users will see their approval requests as Chatter posts and everything works correctly, it is recommended that you follow this checklist when you are ready to activate **Approvals in Chatter** for your organization:

- Create an approval process as described in the *Configuring approval processes* section in this chapter.

- Enable **Chatter feed** tracking for the object on which your approval process is based (this is described in `Chapter 8`, *Introducing Sales Cloud, Service Cloud, and Collaborative Features of Salesforce CRM*).
- Create an approval post template for the object on which your approval process is based. If you want to make this the default template for all approval processes on this object, be sure to check the **Default** checkbox when configuring your post template as described in the *Configuring approval processes* section in this chapter .
- Activate the **Enable Approvals in Chatter** setting.

 Activating the Enable Approvals in Chatter setting as the last step ensures that all approval processes are properly configured to make use of it and, once activated, all existing active approval processes will start generating Chatter approval posts.

Configuring approval processes

To create an approval process, follow these steps:

1. Launch the approval process wizard.
2. Specify **Name**, **UniqueName**, and **Description**.
3. Specify **Criteria** for **EnteringProcess**.
4. Specify **Approver Field** and **Record Editability**.
5. Select **Email Notification Template**.
6. Configure **Approval Request Page Layout**.
7. Specify **Initial Submitters**.
8. Activate the approval process.

Choosing an approval process wizard

When you click on the **Create New Approval Process** button to start creating an approval process, you are presented with the following two options in which to build the process: **Use Jump Start Wizard** or **Use Standard Setup Wizard**. The following sections outline the differences between these two mechanisms.

Jump Start Wizard

The **Jump Start Wizard** is provided as a quick way to create simple approval processes that have a single step. To simplify the settings, with this option the Salesforce CRM application automatically determines some default options for you.

Standard Setup Wizard

The **Standard Setup Wizard** enables the creation of complex approval processes, and is used where multiple processing steps are required. This option provides the mechanisms to define your process and then uses a setup wizard to define each step within that process.

To create an approval process, follow the path **Setup** | **Create** | **Workflow & Approvals** | **Approval Processes**.

Choose the object for the new approval process, click on it, and then select **Use Standard Setup Wizard**, as shown in the following screenshot, where we have selected **Opportunity**:

To set the details for the approval process, carry out the following:

In **Step 1**. Enter Name and Description page (where this is step 1 of 6): enter a **Process Name**, a **Unique Name**, and optionally a **Description**, and then click on **Next**

To specify the entry criteria, which is an optional step on the **Step 2. Specify Entry Criteria** page and is used to determine the records that enter the approval process, you can either choose from the formula logic, or you can select certain fields, operators, and values to specify when the desired criteria are met. This is shown in the following screenshot, which is presented as Step 2 of 6:

Specify Entry Criteria

Use this approval process if the following `criteria are met` ▾ :

Field		Operator		Value		
Opportunity: Amount ▾		greater than ▾		100000		AND
Opportunity: Stage ▾		equals ▾		Proposal/Price Quote	🔍	AND
Opportunity: Closed ▾		equals ▾		False	🔍	AND
Current User: Department ▾		equals ▾		Sales		AND
--None-- ▾		--None-- ▾				

Add Filter Logic...

Previous | Next | Cancel

In **Step 2: Specify Entry Criteria**, either enter the filter criteria for records that are to be included by this approval process, or leave all the filters blank to have all records submitted within the approval process.

Restricting the approval process for specific users:
If only specific users are involved in this approval process, you can specify it here. For example, if only the sales team is to submit opportunity reviews, enter the following filter criteria: **Current User: Department Equals Sales**. As shown in the preceding screenshot, in the fourth entry criteria row where **Field** is **Current User: Department**, **Operator** is **equals** and **Value** is **Sales**.

Click on **Next** to set the **Specify Approver Field andRecord Editability** options.

In this step (step 3 of 6), you would specify who the users are for the approval steps in Salesforce CRM. Here, a user field can be used to automatically route approval requests. This field can be the **Manager** field on an individual's user record, or you can create a custom hierarchical (User to User) field on the User object.

In **Step 3. Specify Approver Field and Record Editability Properties**, using the **Next Automated Approver Determined By** picklist, select a user field if you want the Salesforce CRM application to automatically assign approval requests to an approver based on the value in the user field. For example, you may want to automatically send approval requests to a user's manager as specified in the user's **Manager** field, as shown in the following screenshot:

To allow users to manually choose another user that will approve any approval requests, leave the **Next Automated Approver Determined By** field blank:

- By selecting the **Use Approver Field of Record Owner** checkbox, you can set the approval process to use the standard **Manager** field or a custom field on the record owner's user record instead of the submitting user's record.

If you set the Use Approver Field of Record Owner checkbox (applying the manager of the record owner instead of the manager of the submitting user), it is applied to all subsequent steps.

- Select the appropriate **Record Editability Properties** and click on **Next**.

When a record is in the approval process, it is always locked, and only you as system administrator can edit it. However, you can specify that the currently assigned approver can also edit the record.

- When an approval process assigns an approval request to a user, Salesforce.com automatically sends the user an approval request e-mail. This e-mail contains a web link that the user can click on to access the approval page within the Salesforce CRM application, which lets the user approve or reject the request and also enter comments.

By enabling e-mail approval response, the user can alternatively reply to the e-mail by typing approve, approved, yes, reject, rejected, or no in the first line of the e-mail body, and then add comments in the second line. This option makes it easy to approve or reject approval requests, and is especially useful for users who access approval requests using a mobile device.

- In **Step 4. Select Notification Templates**, you can choose a custom e-mail template to be used when notifying an approver that an approval request has been assigned to them, as shown in the following screenshot for the example **Approval Request** template. Alternatively, by leaving this field blank, a simple default e-mail template is used. In addition, if **Approvals in Chatter** has been enabled, you can also choose an **Approval Post Template**, as shown in the following screenshot:

E-mail approval response

By enabling e-mail approval response, the user can alternatively reply to the e-mail by typing approve, approved, yes, reject, rejected, or no in the first line of the e-mail body. To enable **Email Approval Response**, navigate to **Setup | Customize | Workflow & Approvals | Process Settings**. Now check the **Enable Email Approval Response** checkbox, as shown in the following screenshot:

Process Automation Settings

Help for this Page

[Save] [Cancel]

Specify a default workflow user. Salesforce recommends choosing a user with system administrator privileges.

Default Workflow User [Paul Goodey]

Enabling email approval response lets users reply to email approval requests by typing APPROVE or REJECT in the first line and adding comments in the second line.

Enable Email Approval Response ☐

⚠ By enabling the email approval response feature, you agree to allow Salesforce to process email approval responses, update approval requests for all active users in your organization, and update the approval object on behalf of your organization's users.

Let users pause flows when they need to wait for more information. Once you enable this setting, the Pause button appears on every screen that has "Show Pause button" selected.

Let Users Pause Flows ☐

Flows launched from a URL or from Setup use the Lightning runtime experience instead of the classic runtime experience. Only Lightning runtime supports two-column flow screens.

Enable Lightning Runtime for Flows (Beta) ☐

Allows Apex code to set and remove approval process locks.

Enable record locking and unlocking in Apex ☐

[Save] [Cancel]

If the e-mail approval response is enabled and the user does not respond correctly, perhaps by misspelling the word *approve* or typing it on the wrong line, the Salesforce CRM application will not process the incorrect response made by the user.

Within the **Step 5. Select Fields to Display on Approval Page Layout** page, the option to configure the approval request page layout can be carried out as shown in the following example:

The approval page is where an approver approves or rejects a request, and it is on **Step 5. Select Fields to Display on Approval Page Layout** of configuring the approval process where you can carry out the following:

1. Select and sort the fields you want to display on the approval request page.

2. Select **Display approval history information** in addition to the field selected previously to include the **Approval History**-related list, which displays the **Date, Status, Assigned To, Actual Approver, Comments**, and **Overall Status** columns on the resulting approval request page, as shown in the following screenshot:

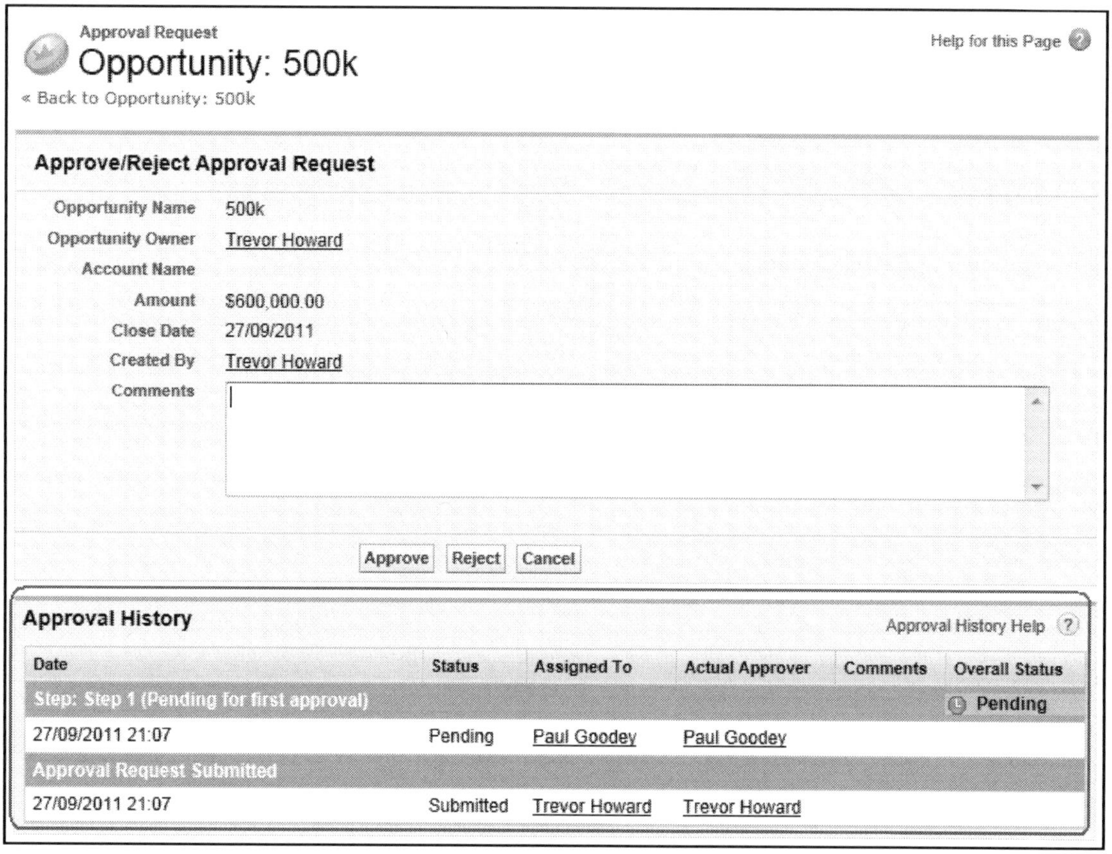

3. To specify how approvers can access an approval page, select either **Allow approvers to access the approval page only from within the application. (Recommended), Allow approvers to access the approval page from within the salesforce.com application**, or **externally from a wireless-enabled mobile device**, and then click on **Next** (as shown previously in the step 5 screenshot).

4. Now specify **Initial Submitters**, as shown in the following screenshot:

5. Specify which users are allowed to submit records for approval.
6. Optionally, select **Add the Approval History related list to all Opportunity page layouts** (as shown for the **Opportunity** object-related approval). This will automatically update all the page layouts for this object and include a related list that allows users to view and submit approval requests.
7. Optionally, select Allow submitters to recall approval requests to give submitters the option to withdraw their approval requests.

When the **Allow submitters to recall approval requests** option is selected, the **Recall Approval Request** button in the **Approval History**-related list is visible for the users that have submitted the record, as well as you, as system administrator.

When a user clicks on **Recall Approval Request**, the pending approval request for the record is withdrawn and the recall action is run.

This option is required for scenarios where changes occur to the record while waiting for approval sign-off. For example, an opportunity might be set to lost or the amount might be lowered below the approval threshold after it has been submitted for approval, or the current approver may be on vacation and the approval needs to be resubmitted and sent to a different user for approval.

Ensure that the recall action resets the state of the record and any field updates that occurred during the initial submission are rolled-back if necessary. If the state of the record is not returned to how it was before the initial submission any attempt to re-submit the approval may fail or the approval may fail to function correctly.

Now click on **Save**, then **Next**, and finally, click on the **Activate** button next to the process.

You will be unable to activate the process until you have created at least one approval step for the approval process.

Creating approval steps

Approval steps in Salesforce CRM set the flow of the record approval process that associates the participating users at each chain of approval. For each approval step, we set who can approve requests for the records, what the record must contain to meet the criteria, and why the record should be allowed to be approved (in the case of a delegated approver).

In addition, the very first approval step in a process also specifies the action required whenever the record fails to reach that step. Later steps then require you to set the action to be taken whenever an approver rejects the request.

To create an approval step, follow the path **Setup | Create | Workflow & Approvals | Approval Processes** and select the name of the approval process, and then carry out the following:

- Click on the **New Approval Step** button from the **Approval Steps**-related list section

 For both Enterprise and Unlimited Editions, there is a limit of 30 steps per process.

- Enter the **Name**, a **Unique Name**, and an optional **Description** for the approval step
- Enter a step number that positions the step in relation to any other step in the approval process, as shown in the following screenshot, and click on **Next**:

Step 1. Enter Name and Description	Step 1 of 3

Next Cancel

Enter a name, description, and step number for your new approval step.

Enter Name and Description   ▌ = Required Information

Approval Process Name	Deals > 100k Review
Name	
Unique Name	ⓘ
Description	
Step Number	1

Next Cancel

On this page, you specify that either all records should enter this step or that only records with certain attributes should enter this step, as shown in the following screenshot:

Step 2. Specify Step Criteria	Step 2 of 3

Previous Next Cancel

Specify whether a record must meet certain criteria before entering this approval step. If these criteria are not met, the approval process can skip to the next step, if one exists. Learn more

Specify Step Criteria

◉ All records should enter this step.

○ Enter this step if the following `criteria are met` ▼ , else `approve record` ▼ :

Previous Next Cancel

If you specified the filter criteria or entered a formula, you can choose what should happen to records that do not meet the criteria or if the formula returns `False`, where the options are as follows:

- **Approve record** to automatically approve the request and perform all final approval actions.
- **Reject record** to automatically reject the request and perform all final rejection actions. This option is only available for the first step in the approval process.

Now click on **Next** to display the page **Step 3. Select Assigned Approver**, where you specify the user who should approve records that enter this step and, optionally, choose whether the approver's delegate is also allowed to approve these requests, as shown in the following screenshot:

Step 3. Select Assigned Approver	Step 3 of 3

Previous | Save | Cancel

Specify the user who should approve records that enter this step. Optionally, choose whether the approver's delegate is also allowed to approve these requests.

Previous Approval Step Information	
Step Number:	1
Name:	Manager Approval
Criteria:	
Assign To:	Manually Chosen

Select Approver

- ◉ Let the submitter choose the approver manually.
- ○ Automatically assign using the user field selected earlier. (**Manager**)
- ○ Automatically assign to approver(s).

☐ The approver's delegate may also approve this request. ⓘ

Reject Behavior

What should happen if the approver rejects this request?

- ◉ Perform all rejection actions for this step **AND** all final rejection actions. (Final Rejection)
- ○ Perform **ONLY** the rejection actions for this step and send the approval request back to the most recent approver. (Go Back 1 Step)

Previous | Save | Cancel

The options are as follows:

- **Let the submitter choose the approver manually**, which prompts the user to manually select the next approver
- **Automatically assign using the user field selected earlier**, which assigns the approval request to the user in the custom field that is displayed next to this option (where this custom field was selected during the earlier configuration of the approval process, which in the preceding screenshot is **(Manager)**
- **Automatically assign to approver(s)**, which allows you to assign the approval request to one or more users or related users, as shown in the following screenshot:

Step 3. Select Assigned Approver		Step 3 of 3

Previous | Save | Cancel

Specify the user who should approve records that enter this step. Optionally, choose whether the approver's delegate is also allowed to approve these requests.

Select Approver

- ○ Let the submitter choose the approver manually.
- ○ Automatically assign using the user field selected earlier. **(Manager)**
- ● Automatically assign to approver(s).

     User ▾   Trevor Howard   🔍

     Related User ▾   --None-- ▾

     Add Row Remove Row

     When multiple approvers are selected:
     ○ Approve or reject based on the **FIRST** response.
     ● Require **UNANIMOUS** approval from all selected approvers.

☐ The approver's delegate may also approve this request. ⓘ

If you specify multiple approvers in the **Automatically assign to approver(s)** option, choose one of the following options:

- **Approve or reject based on the FIRST response**, whereby the first response to the approval request determines whether the record is approved or rejected.
- **Require UNANIMOUS approval from all selected approvers**, whereby the record is only approved if all of the approvers approve the request. If any of the approvers reject the request, then the approval request is rejected.

For custom objects and most standard objects, you can set a queue to be included as part of the automatically assigned approver option. At the time of writing, approval processes for **Opportunities, Solutions**, and **Quotes** cannot be assigned to queues.

Also on this page, there is the option to specify that **The approver's delegate may also approve this request**, where the delegate user is set in the **Delegated Approver** field on the assigned approver's user page.

Delegated approvers cannot reassign approval requests, and they are only permitted to approve or reject approval requests.

If this is not the first step in the approval process, you must specify what will happen if the approver rejects a request in this step, as shown in the following example, where the options are as follows:

- Perform all rejection actions for this step and all final rejection actions (Final Rejection).
- Perform only the rejection actions for this step and send the approval request back to the most recent approver (go back one step).

For both Enterprise and Unlimited Editions, each approval step can have up to 25 approvers.

Now click on **Save** and specify any workflow action you want to set within this step using the following options:

- Yes, I'd like to create a new approval action for this step now
- Yes, I'd like to create a new rejection action for this step now
- No, I'll do this later. Take me to the approval process detail page to review what I've just created.

Finally, click on **Go!** to complete the approval process.

Measuring and refining

Although you will need to plan for successful implementation of approval processes, it is highly likely that they will need to change over time. This could be due to a change of business processing, or refinement of the process within the Salesforce CRM application.

It is therefore a good idea to create analytics to help measure and verify that the approval process is operating successfully. You could, for example, produce reports and dashboards to measure how long approvals take through the process and identify any areas of the process that are not working as expected and refine them accordingly. See Chapter 6, *Generating Data Analytics with Reports and Dashboards* for details of how to produce reports and dashboards.

Process visualizer

The process visualizer provides a read-only representation of your saved approval processes. It can be accessed by clicking on the **View Diagram** button from within the saved approval process, as shown in the following screenshot:

The following screen is displayed for the simple two-step approval process for reviewing opportunity deals that are greater than 100k:

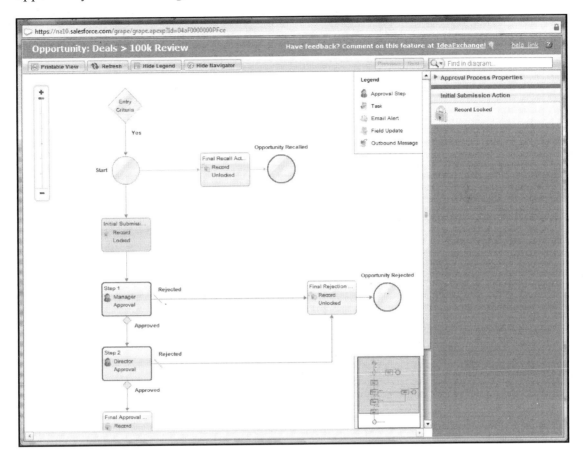

With the process visualizer, you can also print an annotated version of the approval process, where numbers appearing on the diagram correspond to details in a table, which is included in the printable view.

Having the process set out diagrammatically can help in the understanding of the following:

- The steps necessary for a record to be approved
- The designated approvers for each step

- The criteria used to trigger the approval process
- The specific actions taken when a record is approved, rejected, recalled, or first submitted for approval

In summary, approval processes can be a powerful tool to monitor an internal process that must be completed prior to moving forward with the business activities. They also provide great visibility into the timeliness of the business process. Here, you can use approvals to capture the length of time it takes to get expenses, say, approved, which can then help to put measures in place to improve organizational processes.

Visual Workflow

Visual Workflow allows you to build collections of screens, known as **flows**, to guide users through the process of collecting and updating data.

Working with flows involves the creation of a structured set of steps to enable users to complete specified business processes. These business processes could be, for example, call scripts for a customer support team, questionnaires and surveys for customers or employee interaction, or processes to handle incoming sales enquiries for your organization.

Use cases for flows are many and varied, and the **Visual Workflow** options allow you to create screens that collect and display information, create and update Salesforce records, and carry out logic based on input from users, all from within the drag-and-drop **Visual Workflow** user interface.

Configuring Visual Workflow

Working with Visual Workflow involves the following three concepts: flow design, flow management, and runtime. Flow design and management are carried out using the Flow Designer, which is part of the Salesforce CRM setup options. Once the flow has been designed and created, you can then manage it by setting properties, activating, deactivating, deleting, or running it all from within the Salesforce CRM application. Finally, users can then run activated flows, again from within Salesforce. Here, you can configure the flow to be run from a custom button, link or tab, from within a Visualforce page, or directly, using the Salesforce flow URL.

Flow Designer

Visual Workflow and Flow Designer are accessed by following the path **Setup** | **Create** | **Workflow** | **Flows**.

To create and manage flows in Cloud Flow Designer, click on **New Flow** or edit an existing flow.

Flow Designer has a drag and drop user interface that lets you configure screens and define branching logic without writing any code, as shown in the following screenshot:

The Flow Designer user interface has the following features and functional sections:

- Buttons in the button-bar section let you save, close, undo or redo, view properties of, or run the flow.
- Status indicator on the right-hand side of the bar indicates that the flow is active, saved, or whether it has any warnings or errors.

- The **Palette** tab lists all the element types available for the flow. Here you can drag and drop elements from the **Palette** onto the **Canvas** to configure them.
- The **Resources** tab lets you create new resources for the flow, such as variables, constants, formulas, and so on. Once created, the new resources will appear in the **Explorer** tab.
- The **Explorer** tab is a library of all the elements and resources that have been created for the flow.
- The **Description** pane is used to show details for the selected item when you click on them in the **Pallet**, **Resources**, and **Explorer** tabs.
- The **Canvas** is where your flow is built. Here, elements are added from the **Palette** then configured and connected to create the structured set of steps for the flow.

Flow Designer considerations

It is useful to have a general idea for how the flow will be built in Salesforce CRM to help ensure a successful and smooth implementation. Consider the following considerations before starting to configure your flow:

- Use a **Step** element as a placeholder if you are unsure of exactly which element you need at a given point in the flow. This allows for the iterative building of the flow, allowing you to further refine it as your understanding of the process develops.
- To select multiple elements, either use the left-mouse to click and select an area around the multiple elements to highlight them, or use control-click to select individual elements. You can then press the *Delete* button on your keyboard to delete them all at once.
- To view the description or details for an item in the **Palette**, **Resources**, or **Explorer** tab, click on the item and look at the caption in the **Description** pane.

Now, let's look at the **Palette**, **Resources**, and **Explorer** tabs in more detail.

The Palette tab

The **Palette** tab lists the element types available for the flow. Here, you can drag and drop elements from the **Palette** tab onto the main canvas. Once created, the new elements appear in the **Explorer** tab.

Elements are the key aspects of building flows. They represent an action such as collecting or displaying information from users, or querying, creating, updating, and deleting data records. Elements can be connected to create a structured set of steps consisting of screens, inputs, outputs, and branch logic through which users are guided.

Elements

The following elements are available in Cloud Flow Designer:

- **Step**: A placeholder element you can use to quickly sketch out a flow and then convert into a Screen element
- **Screen**: A user-facing screen that can be used to collect input or display output
- **Decision**: Uses conditions to determine where to route users next in the flow
- **Assignment**: Set or change the value of variables
- **Record Create**: Create a new record and insert resource values into its fields
- **Record Update**: Update one or multiple records' fields with resource values
- **Record Lookup**: Find a record and assign its fields to variables
- **Record Delete**: Delete records that match certain criteria
- **Subflows**: Nested flow
- **Apex Plug-In**: Logic built in Apex code via apex classes or AppExchange packages

Using the Step element

From within the **Draft Tools** section, the **Step** element can be used to diagram the flow of your business process. The **Step** element is simply a placeholder, and it cannot be used in an active flow. It is used instead to quickly diagram out the series of steps for the business process that is being built. Once you have each **Step** in place and you want to get the flow activated, you can hover over the **Step** and click on the **Convert Element** (double arrow icon) option. This then enables the conversion of the draft **Step** into a **Screen** element, which is the building block for every flow.

Using the Screen element

The **Screen** element can be created by using the **Convert Element** option on a **Step** element as described previously, or it can be created from within the **USER INTERFACE** section. The screen elements contain the series of windows that the user will see, along with the built-in navigational buttons (for previous and next).

The **Screen** element has various options for user interaction, and it is from the **Add a Field** tab on the **Edit** screen where you can select from the following sections: **INPUTS**, **CHOICES**, **MULTI-SELECT CHOICES**, or **OUTPUTS**, as shown in the following screenshot:

Using the Decision element

Having interacted with a **Screen** element, the user may then need to be directed along a specified path in the flow depending on how they responded. The **Decision** element under the **LOGIC** section allows you to configure how users move through the flow by setting up conditions for each decision outcome.

The **Decision** element is used to navigate the flow and route the user to the next screen or interaction based on their response within the previous **Screen** element. Within the **Decision** element, you can create an **Editable Outcome** for each of the responses, as shown in the following screenshot:

The Resources tab

The **Resources** tab lets you create new resources for the flow, such as **Variable**, **Constant**, **Formula**, and so on, as shown in the following screenshot:

After new resources have been created or items from the **Palette** tab have been added to a flow, they appear in the **Explorer** tab.

The Explorer tab

By double-clicking on items in the Explorer tab, you can access the edit page for them. You can click on an item to view details for the item in the **Description** pane. When viewing items within the **Explorer** tab, the **Description** pane includes two subtabs:

- **Properties**: Shows you information about the element or resource you have selected, such as its label, unique name, description, and data type.

- **Usage**: Lists the elements where the selected item is used. To see where one of the listed elements is located on the canvas, hover over it and click on the magnify icon, as shown in the following screenshot:

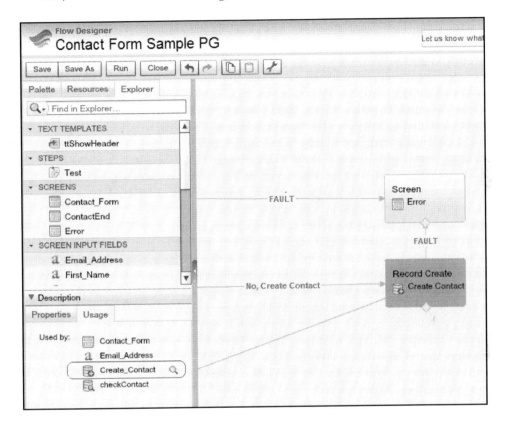

Saving a flow

After you have created a flow in Flow Designer, the options for saving are as follows:

- **Initial save**: When saving for the first time, a dialog box appears. Enter a flow name, unique name, and description. Once the flow has been saved, the unique name cannot be modified.

- **Quick save**: Once you have saved the flow, the **Save** button works as a quick-save, overwriting your previous work. Note that the **Save** button is unavailable when editing active flows. Here, you must use **Save As** to save the changes as either a new flow or a new version of the flow.
- **Save as**: Once you have saved the flow, this button is available with two options: **Save As New Flow**, which opens a dialog box where you can input new details and save as an entirely new flow, or **Save As New Version**, which saves the flow as a new version of the current flow (as shown in the following screenshot). This option is useful if you are about to make changes to a flow and want to keep the old flow as a backup, just in case you need to retrieve it later:

Flow Properties		✕
Save As	New Version ▾	
	New Version	
Name *	New Flow	e PG
Unique Name *		le_PG	i
Description		
	OK Cancel	

Consider the following when saving a flow or flow version:
If you have the flow detail page open in one browser tab, then open a flow version in a new browser tab to edit it, after saving and closing it, you must refresh the first flow detail page before you can successfully run the flow version you just edited. If you have changed the flow properties and for some reason the save fails, the flow properties do not revert to the previous values. Each flow can have up to 50 versions. You can update the flow name and description when you save a new version, but not the unique name.

Flow runtime considerations

Flows can be run directly from the flow URL or from a custom **Web** tab, link, or button pointing to the flow URL.

Depending on how you wish to set up flows for your users, you have the following specific options:

- Add it as a custom link on a detail page
- Add it as a custom button on a detail page
- Add it as a link on the Home page
- Add it as a flow within a Visualforce page

In order to run flows, users require either one of the following permissions to be set up:

- **Run Flows** profile permission
- Force.com **Flow User** field enabled on the user detail page

Consider the following when running flows:

- Do not use the browser's back or forward buttons to navigate through a flow. This may result in inconsistent data between the flow and Salesforce.
- A single flow may have up to 50 different versions. When users run a flow, they see the active version, which may not necessarily be the latest version.

Introduction to Lightning Process Builder

Lightning Process Builder is a workflow automation tool that allows you to automate business processes. At the time of writing the capabilities of Lightning Process Builder is evolving, but the tool allows you to generate a graphical representation of the process as it is developed and built.

Lightning Process Builder allows you to carry out the following:

- Create processes using a user-friendly, visual interface layout with point-and-click features.
- Design a full end-to-end process in one location instead of multiple dependent workflow rules.
- Automate some simple actions that previously needed Apex development and apply the **clicks not code** approach.

At the time of writing, the usefulness and capabilities of the Lightning Process Builder tool hovers between the two other workflow automation tools of Workflows and Visual Workflows (covered in detail earlier in this chapter) and perhaps is the future tool for Salesforce.

Due to the current limitations and the evolving nature of the Lightning Process Builder, this book provides an introduction and a comparison with the other workflow tools at this time.

 For more information on the current capabilities of Lightning Process Builder navigate to the URL `https://developer.salesforce.com/page /Cheat_Sheets` provided by Salesforce and refer to the downloadable *App Logic: Process Automation Cheatsheet* documentation.

Lightning Process Builder provides a visual interface to build a process comprised of if/then statements with actions that allow you to carry out the following:

- Create a record
- Update any related record
- Create or update a record, and log a call using Quick actions
- Send an e-mail alert
- Post to Chatter
- Submit an approval process
- Invoke a different process from a process
- Launch a Visual Workflow flow
- Call Apex code
- Send SOAP messages to external web services

Actions can be run immediately or scheduled. However, at the time of writing, the scheduling capability in Lightning Process Builder is limited compared to Workflow (described earlier in this chapter).

Generally, the Lightning Process Builder actions described previously can be set to trigger from if/then statements and are fired when:

- Records are created
- Records are created or edited

The if/then decision statements can be evaluated based on data in fields within the record that started the process, via a formula, or skipped entirely (by returning true every time). In addition, decisions can be evaluated as true or false by comparing the criteria with static data, global variables, data on the present record, or data on related records.

Comparison of Workflow Automation Tools

The following sections compare the features and supported actions for Workflow Automation Tools in Salesforce CRM.

Feature comparison of Workflow Automation Tools

The following table shows the features of Workflow, Visual Workflow, and Lightning Process Builder at the time of writing:

	Workflow	Visual Workflow	Lightning Process Builder
Single or multiple steps	Single step and a single set of results	Multiple steps and different sets of results	Multiple steps and different sets of results
Able to design the logic using a visual interface?	No	Yes	Yes
Browser support	All	All (Safari not recommended)	All (Chrome recommended)
Can be triggered when a record is changed	Yes	No	Yes
Can be triggered when a user clicks a custom tab, button, or link	No	Yes	No
Can be triggered by another process	No	No	Yes
Can be triggered when Apex is called	No	Yes	No
Supports time-based actions	Yes	Yes	Yes
Supports user interaction	No	Yes	No

Supported actions comparison of Workflow Automation Tools

The following table shows the supported actions for Workflow, Visual Workflow, and Lightning Process Builder at the time of writing:

	Workflow	Visual Workflow	Lightning Process Builder
Call Apex Code	No	Yes	Yes
Create records	Tasks only	Yes	Yes
Invoke processes	No	No	Yes
Delete records	No	Yes	No
Launch a flow	No	Yes	Yes
Post to Chatter	No	Yes	Yes
Send e-mail	Yes (e-mail alerts only)	Yes (e-mail alerts only)	Yes (e-mail alerts only)
Send outbound messages	Yes	No	No
Submit for approval	No	Yes	Yes
Update fields	Yes (the record or its parent)	Yes	Yes (any related record)

Questions to test your knowledge

You are now presented with some questions about the key features of Salesforce CRM administration in the area of Workflow Automation which have been covered in this chapter. The answers can be found at the end of the chapter.

Questions

We present six questions about workflow automation, workflow processes, time-dependent workflow, initiating Approval Processes, approving or rejection Approval Processes, and capabilities during Approval Processes to verify your understanding of workflow automation and approval processes.

Question 1 – Workflow Automation

What are the key concepts of workflow automation in Salesforce CRM? Select one:

a) Workflow rules and time-dependent features.

b) Workflow rules and actions.

c) Workflow e-mail alerts and task actions.

d) Workflow field updates and task actions.

Question 2 – Workflow Processes

Which of the following processes can workflow rules be used to automate? Select all that apply:

a) Sending an e-mail alert to an account owner whenever updates are made to the account by another user.

b) Assigning a follow-up task to a marketing executive whenever a new lead is entered in the system.

c) Assigning a new lead to a queue.

d) Automatically updating an opportunity field whenever the opportunity reaches a specified sales stage.

Question 3 – Time-dependent Workflow

Which scenarios or criteria settings prevent you from adding time-dependent workflow actions? Select all that apply:

a) The rule is already active.

b) The rule criteria are set to evaluate when the record is created, and any time it's edited to subsequently meet criteria.

c) The rule is deactivated, but has pending actions in the workflow queue.

d) The rule criteria are set to evaluate when the record is created, and every time it's edited.

Question 4 – Initiating Approval Processes

Which statements are correct when initiating an approval process? Select all that apply:

a) Approval processes can be set to automatically filter which users are initially involved with the approval process.

b) Approval processes can be set to allow users to choose a user to send the approval to.

c) Approval processes can be set to allow users to choose a queue to send the approval to.

d) Approval processes show an error message if the record does not meet the entry criteria.

e) Approval processes show a warning message showing the entry criteria if the record does not meet the entry criteria.

Question 5 – Approving or Rejectioning approval processes

Which statements are correct when approving or rejecting approval requests? Select all that apply:

a) If enabled, approvers can approve or reject approval requests by e-mail.

b) Approval requests must always be approved or rejected by a specified user.

c) If enabled, approvers can approve or reject approval requests by Chatter.

d) If enabled and a user is set, an approver's delegate can approve or reject approval requests.

Question 6 – During approval processes

Which statements are correct during an approval process? Select all that apply:

a) During an approval process, the record is always locked for all users.

b) If enabled and a user is set, an approver's delegate can reassign approval requests.

c) During an approval process, approvers can reassign approval requests.

d) Approvers can only access an approval page from within the Salesforce application.

e) During an approval process, approvers can view approval requests on their Salesforce homepage.

Answers

Here are the answers to the six questions about workflow automation, workflow processes, time-dependent workflow, initiating Approval Processes, approving or rejection Approval Processes, and capabilities during Approval Processes to verify your understanding of workflow automation and approval processes.

Answer 1 – Workflow Automation

The answer is, **a**) Workflow rules and actions.

Answer 2 – Workflow Processes

The answer is, **a**) Sending an e-mail alert to an account owner whenever updates are made to the account by another user, **b**) Assigning a follow-up task to a marketing executive whenever a new lead is entered in the system, and ,**d**) Automatically update an opportunity field whenever the opportunity reaches a specified sales stage.

The answer **c**) Assigning a new lead to a queue, is not possible using workflow rules and instead can be carried out using lead assignment rules (see Chapter 8, *Introducing Sales Cloud, Service Cloud, and Collaborative Features of Salesforce CRM*).

Answer 3 – Time-dependent Workflow

The answer is, **a**) The rule is already active (here, you must deactivate the rule first), **c**) The rule is deactivated, but has pending actions in the workflow queue (here, you must allow the pending actions to complete or delete the pending action using the time-based workflow queue, and, **d**) The rule criteria is set to evaluate when the record is created, and every time it's edited.

Answer 4 – Initiating Approval Processes

The answer is, **a**) Approval processes can be set to automatically filter which users are initially involved with the approval process, **b**) Approval processes can be set to allow users to choose a user to send the approval to, and **d**) Approval processes show an error message if the record does not meet the entry criteria.

The answer, **c**) and **e**) are not correct for the following reasons, respectively: Approval processes can be set to automatically assign approvers from a queue but not to allow users to choose a queue to send the approval to. Approval processes show an error message only, and not a warning message showing the entry criteria if the record does not meet the entry criteria.

Answer 5 – Approving or Rejecting approval Processes

The answer is, **a**) If enabled, approvers can approve or reject approval requests by e-mail, **c**) If enabled, approvers can approve or reject approval requests by Chatter, and **d**) If enabled and a user set, an approver's delegate can approve or reject approval requests.

The answer **b**) is not correct because approval requests can be set to be approved or rejected by individuals in a queue.

Answer 6 – During Approval Processes

The answer is, **c**) During an approval process approvers can reassign approval requests and **d**). During an approval process, approvers can view approval requests on their Salesforce homepage.

The answers **a**), **b**), and **c**) are not correct for the following reasons, respectively: during an approval process, the record is not locked for admins and can also be edited by the approver. An approver's delegate can approve requests, but cannot reassign approval requests. Approvers can access an approval page from outside Salesforce as well as from within the Salesforce application.

Summary

In this chapter, we looked at the workflow automation features within the Salesforce CRM application through the use of workflow rules and approval processes. We walked through the configuration of these functions and discovered how they can be used to automate and streamline the key business processes for your organization.

We also looked at Visual Workflow and learned how flows and the Lightning Process Builder can be used to build screens that guide users through the process of collecting and updating data. By leveraging workflow automation, your users benefit from greater control over routine activities and elimination of redundant tasks.

Finally, we posed some questions to help clarify some of the key features of Salesforce workflow automation and approval processes.

In the following chapter, we will look at the functional areas of Salesforce CRM and the facilities for sales and marketing automation, service and support, and enterprise social networking.

8
Introducing Sales Cloud, Service Cloud, and the Collaborative Features of Salesforce CRM

In the previous chapter, we looked at the methods to automate business tasks and activities along with approval processes to align business rules with process automation in Salesforce.

This chapter will give you an overview of the functional areas within Salesforce CRM, where we will look at the process from campaign to customer and beyond.

Within the functional areas of this chapter, we will touch on points where business teams concerned with marketing, sales, and customer service have to agree on roles and responsibilities for aspects of the business process. These functional areas of the business can all be managed in Salesforce CRM, and in this chapter we will look at the Sales Cloud, Service Cloud, and Collaboration Cloud features provided by Salesforce.

Finally, you will be presented with a number of questions about the key features of Salesforce CRM administration in the functional areas of Sales Cloud, Service Cloud, and Chatter, which are all covered in this chapter.

We will now look at each of the following core Salesforce CRM functions:

- Marketing administration
- Sales automation

- Customer service and support automation
- Enterprise social networking and collaboration with Salesforce Chatter

Functional overview of Salesforce CRM

The Salesforce CRM functions are related to each other and, as mentioned previously, have cross-over areas, which can be represented as shown in the following diagram:

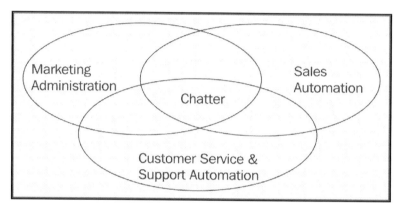

Marketing administration

Marketing administration is available in Salesforce CRM under the application suite known as the **Marketing Cloud**.

The core functionality enables organizations to manage marketing campaigns from initiation to lead development in conjunction with the sales team. The features in the marketing suite can help to measure the effectiveness of each campaign by analyzing the leads and opportunities generated as a result of specific marketing activities.

Salesforce automation

Salesforce automation is the core feature set within Salesforce CRM and is used to manage the sales process and activities. It enables salespeople to automate manual and repetitive tasks and provides them with information related to existing and prospective customers. In Salesforce CRM, Salesforce automation is known as the **Sales Cloud** and helps salespeople manage sales activities, leads and contact records, opportunities, quotes, and forecasts.

Customer service and support automation

Customer service and support automation within Salesforce CRM is known as the **Service Cloud** and allows support teams to automate and manage the requests for service and support by existing customers. Using the Service Cloud features, organizations can handle customer requests such as the return of faulty goods or repairs, complaints, or provide advice about products and services.

Associated with the functional areas described previously are features and mechanisms to help users and customers collaborate and share information known as enterprise social networking.

Enterprise social networking with Salesforce Chatter

Enterprise social network capabilities within Salesforce CRM enable organizations to connect with people and securely share business information in real time. Social networking within an enterprise serves to connect both employees and customers and enables business collaboration. In Salesforce CRM, the enterprise social network suite is known as **Salesforce Chatter**.

Salesforce CRM record life cycle

The capabilities of Salesforce CRM enables the processing of campaigns through to customer acquisition and beyond, as shown in the following diagram:

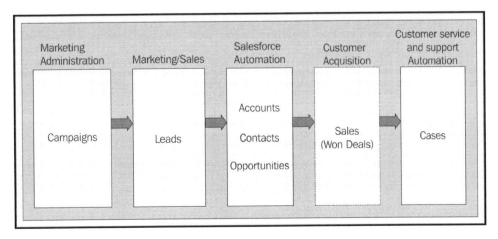

At the start of the process, it is the responsibility of the marketing team to develop suitable campaigns in order to generate leads. Campaign management is carried out using Marketing Administration tools and has links to the lead, as well as any opportunities that have been influenced by the campaign.

When validated, leads are converted to accounts, contacts, and opportunities. This can be the responsibility of either the marketing or sales teams and requires a suitable sales process to have been agreed upon. In Salesforce CRM, an account is the company or organization and a contact is an individual associated with an account.

Opportunities can either be generated from lead conversion or may be entered directly by the sales team. As described earlier in this book, the structure of Salesforce requires account ownership to be established – which sees inherited ownership of the opportunity. Account ownership is usually the responsibility of the sales team.

Opportunities are worked through a sales process using sales stages, where the stage is advanced to the point where they are set as Closed Won/Closed and represent final sales. Opportunity information should be logged in the organization's financial system.

Upon acceptance of the deal by the finance team (and perhaps delivery of the goods or service), the post-customer acquisition process is then enabled, which is when the account and contact can be recognized as a customer. Here, the customer relationships concerning incidents and requests are managed by escalating cases within the customer services and support automation suite.

Marketing administration

Marketing administration in Salesforce CRM provides closed-loop marketing automation from within the marketing app, which can be accessed from the **App Menu** at the top-right corner of the Salesforce CRM screen.

Marketing administration enables integrated marketing functions such as campaign management, lead management, reporting and analysis, response tracking, and campaign effectiveness and it allows users from various departments to centrally access marketing activity.

By default, the marketing administration features provide some level of read-only access to all users. However, to create, edit, and delete campaigns, and carry out advanced campaign and lead management functions, users must have the Marketing User License set on their user record, shown as follows:

User Edit
Paul Goodey

User Edit		Save	Save & New	Cancel

General Information

First Name	Paul		Role	CEO
Last Name	Goodey		User License	Salesforce
Alias	pgood		Profile	System Admin Custom
Email	paul.goodey@widgetsxyz		Active	☑
Username	paul.goodey@widgetsxyz		Marketing User	☑
Community Nickname	admin		Offline User	☑
Title			Knowledge User	☑
Company			Force.com Flow User	☑
Department			Service Cloud User	☑
Division			Mobile User	☑

The Marketing User License is available as standard for organizations with Enterprise or Unlimited editions and can be applied to any active user.

The following key features are available within Salesforce CRM marketing administration:

- Campaign management
- Lead management

Campaign management

With targeted marketing campaigns, companies can build market awareness, generate leads, and learn from their campaign results to fine-tune offers to various customer segments.

The campaign management feature in Salesforce CRM allows your users to manage and track outbound marketing activities. These can be direct mail, roadshow, online or print advertising, e-mail, or other types of marketing initiatives.

Some CRM systems have sales and marketing features separated, requiring marketing and sales users to log on to two separate modules; however, with Salesforce CRM, a dedicated **Campaign tab** is provided to enable marketing and sales users to work together within a single system.

Within the **Campaign tab**, the marketing team can access sales information for their campaigns and the sales team have insight into the marketing activities that affect their accounts, contacts, and leads. Campaigns can also be organized into hierarchies for flexible analysis of related marketing initiatives.

By integrating the marketing and sales effort for campaign and lead management activities, far greater collaboration can be achieved.

Essential success criteria for campaigns can be captured and used to further develop the definition of marketing targets. This enables marketing departments to become more accountable and to better demonstrate their marketing **Return On Investment (ROI)**

The steps to consider when managing and working with campaigns in Salesforce CRM are as follows:

- Campaign planning
- Campaign setup
- Campaign creation
- Campaign execution
- Campaign responses
- Campaign effectiveness

Campaign planning

Before starting to build and run campaigns, it is useful to have an overall plan of the goals and objectives of the campaign, such as the core processes and the type of campaign, such as mass marketing e-mails, hosting a conference, sending direct mail, and so on.

The targets for the campaign also need to be identified and whether they are existing customers, existing leads, or new leads should be defined. With existing leads, you can use lead scoring and lead status to facilitate customer segmentation. For example, a series of archived status definitions could be used, such as No Interest, Future Interest, Nurture, and so on.

Consider how you need to analyze and report on campaigns.

It is worth considering this at an early stage so you can look to create custom campaign fields. You can customize campaigns so that you can improve the targeting and customer segmentation and help to compare and analyze which types of campaigns are the most effective for your sales and marketing teams.

Your marketing team may also want to target new leads through the use of third-party lists. These third-party lists of suspects, prospects, or leads can be flagged in Salesforce with a specific indicator. By flagging with a different record type, or assigning to a different queue, these lead records can be kept apart from existing prospects so that any pre-qualification or de-duplicating can be done before they are available for use in campaigns.

Campaign setup

When setting up campaign management, you should identify who should have access to your campaigns.

 To create, edit, and delete campaigns and configure advanced campaign setup, users must have the **Marketing User license** checked on their user record.

By default, all users have read access to campaigns, but to create, edit, or delete campaigns, users must have the **Create** permission on their profile, shown as follows:

Standard Object Permissions

The permissions defined here control access at the object level. Access to individual records within that object type is controlled by the sharing model. Set access levels based on the functional requirements for the profile. For example, create different groups of permissions for individual contributors, managers, and administrators. How do I choose? ?

	Basic Access				Data Administration			Basic Access				Data Administration	
	Read	Create	Edit	Delete	View All	Modify All		Read	Create	Edit	Delete	View All	Modify All
Accounts	✓	✓	✓	✓	☐	☐	Ideas	☐	☐	☐	☐		
Assets	✓	✓	✓	✓	☐	☐	Leads	✓	✓	✓	✓	☐	☐
Campaigns	✓	✓	✓	✓	☐	☐	Opportunities	✓	✓	✓	✓	☐	☐
Cases	✓	✓	✓	☐	☐	☐	Price Books	✓	☐	☐	☐		
Contacts	✓	✓	✓	✓	☐	☐	Products	✓	☐	☐	☐		
Contracts	✓	☐	☐	☐	☐	☐	Quotes	☐	☐	☐	☐	☐	☐
Documents	✓	☐	☐	☐	☐	☐	Solutions	✓	✓	☐	☐	☐	☐

When starting new types of campaigns, your marketing and sales teams should collaborate to agree on the customer information that is to be captured. Here, you can use the standard fields for both the Campaign and Campaign Member objects or create new custom fields as appropriate.

Standard campaign fields

The following key standard fields are available on the Campaign object:

Field	Type	Description
Campaign Name	Text	This is the name of the marketing campaign. A relevant name should be chosen that is useful for both the marketing and sales teams. For example, Webinar Widgets EMEA FY12Q1.
Type	Picklist	This field is used for the type of campaign. Salesforce provides the following standard list: Conference, Webinar, Trade Show, Public Relations, Partners, Referral Program, Advertisement, Banner Ads, Direct Mail, E-mail, Telemarketing, and Other.
Status	Picklist	This field is used for the current status of a campaign. Salesforce provides the following standard list: Planned, In Progress, Completed, and Aborted.
Start Date	Date	This field is used for the date when a campaign starts.
End Date	Date	This field is used for the date when a campaign ends.
Expected Revenue	Currency	This field is used to set the amount of revenue the campaign will generate.
Budgeted Cost	Currency	This field is used to set the amount of money that has been budgeted for the running of the campaign.
Actual Cost	Currency	This field is used to set the amount of money that the campaign actually cost to run. This field must be recorded to calculate ROI. Note: The ROI is calculated as the net gain using the following expression: **((Total Value Won Opportunities – Actual Cost) / Actual Cost)) * 100**.
Expected Response (%)	Percentage	This field is used to set the expected response rate for the campaign.

Num Sent	Number	This field is used to set the quantity of individuals targeted in the campaign. For example, if a webinar campaign involved sending out invites to 25,000 people, then 25000 would be entered as the number sent.
Active	Checkbox	This field is used to set the campaign to either active or not active. Note: If the campaign is not active, it will not appear in reports or campaign selection picklists (found on lead, contact, opportunity edit pages, and related lists).
Description	Text (long-text area)	This field allows up to 32,000 characters to be entered to add detailed information for the campaign.
Total Leads	Number	This field is the sum of all leads linked to this campaign.
Total Contacts	Number	This field is the sum of all contacts linked to this campaign.
Converted Leads	Number	This field is the sum of all leads linked to this campaign that have been converted.
Total Responses	Number	This field is the sum of all Campaign Members that are linked to this campaign and have their member status set to **Responded**.
Total Value Opportunities	Currency	This field is the total amount of all opportunities linked to this campaign.
Total Value Won Opportunities	Currency	This field is the total amount of all Closed/Won opportunities linked to this campaign

The complete set of fields is shown in the following screenshot, where the picklist values can be adapted to suit your organization.

They are accessed by following the path **Setup** | **Customize** | **Campaigns** | **Fields**:

Campaign Fields

Help for this Page ⑦

This page allows you to specify the fields that can appear on the Campaign page. You can create up to 500 Campaign custom fields.

Note that deleting a custom field will delete any filters that use the custom field. It may also change the result of Assignment or Escalation Rules that rely on the custom field data.

Campaign Standard Fields

Campaign Standard Fields Help ⑦

Action	Field Label	Field Name	Data Type	Controlling Field
Edit	Active	IsActive	Checkbox	
Edit	Actual Cost	ActualCost	Currency(18, 0)	
Edit	Budgeted Cost	BudgetedCost	Currency(18, 0)	
Edit	Campaign Member Type	CampaignMemberRecordType	Lookup(Record Type)	
Edit	Campaign Name	Name	Text(80)	
Edit	Campaign Owner	Owner	Lookup(User)	
Edit	Converted Leads	NumberOfConvertedLeads	Number(9, 0)	
	Created By	CreatedBy	Lookup(User)	
Edit	Description	Description	Long Text Area(32000)	
Edit	End Date	EndDate	Date	
Edit	Expected Response (%)	ExpectedResponse	Percent(8, 2)	
Edit	Expected Revenue	ExpectedRevenue	Currency(18, 0)	
	Last Modified By	LastModifiedBy	Lookup(User)	
Edit	Num Sent	NumberSent	Number(18, 0)	
Edit	Num Total Opportunities	NumberOfOpportunities	Number(9, 0)	
Edit	Num Won Opportunities	NumberOfWonOpportunities	Number(9, 0)	
Edit	Parent Campaign	Parent	Lookup(Campaign)	
Edit	Start Date	StartDate	Date	
Replace | Edit	Status	Status	Picklist	
Edit	Total Actual Cost in Hierarchy	HierarchyActualCost	Currency(18, 0)	
Edit	Total Budgeted Cost in Hierarchy	HierarchyBudgetedCost	Currency(18, 0)	
Edit	Total Contacts	NumberOfContacts	Number(9, 0)	
Edit	Total Contacts in Hierarchy	HierarchyNumberOfContacts	Number(9, 0)	
Edit	Total Converted Leads in Hierarchy	HierarchyNumberOfConvertedLeads	Number(9, 0)	
Edit	Total Expected Revenue in Hierarchy	HierarchyExpectedRevenue	Currency(18, 0)	
Edit	Total Leads	NumberOfLeads	Number(9, 0)	
Edit	Total Leads in Hierarchy	HierarchyNumberOfLeads	Number(9, 0)	
Edit	Total Num Sent in Hierarchy	HierarchyNumberSent	Number(18, 0)	
Edit	Total Opportunities in Hierarchy	HierarchyNumberOfOpportunities	Number(9, 0)	
Edit	Total Responses	NumberOfResponses	Number(9, 0)	
Edit	Total Responses in Hierarchy	HierarchyNumberOfResponses	Number(9, 0)	
Edit	Total Value Opportunities	AmountAllOpportunities	Currency(18, 0)	
Edit	Total Value Opportunities in Hierarchy	HierarchyAmountAllOpportunities	Currency(18, 0)	
Edit	Total Value Won Opportunities	AmountWonOpportunities	Currency(18, 0)	
Edit	Total Value Won Opportunities in Hierarchy	HierarchyAmountWonOpportunities	Currency(18, 0)	
Edit	Total Won Opportunities in Hierarchy	HierarchyNumberOfWonOpportunities	Number(9, 0)	
Replace | Edit	Type	Type	Picklist	

Standard campaign member fields

The following key standard fields are available on the Campaign Member object:

Field	Type	Description
Campaign	Lookup (Campaign)	This field is the campaign name. Set using a link to the campaign record.
Contact	Lookup (Contact)	This field is the contact name. Set using a link to the contact record. Note: Either a Contact is set or Lead is set (not both).
Lead	Lookup (Lead)	This field is the lead name. Set using a link to the lead record. Note: Either a Contact is set or Lead is set (not both).
Status	Picklist	This is the status of the Campaign Member as part of the linked campaign. Salesforce provides the following standard values: Planned, Sent, Received, and Responded. Every campaign has a specific outcome, which can be captured on the member status and response fields. With well-defined member status and response values, reporting can be carried out much easier.

The complete set of fields is shown in the following screenshot, where the picklist values can be adapted to suit your organization. They are accessed by following the path **Setup | Customize | Campaigns | Campaign Members | Fields**:

Campaign Member Standard Fields

Campaign Member Standard Fields Help ?

Action	Field Label	Field Name	Data Type	Controlling Field
Edit	Campaign	Campaign	Lookup(Campaign)	
Edit	City	City	Text(40)	
Edit	Company (Account)	CompanyOrAccount	Text(255)	
Edit	Contact	Contact	Lookup(Contact)	
Edit	Country	Country	Text(80)	
	Created By	CreatedBy	Lookup(User)	
	Created Date	CreatedDate	Date/Time	
Edit	Description	Description	Text(255)	
Edit	Do Not Call	DoNotCall	Checkbox	
Edit	Email	Email	Email	
Edit	Email Opt Out	HasOptedOutOfEmail	Checkbox	
Edit	Fax	Fax	Fax	
Edit	Fax Opt Out	HasOptedOutOfFax	Checkbox	
Edit	First Name	FirstName	Text(40)	
Edit	First Responded Date	FirstRespondedDate	Date	
	Last Modified By	LastModifiedBy	Lookup(User)	
	Last Modified Date	LastModifiedDate	Date/Time	
Edit	Last Name	LastName	Text(40)	
Edit	Lead	Lead	Lookup(Lead)	
Replace | Edit	Lead Source	LeadSource	Picklist	
Edit	Mobile	MobilePhone	Phone	
Edit	Phone	Phone	Phone	
Edit	Responded	HasResponded	Checkbox	
Replace | Edit	Salutation	Salutation	Picklist	
Edit	State/Province	State	Text(40)	
Replace | Edit	Status	Status	Picklist	
Edit	Street	Street	Text(255)	
Edit	Title	Title	Text(80)	
Edit	Zip/Postal Code	PostalCode	Text(20)	

Both your marketing and sales teams should also help to define and agree on any required custom fields or picklist values; for example, segmentation definitions, status, and responses.

Campaign creation

To create campaigns, users must have the **Marketing User** checkbox selected in their user record and have the **Create** permission on campaigns in their profile as shown previously.

To create a campaign, follow the required steps:

1. Click on the **Campaigns** tab to view the campaign's home page or select **Campaign** from the **Create New** drop-down list in the sidebar.
2. Enter values for the fields that apply to the campaign, as shown in the following screenshot:

3. Now click on **Save**, or click on **Save & New** to save the campaign, and then add another.

Member status values

New campaigns have two default member status values: **Sent** and **Responded**. These are populated from the **Campaign Member Status** picklist that we looked at earlier.

Non-system administrator users can, however, overwrite the status values (for the specific campaign record only) from within the campaign detail page by clicking on the **Advanced Setup** button, as shown in the following screenshot:

Campaign
Webinar Widget FY12Q1

Customize Page | Edit Layout | Print

« Back to List: Leads

Campaign Hierarchy [1] | Open Activities [0] | Activity History [0] | Attachments [0] | Opportunities [0] | Campaign Me

Campaign Detail   [Edit] [Delete] [Clone] | [Manage Members ▾] | [Advanced Setup]

| Campaign Owner | Paul Goodey [Change] | Total Leads | 0 |
| Campaign Name | Webinar Widget FY12Q1 [View Hierarchy] | Converted Leads | 0 |

Here, your users can edit or replace them, or create new ones as necessary:

Campaign Member Status
Webinar Widget FY12Q1

Help for this Page

| Current Campaign | Webinar Widget FY12Q1 | Status | Planned |
| Type | Webinar | Active | |

Member Status Values   [Edit] [Replace]

Status	Responded	Default
Sent		✓
Responded	✓	

Create multiple responded values:
You can have more than one **Responded** value. These are summed together to produce the calculated field **Total Responses**.

Target lists

Target lists is a marketing term used to describe the individuals or types of people that are to be included as part of the marketing campaign.

In some situations, such as with an online advertising campaign, people are not specifically set up as individual targets. Here, the campaign would usually be set up in Salesforce as one without members.

If your campaign is targeting individuals, it is important to create a target list that has been segmented according to criteria that will result in the highest quality returns.

Targeting existing leads or contacts

To target existing leads or contacts, you can use the following methods in Salesforce CRM:

Method	Description
Use the **Campaign Detail** page	Click on the **Manage Members** button to add multiple campaign members
Create **Lead** or **Contact** reports	Click on the **Add to Campaign** button to add multiple campaign members
Use **Lead** or **Contact List** views	Click on the **Add to Campaign** button to add multiple campaign members
Use the **Lead** or **Contact Detail** pages	Click on the **Add to Campaign** button to add a single campaign member

Using the campaign detail page

To add multiple campaign members from the **Campaign Detail** page, users should select the **Manage Members** button, as shown in the following screenshot:

You can add existing contacts or leads by selecting **Add Members – Search** from the **Manage Members** drop-down button on a **Campaign Detail** page.

Creating lead or contact reports

To add multiple campaign members from either lead or contact reports, carry out the following steps:

1. Create a custom lead or contact report.
2. In the **Select Criteria** step, enter up to three criteria to segment the report data.

For example, to target all CFOs at Electronics or Energy companies with an annual revenue greater than ten million, you would set the following:

- Title equals CFO
- Industry equals Technology, Telecommunications (using a comma to indicate an OR Boolean result)
- Annual Revenue greater than 10,000,000

Now you can run the report and use the **Add to Campaign** button, as shown in the following screenshot:

Using lead or contact list views

From within a lead or contact list view, you can click on the **Add toCampaign** button to add multiple Campaign members.

Using the lead or contact detail pages

You can use the **Add to Campaign** button within the **Lead Detail** and **Contact Detail** pages to add that record as an individual campaign, as shown in the following screenshot:

Targeting new leads or prospects

When using externally purchased lists of new prospects within Salesforce, it is advisable to flag the records with a specific third-party designation (say by record type or custom picklist value). These records can then be pre-qualified before being added to any campaign or sales activity. What is particularly important is the de-duplication of any new leads against existing records in your Salesforce database so that you can determine which are existing customers or leads.

Salesforce does not recommend mass importing rented or purchased lists of prospects into Salesforce, as these lists are usually controlled by the list vendor and may have restriction or limited use policies. Here, you should simply make use of the list of names as your target list and only after the prospect has responded to your campaign should you import the lead record.

Campaign execution

Although campaign execution activities occur outside the Salesforce CRM application during the execution of either an offline or an online campaign, there are some features of the campaign activity that can aid using the export facilities within Salesforce.

Users can use Salesforce to generate lists of accounts and individuals for mailing houses. or e-mailing specialist partners to send out mass marketing e-mails used in both online and offline events (such as trade shows, advertisements, direct mail, and so on).

There are various options available for integrating Salesforce with other solutions, including provision for mass e-mailing. Integration solutions are covered later in this book, where sources include the AppExchange directory (a Salesforce.com sponsored market place for accredited products and services).

Salesforce can be used to deliver mass e-mails, but the application is not intended for large volume mass e-mail marketing, and there are limits to the quantity of e-mails that can be sent.

For each Salesforce application, a total of 1,000 e-mails can be sent per day to external e-mail addresses. Using the Enterprise Edition, the maximum number of external addresses (unique or non-unique) you can include in a mass e-mail is 500, and for Unlimited and Performance Edition the limit is 1000.

 The mass e-mail limits do not take unique addresses into account. For example, if you have john.smith@widgetsXYZ.com in your mass e-mail 500 times, that counts as 500 against any limit.

You can build an integrated web form to automatically capture individuals as leads in Salesforce. This is detailed later on in this chapter in the **Lead Management** section under **Marketing administration**.

Campaign responses

After the campaign has been executed, your company will want to track the responses, which can include:

- Website responses using a form on your website where you can set up a **Web-to-Lead** form to create a target page with a response form. All responses appear in Salesforce as leads but can be linked to the campaign. This is covered later in this chapter.

- Mass update or offline responses using the campaign member import wizards to import a list of leads or contacts and their responses. Users need the **Marketing User** profile or the **Import Leads** permission to use these wizards.
- Manual responses; for example, when prospects and customers respond by phone or e-mail, users can manually record these responses on the **Campaign History** related list on the lead or **Contact Detail** page.

	Open Activities [0]	Activity History [0]	Campaign History [1]	HTML Email Status [0]	Links to Objects [0]	

Campaign History   [Add to Campaign]   Campaign History Help (?)

Action	Campaign Name	Start Date	Type	Status	Responded	Member Status Updated
Edit	Del	View	Webinar Widget FY12Q1	20/01/2012	Webinar	Sent		05/06/2011 16:26

Title   SVP, Procurement   Email   jeffg@jackson.com

Campaign influence

To ensure existing opportunities are included in the results for the campaign, you can add the campaign to the **Campaign Influence** related list on the opportunity, shown as follows.

The **Campaign Influence** related list is not included in the set of related lists on the **Opportunity Page Layout** by default, so you may need to include it on your chosen **Opportunity Page Layout**.

By setting the **Primary Campaign Source flag** (a checkbox on the **Campaign Influence** record), the opportunity amount is included in the campaign statistics and reports, shown as follows:

Opportunity
Opportunity Y

Customize Page | Edit Layout | Printable View | Help for this Page (?)

Show Chatter   Follow

« Back to List

	Similar Opportunities [0]	Products [0]	Open Activities [0]	Activity History [0]	Notes & Attachments [0]	
	Contact Roles [0]	Partners [0]	Campaign Influence [1]	Competitors [0]	Stage History [3]	Activity Tracker [0]

Campaign Influence   [Add to Campaign]   Campaign Influence Help (?)

Action	Campaign Name	Contact Name	Contact Role	Responded	Primary Campaign Source
Edit	Del	Webinar Widget FY11Q2				✓

Campaign effectiveness

Campaign effectiveness can be analyzed using either the statistics on the campaign record or by running campaign reports.

Campaign statistics

The summary fields on the **Campaign Detail** page, as shown in the following screenshot, allows various statistics to be seen, such as the total number of responses, the amount of business generated from the campaign, and so on:

Campaign
Webinar Widget FY11Q2

Customize Page | Edit Layout | Printable View |

« Back to List

Campaign Hierarchy [1] | Open Activities [0] | Activity History [0] | Attachments [0] | Oppor
Campaign Members [5+] | Links to Objects [0]

Campaign Detail | Edit | Delete | Clone | Manage Members ▼ | Advance

Campaign Owner	Paul Goodey [Change]	Total Leads	1
Campaign Name	Webinar Widget FY11Q2 [View Hierarchy]	Converted Leads	1
Active	✓	Total Contacts	39
Type	Webinar	Total Responses	31
Status	Completed	Num Total Opportunities	3
Start Date	01/06/2011	Num Won Opportunities	2
End Date	01/06/2011	Total Value Opportunities	$30,000
Expected Revenue	$25,000	Total Value Won Opportunities	$30,000
Budgeted Cost	$3,000		

The campaign statistics are automatically recalculated every time a campaign is saved. When a lead gets converted to an opportunity, the campaign that was most recently associated to the lead will automatically pass over to the opportunity.

Campaign reports

Reports can be accessed from the **Reports** tab by selecting the **Campaign Reports** folder, as shown in the following screenshot:

As an example, the **Campaign ROI Analysis Report** shows performance metrics and gives you a figure for the return on investment for the campaign, as shown in the following screenshot:

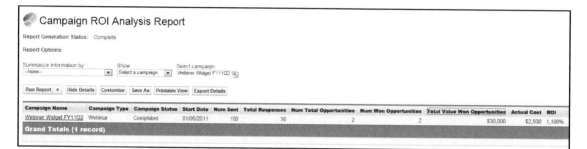

ROI calculation:

The ROI percentage calculation taken from the Campaign ROI Analysis Report uses the following equation:((Total Value of Won Opportunities - Actual Cost) / Actual Cost)) * 100. In the example shown, we have: ((30,000 – 2500)/2500))*100 = 1100%.

Note: all opportunities that are linked to the Campaign must be set to Closed Won and the Campaign must be set as the Primary campaign for them to be included in the Total Value of Won Opportunities amount.

Customizable Campaign Influence overview

Salesforce has improved upon the campaign influence mechanism described previously and provides the **Customizable Campaign Influence** functionality.

Customizable Campaign Influence allows you to choose how the revenue from an opportunity is attributed to multiple campaigns that are associated with it.

At the time of writing, the features that are common to Campaign Influence and Customizable Campaign Influence are:

- Auto-association with an opportunity
- Can use a Salesforce Default Model which attributes 100% of revenue to the primary campaign on the opportunity
- Applies Campaign Influence on the opportunitiy as per the specified Model

At the time of writing, the features that are only available in Customizable Campaign Influence are:

- Ability to create custom Campaign Attribution Models
- Allows Flexible Influence Attribution
- Enables Campaign Attribution Models to be locked
- Allows Campaign Influence to be applied on an opportunity for the given Campaign Attribution Model
- Produces Campaign Results on Campaigns for the given Campaign Attribution Model
- Allows API access

With **Customizable Campaign Influence** you can configure multiple ways to track how an opportunity has benefited and been influenced by one or more campaigns. Each method of tracking is achieved by creating a custom Campaign Attribution Model.

A default Attribution model which attributes 100% of revenue to the primary campaign on an opportunity and 0% to any other campaigns that users assign to the opportunity is the standard model for **Customizable Campaign Influence**.

The benefit of **Customizable Campaign Influence** is that it allows you to build more flexibility in how revenue is attributed to campaigns by creating custom attribution models. Examples of custom attribution models are:

- Attributing 100% of the revenue to the initial campaign to have been associated with the opportunity.
- Attributing 100% of the revenue to the latest campaign to have been associated with the opportunity.

- Evenly distributing the revenue across all campaigns that have been associated with the opportunity.

With **Customizable Campaign Influence** you can prevent users from manually creating or updating campaign influence records which are associated to opportunities by locking the Attribution Model. Here, the records that are a part of a locked Attribution Model can only be updated via the Salesforce API.

 With **Customizable Campaign Influence** the default Salesforce model is always locked.

Lead management

Managing prospective customers appropriately often raises issues within companies. The status and quality of prospect data can cause obstacles when trying to automate the processing through the sales process. Prospect data often comes from various sources which, if not carefully controlled, can make them difficult to accurately process.

Without a central system and agreed approach, there can be conflict between the marketing team, who are often unable to trace what is happening to the prospects after distributing them to sales, and the sales team, who are unable to verify the quality of the data. Salesforce CRM helps bridge any gap between sales and marketing, and by using lead management mechanisms it offers a way to improve the management and automation of the flow from potential customers to a closed sales deal.

Leads are prospects or potential opportunities and are accessed in Salesforce CRM from the **Leads** tab. They are sources of potential deals that usually need more qualification, and they may be visitors to your website who requested more information, respondents to marketing campaigns, trade show visitors, and so on. Leads are stored and managed separately to account, contact, and opportunity records, which are covered later in this chapter.

Standard lead fields

The following key standard fields are available on the Lead object:

Field	Type	Description
Lead Owner	Lookup (to lead or queue)	This field is the user or queue who owns the lead. A lead can be owned by a person or stored in a queue. Here, you can allow specified users to accept (and return) leads from a queue. This is covered in more detail later in this section.
Last Name	Text	This field is the last name and is a required field. The last name is copied over to the Last Name field on a contact record during the lead conversion process.
Company	Text	This field is the company name and is a required field. The company name is copied over to the company name on an account record during the lead conversion process.
Lead Status	Picklist	This field is the status and is a required field. Salesforce provides the following standard values: Open – Not Contacted, Working – Contacted, Closed – Converted, and Closed – Not Converted. Lead Status is an important field used in the lead process settings, as we will discover later on in this section.
Lead Source	Picklist	This field is used to set the source from which the lead appeared. Salesforce provides the following standard values: Web, Phone Inquiry, Partner Referral, Purchased List, and Other.

The complete set of fields is shown in the following screenshot, where the picklist values can be adapted to suit your organization. They are accessed by following the path **Setup | Customize | Leads | Fields**:

Lead Standard Fields

Action	Field Label	Field Name	Data Type
	Address	Address	Address
Edit	Annual Revenue	AnnualRevenue	Currency(18, 0)
Edit	Campaign	Campaign	Lookup(Campaign)
Edit	Company	Company	Text(255)
	Created By	CreatedBy	Lookup(User)
Edit	Description	Description	Long Text Area(32000)
Edit	Do Not Call	DoNotCall	Checkbox
Edit	Email	Email	Email
Edit	Email Opt Out	HasOptedOutOfEmail	Checkbox
Edit	Fax	Fax	Fax
Edit	Fax Opt Out	HasOptedOutOfFax	Checkbox
Replace	Edit	Industry	Industry	Picklist
	Last Modified By	LastModifiedBy	Lookup(User)
Edit	Last Transfer Date	LastTransferDate	Date
Edit	Lead Owner	Owner	Lookup(User,Queue)
Replace	Edit	Lead Source	LeadSource	Picklist
Replace	Edit	Lead Status	Status	Picklist
Edit	Mobile	MobilePhone	Phone
	Name	Name	Name
Edit	Replace	Salutation	Picklist	
	First Name	Text(40)	
	Last Name	Text(80)	
Edit	No. of Employees	NumberOfEmployees	Number(8, 0)
Edit	Phone	Phone	Phone
Replace	Edit	Rating	Rating	Picklist
Edit	Title	Title	Text(80)
Edit	Website	Website	URL(255)

Lead business process

Creating a business process within the lead management function involves agreeing on and implementing the steps and field values that are to be recorded by the sales and marketing teams during the lead life cycle.

The lead processes are accessed by following the path **Setup | Leads | Lead Processes,** where processes can be created or edited, as shown in the following screenshot:

Lead Process Edit
New Lead Process

Enter a name and description for the Lead Process. Select an existin
the new process. Selecting "master" copies all available picklist value

Lead Process

Existing Lead Process	--Master-- ▾
Lead Process Name	Lead Process
Description	This is a lead process for WidgetsXYZ

Save   Cancel

You can now assign the status values for the lead, as shown in the following screenshot:

Finally, by associating the lead business process with one or more record types, this will make it available to your users (based on their profile).

Creating leads in Salesforce CRM

There are several ways of creating lead records within the Salesforce CRM application. This includes the manual entry of single leads by your users, the manual entry of leads by the prospect themselves (using public facing web forms known as **Web-to-Lead**), or the manual importing of multiple leads within the application by you or your users.

Creating lead records within the application

Leads can be manually created from either the **Leads** tab by clicking on the **New** button, or from the **Create New** selection in the left-hand side bar, as shown in the following screenshot:

Manually creating leads with Web-to-Lead

With the Web-to-Lead functionality in Salesforce CRM, leads can be directly entered into your Salesforce application from a public-facing website. This means prospective information can be gathered directly from the individual. This feature is used to generate **Hyper Text Markup Language** (**HTML**) code, which can then be incorporated into the required web page.

Lead settings

To enable the **Web-to-Lead** feature, you must first configure the appropriate lead settings by following the path **Setup | Customize | Leads | Settings**. Now click on the **Edit** button to display the page, as shown in the following screenshot:

Edit Lead Settings

Use the lead settings below to specify default lead behavior for your organization.

Lead Queue Settings

The queue or user that will own a lead when assignment rules fail to locate an owner:
• when a lead is saved with the auto-assign checkbox selected
• when a lead is captured online

| User ▾ | | Paul Goodey | 🔍 |

Notify Default Lead Owner ☐

Lead Conversion Settings

Require Validation for Converted Leads ☑ ⓘ

Preserve Lead Status ☑ ⓘ

Enable Conversions on the Salesforce1 App ☐ ⓘ

[Save] [Cancel]

Now select a **Default Lead Owner** and select the **Notify Default Lead Owner** checkbox to automatically notify the default lead owner whenever a lead is assigned to them.

The default lead owner becomes the owner of any leads that are not auto-assigned by lead assignment rules.

The Web-to-Lead settings

To enable the Web-to-Lead feature, you must first configure the **Web-to-Lead Settings** by following the path **Setup** | **Customize** | **Leads** | **Web-To-Lead Settings**. Now click on the **Edit** button to display the page, as shown in the following screenshot:

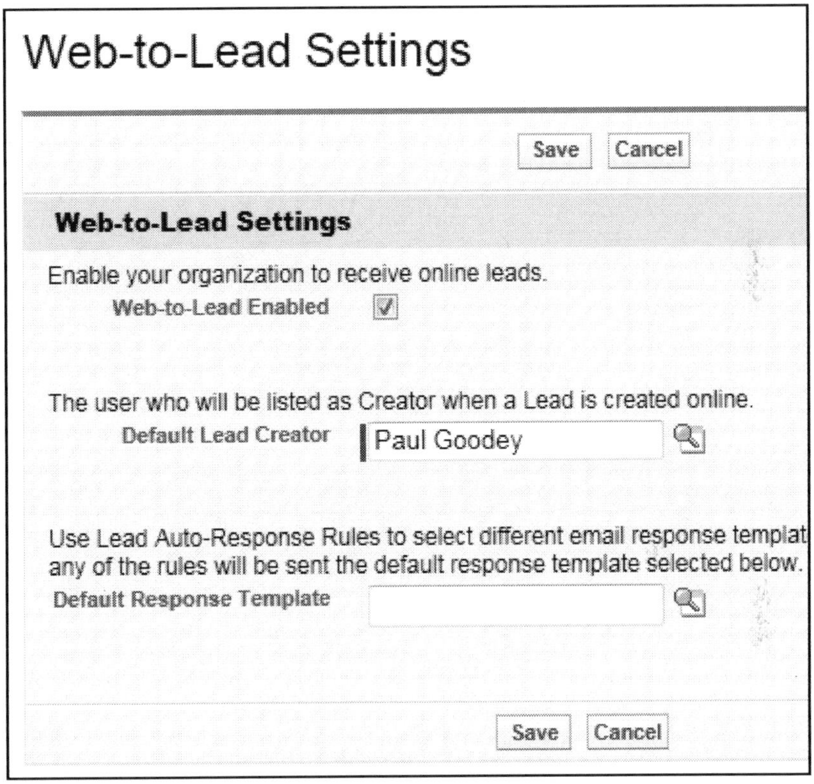

Now check the **Web-to-Lead Enabled** checkbox, select the user who will be set as the creator whenever the lead is entered from an online web form, and finally create **Web-to-Lead** e-mail auto-response rules to determine which e-mails to send to prospects when they submit information online. Then, click on **Save**.

Generating the Web-to-Lead HTML code

To generate the **Web-to-Lead** HTML code, follow the path **Setup | Customize | Leads | Web-To-Lead**. Now click on the **Create Web-To-Lead Form** button to display the page, as shown in the following screenshot:

Web-to-Lead Setup   Help fo

Easily set up a page on your website to capture new leads.

Create a Web-to-Lead Form

Select the fields to include on your Web-to-lead form:

Available Fields		Selected Fields		NOTE: W
Salutation		First Name	Up	like to ad
Title	Add	Last Name		fields tha
Website	▶	Email	▲	not see li
Phone		Company		Available
Mobile	◀	City	▼	You can
Fax	Remove	State/Province	Down	custom l
Address				gather a
Zip				informati
Country				your web
				me more.

After users submit the Web-to-Lead form, they will be taken to the specified return U website, such as a "thank you" page.

Return URL: `http://`

[Generate] [Cancel]

Now select the fields to include in the form and specify a URL that users will be taken to after submitting the form. Finally, click on the **Generate** button and then copy the generated HTML code and send it to the team responsible for the website in your organization.

The page style can be customized for your website, but the core form elements that have been generated within the HTML code should not be changed.

With the **Web-to-Lead** feature, you can capture up to 500 leads per day.

To increase the limit of 500 leads per day:
This feature may be increased by sending a request to Salesforce customer support, although there may be additional costs for this increase.

Web-to-Lead auto-response rules

Auto-response rules provide a method to customize any communication that is sent back to an individual after they have filled out a web lead form. These auto-response rules can contain logic to determine which e-mail template and what content to send to leads that have been generated using **Web-to-Lead**.

To enable auto-response rules, follow the path **Setup** | **Leads** | **Auto-response Rules**. Then, click on the **New** or **Edit** button, as shown in the following screenshot:

Here, you first create the rule detail and name and activate the rule. Then, you add the rule entries that contain the logic and where multiple rule entries may be created. Rule entries require the following:

- An order of execution
- The criteria for when the rule is triggered
- A sent from e-mail address detail
- An e-mail template to be used to send to the respondent

Any e-mails that are sent are included in the daily limit of 1,000 mass e-mails for an organization.

Manual importing of multiple leads

To import leads, follow the path **Setup | Data Management | Import Leads**. Now follow the on-screen instructions to export your data from its current source and label each column in the file with the correct field name, as shown in the following screenshot:

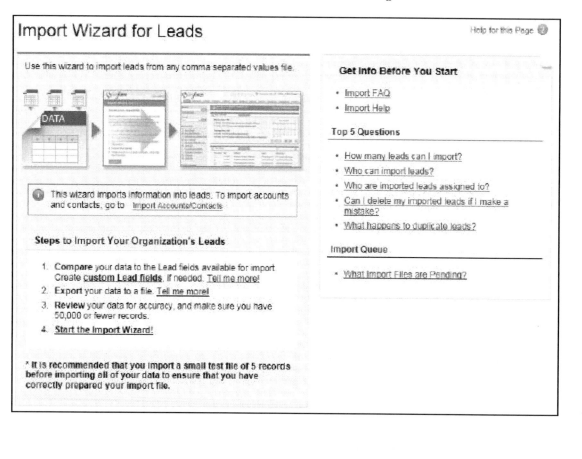

Only users with the **Import Leads** permission on their profile (in the general user permissions section) have access to the importing leads feature, where files of up to 50,000 leads can be imported.

A lead assignment rule can automatically assign leads to users or queues based on values in lead fields. Alternatively, a **Record Owner** field in the import file can determine lead ownership for each imported lead.

Without a lead assignment rule or **Record Owner** field, imported leads are automatically assigned to the user that has carried out the import.

The **Import Queue** shows the status of the import. You will be notified by e-mail when your import is complete (this notification may take up to 24 hours).

Marketing users with the **Marketing User** profile can also import new leads by selecting **Add Members – Import File** from the **Manage Members** drop-down button on the **Campaign Detail** page.

Lead queue

Queues can be thought of as a storage location to group leads together, usually by geographic region or business function. **Leads** remain in the queue until they are assigned or accepted by users. Users who have been included as part of the queue can access and accept the records by clicking on the **Accept** button, as shown in the following screenshot:

Action	Name ↑	Company	State/Province	Email	Lead Status	Created Date	Owner Alias
Edit | Del	Chubbe, Mos	Ideal Homes			Open - Not Contacted	05/06/2011	US Leads

US Leads | New Lead | Accept | Change Status | Change Owner | Add to Campaign

Create New View | Edit | Delete | Refresh   A | B | C | D | E | F | G | H | I | J | K | L | M | N | O | P | Q | R | S | T | U | V | W | X | Y | Z | Other | All

Whenever you create a lead queue, Salesforce automatically generates a lead list view to enable users to access the records in the queue.

Creating and adding users to a lead queue

To create and provide users with access to a lead queue, follow the path **Setup | Manage Users | Queues | New**.

Here, you can carry out the following: name the queue, select the supported object (selection being either lead or case), and assign the queue member (selection being either users, public groups, roles, or role and subordinates).

You can also set up the queue so that e-mails are sent to the queue members (using a default e-mail address for the queue) whenever a case is assigned to the queue.

Lead assignment rules

Lead assignment rules determine how leads are automatically assigned to users or a queue. They contain rule entries, which are predefined business rules that determine the lead routing.

Lead assignment rules can be accessed by following the path **Setup | Customize | Leads | Assignment Rules**.

Only one lead assignment rule can be active at any given time but each rule can have multiple criteria, as shown here:

Lead Assignment Rules　　　　　　　　　　　Help for this Page

Lead Assignment Rules allow you to automatically route leads to the appropriate users or queues. A Lead Assignment Rule consists of multiple rule entries that define the conditions and order for assigning leads.

New

Action	Rule Name	Active	Created By	Created On
Rename | Del	Standard	✓	Paul Goodey	19/12/2009
Rename | Del	test	☐	Paul Goodey	03/02/2010

Criteria are evaluated in the order in which they appear in the list. When there are multiple rules that can be applied, you can set the priority for the criteria by setting the most specific criteria at number one and then adding more criteria numbers that are more generic. The following screenshot shows a simple example and use case of multiple criteria rules, which is used to assign leads according to a geographic flag by using the **Country** field:

Lead Assignment Rule				Help for this Page ⓘ

Standard

Create the rule entries to automatically assign leads to users or queues based on the criteria specified in the rule entries. You can reorder the entries from this page after creating them.

Rule Detail   [Edit]

Rule Name	Standard	Active	✓
Created By	Paul Goodey, 19/12/2009 13:01	Modified By	Paul Goodey, 15/06/2011 20:45

[Edit]

Rule Entries   [New] [Reorder]

Action	Order	Criteria	Assign To	Email
Edit | Del	1	Lead: Country EQUALS US,USA,United States,United States of America	Paul Goodey	☐
Edit | Del	2	Lead: Country NOT EQUAL TO US,USA,United States,United States of America	Trevor Howard	☐

Lead conversion

Lead qualification depends on your business process and should have been developed in conjunction with both the marketing and sales team.

As part of the lead conversion routine, certain key information contained on the lead record is mapped to the Salesforce CRM object's accounts, contacts, and optionally the opportunity records. During lead conversion, new records are created for these objects, where the account record name field will contain the **Company Name** field value from the lead, and the contact record name field will be populated from the **Name** field within the lead record.

Any existing account or contact records are automatically checked before the lead conversion to avoid record duplication.

Opportunities that are created upon lead conversion contain default values for the required fields, where the **Close Date** defaults to the last day of the current quarter and **Sales Stage** is set to the first value in the Stage picklist.

 During the lead conversion, there is no opportunity amount value set on the resulting opportunity.

To convert a lead, select the lead that is to be converted either by clicking on the **Lead** tab and selecting from the list view or by searching and then clicking on **Convert** on the **Lead Detail** page, as shown in the following screenshot:

Lead
Mr Jeff Glimpse

Customize Pag

« Back to List: Leads

Open Activities [0] | Activity History [0] | Campaign History [1] |

Lead Detail   Edit   Delete   Convert   Cl

Lead Owner	Paul Goodey [Change]
Name	Mr Jeff Glimpse
Company	Jackson Controls

The lead conversion screen will be displayed where you can check the owner of the new records. Here, you can choose to send the record owner an automated notification e-mail. You can also set the status of the converted lead and also specify that a new task is created for the record owner to act as a follow-up task, as shown in the following screenshot:

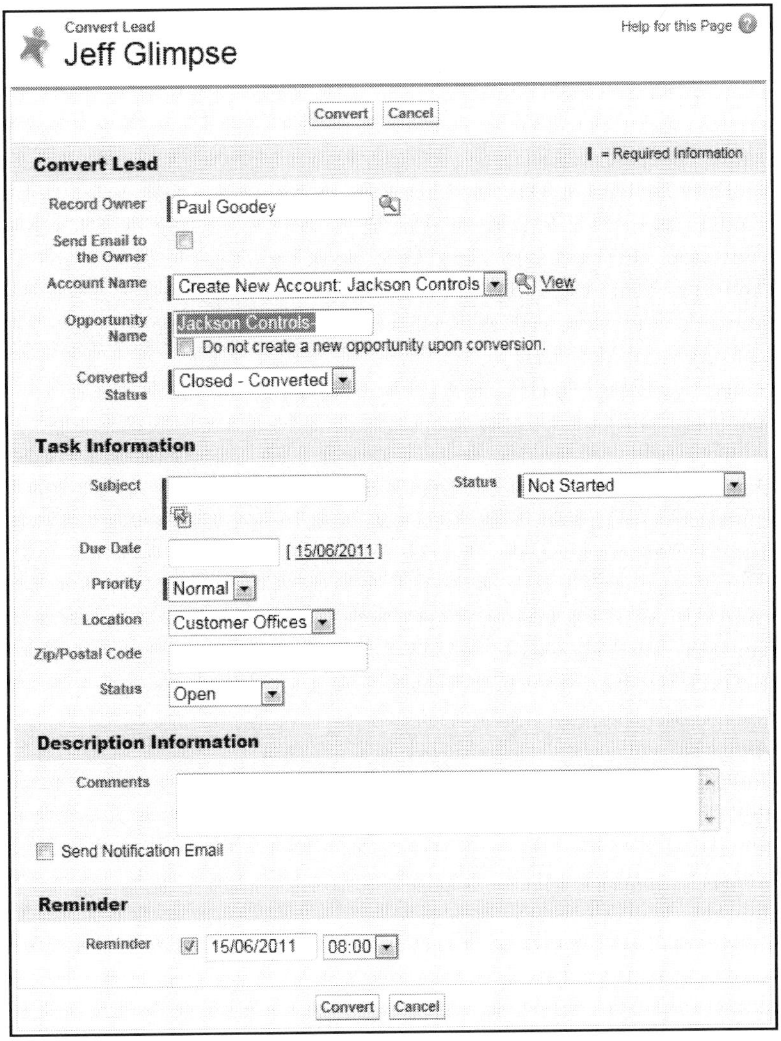

Before creating any new account or contact records, the Salesforce CRM application attempts to match an existing account, contact names, and the name of the lead. Where there is a match you will have the option of selecting the existing records, as shown in the following screenshot:

Convert Lead

Record Owner	Paul Goodey
Send Email to the Owner	☐
Account Name	--None-- ▾ View
Opportunity Name	--None--
	Create New Account: Jackson Controls
	Attach to Existing: Jackson Controls
Converted Status	Closed - Converted ▾

Clicking on the **Convert** button completes the lead conversion process and results in the following:

- The company name from the lead becomes the account name
- The lead name from the lead becomes the contact name
- The opportunity and contact are associated with the account
- Any campaigns related to the lead are associated with the opportunity

Converted leads can no longer be viewed in the **Leads** tab, and the only way to view the record is to create a lead report. When customizing your report, enter a filter option of **Converted equals True** to view converted leads.

Lead conversion field mappings

There are standard field mappings between the lead and account, contact, and opportunity records that are provided by Salesforce for the lead conversion process; however, you can extend these. To extend the mappings, follow the path **Setup | Customize | Leads | Fields**. Now navigate to the **Lead Custom Fields & Relationships** section at the bottom of the page, as shown in the following screenshot:

Action	Field Label	API Name	Data Type	Controlling Field	Modified By
		New **Map Lead Fields** **Field Dependencies**			Lead Custom Fields & Relationships Help
Edit | Del	Current Generator(s)	CurrentGenerators__c	Text(100)		Paul Goodey, 19/12/2009 13:01
Edit | Del	Number of Locations	NumberofLocations__c	Number(3, 0)		Paul Goodey, 19/12/2009 13:01
Edit | Del	Offer	Offer__c	Lookup(Offer)		Paul Goodey, 04/06/2011 11:42

Extending the field mappings may become necessary whenever you add required custom fields on either the account, contact, or opportunity records, which are to be populated from the lead records. This is done as shown in the following screenshot:

Lead Custom Field Mapping

Map each of your organization's lead custom fields to one of your custo
be used when you convert leads.

Lead Custom Field Mapping

Take this lead custom field...	...and map it to this field
Current Generator(s)	--None--
Number of Locations	--None--
Offer	None Available
Primary	--None--
Product Interest	--None--
SIC Code	--None--

Save   Cancel

It is important to ensure the field mapping is in place whenever you have certain mandatory fields or rules for your account, contacts, or opportunities. This ensures that the quality of data is preserved. You can enable the setting **Require Validation for Converted Leads** as shown in the screenshot shown in the section Lead settings to enforce the validation logic during the lead conversion process. By disabling the setting **Require Validation for Converted Leads** the validation logic for required custom fields and workflow or validation rules is not enforced during the lead conversion process.

Salesforce automation

Salesforce automation allows the management and control of the phases required for the sales process within a **Customer Relationship Management** (**CRM**) system. Enabling and automating these phases within CRM systems helps to improve the quality and also minimizes the time that sales representatives spend on each phase.

Salesforce automation in Salesforce.com is performed within the **Sales App,** which can be accessed from the **App** Menu at the top-right corner of the Salesforce CRM screen.

At the core of the **Sales App** in Salesforce CRM are the account, contact, and opportunity management functions for tracking and recording each stage in the sales process for new and existing customers.

Accounts can be sorted by standard views or customized views, and users can add new accounts and edit existing accounts. Associated contacts and activities are also listed in the same page of the account where users can manipulate other operations, such as viewing, adding, and editing as necessary. Account views can be filtered based on time variables, such as by viewing recently modified or created accounts, new accounts this week, and so on.

Account management

In Salesforce CRM, account management is carried out using the facilities found in the **Accounts** tab and is typically where customer information is located.

Account records are used to store the company information from converted leads and can also be used for the storage of company information for partners, suppliers, and even competitors.

Accounts may be considered as business accounts from a Business-to-Business (B2B) perspective and are usually the company records stored within the application. However, Salesforce provides another variety of account called a Person Account, which allows organizations with a Business-to-Consumer (B2C) business model to manage the relationships with individuals. The `Business account` and `Person Account` records offer very similar features and fields; however, Person accounts do not have certain fields or features, such as a **Reports To field**, a **Parent Account field**, or the Account Hierarchy feature.

 Person accounts are not enabled by default in the Salesforce CRM application and are only available by request to Salesforce customer support.

Business account information consists of company name, type, company website, industry, annual revenue, billing and shipping addresses, account record owner, date of creation and modification, and so on.

 Naming convention for accounts:
Having consistent account names is essential for ensuring clean and accurate account data. It can be useful to adopt an appropriate account naming policy to be used by all users in Salesforce. One way to achieve this is to ensure that accounts are named using their full legal name wherever possible.

As described earlier in this book, accounts are also the primary mechanism used in the organization of records.

They are used within the record sharing and ownership hierarchy and are the parent object for standard objects, such as contacts, opportunities, and so on. When changing ownership of account records, you have the option to re-assign these child records, as shown in the following screenshot:

Select New Owner

Transfer this account   Company X

Owner [   ] 🔍

☐ Transfer open opportunities not owned by the existing account owner
☐ Transfer closed opportunities
☐ Transfer open cases owned by the existing account owner
☐ Transfer closed cases
☐ Send Notification Email

[Save] [Cancel]

Contact management

Contact management is performed using the facilities found in the **Contacts** tab. **Contacts** are the individuals that your users want to keep in touch with. For the sales team, this is likely to be people such as purchasers and key decision makers. For the marketing team, this may include the CEOs and CFOs and other influencers. For support, the contacts could be any of the users of the product or service that your organization provides.

Salesforce CRM provides the facility for users to store, view, sort, filter, delete, edit, and find contact information which may or may not be associated with accounts. Each contact is recorded with details such as title, contact details (address, cell phone, work phone, fax, and e-mail address), date of creation and modification, and contact record owner.

Activity management

Activities in Salesforce are made up of tasks and events. Unlike other areas of functionality, there is no access to Activities from the tab; instead, they are created and viewed from related lists on other types of records, such as accounts, contacts, cases, and so on. Users can view activities both in the context of a relevant item (such as where they relate to an account, for example) or as a standalone mechanism from their calendar and task list from the Salesforce CRM homepage.

The Activity History-related list of a record shows all completed tasks, logged phone calls, and expired events, such as meetings, outbound e-mails, and so on, for the record and any linked records.

Cloud Scheduler

Creating and scheduling appointments with customers is a central activity of most customer-oriented businesses. Marketing, sales, and customer support teams spend time getting in touch with prospective leads and customers and use a variety of means to agree on a time and place to meet.

To improve this activity, Salesforce provides the **Cloud Scheduler** facility, which is an automated system used to manage the scheduling and presentation of suitable appointment times to individuals through a Web interface.

 Salesforce has announced the planned retirement of Cloud Scheduler at the time of writing. From Winter '17 onwards Cloud Scheduler is no longer available for new orgs and will be disabled in the Winter '18 release and no longer available for all existing organizations.

All the responses from invitees are then tracked by Salesforce and a date and time that fits with everyone can then be selected and chosen as confirmation for the meeting.

 As part of the **Cloud Scheduler** feature, Salesforce creates a unique web page for the meeting which displays the proposed meeting times. When invitees visit the web page, they can select the times that are suitable for them , and then send a response. Cloud Scheduler setup.

The settings for the Cloud Scheduler can be configured by following the path **Setup | Customize | Activities | Cloud Scheduler**. The **New Meeting Request** button for the Cloud Scheduler can be added to page layouts with an **Open Activities**-related list, such as contacts, leads, or **Person Accounts** (if enabled).

For users to request a meeting with a person account, you may also need to add the **Email** field to the page layout by following the path **Setup | Customize | Accounts | Person Accounts | Page Layouts**.

You can also include the **New Meeting Request** button on the user's home page. This is displayed above the **Scheduled Meetings** and **Requested Meetings** tabs, as shown in the following screenshot:

Calendar	New Event	New Meeting Request
Scheduled Meetings	Requested Meetings	
You have not proposed any meetings.		

If this section is not displayed on the homepage, then **Show Requested Meetings** in the **Calendar Section** on the **Home Tab** needs to be selected by following the path **Setup | Customize | Activities | Activity Settings,** as shown in the following screenshot:

Cloud Scheduler requesting a meeting

The following offers an overview of how users within your organization can request a meeting with co-workers and customers using the Cloud Scheduler.

Requesting a meeting

Users can either navigate to the contact or **Lead Detail** page of the individual they want to request a meeting with through the **Open Activities**-related list or navigate to the calendar section on their homepage. They then click on the **New Meeting Request** button to display the **Meeting Request** page. Here, users click to invite other Salesforce users, leads, contacts, or **Person Accounts** to the meeting and click in the calendar to propose up to five meeting times, or they can choose to let the Salesforce application automatically propose times, as shown in the following screenshot:

Invitees response

Salesforce e-mails a meeting request to the invitees so they can pick the times they are available. Within the e-mail is a link which the invitees click called **Respond toThis Request**, which opens the meeting's web page. Within the web page, invitees can then pick the proposed times that are suitable for them and then send a reply, as shown in the following screenshot:

Meeting Request from:
Paul Goodey

Subject	Demo Meeting
Who	Trevor Howard, Paul Goodey, Shelly Brownell
When	Between 20/06/2011 – 22/06/2011 BST
Duration	1 hour
Where	To be determined

Trevor Howard, select times that work for you.

Messages

☐ **Mon 20/06/2011**
10:00 - 11:00 (BST)

☐ **Tue 21/06/2011**
10:00 - 11:00 (BST)

☐ **Wed 22/06/2011**
10:00 - 11:00 (BST)

☐ **None of these times works for me.**

Write your message . .

Reply

Paul Goodey (6 minutes ago) Selected 3 times

Demo Meeting

Powered by salesforce.com
http://www.salesforce.com/

Confirmation of the meeting

Salesforce keeps track of all the responses sot users can see when each invitee is available, and they can then select the best time to meet and confirm the meeting, as shown in the following screenshot:

Opportunity management

Opportunity management is performed using the facilities found in the **Opportunities** tab.

Opportunities in Salesforce CRM are the sales deals that the sales team in your organization creates and updates. By adding new opportunities, the sales team is building the sales pipeline, which will be used to produce figures for both individual sales forecasts, as well as the wider company sales forecast.

Opportunity records are also important for other users in your organization to track, such as the marketing team, who may want to monitor the effectiveness of marketing campaigns, or the customer support teams who may need to have an up-to-date view of customer spending when negotiating support contracts.

Product, Price Book, and Price Book Entry

A Product in Salesforce CRM is an item that your organization provides quotes for and ultimately sells to customers. These product items can be goods or services with which your sales users can add to quotes and opportunities. As an administrator you can create a Product and associate it with a price in a Price Book.

A Price Book contains products along with the associated price. A Product can be listed in multiple Price Books to allow the selling of goods and services at different prices for different categories of sales (this might depend on which customer a product is being sold to, to which geographic location, or by the total quantity of the products).

The variation and combination of a Product with a price in a Price Book is managed in Salesforce CRM using a junction object called a Price Book Entry.

Service cloud

At the core of the service cloud in Salesforce CRM is the case management functionality, which is used to track and record activities dealing with customers, service, and support automation. Case records, in Salesforce, are associated with contacts and/or accounts.

A case is a detailed description of a customer's feedback, problem, or question. Your organization can use cases to track and solve your customer's issues. Cases can be manually entered from within the **Cases** tab by the support or sales team after, say, a phone call or e-mail to or from a customer. However, you can also set up more complex **Web-to-Case** and **Email-to-Case objects** to obtain customer responses from your company's website and customer e-mails.

Case management

There are number of ways case records, which may consist of recording phone calls or e-mail communication, can be entered into the Salesforce CRM application. Case records can be entered manually by users accessing the **Cases** tab, but there are other methods available for you to consider, which include:

- Automatic creation from an e-mail using**Email-to-Case** sent by a customer
- Automatic creation from a web form using **Web-to-Case** entered by a customer

Email-to-Case

Email-to-Case provides the facility for automatic case creation when an e-mail is sent to a preconfigured e-mail address.

Web-to-Case

Web-to-Case provides the facility where customers can submit support cases online.

 The **Web-To-Case** feature can be used to generate up to 500 new cases a day.

When setting up **Web-to-Case**, auto-response rules can be created to use e-mail templates to send an acknowledging e-mail to customers who have created cases using the web form.

Case queues

Queues can be thought of as a storage location to group cases together, usually by a geographic region or business function. Cases remain in the queue until they are assigned to or accepted by users.

Whenever you create a case queue, Salesforce automatically generates a case list view to enable users to access the records in the queue.

Case records can be assigned to queues manually or automatically using assignment rules. Case queues and assignment rules are very similar to the queues and assignment rules available for leads.

Assignment rules

Only one case assignment rule can be active at any one time, and each rule can contain multiple criteria up to a maximum of 25 criteria.

Escalation rules

Escalation rules are used to automatically escalate an unresolved case within a certain period of time. This escalation is triggered on the **Age Over** setting (when the **Age** field is overdue).

The modification of a field on a case is the only thing that stops the clock for escalation rules if the rule is set to disable after the field is first modified, or based on the last modification time of the case.

 For each escalation rule you can specify up to five actions to escalate the case over increasing periods of time. The **Age Over** field specifies the number of hours after which a case should be escalated if it has not been closed. This time is calculated from the date field set in the **Specify how escalation times are set** field. No two escalation actions can have the same set time period.

Sending an e-mail to a customer from the case record does not reset the case escalation. Only when the record – and not a related list – is changed is the case escalation time reset.

Escalation rules use business hours to determine when to escalate a case. The case feature can include business hours in multiple time zones and can associate cases to various time zones.

Each escalation rule can have multiple criteria settings and up to five escalation actions per entry. An example of one such action is shown in the following screenshot:

Early triggers

The early triggers mechanism enables case escalation to get expedited to the previous quarter hour slot. The setting is activated for the organization as a whole and is used to ensure that customer **Service Level Agreements (SLAs)** are met.

The early triggers on the escalation box allow you to specify whether cases should escalate sooner than the **Age Over** time specified.

As an example, we can consider that the escalation logic is currently running on the hour and the escalation triggers are fired every 15 minutes.

Now, say a case is created at 16:16 and the Escalation Rule is set to trigger after one hour. The case will not be escalated until 17:30 because it missed the 17:15 escalation trigger by one minute. This can be an issue when precise escalation is required, and hence by enabling early triggers, this issue can be eliminated.

To enable early triggers in the escalation box, follow the path **Setup** | **Customize** | **Cases** | **Support Settings**. Now click on **Edit** and set the **Early Triggers Enabled** checkbox, as shown in the following screenshot, and then click on the **Save** button:

Salesforce Chatter

Salesforce**Chatter** is an enterprise social networking application that helps users connect with people and share business information. It can be accessed from the **App** Menu at the top-right corner of the Salesforce CRM screen. **Chatter** feeds can also be accessed from within the Salesforce CRM record pages. All users with a Salesforce license have access to **Chatter**, and you can also create new users that do not have Salesforce licenses but wish to have access to **Chatter**. These user licenses can access **Chatter** users, profiles, groups, and files. However, they cannot access any Salesforce object data.

Chatter Only user licenses can be created for users within your company, known as **Chatter Free**, as well as for employees not in your organization, such as customers, known as **Chatter External**. These are shown in the following screenshot.

New User

User Edit	Save	Save & New	Cancel

General Information

First Name		Role	<None Specified>
Last Name		User License	Chatter Free
Alias		Profile	Chatter External / Chatter Free / Salesforce Platform
Email		Active	
Username		Marketing User	
Community Nickname		Offline User	

A further **Chatter** license (not shown in the previous screenshot of User License selection) is the **Chatter Only** license. This license is also known as **Chatter Plus** and is for users that do not have Salesforce licenses but require access to some Salesforce objects in addition to **Chatter**. This provides access to **Chatter** users, profiles, groups, and files, in addition to the viewing of Salesforce accounts and contacts and the ability to modify up to ten custom objects.

 You can upgrade a user's **Chatter Free** license to a standard Salesforce license whenever you wish; however, you cannot change a standard Salesforce license or Chatter Only license for a user to a Chatter Free license.

As mentioned previously, Salesforce **Chatter** can be accessed from the **App** Menu by selecting the Salesforce**Chatter** option, within which the following tabs are available: **Chatter, Profile, People, Groups,** and **Files,** as shown in the following screenshot:

These tabs are available by default in the **Chatter** app, however you can also add these tabs to other apps if required.

Chatter's primary features

The following primary features exist in Salesforce**Chatter**.

Feed

A **Chatter** feed is a list of recent activities in Salesforce that are displayed on:

- The **Chatter** tab and **Home** tab. Here, users can see their posts, posts from people they follow, updates to records they follow, and posts to groups they are a member of.
- Profiles, where users can see posts made by the person whose profile they are viewing.
- Records, where users can see updates to the record they are viewing.
- **Chatter** groups, where users can see posts to the group they are viewing.

Post

A **Chatter** post is a top-level comment in a **Chatter** feed.

Invitations

As the name suggests, a **Chatter** invitation sends an invite by e-mail to co-workers (either with or without a Salesforce license) or people outside your company (such as customers).

Chatter settings

Chatter settings provide options for feeds, posts, and invitations. We will first look at the setting to enable **Chatter,** and then in the following sections we will look through the various settings you can apply in Salesforce**Chatter**.

Enabling Chatter

Enabling **Chatter** also enables the Classic 2010 interface theme, which updates the look and feel of Salesforce.

Chatter is enabled by default for organizations created after June 22, 2010. For existing organizations, you must enable **Chatter**, as shown shortly.

When **Chatter** is enabled, the global search, which allows searching across Salesforce, including **Chatter** feeds, files, groups, and people is activated.

Where there are 15 or fewer users, all users automatically follow each other when **Chatter** is enabled.

The selection of the Salesforce Chatter options can be carried out by following the path **Setup | Customize | Chatter | Chatter Settings,** as shown in the following screenshot:

Let's look at each of the Salesforce Chatter setting options.

Chatter Settings – Enable Chatter

Check the **Enable** checkbox to turn on **Chatter** and the **Global Search** features.

Groups

This option allows you to modify **Chatter** group settings. By checking the **Allow Group Archiving** you will allow automatic and manual archiving for groups.

Groups can be activated even if this feature is not enabled.

Rich link previews in feed

Check the **Allow Rich Link Previews** checkbox to display rich content in the **Chatter** feed. By enabling this option, links in posts are converted into embedded videos, images, and article previews.

The rich content is provided by `Embed.ly`, which is a third-party web hosting service and previews are only available for links to supported sites. Salesforce does not share any private content with `Embed.ly`, just the URL.

Approval posts

Check the **Allow Approvals** checkbox to permit users to use **Chatter** posts within Salesforce Workflow approval processing. By enabling this option, users can approve any business process from within their **Chatter** feed.

Coworker Invitations

Check the **Allow Coworker Invitations** checkbox to enable everyone in your company to access **Chatter**. This allows all colleagues, even those who do not have Salesforce licenses, to collaborate using Salesforce **Chatter**.

Invited users can access **Chatter** users, profiles, groups, and files but cannot access Salesforce records unless they have a Salesforce license. To make **Chatter** available for company colleagues, you can either manually add **Chatter** users or use the **Invitations** option.

Invitations are automatically turned on for new organizations, and the **Company Email Domains** field is populated based on the first user's e-mail address.

 Salesforce recommends that you do not enter public e-mail domains such as `hotmail.com` or `gmail.com`. Anyone with an e-mail address in these domains could then join and access Chatter features and data within your organization.

You must provide at least one e-mail domain. You can add a maximum of 200 domains. The domains that you enter should be those used in e-mail addresses within your company.

 As security, the **Allow Coworker Invitations** checkbox will not be activated if the domain is a free e-mail provider such as `yahoo.com`, `gmail.com`, and so on.

Customer Invitations

Check the **Allow Customer Invitations** checkbox to permit users to invite people from outside your company network.

File Sync

This option allows users to access files saved in their Salesforce Files folder on their desktops from the Synced filter on the Files tab in **Chatter,** and in Salesforce1 Mobile (this was covered in `Chapter 10`, *Administrating the Mobile Features of Salesforce CRM*).

Your users need to install a desktop client called Salesforce Files. They can then securely store, sync, and share files between **Chatter**, their desktops, and mobile devices.

 These following limits apply when using the Salesforce Files Client: 10 GB is the maximum amount of data that individual users can sync in their Salesforce Files folder. Should the folder reach this limit, new files will not sync until other files are deleted from the folder. 500 MB is the maximum size of file that can be uploaded using the Salesforce Files folder.

Publisher Actions

Publisher Actions (or simply Actions) let you create actions and add them to the **Chatter** publisher on the homepage, on the **Chatter** tab, in **Chatter** groups, and on record detail pages. Actions also appear in the action tray in Salesforce1.

Actions can be set up to provide your users with the option to create or update records and log calls directly in the **Chatter** feed or from the users' mobile devices. Actions can be regular actions, such as create and update, or you can configure and develop custom Actions based on your company's needs.

The following lists the various types of actions:

- Standard actions that are automatically included when **Chatter** is enabled, such as **Post, File, Link**, and **Poll**. Here, you can customize the order in which these appear, but you cannot edit their properties.
- **Create actions** allow users to create records. You can choose the fields used in **Create actions** and when the record is saved any validation rule or mandatory field is fired.
- **Log a call actions** permit users to enter the details of phone calls where these call logs are saved as completed tasks.
- **Send email actions** (only available on Case records) provide a Case feed e-mail action on Salesforce1 Mobile (albeit, at the time of writing, a simplified version of the **Case Feed Email** function).
- **Update actions** let users amend a record from the feed associated with the record.
- **Question actions** let users ask and search for questions about the record.
- **Custom actions** are extended functionality developed with **Visualforce pages** or **Canvas** apps or Lightning Components.

Feed tracking

When you enable feed tracking, users will see updates for the objects and records that they follow in their **Chatter** feed. Many objects and fields are tracked by default, but you can further customize feed tracking to include or exclude specific objects and fields.

You can set feed tracking for users, **Chatter** groups, and the following standard objects: accounts, assets, campaigns, cases, contacts, contracts, dashboards, events, leads, opportunities, products, reports, solutions, and tasks. You can also configure feed tracking for custom objects.

The selection of the **Salesforce Feed Tracking** options can be carried out by following the path **Setup | Customize | Chatter | Feed Tracking**, as shown in the following screenshot.

Chat settings

This feature allows users to chat with people they follow in **Chatter** without having to use external chat clients.

Chat was no longer available for new orgs that were created from Spring '16 onwards and the feature will no longer be supported for existing orgs in the Spring '17 release.

The selection of the Salesforce Feed Tracking options can be carried out by following the path **Setup | Customize | Chatter | Chater Settings**, as shown in the following screenshot.

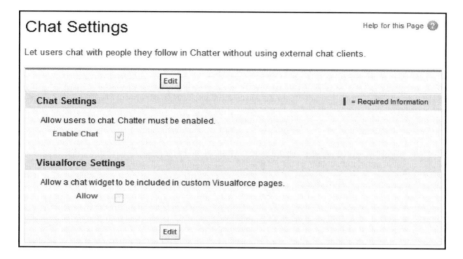

In the **Chat Settings** section, check the **Enable Chat** checkbox to permit users to use the chat facility directly in Salesforce CRM.

In the **Visualforce** Settings section, check the **Allow** checkbox to permit developer and administrators to include the **Chat** widget within custom **Visualforce** pages.

Influence

This setting allows you to control how much activity users must have before they are included in influence-level calculations.

The selection of **Salesforce Feed Tracking** options can be carried out by following the path
Setup | Customize | Chatter | Influence, as shown in the following screenshot.

Influence

Help for this Page

Activity Thresholds

▌ = Required Information

Do you want to control how much activity users must have before they're included in the influence level calculations? Users who don't meet all three minimums are considered observers and aren't counted when calculating the relative rank of people in your organization. Use caution when setting new thresholds because users' influence levels can change immediately.

Posts & Comments	0
Comments Received	0
Likes Received	0

[Save] [Cancel]

Chatter e-mail settings

This setting allows you to apply custom e-mail branding for **Chatter** e-mails and control whether your users are able to receive e-mails, and send posts using e-mail.

The options for the **Chatter Email Settings** can be set by following the path **Setup |
Customize | Chatter | Email Settings,** as shown in the following screenshot:

Chatter Email Settings

Help for this Page

Allow users to receive Chatter emails, apply custom branding, and more.

Save

General Settings

Allow Emails	☑ i
Allow Email Replies	☑
Allow Posts via Email	☐

Sender

From Name	Salesforce Chatter Name
Email Address	Salesforce Chatter Address

Branding

Logo	Salesforce Chatter logo

150 x 50 pixels or less on a transparent background is best.

Footer Text	salesforce.com Level 1, Atrium A Sandyford Business Park Dublin 18 Ireland

We strongly recommend including your company's physical address to comply with applicable
anti-spam laws.

Save

E-mail notifications

The following are the steps required for granting users the permission to receive and reply to e-mails:

- Check the **Allow Emails** checkbox to permit users to receive personal **Chatter** e-mail notifications
- Check the **Allow Email Replies** checkbox to permit users to reply to **Chatter** posts by e-mail

Questions to test your knowledge

You are now presented with questions about the key features of Salesforce CRM administration in the area of workflow automation, which have been covered in this chapter. The answers can be found at the end of the chapter.

Questions

We present ten questions about the functional areas of Sales Cloud, Service Cloud, and **Chatter,** which have been outlined in this chapter.

Question 1 – Lead Automation

What feature should you use to route a Lead record to a specific Lead Queue? (Select one)

a) Workflow rules.

b) Escalation rules.

c) Assignment rules.

d) Early triggers.

Question 2 – Lead Conversion

Leads are converted to which of the following objects? (Select one)

a) Contact, Opportunity, and optionally an Account.

b) Account, Opportunity, and optionally a Campaign or Contact.

c) Account, Contact, and optionally an Opportunity.

d) Account and optionally a Contact or Opportunity.

Question 3 – Converted Leads

Converted leads can be accessed in Salesforce CRM by carrying out which of the following? (Select all that apply)

a) Create a converted lead view in the Contacts Tab.

b) Create a converted lead view in the Leads Tab.

c) Create a converted lead report.

d) Create a converted lead view in the Accounts Tab.

Question 4 – Add to Campaign

Where will you find an **Add to Campaign** button in Salesforce CRM? (Select all that apply)

a) On the detail page for a Lead record.

b) On the results page of a Contact report.

c) On the detail page for an Opportunity record.

d) On the detail page for a Contact record.

e) On the results page of a Lead report.

Question 5 – Campaign Leads

How should you track the leads that are involved in a Campaign?

a) Link the lead using a custom lead lookup field on the Campaign.

b) Convert the lead to a Contact and link the Contact using a custom contact lookup field on the Campaign.

c) Associate the lead as a Campaign Member on the Campaign.

d) Create a Contact with the same details as the lead and then associate the contact as a Campaign Member on the campaign.

Question 6 – Campaign ROI Calculation

What must be set on the opportunities to include their values within the Campaign ROI calculation for a campaign? (Select all that apply)

a) All opportunities that are associated with the Campaign must have a value set on the opportunity Actual Cost field.

b) All opportunities that are associated with the Campaign must be Closed/Won.

c) All opportunities that are associated with the Campaign must have a value set on the opportunity Total Value of Won Opportunities field.

d) All opportunities that are associated with the Campaign must be set as the primary campaign for the Campaign.

Question 7 – Case Automation

What feature should you use to route a Case record to a specified Case Queue? (Select one)

a) Workflow rules.

b) Escalation rules.

c) Assignment rules.

d) Early triggers.

Question 8 – Unresolved Case

What feature can be used to automatically escalate an unresolved Case within a certain period of time? (Select one)

a) Workflow rules.

b) Escalation rules.

c) Assignment rules.

d) Early triggers.

Question 9 – Activities

Name the two types of activities that are found in Salesforce CRM. (Select one)

a) Tasks and Calendars.

b) Events and Calendars.

c) Log a call and Events.

d) Tasks and Events.

Question 10 – Chatter

Select the feature that can be used to automatically generate a **Chatter** post when fields within a record are updated. (Select one)

a) Publisher Actions.

b) Customer Invitations.

c) Feed tracking.

d) Coworker Invitations.

Answers

Here are the answers to the six questions about the functional areas of Sales Cloud, Service Cloud, and **Chatter**.

Answer 1 – Lead Automation

The feature that you should use to route a Lead record to a specific Lead Queue is **c)** Assignment rules.

Answer 2 – Lead Conversion

The objects that Leads are converted is **c)** Account, Contact, and optionally an Opportunity.

Answer 3 – Converted Lead

Converted leads can be accessed in Salesforce CRM by carrying out **c)**. Create a converted lead report.

Answer 4 – Add to Campaign

The **Add to Campaign** button is found in Salesforce CRM in: **a)** On the detail page for a Lead record, **b)** On the results page of a Contact report, **d)** On the detail page for a Contact record, and **e)** On the results page of a Lead report.

Answer 5 – Campaign Lead

You should track the leads that are involved in a campaign by carrying out **c)** Associate the lead as a Campaign Member on the Campaign.

Answer 6 – Campaign ROI Calculation

The following must be set on the opportunities to include their values within the Campaign ROI calculation for a campaign: **b)** All opportunities that are associated with the Campaign must be Closed/Won, and **d)** All opportunities that are associated with the Campaign must be set as the primary campaign for the Campaign.

Answer 7 – Case Automation

The feature that you should use to route a Case record to a specified Case Queue is **c**) Assignment rules.

Answer 8 – Unresolved Case

The feature that can be used to automatically escalate an unresolved Case within a certain period of time is **b**) Escalation rules.

Answer 9 – Activities

The two types of activities that are found in Salesforce CRM are **d**) Tasks and Events.

Answer 10 – Chatter

The feature that can be used to automatically generate a **Chatter** post when fields within a record are updated is **c**) Feed tracking.

Summary

In this chapter, we looked at the functional areas within Salesforce CRM, where we described the process from campaign to customer and beyond. We saw how leads in Salesforce CRM can be converted to generate the accounts, contacts, and opportunity records, which would then be processed through the sales cycle to form customer records, and we also saw how these customers can be supported by the customer service and support teams using the case management features.

Within the functional areas, we touched on when business teams concerned with marketing, sales, and customer service have to agree on roles and responsibilities for aspects of the business processes. We also looked at Salesforce **Chatter**, a collaboration application that helps in this respect by connecting people and sharing business information.

Finally, we posed some questions to help clarify some of the key features of Salesforce's Sales Cloud, Service Cloud, and Chatter.

In the next chapter, we will look at the ways in which the Salesforce CRM platform can be extended further through the use of customization technologies, such as Visualforce, where you can leverage further benefits for your organization and enhance the system without the need for expensive IT development resources.

9
Extending and Enhancing Salesforce CRM

In this chapter, we will look at how to extend and enhance the functionality within the Salesforce CRM application and how to move beyond the standard Salesforce Apps and features that we have looked at so far.

We will look at how additional functionality can be added to your Salesforce environment by using external applications from the **AppExchange Marketplace** to extend the capability of the core Salesforce CRM platform.

An overview of the technologies and techniques that allow advanced customization will be presented, which will help you gain an understanding of the features and considerations required to create web mashups in your Salesforce CRM applications.

You will discover how, with the use of platforms and technologies such as Visualforce, you can extend the core functionality of the application and leverage significant benefits for your organization, as well as how to enhance the system without the need for expensive IT development resources.

The following topics will be covered in this chapter:

- Salesforce AppExchange Marketplace
- Enterprise mashups in web applications
- Mashups in Salesforce CRM
- Introduction to Visualforce
- Creating an example mashup with Visualforce
- Overview of Visualforce controllers
- Introduction to Apex code and triggers
- Change management overview
- User adoption

Salesforce AppExchange Marketplace

The Salesforce **AppExchange Marketplace** is a website provided by Salesforce.com that enables organizations to select additional applications, known as **Apps**, to add new features to their Salesforce CRM application

Both the Salesforce CRM application and the AppExchange provide web-delivered platforms for using and building applications. This integrated web-delivered approach allows for the installation of applications and new functionality from AppExchange into Salesforce, which is often far simpler and more cost effective than traditional software update mechanisms. The benefits of the AppExchange are that system administrators can easily extend the Salesforce CRM application as your company's business requirements change.

There is a wealth of solutions available to help achieve most requirements that you can access from the Salesforce **AppExchange Marketplace**, and in this section we will describe and take you through the process of installing an example app.

The apps and services listed on AppExchange are provided by the Salesforce community of third-party developers and system integrators. Many of the apps are also provided by Salesforce themselves through their team known as the **Force.com Labs**. The apps can range from highly complex multiple screen solutions to simple sets of dashboards or reports.

Apps can sometimes incur additional costs, but there are many which are provided for free or a small fee. In general, apps provided by the Salesforce.com Force.com Labs team tend to be free. To access AppExchange, navigate to **Setup | AppExchange Marketplace**, as shown in the following screenshot:

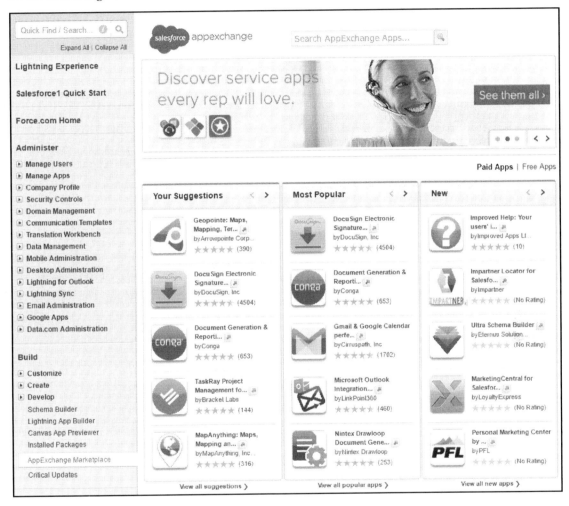

You can also access the **AppExchange Marketplace** website directly by navigating to `http://www.appexchange.com/`, as shown in the following screenshot:

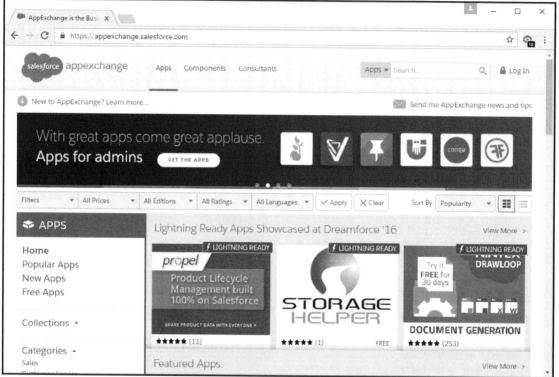

As a directory, Salesforce AppExchange is similar to consumer websites, such as the App Store from Apple, in the way that it seeks to provide an open, community-based channel for the distribution, retrieval, and installation of applications.

AppExchange differs, however, in that it provides not only the facilities for the third-party distribution of apps, but also the listing of services by system integrators. This enables the Salesforce community to search for and review both apps and services from a central site.

Managed and unmanaged packages

Salesforce terms the collection of components and applications that are distributed through AppExchange as a **package**. There are two main types of packages, namely, managed and unmanaged.

Managed packages differ from unmanaged packages by the use of protected components that allow the managed packages to be upgraded by the developers, allowing them to add new functionality or to refactor in any changes in the Salesforce environment. By protecting certain components such as Apex Code, managed packages also serve to protect the intellectual property of the developer organization.

Unmanaged packages, on the other hand, do not protect components and are therefore static within your organization, as they cannot be upgraded by the publishing developer. They allow you to access all of the implemented customization or code and can be useful if you want to change or extend the functionality yourself.

 Users with the permission **Download AppExchange Packages** enabled for their profile can install or uninstall the AppExchange packages from the AppExchange website.

Sometimes apps are distributed by **Independent Software Vendors (ISVs)**, which use the AppExchange package as a channel to advertise their presence and to showcase their range of products.

External and third-party tools

By showcasing on the **AppExchange Marketplace** website, ISVs often provide free apps, which help drive traffic and interest in their core products that complement Salesforce CRM, and they are usually provided as web-based solutions in the same way as Salesforce.

These complementary applications are typically deployed alongside Salesforce CRM in support of a specific business process or function. For example, **incentive and commission management**, **project management**, **product configuration**, **expense management**, **address checking**, and so on, are all examples of apps for Salesforce that are available from AppExchange.

App security

Salesforce inspects all registered apps to be sure that they have no obvious security risks. However, it is worth noting that since the apps are developed by third-party providers, you should also carry out extensive testing and employ due diligence to eliminate any risk before installing the app into your production instance.

After an app has passed the Salesforce inspection, the core functionality and code can no longer be changed. However, custom links and web tabs are allowed to be changed because they may need to be altered after installation, for example, simple target URLs might need to be changed from one organization to another.

You need to be aware how these links may introduce risks as part of your decision whether to trust the source of an app before installing it to production. This is described in more detail in the following section.

Before installing an app

The following steps are recommended to help you understand more about the app and to determine any risk or need for further setup in your organization before you actually install the app into your production instance:

1. Read the specifications and reviews.
2. Review the screenshots and customization guides.
3. Take a test drive.

Reading specifications and reviews

Before installing, read the specification associated with the app, where you will see the following details: which Salesforce editions are supported, what languages are supported, the components summary, and package details.

It is often also worth looking at the reviews that have been left by others that have attempted to install the app. Although there is no guarantee that the review is 100% accurate, and it may be subjective, it can give you an indication of the complexity in the use and successful installation of an app by other system administrators.

Reviewing screenshots and customization guides

Most apps that have been listed on the AppExchange website provide screenshots and guides for any post-install customization that may be required. These are useful and provide a quick indicator of whether the app will be of use to you and your organization.

Taking a test drive

Apps typically offer a test drive option (especially the more complex apps), where you are directed to an external Salesforce application where you can use the app as a read-only user before installation. A test drive gives you a far better way of determining whether the app is suitable for your organization before installing.

Within the test drive, you have the opportunity to check the app and its components to ensure that they are suitable, and also that they pose no security risks. For example, components such as custom links, formula fields, and web tabs can send Salesforce session IDs to external web services.

 Session IDs are tokens that allow users to access Salesforce CRM without re-entering the login name and password.

Salesforce.com recommends checking all links to external services that include a `session ID merge` field, because if these `session IDs` are shared with an external service, then they can expose your data, potentially leading to a significant security risk that we need to be aware of.

Installing an app

The following steps describe the process of how to install an app into your Salesforce CRM application from the **AppExchange Marketplace**:

1. Click the **Get It Now** button.
2. Examine the package.
3. Review the security.
4. Install the app.
5. Perform the post-installation configuration.

The best way to guide you through the use of new technology is by demonstrating with an example.

Here, we are going to install an application called **Mass Delete**, which has been developed and published by Salesforce.com's Force.com Labs team. This is a free app that provides a set of custom buttons that allow users to select any number of records and then delete them with a single click.

 The `Mass Delete` app from Salesforce.com's Force.com Labs is available from the **AppExchange Marketplace** directly through the following URL: `http://appexchange.salesforce.com/listingDetail?listingId=a0N 300000016YuDEAU`

The **Mass Delete app** page looks as follows:

![Mass Delete app page on AppExchange showing the Overview tab with app description, rating, and Get It Now button](screenshot)

Get It Now

By clicking on the **Get It Now** button, you will start the process of installing the application, where you will be prompted to log in to AppExchange using your Salesforce credentials, as shown in the following screenshot:

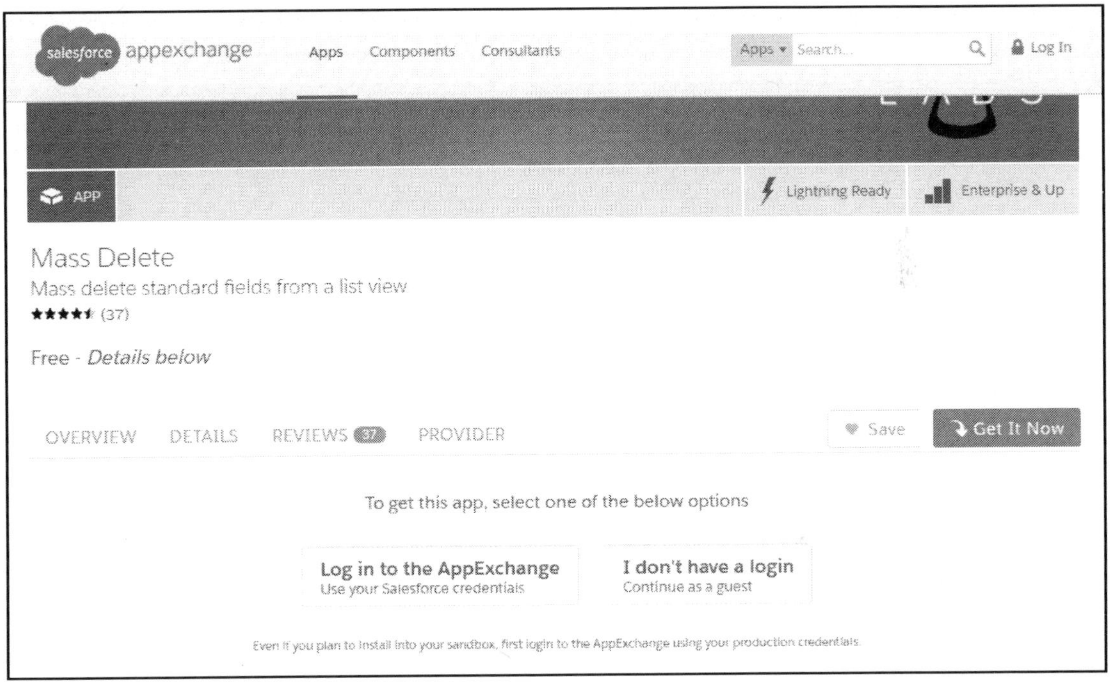

You will then be asked to select the location for the installation, where the options are to either **Install in production** or to **Install in sandbox,** as shown in the following screenshot:

You will then be presented with details of the app that will be installed (listed in the *What you are installing* section) and the Salesforce organization where the app will be installed (listed in the *Where you are installing* section), as shown in the following screenshot:

This page shows information about the **Package** and **Version,** along with the **Subscription**, **Duration**, and **Number of Subscribers** information that are a part of the app package.

Click on the checkbox labeled **I have read and agree to the terms and conditions** to confirm that you agree to proceed with the installation and then click on the **Confirm** and **Install!** to continue to the Salesforce login screen, as shown in the following screenshot:

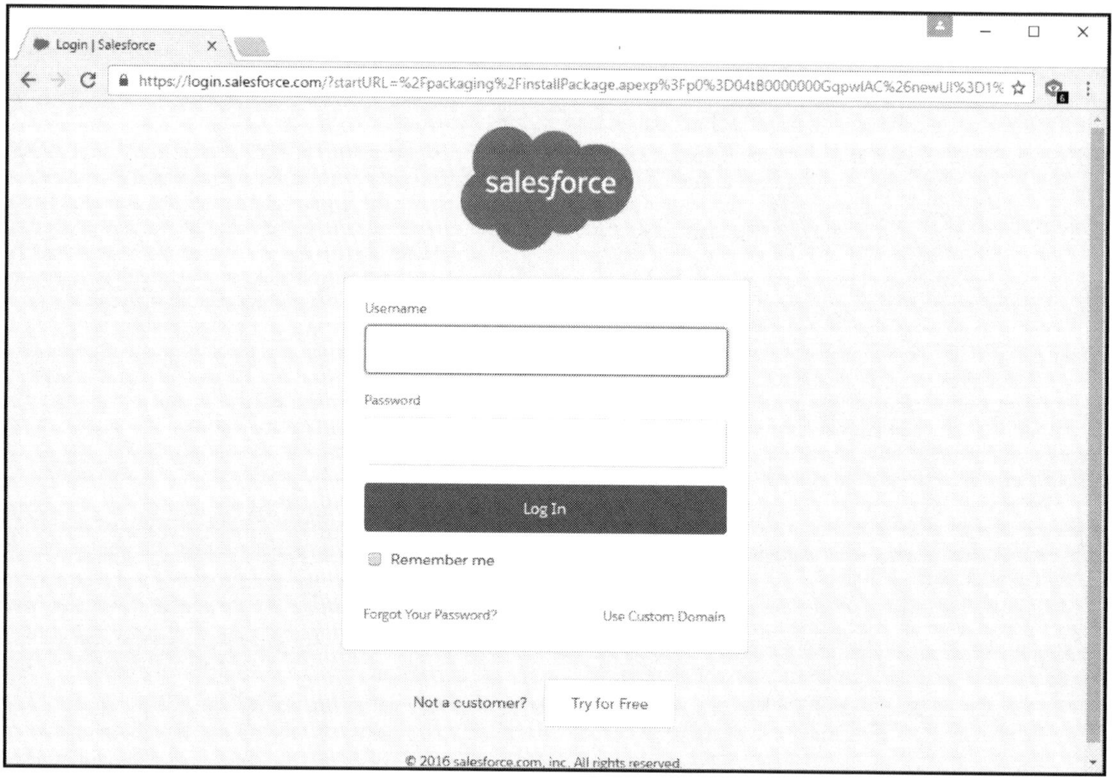

This screen allows you to log into the Salesforce app. If you wish to install the app into your production organization, you would use your production login details along with the Salesforce production URL, which may be `https://login.salesforce.com`. If you want to install it into a sandbox org, you must change the login URL to that of the sandbox, which is `https://test.salesforce.com`, and use your sandbox login details.

Now enter your **User Name** and**Password** and then click on **Login** to proceed to the next screen:

In this screen you are presented with options of how to handle a situation when an existing component's name conflicts with a component being installed. Here, the options available are **Do not install and Rename conflicting components in package**. You are also presented with options for the users' profile permissions that will be applied when the app is installed.

Now click on the **Install** button to proceed with the installation, and when complete the following confirmation screen appears:

In this final screen you are presented with information about the **App Name**, **Publisher**, **Version Name**, and various other details that make up the app package.

This screen provides confirmation that the app package has been successfully installed.

For large and complex apps, you may not see the **Installation Complete Confirmation** screen straight away. Instead, a screen is sometimes displayed that shows a message that the installation has been scheduled, and you will then later receive an e-mail notification when the deployment is complete.

Post-install configuration

Included in the package components of this **Mass Delete** app is a PDF guide describing the post-installation configuration that must be applied to the app before the functionality can be used. The guide can be accessed from within the **Documents** tab (which is accessible from the main **Documents** tab), as shown in the following screenshot:

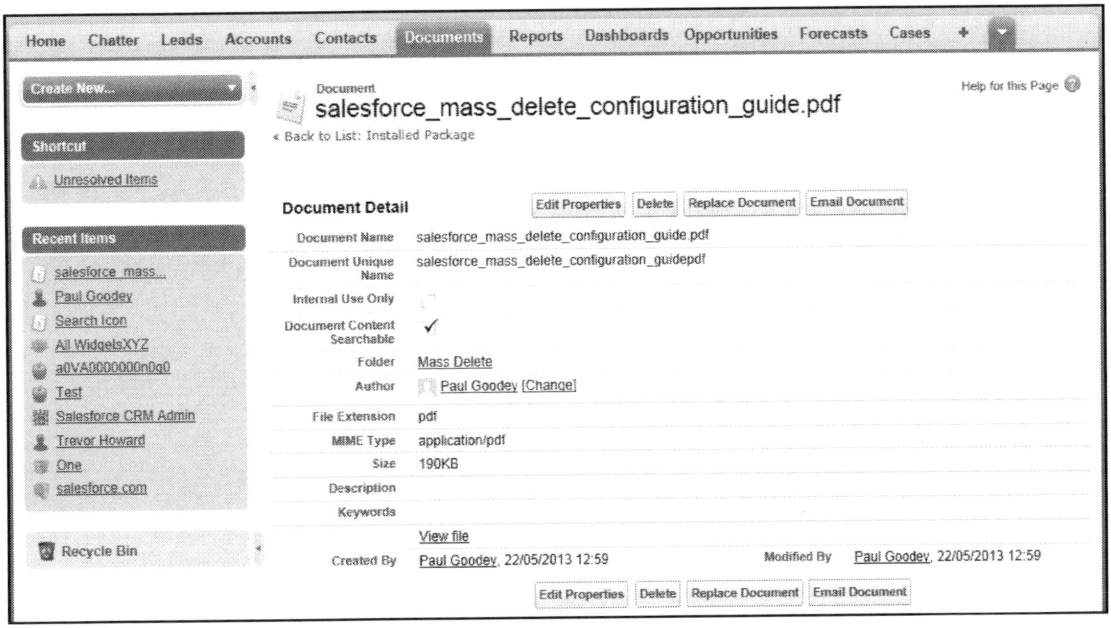

The guide describes how to complete the installation and customization of the app:

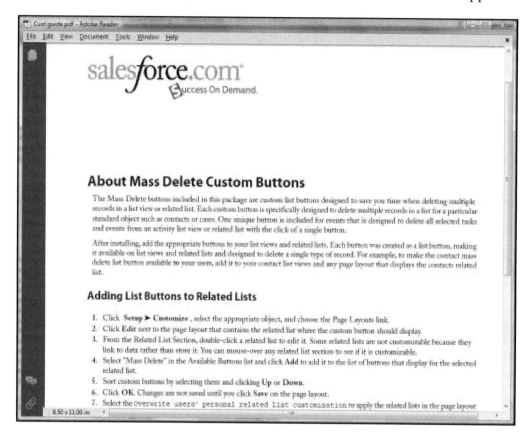

Using the guide, we add the **Custom list** button to the Contacts-related list within the
Accounts detail page, as shown in the following screenshot:

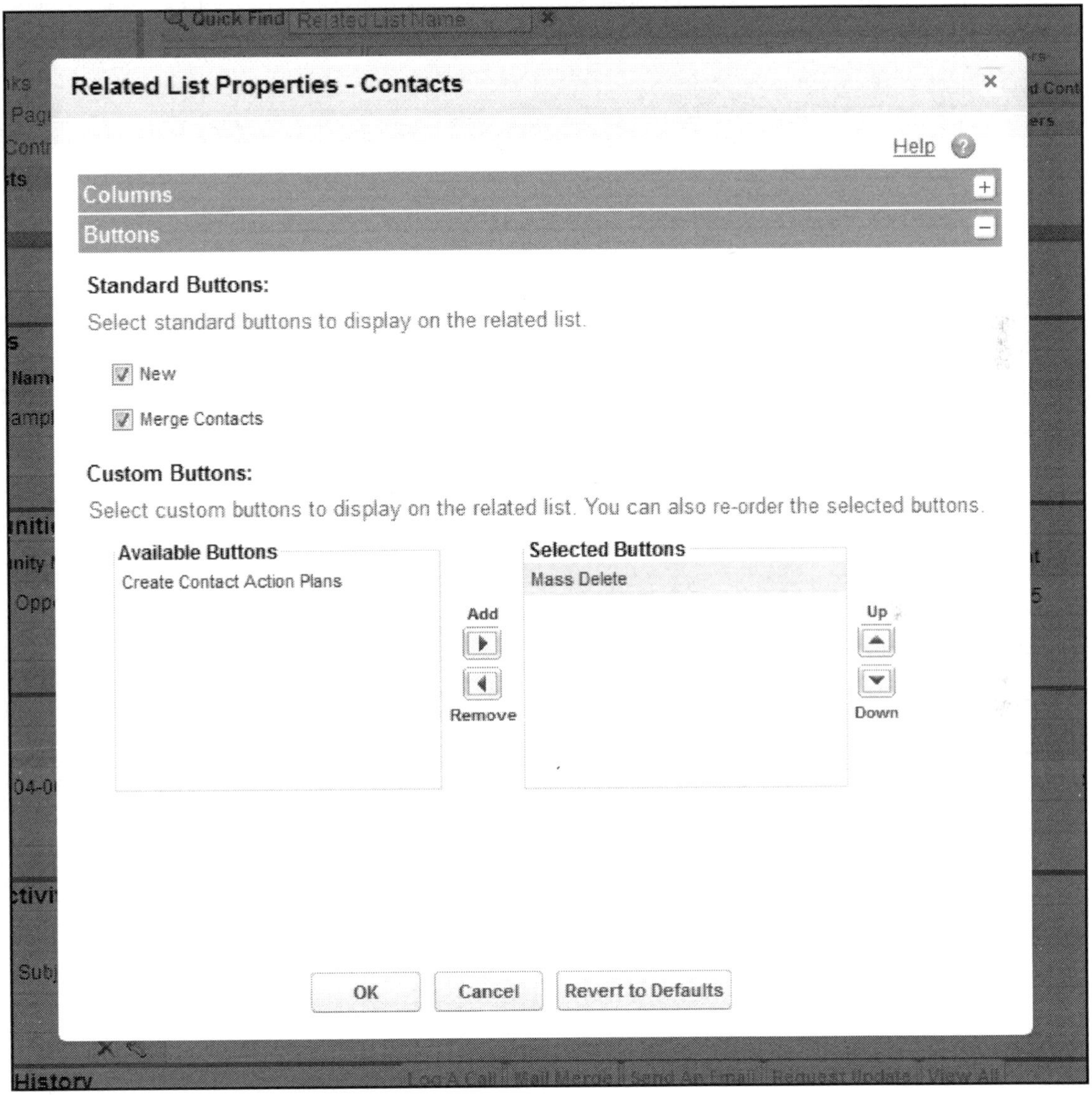

Finally, to verify the installation and customization, we can navigate to the **Accounts detail** page and access the **Contacts related list** section, whereupon we can access the **Mass Delete** custom button and associated functionality:

Account				
Edge Communications				

Customize Page | Edit Layout | Printable View | Help for this Page

Show Chatter ✔ Following

Contacts [2] | Opportunities [4] | Cases [3] | Open Activities [0] | Activity History [0] | Notes & Attachments [0] | Partners [0]

Contacts   [New Contact] [Merge Contacts] [Mass Delete]   Contacts Help (?)

✔ Action	Contact Name	Title	Email	Phone
✔ | Edit | Del	Sean Forbes	CFO	sean@edge.com	(512) 757-6000
✔ | Edit | Del	Rose Gonzalez	SVP, Procurement	rose@edge.com	(512) 757-6000

In Salesforce CRM Unlimited Edition, you can install an unlimited number of apps. In the Enterprise Edition, there is a maximum limit of ten apps.

Uninstalling an app

You can uninstall an app that has been installed from the AppExchange; however, there are some considerations. If you uninstall a package that includes a custom object, all components associated with that custom object are deleted, such as custom fields, validation rules, workflow rules, approval processes, custom buttons and links, and so on.

You cannot uninstall a package if any component in the package is referenced by a component that will not be included in the uninstall, or if a field added by the package is being updated by a scheduled job, such as a time-based workflow field update (here, you must wait until the background job finishes and retry).

After an uninstall, Salesforce automatically creates an export file containing the package data. When the uninstall is complete, Salesforce sends an e-mail containing a link to the admin user carrying out the uninstall.

The export files (plus related notes and attachments) are listed below the list of installed packages.

> Salesforce recommends backing up and storing the export file elsewhere because it will only be available for a limited period after the uninstall.To uninstall an AppExchange app, navigate to **Setup | Installed Packages**, as shown in the following screenshot:

packages							Help for this Page		
		Installed Packages							
Expand All	Collapse All		On Force.com AppExchange you can browse, test drive, download, and install pre-built apps and components right into your salesforce.com environment. Learn More about Installing Packages							
Build		Apps and components are installed in packages. Any custom apps, tabs, and custom objects are initially marked as "In Development" and are not deployed to your users. This allows you to test and customize before deploying. You can deploy the components individually using the other features in setup or as a group by clicking Deploy.							
Create							**Visit AppExchange »**		
Packages									
Installed Packages		To remove a package, click Uninstall. To manage your package licenses, click Manage Licenses.							

Installed Packages

Action	Package Name	Publisher	Version Number	Namespace Prefix	Install Date	Limits	Apps	Tabs	Objects
Uninstall	Mass Delete		0.3		1/6/2015 4:50 PM	✓	0	0	0

Now select the installed package and either click on the **Uninstall,** or click on the package name to review the details of the package, set the uninstall confirmation checkbox, and finally click on the **Uninstall** button, as shown in the following screenshot:

Uninstalling a Package

Help for this Page

⚠ Uninstalling this package will:

- Permanently delete all components in this package (listed below)
- Permanently delete all customizations you have made to these components

When you uninstall a package, by default, all its data as well as related notes and attachments are automatically saved as an export file. This file is available for 48 hours in case you need to recover the data. To reload the data, import the export file manually and recreate any relationships between objects. Some components can't be recreated and others require special treatment. You can also prevent the package data from being exported by selecting the appropriate radio button below.   Tell me more

Package Components

Action	Name	Parent Object	Type
	Mass_Delete_Records	Case	Button or Link
	Mass_Delete_Records	Contact	Button or Link
	Mass_Delete_Records	Contract	Button or Link
	Mass_Delete_Records	Lead	Button or Link
	Mass_Delete_Records	Account	Button or Link
	Mass_Delete_Records	Asset	Button or Link
	Mass_Delete_Records	Campaign	Button or Link
	MassDeleteExtensionTest		Apex Class
	MassDeleteExtension		Apex Class
	Mass_Delete_Lead		Visualforce Page
	Mass_Delete_Opportunity		Visualforce Page
	Mass_Delete_Case		Visualforce Page
	Mass_Delete_Account		Visualforce Page
	Mass_Delete_Asset		Visualforce Page
	mdslds212		Static Resource
	Mass_Delete_Records	Opportunity	Button or Link
	Mass_Delete_Records	Product	Button or Link
	Mass_Delete_Product2		Visualforce Page
	Mass_Delete_Records	Solution	Button or Link
	Mass_Delete_Solution		Visualforce Page

⦿ Save a copy of this package's data for 48 hours after uninstall
◯ Do not save a copy of this package's data after uninstall

☑ Yes, I want to uninstall this package and permanently delete all associated components

[Uninstall]

AppExchange best practices

The following best practices should be applied when installing apps from the **AppExchange Marketplace** website:

- Clarify that the specification for the app meets the requirements and assess any reviews and comments
- Take a test drive, if available
- Review all the components that are included in the package and be aware of any security issues concerning links and session IDs
- Test the app in a sandbox before deploying into production
- Try to enlist business support to own and validate the app before deploying into production
- Consider undertaking a pilot deployment for selected users if the app is particularly complex
- Communicate the app to the business prior to deployment and activation in production
- Prepare training material for all affected users if the app is particularly complex

Enterprise mashups in web applications

A **mashup** is a general term that is commonly used to describe the merging of functionality and content from multiple sources. It is typically applied to describe the merging of web applications where the sources may often be using different technology to provide the service or application. As part of the distinction of a web application mashup, there is a common feature that provides connectivity, which is the Internet.

The connections between the various sources may require different levels and complexities of integration, depending on whether the associated information or content is to be simply viewed or whether it is also to be amended, and therefore whether data is to be distributed across various systems. When mashups first started appearing on the Web, they were created to enable the viewing of content from another web source within an Internet browser, and did not transfer any data or functionality between the source systems.

An example of such a mashup is a website that displays a *how to find us* type of page within one of its web pages, such as the contact page. Within the HTML code, there might be an embedded piece of functionality showing a static Google Map or a similar web control, as shown in the following screenshot:

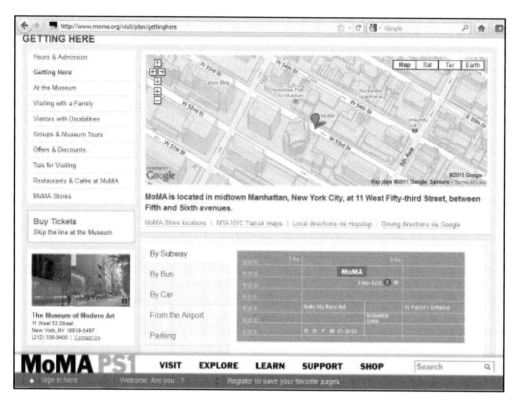

This type of mashup is an example of a simple client-side mashup, where the connectivity occurs inside the web browser. This coding inside the web page provides a way to combine static information from multiple Internet sources and generate an elegant visual presentation.

As mashups have evolved, far more complex functionality can now be achieved. It is possible to have sophisticated integration between web applications where information and functionality are seamlessly shared. As you might expect, this requires more complex coding to achieve, and also may require the use of server-side infrastructures. We will look at the distinction between client-side and server-side mashups shortly.

Mashups in Salesforce CRM

It may seem daunting at first, especially if you are less familiar with Internet scripting technologies such as HTML, but certain types of mashups can be accomplished by most people and do not require professional software developers or an IT team.

 HTML is the main markup language for creating web pages and other information that can be displayed in a web browser (`https://en.wikiped ia.org/wiki/HTML`).

Before starting out, it is always useful to first evaluate how and where the mashup needs to be done, and in particular, the type of data and service that is to be mashed up. Once this is understood, you can then begin to consider the coding effort and plan the resources required to implement them.

To understand the flavor of mashups as far as Salesforce CRM is concerned, and as suggested, at a high-level, there are two main categories of mashup development, and these can be classed as either server-side or client-side, as shown in the following diagram:

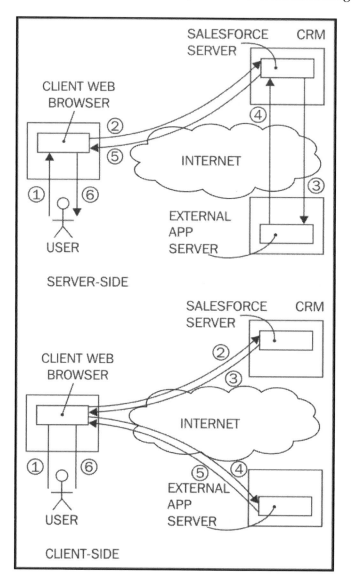

Looking at the previous diagram, we see that the server-side mashup goes through the following high-level steps:

1. User makes a page request to Salesforce CRM using their web browser.
2. The web browser calls the Salesforce CRM servers, which invoke custom Apex code.
3. The custom Apex code in Salesforce CRM calls a function on an external application server.
4. The external application returns the response to Salesforce CRM.
5. Salesforce CRM processes the response and returns the details to the user's web browser.
6. The user's web browser finally presents the overall response back to the user.

Client-side mashups are far more simple, as they use the browser to link the requests and responses required for the mashup, where the following typical high-level steps can be considered:

1. User makes a page request to Salesforce CRM using their web browser.
2. The user's web browser requests details from Salesforce CRM.
3. Salesforce CRM returns the response to the user's web browser.
4. The user's web browser requests details from the external application.
5. The external application returns the response to the user's web browser.
6. The user's web browser finally presents the overall response back to the user.

As indicated, server-side mashups often require sophisticated coding and require external infrastructure, which is generally provided by IT resources. As this book does not aim to be a resource for developers, we will look at server-side technology at a high level, but we will not go into the details.

We will, however, cover the use cases and provide some step-by-step instructions on how you can compose client-side mashups, as well as the tools that are available within your Salesforce CRM application.

Server-side mashups

By way of introduction, and for the sake of completeness, the following section describes the core features of external server-side mashups. We will briefly look at, in a little more detail, the capabilities, features, and implications associated with the use of server-side mashups.

Server-side mashups are a specific example of an external services mashup. This is where external systems may either serve the request for data from Salesforce as a client or use data presented by Salesforce and mash the composite data in an external system.

These mashups typically use web services, and are most often provided by organizations using web APIs, which describe how the service can be accessed by a client application over the Internet and which are executed on the remote system that is hosting the service.

A more formal definition of a web service is provided by the **World Wide Web Consortium (W3C)**, which as detailed on their web page (http://www.w3.org), is an international community where member organizations, a full-time staff, and the public work together to develop web standards.

The definition of a web service by the W3C is as follows (http://www.w3.org/TR/ws-gloss/):

A Web service is a software system designed to support interoperable machine-to-machine interaction over a network. It has an interface described in a machine-processable format (specifically WSDL). Other systems interact with the Web service in a manner prescribed by its description using SOAP-messages, typically conveyed using HTTP with an XML serialization in conjunction with other Web-related standards.

Although the web service definition for the machine-to-machine interaction by the W3C refers to machine-to-machine interaction using **Simple Object Access Protocol (SOAP)**, there is another protocol that is becoming increasingly popular today, known as **Representational State Transfer (REST).** This is mentioned for information only, and we will not go into any further detail about web services in this book.

Client-side mashups

Within Salesforce CRM, there are typically two types of client-side mashup, namely, client-side services mashups and client-side presentation mashups.

Client-side services mashups

Similar to server-side mashups, client-side services mashups can also be used to call web services or consume websites and feeds. They can be used to invoke the Salesforce CRM web services API from within the browser. Client-side services mashups require more complex programming than client-side presentation mashups, and typically rely on the technologies associated with web services.

Client services mashups and external services mashups are useful to organizations that need to access information from various systems that usually serve a business data process and interact in real time. Specifying and developing these types of mashups needs to be carefully evaluated to determine the required effort and resources.

Client-side presentation mashups

Client-side presentation mashups are the least complex mashups and can be composed relatively quickly. Here, live data and functionality from multiple sources are embedded on a web page that requires data from the Salesforce platform with which to mashup with the non-Salesforce data and functionality.

Client presentation mashups in Salesforce can be composed using Visualforce, HTML, and JavaScript, and which can often be copied and pasted by nontechnical users, immediately adding value to a web application.

Having briefly outlined the nature of client-side mashups, we are now going to look at how they can actually be created in Salesforce CRM. As shown earlier, the enabling technology is provided by the Salesforce platform with the use of the web page framework known as Visualforce.

The best way to guide you through the use of new technology is by demonstrating how to use it with an example. Here, we are going to compose a client-side presentation that displays a Google Map widget displaying Google Map location details for a given company record in Salesforce.

The Google Map will be presented to the user in Salesforce CRM after selecting an appropriate account record, and live Google Map information will be displayed right from within the relevant account detail page. The mashup will be composed by creating a new Visualforce page with the required Google Map widget and then adding a new section to the account detail page where the Visualforce page will be included.

Introduction to Visualforce

Visualforce is the framework in Salesforce CRM that allows you to further customize your organization's user interface beyond the standard functionality we have previously covered.

As described previously, using Visualforce you can combine data from multiple objects, create mashups with data from external web services, and even override some of the logic and the behavior found within standard Salesforce CRM application functions. Visualforce consists of the following three elements:

- Visualforce pages: These are used to define the user interface
- Visualforce components: These can be thought of as a library of standard or custom-built sections of Visualforce code
- Visualforce page controllers: These are used to control the behavior of Visualforce pages, and can either be controlled by standard logic or you can create custom logic to change or extend the standard Salesforce CRM behavior

Visualforce pages

The Visualforce framework allows for the creation of Visualforce pages. These pages are a little like documents that are stored in Salesforce, and they are comprised of instructions that specify how the page is to appear and function. Similar in nature to HTML, Visualforce pages comprise of a tag-based markup language, with each Visualforce tag type corresponding to a particular user interface component.

 The maximum size of a Visualforce page cannot be greater than 15 MB.

For the more technical readers, Visualforce performs similar functions as, say, Java Server Pages or Active Server Pages and is used to manage the retrieval of data from the Salesforce platform and the rendering of results via the Internet browser user interface.

Creating a Visualforce page

Now that you are aware of the basic building blocks provided by Visualforce, we will describe the creation of Visualforce pages. This section looks at how the creation and modification of pages can be done and shows the following two ways of doing so:

- Using the Visualforce pages setup page
- Using development mode

Visualforce pages setup page

To navigate to the setup page for creating Visualforce pages, go to **Setup | Develop | Pages.** Now click on the **New** button to create a new Visualforce page. Select an existing entry to view the page or click on **Edit** to modify it, as shown in the following screenshot:

Visualforce development mode

We can also use something called Visualforce development mode to initially create and edit Visualforce pages. This can be a better choice because it provides several useful features that make it easier to build **Visualforce pages**.

To start using the development mode, it needs to be activated on your user record by navigating to **Your Name** | **Setup** | **My Personal Information** | **Personal Information**. Now click on the **Edit** button, select the **Development Mode** checkbox (as shown in the following screenshot), and then finally click on **Save**:

When in Visualforce development mode, you can create a new page simply by entering a unique URL into the browser's address bar.

Automatic creation of new Visualforce pages can be done by entering a unique URL (for a Visualforce page that does not exist) into the browser's address bar. For example, typing the URL `https://na10.salesforce.com/apex/GoogleMap` will enable a new page called Google Map to be created.

You need to be careful that you are entering the correct URL text, as it is the `/apex/GoogleMap` part in the preceding example that prompts Salesforce CRM to check and create a new page if it does not currently exist. It is also important that the start of the URL is entered correctly. The `https://na10.salesforce.com` part refers to the Salesforce instance for your Salesforce CRM application.

When entered correctly, the following screen, which allows you to create the Visualforce page, will be presented:

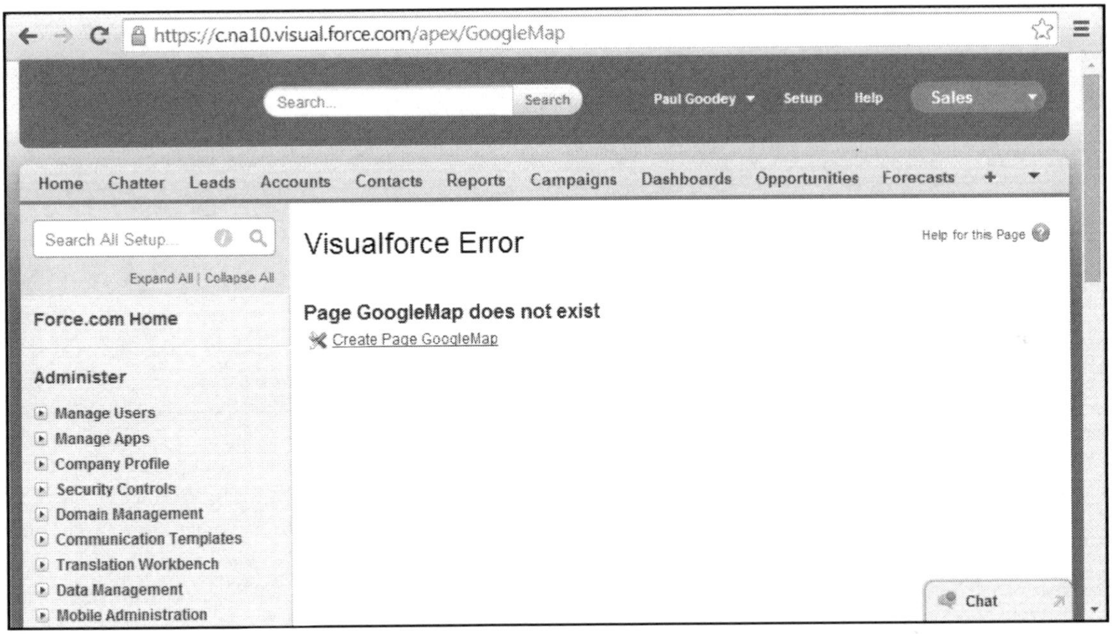

This, as you can appreciate, can save a lot of time when creating multiple pages, as you do not need to keep navigating to the setup section, saving you a number of mouse clicks.

The resulting edit page when you click on the **Create Page Google Map** link is the same edit page as when accessed through the setup route, as shown in the following screenshot:

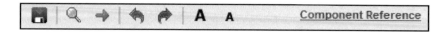

When development mode is enabled, a development section is automatically presented below the Visualforce page that you are creating or editing, which displays an editor section. To show or hide the development section, click on the following icon:

The editor allows you to write Visualforce component tags directly within the browser window and also offers the following features:

As shown, the seven menu functions are provided for:

- Saving the page
- Searching for text
- Navigating to a specified line in the code

- Undoing changes
- Redoing changes
- Increasing the font size of the text
- Decreasing the font size of the text

Clicking on the **Component Reference** link will take you to online documentation, which provides descriptions as well as example code for all the Visualforce components, as shown in the following screenshot:

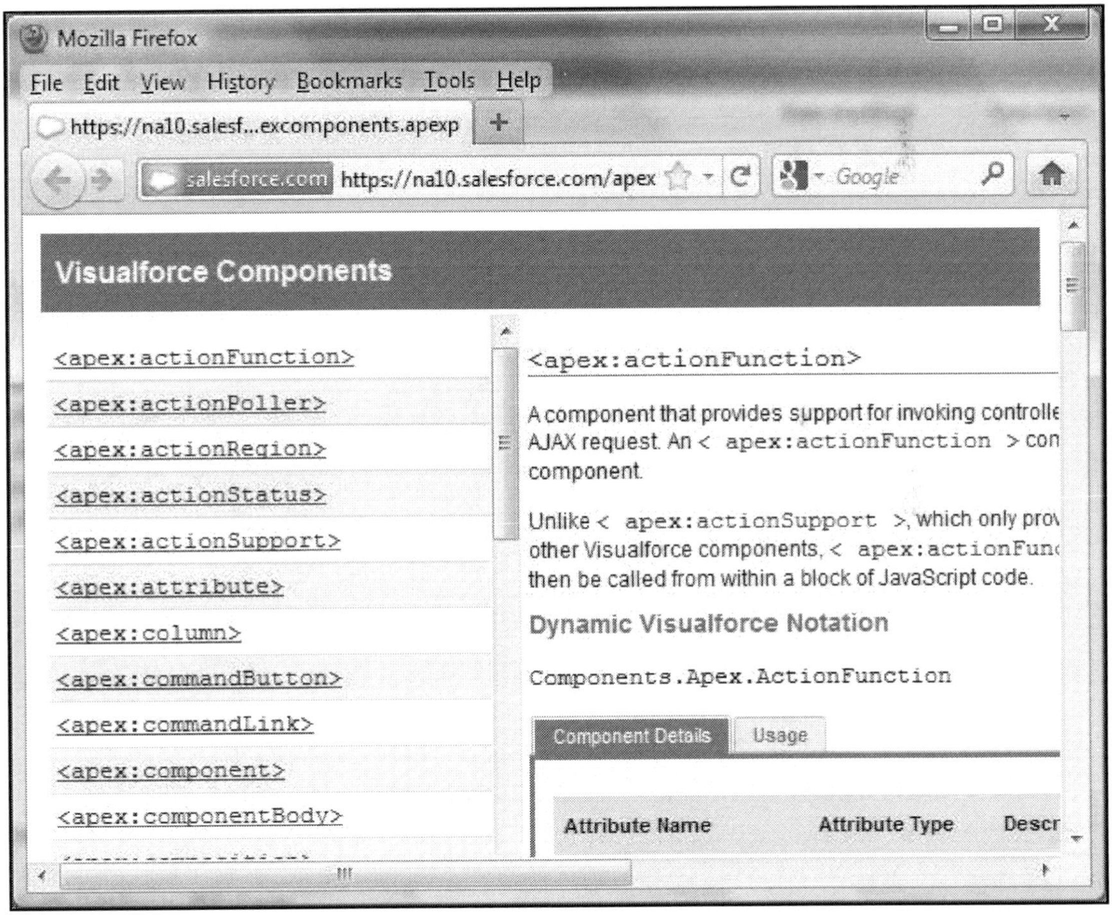

In addition, the page editor also provides highlighting and an autocomplete feature that automatically displays available component markup tags, as shown in the following screenshot:

The greatest benefit of having development mode enabled when building Visualforce pages using the Salesforce CRM platform is that as you add component tags and build up the code in the page, you can click on the save icon and view the resulting changes immediately.

> The Visualforce page must be free from errors before the page can be saved.

Visualforce components

We have seen in the previous section that Salesforce provides a set of standard, pre-built components, such as `<apex:actionFunction>` and `<apex:actionStatus>`, which can be added to Visualforce pages to construct pages of functionality. In addition, you can build your own custom components to augment this library of components.

Similar to the way functions work in a programming language, a custom Visualforce component allows you to construct common code and then re-use that code in one or more Visualforce pages.

Custom components allow you to define attributes that can be passed to each component. The value of an attribute can then change the way the markup is displayed on the final page and the controller-based logic that executes for that instance of the component.

Visualforce custom components consist of Visualforce markup tags using the standard `<apex:component>` tag, and so rather than repeating the Visualforce markup required for every page that you need the common code on, you can define a custom component that has certain attributes and then uses those attributes to display the functionality on the page. Once defined, every Visualforce page in your organization can leverage the custom component in the same way as a page can leverage standard components such as `<apex:dataTable>` or `<apex:actionStatus>`.

Creating an example mashup with Visualforce

To construct our example mashup we will follow these steps:

1. Delete the default new Visualforce markup content.
2. Change the Visualforce Controller to specify an Account Standard Controller.

Copy and paste the Google Map code and add Salesforce-specific merge fields.

Deleting the default new Visualforce markup content

Delete the existing Visualforce page text (lines 2 to 5 in the following screenshot) and leave just the starting and ending tags, `<apex:page>` and `</apex:page>`, as shown in the following screenshot:

Changing the Visualforce Controller to specify an Account Standard Controller

We also need to change the Visualforce page controller so that we can read the value of the fields stored on the Account record. Controllers will be looked at in more detail later on in this chapter, but for the moment we will change the opening tag `<apex:page>` and add the `standard Controller` attribute, which allows the call to the **Account** record, as shown using the code `<apex:page standard Controller="account">`:

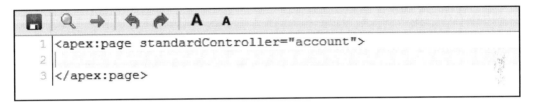

```
1 <apex:page standardController="account">
2
3 </apex:page>
```

Copy and paste the Google Map code and add Salesforce-specific merge fields.

We will copy and paste the following code, which contains Salesforce merge fields, to render a Google Map on our account records:

```
<script type="text/javascript" src="https://maps.google.com
/maps/api/js?sensor=false"></script>
<script type="text/javascript">
function initialize()
{
  var map;
  var mapOptions =
  {
    zoom: 13,
    mapTypeId: google.maps.MapTypeId.ROADMAP,
    mapTypeControl: false
  }
  var mapMarker;
  var geocoder = new google.maps.Geocoder();
  var address =
   "{!SUBSTITUTE(JSENCODE(Account.BillingStreet),'\r\n','
   ')}, " + "{!Account.BillingCity}, " +
   "{!Account.BillingPostalCode}, " +
   "{!Account.BillingCountry}";geocoder.geocode( {address:
   address}, function(results, status)
   { if(status ==
     google.maps.GeocoderStatus.OK && results.length)
     { if(status !=
     google.maps.GeocoderStatus.ZERO_RESULTS)
```

```
        {
            map = new
            google.maps.Map(document.getElementById("map"),
            mapOptions);
            map.setCenter(results[0].geometry.location);
            mapMarker = new google.maps.Marker({
                position: results[0].geometry.location,
                map: map,
                title: "{!Account.Name} " + address
            });
        }
    } else {
        document.getElementById("map").innerHTML = "Unable to find or
display a map
        for {!Account.Name}'s billing address : " + address;
    }
    });
    }
</script>
    <div id="map" style="width:100%;height:300px"></div>
<script>
    initialize();
</script>
```

We use Salesforce merge fields for the **Account** record to pass the **Billing Address** data to the Google map API, as shown in the following snippet:

```
var address = "{!SUBSTITUTE(JSENCODE(Account.BillingStreet),'\r\n',' ')}, "
+ "{!Account.BillingCity}, " + "{!Account.BillingPostalCode}, " +
"{!Account.BillingCountry}";
```

The final code will appear within the Visualforce page, as in the following screenshot:

When saving the Visualforce page, the page is rendered immediately. However, at this point, there is no billing address data that can be passed to the Google Map widget (this will be rendered properly after we have added the Visualforce page to the Account Page Layout), and therefore an error will initially be presented, as shown in the following screenshot:

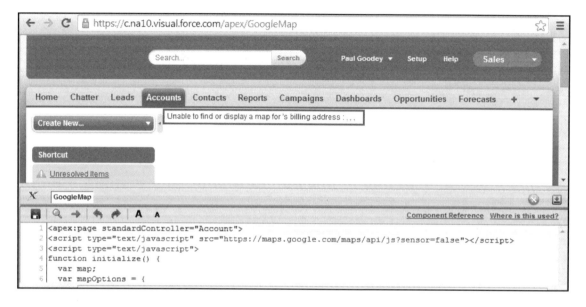

 Notice how with the use of the `<apex:page standardController="account">` tag, the **Accounts** tab is now automatically highlighted.

Adding the Visualforce page to the Account page layout

Now that we have completed and saved the Visualforce page, we can add the **Google Map** page to the Account page layout. To add Visualforce pages to Accounts, navigate to **Setup |Customize | Accounts | Page Layouts**. Now select the appropriate page layout. Here, we are going to add it to the page layout called Account Layout by carrying out the steps discussed in the following section.

Adding a new section to the Account page layout

The new section has been given the title **Google Map** and has been set to **1-Column** width and positioned by dragging and dropping below the **Account System and Description Information** section, as shown in the following screenshot:

Adding the Visualforce page to the new page layout section

Now drag and drop the **Google Map Visualforce** page to the **Google Map** section on the page layout, as shown in the following screenshot:

Now click on **Save**; we are ready to test by navigating to an account page.

Running the completed Visualforce page

Navigate to the **Account** tab and select an existing account to verify that the mashup is working as expected.

You will need to ensure a Billing Address is completed for the account record. **The Billing Address** composite field is a standard **Account** field in Salesforce CRM.

Here we have an existing account for Salesforce.com with the **Billing Address** populated and which displays a **Google Map** when the account detail page is loaded, as shown in the following screenshot:

Account
salesforce.com

Customize Page | Edit Layout | Printable View | Help for this Page

Show Feed

« Back to List: Pages

Action Plans [0] | Contacts [0] | Opportunities [0] | Cases [0] | Open Activities [0] | Activity History [0] | Notes & Attachments [0]

Account Detail Edit Delete Include Offline

Account Owner	Paul Goodey [Change]	Active
Account Name	salesforce.com [View Hierarchy]	Upsell Opportunity
Parent Account		Type
Billing Address	The Landmark @ One Market Suite 300 San Francisco, California 94105 United States	Shipping Address

▼ Google Map

How do I suppress browser security warnings in Internet Explorer?

By default, Internet Explorer displays the following security warning message when a page contains a mixture of secure (HTTPS) and nonsecure (HTTP) content: **This page contains both secure and nonsecure items. Do you want to display the nonsecure items?** When you create a mashup with a nonsecure URL, users may see this warning message depending on their browser security settings. To suppress this warning in Internet Explorer, follow these steps: from the Internet Explorer tools menu, select **Internet Options**, click on the **Security** tab, click on the **Custom Level** button and, finally, in the miscellaneous section, set **Display mixed content** to **Enable**, as shown in the following screenshot:

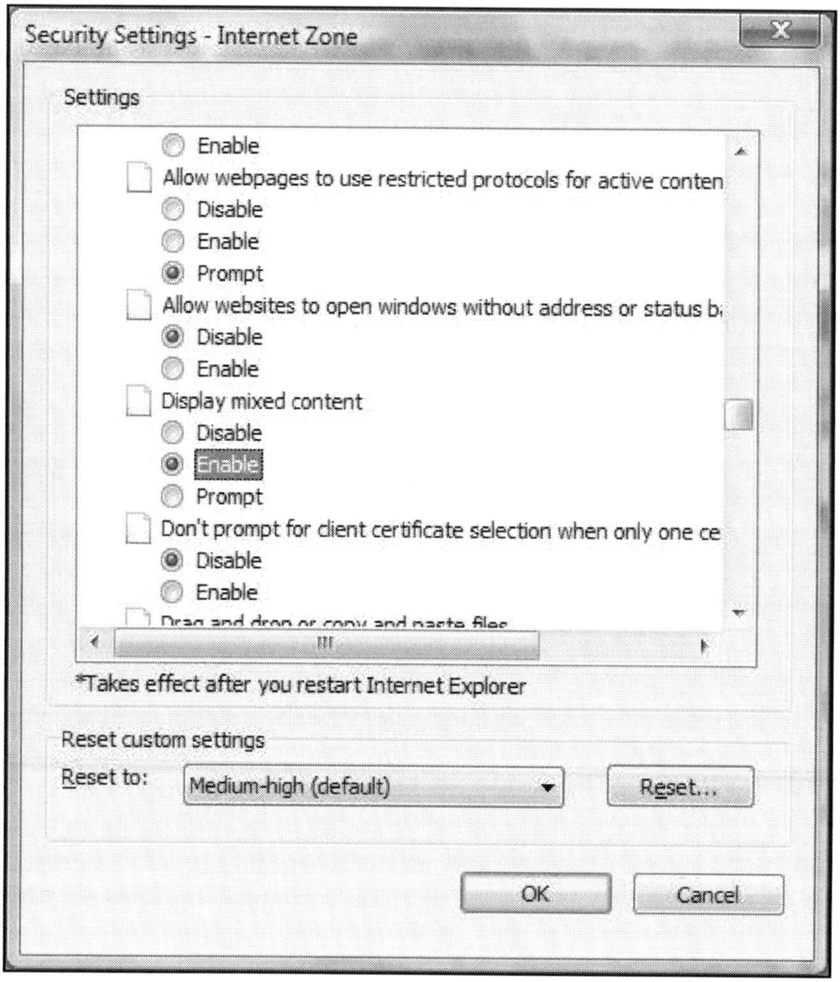

Visualforce page controllers

As described earlier in this chapter, there are four types of controllers that can be used to control the functionality behind a Visualforce page.

Standard controllers

A standard controller provides access to standard Salesforce CRM behavior and, as shown in our example client-side mashup, can be specified using the following tag and attribute as the first line in the Visualforce page:

```
<apex:page standardController="Account">
```

Standard controllers are available for standard objects, such as Account, Contact, Opportunity, and so on, as well as custom objects, and they provide access to standard Salesforce CRM data operations and behavior for actions such as save, edit, and delete.

Custom controllers

Custom controllers are used for fully customized behavior and are implemented using the Visualforce tag and attribute as follows:

```
<apex:page controller="CustomAccount">
```

Controller extensions

Controller extensions are used to extend the behavior of standard controllers and allow the addition of customized functionality. Controller extensions are provided using the Visualforce tag and attribute as follows:

```
<apex:page standardController="Account"
extensions="CustomAccountExtension">
```

Standard list controllers

Salesforce record pages allow users to filter the records displayed on the page using list views (covered in Chapter 3, *Configuring Objects and Apps*). For example, on the accounts home page, users can choose to view a list of only the accounts they own by selecting **My Accounts** from the list view drop-down menu.

Standard list controllers provide the same list view picklist and are implemented using the following tag and attribute as the first line in the Visualforce page:

```
<apex:page standardController="Account" recordSetVar="accounts">
```

Apex code

The Apex code language in Salesforce CRM is based on Java, which is one of the most popular programming languages for Internet and web-based applications, and is executed on the Salesforce platform servers.

Although based on Java, the Apex code and the Salesforce CRM platform is not a general-purpose computing platform that can be used to run any type of program that developers may choose to run. Instead, Apex is kept intentionally controlled and limited and is, therefore, designed with the needs of the business and platform in mind.

Apex code in Salesforce is not intended to solve every programming problem and is instead concerned principally with helping developers gain advantages in development time, code conciseness, and reduction in maintenance costs.

Apex is used in Salesforce CRM to develop the code within Custom controllers and Controller extensions, as well as Apex triggers, which we will look at shortly.

Apex is specifically designed for building business applications to manage data and services, and the language provides a highly productive approach to creating applications and business logic. Developers can focus on the functionality required to solve the business problem and domain and need not be concerned with building the infrastructures, such as database connection, error handling, and so on, which is instead managed by the platform.

It should be noted that since the Salesforce CRM platform is a multi-tenant platform, there are certain limits as to what and how much processing can be performed within certain operations. Such limits are known, such as **Governor Limits**, and there are some restrictions and requirements – for example, Apex code must be developed in a developer or sandbox organization and must have test methods to verify each line of code. Only then is it allowed to be deployed to production.

 For successful deployment to production, Apex code must have associated unit test methods that provide at least 75% successful code coverage.

Apex triggers

Apex triggers are blocks of Apex code that are executed before and/or after any record action such as create, update, or delete in the Salesforce CRM application.

Triggers are very powerful and can include complex code for controlling your process. They are used for complex business logic automation and where such functionality is too complicated to be implemented using validation rules or workflow rules, such as field updates. The development of Apex triggers usually requires the resource of a software developer, as they have certain restrictions and implications for the overall system.

When using multiple triggers, and alongside any existing workflow field updates, there needs to be a thorough understanding of any dependencies so as to avoid any ripple effect when records are created or updated. As trigger code can make changes to the record being updated within its own operation, any likely recursion effect needs to be understood and avoided.

Apex triggers offer many benefits to an organization, but they also introduce some risks as there needs to be awareness of certain patterns and limits (bulkifying triggers, governors, and so on.) imposed by the underlying platform. It is particularly important to understand the timing, order of execution, and dependencies of the various rules and triggers within an organization.

Change management overview

As outlined in the section on installing apps from **AppExchange Marketplace**, you should properly evaluate the functionality and results of deploying an app within your Salesforce CRM organization. This concept is part of a wider concern, which addresses the way changes are applied to the Salesforce CRM application.

With the use of Salesforce sandboxes, you can properly evaluate and perform due diligence for new Salesforce functionality before deciding to roll it out to your users in the production system. In the case of an AppExchange app, if the app proves to be unsuccessful, then it need not be uninstalled.

Salesforce sandboxes

Sandboxes are separate Salesforce CRM environments that are isolated from your Salesforce production organization, so actions that you carry out in your sandboxes do not affect your Salesforce production environment, and vice versa.

To view and manage your existing sandboxes or create new ones in Salesforce CRM, navigate to **Setup | Sandboxes.**

You can view the list of any existing sandboxes that have been created, and clicking on a sandbox name allows you to view details about the sandbox, such as when it was created.

In the Sandbox List, you can see the **Name**, **Type**, **Status**, **Location**, **Current Org Id**, **Completed On**, and **Description** Sandboxes where there are the following types: **Developer**, **Developer Pro**, **Partial Data**, and **Full,** as shown in the following screenshot:

Sandboxes   Help for this Page 🔘

Sandboxes are special organizations that are used to test changes or new apps without risking damage to your production data or configuration. Sandbox Templates are used to create new Sandboxes containing specific data sets.

Available Sandbox Licenses

Developer	**Developer Pro**	**Partial Data**	**Full**
10 Available (1 in use)	1 Available (1 in use)	0 Available (0 in use)	0 Available (1 in use)

Sandboxes | Sandbox Templates | Sandbox History

New Sandbox

Action	Name	Type	Status	Location	Current Org Id	Completed On	Description
Edit | Del | Refresh | Login Dev	Developer	Completed	CS2	0000000000000000	30/05/2012 14:16	Developer sandbox
Edit | Del | Refresh | Login Dev1	Developer Pro	Completed	CS17	0000000000000000	05/08/2018 11:07	Developer Pro sandbox
Edit | Del | Refresh | Login Test	Full	Completed	CS18	0000000000000000	12/02/2018 08:14	Full Sandbox

Sandbox availability is dependent on your edition of Salesforce CRM. Some types are provided as standard while others are available for additional cost.

Developer sandbox

A Developer sandbox is intended to be used for coding and testing and contains a copy of all the configuration setup from your production system. It does not, however, contain any of the data. There is a maximum of 200 MB of data storage and 200 MB of file storage that can be created. The Developer sandbox can be refreshed once per day.

Developer Pro sandbox

A Developer Pro sandbox is intended to be used for coding, testing, and user training and contains a copy of all the configuration setup from your production system. It does not, however, contain any of the data. There is a maximum of 1 GB of data storage and 1 GB of file storage that can be created. The **Developer Pro** sandbox can be refreshed once per day.

Partial Copy sandbox

A Partial Copy sandbox is intended to be used as a testing environment and contains a copy of your production organization's configuration setup. Unlike the **Developer** and **Developer Pro** sandboxes, a Partial Copy sandbox permits a sample of your production organization's data that you define by using a sandbox template.

To create a Partial Copy sandbox, you must apply a sandbox template at creation time, although there is a maximum of 5 GB of data storage and 5 GB of file storage that can be stored. For each selected object in the sandbox template, up to 10,000 records are brought over from the production environment. For example, if you have a template that includes only accounts to create a Partial Copy sandbox, up to 10,000 Account records will be copied into the new sandbox – no other records. Unlike the Developer and Developer Pro sandboxes, the Partial Copy sandbox can only be refreshed once every five days.

Full Copy sandbox

A **Full Copy sandbox** contains a copy of your entire production setup, including all the data. Because the data is also copied over during a refresh, there is a limit of refreshing the Full Copy sandbox to once every 29 days. Full Copy sandboxes have the same storage limit as the production organization.

The **Full Copy sandbox** is generally used for **User Acceptance Testing (UAT)**.

Clicking on the **New Sandbox** button allows you to create a new sandbox.

The **Sandbox Templates** tab is used with **Partial Copy** sandboxes and determines the types of record and data that is to be copied over from the production environment.

The **Sandbox History** tab allows you to see the sandbox refresh history, showing when sandboxes were created and who created them.

The **Refresh** link allows you to replace an existing sandbox with a new copy. The existing copy of the sandbox remains available while the refresh completes and until you activate the new copy.

When creating or refreshing a **Full** sandbox, you can reduce the time taken for the refresh by reducing the amount of data that is copied. The following options allow you to reduce the amount of data that is copied:

- The **Case History** option allows you to select the number of days of case history from your production organization to copy to your sandbox. You can copy from 0 to 180 days in 30-day increments. The default value is 30 days.
- The **Opportunity History** option allows you to select the number of days of opportunity history from your production organization to copy to your sandbox. Here, you can copy from 0 to 180 days in 30-day increments. The default value is 0 days.

By default, **Chatter** data is not copied to your sandbox. **Chatter** data includes feeds, messages, and discovery topics. Select the **Copy Chatter Data** checkbox if you wish to copy it. Salesforce does not recommend increasing the default selections as too much data can cause delays in the time it takes to copy or refresh the sandbox. The **Refresh** option is only shown for each sandbox that is available for refreshing.

- An **Activate** link allows you to activate a refreshed sandbox, which must be done before you can start using the new sandbox.

The **Activate** option is only displayed for refreshed sandboxes that have yet to be activated.

Activating a refreshed sandbox replaces the existing sandbox with the refreshed version and permanently deletes the old version and any data in it.

- The **Login** option allows you to log in to a sandbox.

The **Login** button is only displayed for system administrators and may not always be available. Users can log in to an active sandbox by using the following URL: `https://test.salesforce.com` and entering a modified username, which is `<username>` from production, with a suffix for the name of the sandbox. So, for a sandbox called **Test**, it would be `martin.brown@widgetsXYZ.com.test`.

Sandboxes that no one has logged in to for 180 days are deleted. Users who have created or most recently refreshed any sandbox within your organization will be notified that the sandbox is scheduled for deletion. These users will receive at least three e-mail notifications over 30 days prior to the deletion.

Salesforce recommends keeping a sandbox active by logging in periodically to avoid e-mail notifications.

By using a sandbox, you can ensure that changes are deployed in a structured and controlled manner and any change can be undone easily. This is known as change management.

Effective change management reduces the risk when introducing new areas of functionality and when making changes to existing functionality. It obviously depends on the amount and complexity of the planned change, but for a risk-free and successful implementation of changes in Salesforce CRM, there needs to be a change management strategy, which typically covers the following steps:

1. Changing requests.
2. Configuring, developing, and deploying.

Change requests

When working with a change management process in an organization, change requests are typically gathered from ideas and requests from management and application users.

Case management for change requests
One method of gathering and storing change requests is by utilizing the case management features within Salesforce CRM itself. This feature can be set up to enable users to enter their required changes directly. You can even consider building an approval process so that the change is approved by the user's manager before being considered in any release cycle.

However, before the change requests are captured, you need a process to analyze and prioritize the lists of requests and assess the scope of the work required. It can be useful to classify the changes that are requested for inclusion in either an immediate, minor, or a major release.

Immediate release

Change items that are suitable for immediate release are very small changes that can be quickly implemented; they carry no risk and can be made directly into the production environment. Changes such as new dashboards or reports, or modifications to existing dashboards and reports, and field positioning on page layouts and related lists are considered small changes. This category of release also includes simple data changes, such as data imports and exports.

Changes can be configured, tested, and deployed with minimal impact, and therefore these changes do not usually need to go through the change control process.

 It is worth considering, however, how the changes are applied in any other sandbox such as a developer, user acceptance, or test environment to ensure that all the sandbox environments are kept in sync.

Minor release

Minor releases are for larger changes that can be grouped and scheduled for change perhaps every 30 or 60 days. The types of changes that fall into this category include new fields, new page layouts, new custom objects, and so on, which are more complicated than the immediate release change items.

Minor release change items are medium level changes that can be implemented with minor impact to the production environment and typically require less than a day of additional training for users and overall less than a week of customization or code changes.

 It is worth considering, however, how the changes are applied in any other sandbox such as a **Developer**, **User acceptance**, or **Test environment** to ensure that all the sandbox environments are kept in sync.

Major release

Major releases are large changes that will carry risk and have a major impact to the business or environment. These changes are the ones that require modification to the user interface, to the way data is updated, data migrations, and any integration projects. These types of changes include new or modified role hierarchies, profiles, page layouts, record types, sales and support processes, workflow and approvals, and custom code. These changes can be introduced with the introduction of new AppExchange apps, process-impacting configuration changes, data migrations, and integration

Major release change items carry a high level of risk and are obviously more complicated than a minor release change. These changes may require additional time for training users, and in general require more than a week of customization or code changes.

Configuring, developing, and deploying

Typical compliance requirements for change management are that changes are appropriately tested and validated and that only approved changes are deployed into production.

Configuration, development, and testing should always typically be carried out using a sandbox environment, and a record should be maintained to record the successful testing, validation, and approval of any changes prior to deployment or production. Depending upon the scope and scale of the change request, as described previously, you may need to consider using a different environment for development and testing.

A complex change often sees the need for a developer sandbox and separate testing sandbox. When the changes are finished in the developer sandbox, they are migrated to the testing sandbox, and only when approved are they deployed into the production environment.

Only after appropriate review and agreement by the approval authority can the changes ever be deployed into the production environment.

User adoption

In Chapter 8, *Introducing Sales Cloud, Service Cloud, and Collaborative Features of Salesforce CRM*, we looked at the core functionality that Salesforce CRM provides and also at how the complete sales process, from campaign and lead capture right through to customer service and support, can be captured. Here, we looked in detail at how Salesforce provides the facilities to obtain a full 360-degree view of customer's past, present, and future relationships within our organization.

We looked at how this information enables marketing to measure the return on investment for marketing campaigns, sales to optimize the sales pipeline and sell more to each customer, support to track customer support incidents, and requests to ensure that each one is resolved appropriately and in a timely fashion.

Having this process in place is one thing, but to ensure that the information is captured to support the process is another issue altogether. After all, processes and technologies are only as good as the people who use them. So, it is vital that users are regularly logging in, creating, and updating information into Salesforce CRM.

CRM technology, therefore, must be easy to use, accessible, and scalable to ensure that the efforts of using the system provide significant enhancements in productivity, efficiency, and information accessibility. Once the business goals have been established and can be measured, organizations generally need to address methods of ensuring or increasing user adoption. Here, you can cultivate active product advocates or evangelists from within your business to support certain initiatives for any relevant areas of the business.

A significant factor for successful adoption is to give users incentives to use the system by providing them with functionality that improves the way they work and offers valuable information and tools not available elsewhere within the organization.

Another important consideration is to encourage feedback from the user community. By encouraging feedback and instilling a sense of collaboration, a collective ownership for Salesforce CRM can be obtained that will instill trust. Responding to good suggestions, customizing, and communicating enhancements to the application can lead to better acceptance of changes, and makes people more likely to want to spend their time working with the application.

In spite of the positives mentioned, user adoption cannot be assumed or taken for granted, and your company might need to consider reinforcing adoption with rules as well as rewards.

User adoption seeks to ensure that the business communities, as described previously, are effectively using Salesforce CRM and that the features that have been implemented are being properly utilized and continue to successfully address the business challenges.

To enable the monitoring of user adoption, there needs to be effective reports and dashboards to capture adoption metrics, where the following areas can be considered when building user adoption metrics:

- Usage
- Data quality
- Business performance

Usage

The first key requirement for ensuring that Salesforce CRM is being appropriately used is by measuring the number and frequency of users logging in to the system. You also need to ensure that users are actively and consistently updating data and creating new **Leads**, **Contacts**, **Opportunities**, and/or **Cases** depending on their roles in the organization.

Having a well implemented business application should help to make business processes simple and hide complexity; this all helps to increase user adoption. However, making a computer application appear simple often requires a considered approach and sometimes takes far more effort than leaving it in its natural complex state. Removing obstacles and unnecessary features takes time and effort, but it is time and effort well spent and will yield results and hopefully result in higher adoption rates.

Simplicity

As a platform, Salesforce CRM has proven to be highly successful since its conception a decade ago, and the number of organizations and subscriptions to the service grows year on year. Much of this success can be attributed to the simplicity, ease of use, and focus on user productivity that the platform affords.

While you may feel justified in introducing new mandatory fields and enforcing data capture requirements into the application, this can sometimes make the system less user-friendly. Sometimes, applications that offer the simplest solution for a given problem are more likely to be rewarded with acceptance and adoption by your Salesforce community.

Connectivity

Enabling users to connect information from other tools, such as Microsoft Outlook, and fully integrate Salesforce CRM with other such business systems provides a mechanism for accessing all the information users need.

Salesforce Mobile

In the past, mobile devices that were capable of accessing software applications were very expensive. Often these devices were regarded as a *nice to have* accessory by management and seen as a company perk by field teams. Today, mobile devices are far more prevalent within the business environment and organizations are increasingly realizing the benefits of using mobile phones and devices to access business applications.

Salesforce.com provides several mobile apps and solutions to keep your users connected and productive when using their mobile devices. These solutions are covered in detail in the next chapter, Chapter 10, *Administrating the Mobile Features of Salesforce CRM.*

Communications

Users are far more likely to adopt Salesforce CRM when they know that their peers and colleagues are achieving results from its use. By communicating both the business and personal results, for example, an increase in company sales and the resulting sales commissions paid to the sales team, you can encourage others to adopt the system.

Data quality

Data quality is a valuable metric for measuring adoption. Although outlined previously, it is advisable not to over complicate the entering of information with needless validation; it is important that any critical fields are completed.

When certain fields are consistently filled out, user acceptance will increase as it provides good data integrity and reliability that translates into higher user confidence and higher adoption.

Business performance

Usage should also reflect business performance and compliance metrics that are used to ensure that users are not just using the application, but are using it in a way that enhances business effectiveness. Here, metrics can be built that will uncover patterns and trends that track performance levels, and can then identify areas that need improvement.

This has been a quick overview of areas that can be used to generate metrics that you can track and there is an enormous quantity of metrics that can be generated.

There is a balance, however, in getting accurate views without overcomplicating and spawning too many metrics. Here, it is often best to create the minimum number of metrics that can adequately capture and track the success of the business performance objectives.

Certain performance indicators can be established to identify the business sales revenues, which are listed as follows:

- Compare the current fiscal year against last year's sales by month, say, to measure cyclical variances.
- Compare sales from existing customers against new customers to measure what customer type revenue is coming from and enhance CRM activities accordingly.
- Compare won and lost sales ratios to measure the effectiveness of deal closure, see why deals are getting lost, and learn from the reasons.
- Measure the sales pipeline by sales stage to identify where new opportunities are appearing.
- Measure key opportunities in the sales pipeline to identify the current key opportunities to ensure they get the right attention.
- Measure closed sales actuals against quota. Here, you can introduce a closed sales leaderboard to identify who your top deal-closers are. This can sometimes be seen as a way of shaming bad performers, but sales management can use this information positively to get the top performers to share knowledge and best practices to help the organization.

For marketing-specific metrics, the following examples can be performed:

- Measure campaigns by **Return On Investment (ROI)**, Actual ROI, by campaign type, and average opportunity amount per campaign
- Measure lead conversion rates

There are many dashboards that you can install from AppExchange that give metrics for how Salesforce is being used. The following is called **Salesforce Adoption Dashboards**, which is an example from `labs.force.com`:

 The **Salesforce Adoption Dashboards** app from **Salesforce.com** is available from the **AppExchange Marketplace** directly through the following URL: `http://appexchange.salesforce.com/listingDetail?l istingId=a0N30000004gHhLEAU`.

Questions to test your knowledge

You are now presented with questions about the Salesforce AppExchange, which has been covered in this chapter. The answers can be found at the end of this chapter.

Questions

We present two questions to verify your understanding of the Salesforce **AppExchange Marketplace**.

Question 1 – Salesforce AppExchange Marketplace

What is the purpose of the Salesforce **AppExchange Marketplace**? (Select all that apply):

a) Administrators can download and customize pre-built reports and dashboards.

b) Sales users can install add-ins to synchronize the Contacts and Calendar entries in their desktop e-mail apps with Salesforce.

c) Partners can share and link opportunities to collaborate on sales deals.

d) Salesforce customers can share and install apps published by third-party developers and system integrators.

Question 2 – Salesforce AppExchange Package Types

What are the package types found in the Salesforce **AppExchange Marketplace**? (Select all that apply):

a) Mass Delete.

b) Managed.

c) Sales.

d) Unmanaged.

e) Marketing.

Answers

Here are the answers to the two questions about the Salesforce **AppExchange Marketplace**.

Answer 1 – Salesforce AppExchange Marketplace

The answer is **a**) Administrators can download and customize pre-built reports and dashboards and **d**) Salesforce customers can share and install apps published by third-party developers and system integrators.

Answer 2 – Salesforce Appexchange package types

The answer is **b**) Managed and **d**) Unmanaged. Managed Package Types are packages that may continue to be managed by the publishing developers and the package contents are not visible or editable. Unmanaged packages are not managed by the publishing developers and the package contents are visible and editable.

Summary

In this chapter, we looked at the core features of Salesforce CRM that can be enhanced by adding additional functionality with external applications from the **AppExchange Marketplace**.

We discovered how easy it is to build a mashup in Salesforce CRM using the Visualforce technology and looked at how, with the use of Visualforce pages, we can extend the standard page functionality of the Salesforce CRM.

We looked at the concept of web mashups from the perspective of both the client-side and server-side aspects of web technologies. We also described the difference between presentation mashups, which are rendered in an Internet browser, and services that require more complex features, such as web services.

We were introduced to the ways in which Visualforce pages can be controlled, where we looked at the use of Apex code, which can extend the functionality within the Salesforce CRM platform. Apex triggers were briefly covered, where we considered the need for careful implementation in order to observe the order of execution for workflow rules and triggers to ensure that no unwanted ripple effects were introduced.

We looked at the importance for planning and scheduling the release of changes into the Salesforce application and provided some best practices relating to change management.

We also looked at how to improve user adoption by giving users incentives to use the system by providing them with functionality that improves the way they work and offering valuable information and tools not available elsewhere within the organization.

Finally, we posed questions to help clarify some of the key features of the Salesforce **AppExchange Marketplace**.

In the next chapter, we will look at the administration of mobile features within Salesforce CRM.

10
Administrating the Mobile Features of Salesforce CRM

In the previous chapter, we looked at how external third-party web functionality can be used within Salesforce where we introduced Visualforce and provided a detailed guide to using the Salesforce AppExchange which provides the ability to extend and enhance the core functionality of Salesforce CRM.

In this chapter, we will look at the administration of Salesforce Mobile solutions, which can significantly improve productivity and user satisfaction for users accessing data and application functionality whilst mobile and away from the office.

In the past, mobile devices that were capable of accessing software applications were very expensive. Often these devices were regarded as a nice accessory by management, and seen as a company perk by field-based teams.

Today, mobile devices are almost ubiquitous within the business environment, and organizations of all sizes are realizing the benefits of using mobile phones and devices to access business applications.

Salesforce has taken the lead in recognizing how mobile has become the new standard for being connected in people's personal and professional lives. And how more and more, the users of their apps are living lives connected to the Internet, but rather than sitting at a desk in the office, they are in between meetings, on the road, in planes, in trains, in cabs, or even in the queue for lunch. As a result, Salesforce have developed innovative mobile solutions that help you and your users embrace this mobile-first world in Salesforce CRM.

The following topics are being covered in this chapter:

- Accessing Salesforce mobile solutions
- Salesforce mobile products overview
- SalesforceA
- Salesforce Touch
- Salesforce Classic
- Mobile Administration Console
- Salesforce1
- Mobile Dashboards
- Salesforce Adoption Manager

Accessing Salesforce mobile solutions

Salesforce offers two varieties of mobile solutions, namely mobile browser apps and downloadable apps. Mobile browser apps, as the name suggests, are accessed using a web browser that is available on a mobile device. Downloadable apps are accessed by first downloading the client software from, say, the Apple App Store or Google Play and then installing it onto the mobile device. Mobile browser apps and downloadable apps offer various features and benefits and, as will be covered, are available for various Salesforce mobile products and device combinations.

Most mobile devices these days have some degree of web browser capability, which may be used to access Salesforce CRM, however some Salesforce mobile products are optimized for use with certain devices. By accessing a Salesforce mobile browser app, your users do not require anything to be installed. Supported mobile browsers for Salesforce are generally available on Android, Apple, BlackBerry, and Microsoft Windows 8.1 devices.

Downloadable apps, on the other hand, will require the app to be first downloaded from the App Store for Apple devices or from Google Play for Android devices and then installed on the mobile device.

Salesforce mobile products overview

Salesforce have provided some of their mobile products as downloadable apps while others have been provided as both downloadable and mobile browser-based. The following list outlines the various mobile app products, features, and capabilities used for accessing Salesforce CRM on mobile devices:

- SalesforceA
- Salesforce Touch
- Salesforce Classic
- Salesforce1

 Salesforce Touch is no longer available and is mentioned here for information as this product has been recently incorporated into the Salesforce1 product.

SalesforceA

SalesforceA is a downloadable system administration app that allows you to manage your organization users and view certain information on your Salesforce organization from your mobile device. **SalesforceA** is intended to be used by system administrators as it is restricted to users with the `Manage Users` permission.

The **SalesforceA** app provides the facilities to carry out user tasks such as deactivating or freezing users, resetting passwords, unlocking users, editing user details, calling and emailing users, and assigning permission sets.

These user task buttons are displayed as action icons as shown in the following screenshot:

The available action icons depend on the user and organization. To open the action menu with all available actions for the current user, tap the More Actions ⦁⦁⦁ icon.

The icons represent the following actions.

Action Icon	Action
	Edit the user record
	Freeze or unfreeze the user account
	Reset the user's password
	Deactivate or activate the user account
	Assign permission sets to the user
	Email the user
	Call the user or log a call made outside of the SalesforceA app.

These icons are presented in the action bar at the bottom of the mobile device screen as shown in the following screenshot:

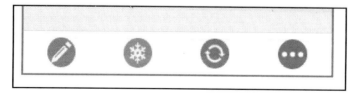

In addition to the user tasks, you can view system status and also switch between your user accounts in multiple organization. This allows you to access different organizations and communities without having to log out and log back in to each user account. By staying logged into multiple accounts in different organization, you will save time by easily switching to the particular orgnizations user account that you need to access.

SalesforceA supported devices

At the time of writing, the following devices are supported by Salesforce for use with the **SalesforceA** downloadable app:

- Android phones
- Apple iPhone
- Apple iPod Touch

SalesforceA can be installed from Google Play for Android phones and Apple App Store for Apple devices.

Salesforce Touch

Salesforce Touch is the name of an earlier Salesforce mobile product and is no longer available. Within the Spring '14 release, Salesforce Touch was incorporated into the Salesforce1 app, hence both the Salesforce Touch mobile browser and Salesforce Touch downloadable apps are no longer available but the functionality that they once offered are available in Salesforce1, which is covered later in this chapter.

Salesforce Classic

Salesforce Classic is a more mature product within the mobile solutions provided by Salesforce and provides mobile access to Salesforce CRM data, tasks, and calendar, and integrates that data with users email and mobile devices.

There are two types of Salesforce Classic, namely a full version and a free version. The full version of the Salesforce Classic app requires mobile licenses, which may be part of your standard Salesforce CRM licenses. There is also a free, limited version of Salesforce Classic that allows any Salesforce CRM user who does not have a mobile license to download a free, restricted version of Salesforce Classic.

Since Summer '16, the free version of Salesforce Classic Mobile has no longer been available for new organizations or for existing organizations that did not previously have it enabled. For organizations that had already enabled the free version before Summer '16, there was no change.

Salesforce Classic supported Operating Systems

At the time of writing, the supported operating systems for Salesforce Classic downloadable apps are as follows:

- Android
- Apple iOS
- BlackBerry

Users can install the downloadable apps from the App Store, Google Play, and Blackberry World. However recently-released mobile devices may not be supported because every device must be put through Salesforce official certification process.

Salesforce Classic data availability

Most standard Sales Objects and some Service Objects are also available; if you are using the full version, custom objects and configurations are also supported. The free version allows your users to view, create, edit, and delete only accounts, assets, contacts, leads, opportunities, events, tasks, cases, and solutions. Users can also access their dashboards.

In the free version of Salesforce Classic, only records that users have recently accessed in the Salesforce CRM browser app are automatically synchronized to their mobile devices. However, users can search for and download any records that are not automatically delivered to their mobile devices.

 In addition to recently accessed records, the default configuration synchronizes activities closed in the past five days and open activities due in the next 30 days.

For both the full and free version of Salesforce Classic, any items that are downloaded from Salesforce become a permanent part of your users mobile data set.

Salesforce Classic Administration

You can manage your organizations access to the Salesforce Classic apps and there are separate features for controlling access depending on whether you are setting up the full or the free version.

Salesforce Classic Full Version Access

The **Mobile User** checkbox on the user record assigns a mobile license to users, which enables use of the full version of Salesforce Classic. This option is set and appears as shown in the following screenshot:

Salesforce Classic User	☑

The Salesforce Classic Mobile app is to be retired in December 1, 2017.
At the time of writing, Salesforce has announced that the Salesforce Classic Mobile app is to be retired and will no longer be available from December 1, 2017. From this date, any current orgnizations and users with Salesforce Classic Mobile apps installed will see their app disabled. Also on December 1, 2017 the Salesforce Classic Mobile app is to be removed from Google Play and the App Store.

Salesforce Classic Free Version Access

Other Salesforce users without an assigned mobile license may be able to access the free version of Salesforce Classic depending upon when the Salesforce organization was created and whether Salesforce Classic Lite has been enabled.

Salesforce Classic Lite is not available for new organizations and any organization that did not have it enabled, or disabled it after the Summer '16 release.

The option that enables Salesforce Classic Lite can be found by navigating as follows:

Don't disable the Enable Salesforce Classic Lite checkbox, even temporarily, if you want your users to retain access to the free version of Salesforce Classic Mobile. If you disable this option, the checkbox is immediately removed from the Salesforce Classic Mobile Settings page and unlicensed users are unable to use the Salesforce Classic Mobile app. Furthermore, if you deselect this option while users are running the app, the Salesforce data on their devices is erased the next time the devices synchronize with Salesforce.

If you disable the free version of Salesforce Classic Mobile in error, contact Salesforce customer support for assistance restoring access for unlicensed users.

Salesforce Classic Lite access is an organization-wide setting. It enables access for all active users and cannot be enabled for individual users.

Now click **Edit** band then deselect the **Enable Salesforce Classic Lite** option as shown in the following screenshot:

Salesforce Classic Settings

Help for this Page

Modify the Salesforce Classic settings for your organization.

Salesforce Classic Settings

Standard Salesforce Classic Settings

Enable Salesforce Classic Lite

This option allows users who do not have a mobile or Unlimited Edition license to use a free, restricted version of Salesforce Classic.

Advanced Salesforce Classic Settings

Permanently Link User to Mobile Device

Select this option only if you want to prevent your users from switching devices. Note that enabling this option requires administrative maintenance when users need to switch to a different device. Without administrative intervention, users who need to switch to a different device will be unable to use Salesforce Classic.

Edit

If you deselect this option while users are running the Salesforce Classic app, the Salesforce data on their mobile devices is deleted the next time that device synchronizes with Salesforce.

Mobile Administration Console

The Mobile Administration Console is available to set up and manage mobile configurations and offers the following five step process to set up Salesforce Classic:

1. **Create a mobile configuration**: This step creates a mobile configuration and allows the selection of users and/or profiles that will be linked to the configuration.
2. **Define the data set**: In this step, you will specify the data set that will be synced to the mobile device and select the objects and record filters for those objects.
3. **Set the mobile data set size**: In this step, the size of the mobile data set is specified and you can test the data size against user accounts. For this test, you should aim to test a mobile configuration with the accounts of specific users that will be assigned to the configuration.
4. **Exclude fields**: In this optional step, you can modify any object's mobile page layout and exclude fields. This is often needed because unnecessary fields consume memory and makes it slow to scroll through pages on the mobile device.
5. **Send a mass email**: This is the final step of the Mobile Administration Console, which will allow you to send a mass email to mobile users to notify them of the availability of the mobile client application.

To access a demo of the setting up of Salesforce Classic and the overview of the setup steps within the Mobile Administration Console, navigate to **Setup | Mobile Administration | Salesforce Classic | Configurations** as shown in the following screenshot:

Introducing the Mobile Administration Console

Help for this Page

The Mobile Administration Console is used to set up and manage mobile configurations so that salesforce.com users can easily and productively access their salesforce.com data from their mobile device, whether or not a wireless connection is available. Salesforce Classic allows users to quickly look up a contact and -- with one click -- place a phone call or send an email, then log the call or email directly into salesforce.com. Users can make appointments, create and assign tasks, follow up on leads, work on cases and much more, all conveniently from their mobile device.

For more information about Salesforce Classic see Mobile Platform

All Customers

Administrators should read the Mobile Implementation Guide before using the Mobile Administration Console. Existing mobile customers can find information in the guide about migrating from earlier versions of the mobile console.

Set up Salesforce Classic with the Mobile Administration Console in 5 steps:

1. **Create a mobile configuration** and choose users and/or profiles that will be linked to the configuration (Note: licenses are required to activate users for Salesforce Classic).
2. **Define the data set** that will be pushed to the mobile device, then select the objects and record filters for those objects. Choose the objects in hierarchical order to create record filter dependencies.
3. **Set the mobile data set size** and test the data size against user accounts. It is important to test a mobile configuration with the accounts of users who will actually be assigned to the configuration, particularly users who own a large number of records.
4. **Optionally exclude some fields** from each object's mobile page layout because unnecessary fields consume memory and make it harder for users to scroll through pages on the mobile device.
5. **Send a mass email to mobile users** to notify them about the availability of the mobile client application.

See a short demo on setting up Salesforce Classic.

☐ Don't show me this page again

[Continue]

Salesforce1

Salesforce1 is Salesforce's next-generation mobile CRM platform, which has been designed for Salesforce's customers, developers, and **ISVs** (**Independent Software Vendors**) to connect mobile apps, browser apps and third-party app services. Salesforce1 has been developed for a mobile-first environment and demonstrates how Salesforce's focus as a platform provider aims to connect the enterprise with systems that can be programmed through APIs along with mobile apps and services that can be utilized by marketing, sales, and customer service.

There are two ways to use Salesforce1; either using a mobile browser app that users access by logging into Salesforce from a supported mobile browser, and downloadable apps that users install from the App Store or Google Play. Either way, Salesforce1 allows users to access and update Salesforce data from an interface that has been optimized for navigating and working on their touchscreen mobile devices.

Using Salesforce1, records can be viewed, edited, and created. Users can manage their activities, view their dashboards, and use **Chatter**. Salesforce1 also supports many standard objects and list views, all custom objects, plus the integration of other mobile apps, and many of your organizations Salesforce customizations, including Visualforce tabs and pages.

Salesforce1 supported devices

At the time of writing, the following devices are supported by Salesforce for the Salesforce1 mobile browser app:

- Android phones
- Apple iPad
- Apple iPhone
- BlackBerry Z10
- Windows 8.1 phones (Beta support)

At the time of writing, Salesforce specifies the following devices as being supported for the Salesforce1 downloadable app:

- Android phones
- Apple iPad
- Apple iPhone

Salesforce1 data availability

Your organization edition, the user's license type, along with the user's profile and any permission sets determines the data available to the user within Salesforce1.

Generally, users have the same visibility of objects, record types, fields, and page layouts that they have while accessing the full Salesforce browser app. However, at the time of writing, not all data is available in the current release of the Salesforce1 app.

In Winter'17, the following key objects will be fully accessible from the Salesforce1 navigation menu: **Accounts**, **Campaigns**, **Cases**, **Contacts**, **Contracts**, **Leads**, **Opportunities**, **Tasks**, **Users**, **Dashboards**, and **Events**, however, are restricted to being only viewable from the Salesforce1 navigation menu.

Custom objects are fully accessible if they have a tab that the user can access.

For new users who have yet to build a history of recent objects, they initially see a set of default objects in the **Recent** section in the Salesforce1 navigation menu.

The majority of the standard and custom fields, and most of the related lists for the supported objects are available on these records, however at the time of writing, the links on formula fields are not supported, which is the Rich Text area field support exception that exists in Salesforce1.

Rich Text area field exception in Salesforce1

Salesforce1 considers Rich Text area fields to be long-text area fields. As such, these fields do not support HTML content or images and are truncated at 1,000 characters (including any HTML content).

 Consider removing Rich Text area fields from Salesforce1 mobile page layouts.
A Rich Text area field that contains an existing text value greater than 1,000 characters will be truncated if it is edited in Salesforce1.

Salesforce1 Administration

You can manage your organizations access to the Salesforce1 apps; there are two areas of administration: the mobile browser app that users access by logging in to Salesforce from a supported mobile browser, and the downloadable app that users install from the App Store or Google Play. The following sections describe the ways to control user access for each of these mobile apps.

Salesforce1 Mobile Browser App access

You can control whether users can access the Salesforce1 mobile browser app when they log into Salesforce from a mobile browser. To select or deselect this feature, navigate to **Setup** | **Mobile Administration** | **Salesforce1** | **Settings**, as shown in the following screenshot:

Salesforce1 Settings

Help for this Page

There are two ways to use Salesforce1: a mobile browser app that users access by logging in to Salesforce from a supported mobile browser, and downloadable apps that users install from the App Store or Google Play.

You can control your organization's access to all of the Salesforce1 apps.

Save   Cancel

Mobile Browser App Settings

| = Required Information

☑ Enable the Salesforce1 mobile browser app i

Downloadable App Settings

Salesforce1 downloadable app settings are now located in Connected Apps

Save   Cancel

By checking the **Enable the Salesforce1 mobile browser app** checkbox, all users are able to access Salesforce1 from their mobile browsers. Deselecting this option turns off the mobile browser app, which means users will automatically access the full Salesforce site from their mobile browser.

 By default, the mobile browser app is turned on in all Salesforce organizations.

Salesforce1 desktop browser access

Checking the **Enable the Salesforce1 mobile browser** app checkbox as described in the previous section also permits activated users access to Salesforce1 from their desktop browsers.

Users can navigate to the Salesforce1 app within their desktop browser by appending `/one/one.app` to the end of the Salesforce URL. As an example, for the following Salesforce URL accessed from the `server na10`, you would enter the desktop browser URL of `https://na10.salesforce.com/one/one.app`.

Salesforce1 downloadable App access

The Salesforce1 app is distributed as a managed package and within Salesforce it is implemented as a connected app. You might already see the Salesforce1 connected app in your list of installed apps as it may have been automatically installed in your organization.

 The list of included apps can change with each Salesforce release but to simplify administration, each package is asynchronously installed in Salesforce organizations whenever any user in that organization first accesses Salesforce1. However, to manually install or reinstall the Salesforce1 package for connected apps, you can use the AppExchange.

To view the details for the Salesforce1 app in the connected app settings, navigate to **Setup | Manage Apps | Connected Apps**. The apps that connect to your Salesforce organization are then listed as shown in the following screenshot:

Connected Apps

Help for this Page

Manage the apps that connect to your Salesforce organization.

App Access Settings   Edit

☐ Allow users to install canvas personal apps

View: All ▾ Create New View

A | B | C | D | E | F | G | H | I | J | K | L | M | N | O | P | Q | R | S | T | U | V | W | X | Y | Z | Other | **All**

Action	Master Label ↑	Application Version	Permitted Users
Edit	Ant Migration Tool	4.0	All users may self-authorize
Edit	Chatter Desktop	7.0	All users may self-authorize
Edit	Chatter Mobile for BlackBerry	7.0	All users may self-authorize
Edit	Dataloader Bulk	6.0	All users may self-authorize
Edit	Dataloader Partner	6.0	All users may self-authorize
Edit	Force.com IDE	4.0	All users may self-authorize
Edit	Salesforce Files	5.0	All users may self-authorize
Edit	Salesforce for Outlook	6.0	All users may self-authorize
Edit	Salesforce Mobile Dashboards	6.0	All users may self-authorize
Edit	Salesforce Touch	7.0	All users may self-authorize
Edit	Salesforce1 for iOS	7.0	All users may self-authorize
Edit	Salesforce1/Chatter for Android	7.0	All users may self-authorize
Edit	SalesforceA	1.0	All users may self-authorize
Edit	Workbench	2.0	All users may self-authorize

Show me fewer ▲ records per list page

Within the **Connected Apps** listing, you can control various features of the Salesforce1 mobile apps such as IP restriction, session timeout, and so on.

Salesforce1 notifications

Notifications allow all users in your organization to receive mobile notifications in Salesforce1, for example, whenever they are mentioned in **Chatter** or whenever they receive approval requests.

To activate mobile notifications, navigate to **Setup** | **Mobile Administration** | **Notifications** | **Settings**, as shown in the following screenshot:

Notifications Settings

Help for this Page

Allow users to receive notifications in the Salesforce1 app.

Notifications   [Save]

☑ Enable in-app notifications [i]

☑ Enable push notifications [i]

☐ Include full content in push notifications [i]

The following settings for notifications can be set as follows:

- **Enable in-app notifications**: Set this option to keep users notified of relevant Salesforce activity while they are using Salesforce1
- **Enable push notifications**: Set this option to keep users notified of relevant Salesforce activity when they are not using the Salesforce1 downloadable app.
- **Include full content in push notifications**: Keep this checkbox unchecked if you do not want users to receive full content in push notifications. This can prevent users receiving potentially sensitive data that may be in comments, for example, If you set this option, a pop-up dialog appears displaying terms and conditions where you must click **OK** or **Cancel**.

Salesforce1 branding

This option allows you to customize the appearance of the Salesforce1 app so it complies with any company branding requirements that may be in place.

 Salesforce1 branding is supported in downloadable app version 5.2 or later and also in the mobile browser app.

To specify Salesforce1 branding, navigate to **Setup | Mobile Administration | Salesforce1 | Branding**, as shown in the following screenshot:

Salesforce1 Branding

Help for this Page 📄

Customize the appearance of the Salesforce1 app so it matches your company's branding. Salesforce1 branding is supported in the mobile browser app and version 5.2 or later of the downloadable apps.

To change the branding of your login page, see the Login Page Settings section on the My Domain page.

Salesforce1 Branding Settings	Edit
Brand Color	None selected
Loading Page Color	None selected
Loading Page Logo	None selected
Publisher Icon	None selected

Edit

Salesforce1 compact layouts

In Salesforce1, compact layouts are used to display the key fields on a record and are specifically designed for viewing records on touchscreen mobile devices. As the space is limited on mobile devices and quick recognition of records is important, the first four fields that you assign to a compact layout are displayed.

> If a mobile user does not have the required access to one of the first four fields that have been assigned to a compact layout, the next field, if more than four fields have been set on the layout, is used.

If you have yet to create custom compact layouts, the records will be displayed using a read-only, predefined system default compact layout and after you have created a custom compact layout, you can then set it as the primary compact layout for that object.

As with the full Salesforce CRM site, if you have record types associated with an object, you can alter the primary compact layout assignment and assign specific compact layouts to different record types. You can also clone a compact layout from its detail page.

The following field types cannot be included on compact layouts: text area, long text area, Rich Text area, and multi-select picklist.

Salesforce1 offline access

In Salesforce1, the mechanism for handling offline access is determined by users most recently used records. These most recently used records are cached for offline access and at the time of writing, are read-only.

> The cached data is encrypted and secured through persistent storage by the Salesforce1 downloadable apps. Offline access is available in the Salesforce1 downloadable apps version 6.0 and later and was first released in Summer '14.

Offline access is enabled by default when the Salesforce1 downloadable app is installed. To manage these settings, navigate to **Setup** | **Mobile Administration** | **Offline**. Now check or uncheck the **Enable Offline Sync for Salesforce1** as shown in the following screenshot:

When offline access is enabled, data based on the objects is downloaded to each user's mobile device and presented in the **Recent** section of the Salesforce1 navigation menu, and on the user's most recently viewed records. The data is encrypted and stored in a secure, persistent cache on the mobile device.

Salesforce1 Setup with the Salesforce1 Wizard

The Salesforce1 Wizard simplifies the setting up of the Salesforce1 mobile app. The wizard offers a visual tour of the key setup steps and is useful if you are new to Salesforce1 or need to quickly set up the core Salesforce1 settings.

The Salesforce1 Wizard guides you through the setting up of the following Salesforce1 configuration steps:

- Choose which items appear in the navigation menu
- Configure global actions
- Create a contact custom compact layout
- Optionally invite users to start to use the Salesforce1 app

To access the Salesforce1 Wizard, navigate to **Setup** | **Salesforce1 Quick Start**. Now click **Launch Quick Start Wizard**, within the Salesforce1 Setup page, as shown in the following screenshot:

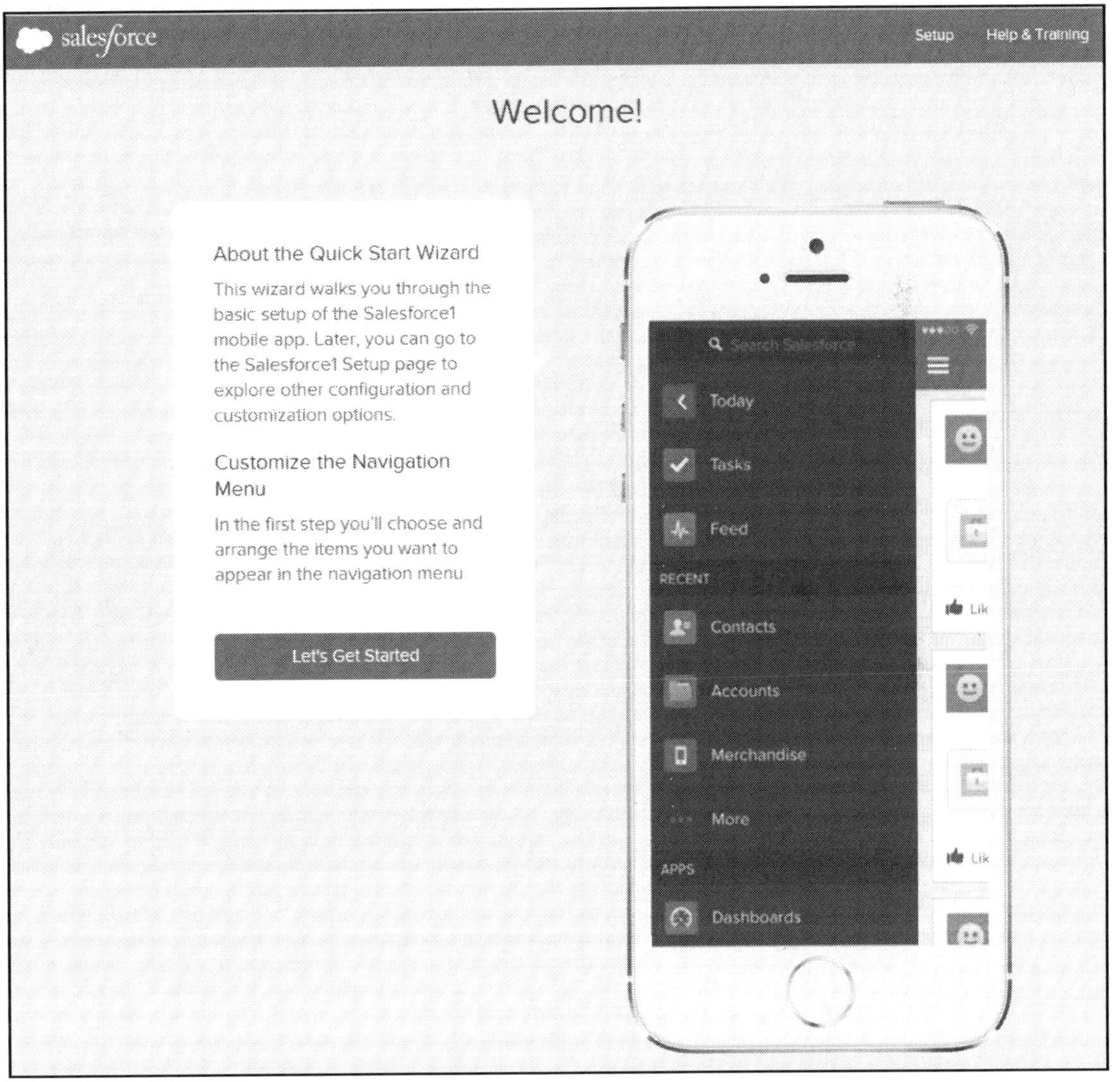

Upon clicking the **Let's Get Started** section link, you will be presented with the **Salesforce1 Setup** visual tour as shown in the following screenshot:

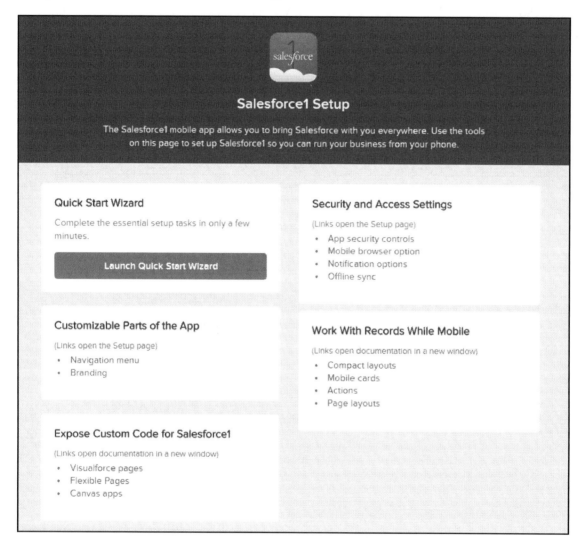

The Quick Start Wizard

The **Quick Start Wizard** guides you through the minimum required configuration steps for setting up Salesforce1. By clicking the **Launch Quick Start Wizard** button, the process for completing the essential setup tasks for Salesforce1 is initiated and provides a five-step, wizard guide. The five steps are as follows:

1. **Customize the Navigation Menu**: This step results in the setup of the navigation menu for all users in your organization. To reorder items, drag them up and down. To remove items, drag them to the **Available Items** list as shown in the following screenshot:

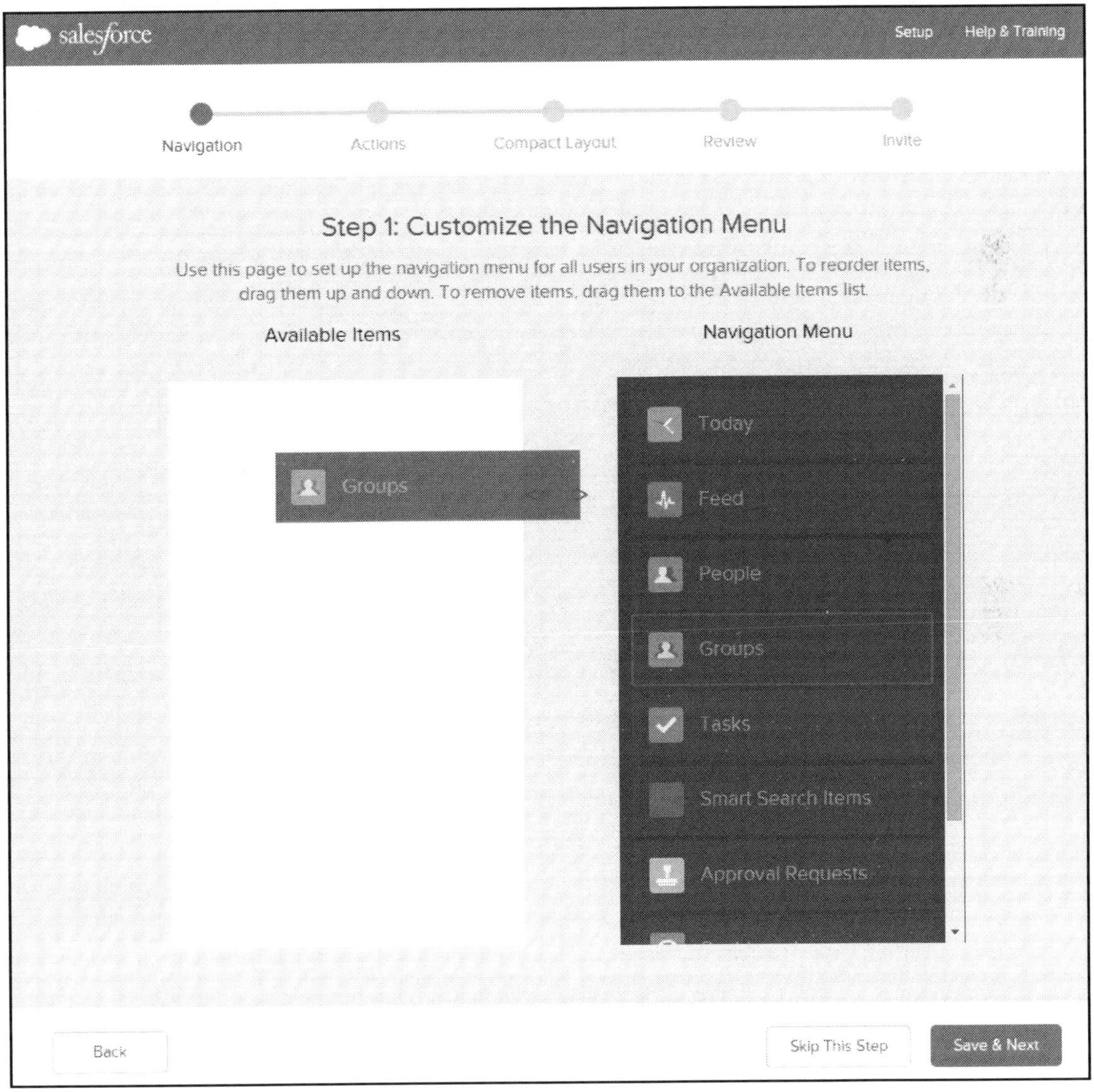

2. **Arrange Global Actions**: Global actions provide users with quick access to Salesforce functions and in this step, you will choose and arrange the Salesforce1 global actions as shown in the following screenshot:

Actions may appear differently dependent upon your version of Salesforce1.

3. **Create a Custom Compact Layout for Contacts**: Compact layouts are used to show the key fields on a record in the highlights area at the top of the record detail. In this step, you are able to create a custom compact layout for contacts, for example a contact's name, email, and phone number as shown in the following screenshot:

However, after you have completed the Quick Start wizard, you can create compact layouts for other objects as necessary.

4. **Review**: In this step you are given the chance to preview the changes to verify the results of the changes as shown in the following screenshot:

The **Review** step screen gives a live preview, which uses your current access as the logged-in user.

5. **Send Invitations**: This is the final step of the Quick Start wizard, which will provide you with a basic setup of Salesforce1 and allows you to get feedback on what you have implemented. In this step, you can invite your users to start using the Salesforce1 app as shown in the following screenshot:

This step can be skipped and you can always send invitations later, from the Salesforce1 Setup page along with other options for customizing the app, such as incorporating your own branding.

Salesforce1 differences from the Full Salesforce CRM browser app

In the Winter' 2017 release and at the time of writing, Salesforce1 does not have all of the features of the full Salesforce CRM site, and in some areas includes functionality that is not available or is different to the full Salesforce site.

As an example, in the full Salesforce CRM site, compact layouts determine which fields appear in the **Chatter feed** item, which appears after a user creates a record via a publisher action. However, compact layouts in Salesforce1 are used to display the key fields on a record.

For details about the current features that differ between the full Salesforce CRM site and Salesforce1, please refer to **Salesforce1 Limits and Differences** from the Full Salesforce Site within the Salesforce **Help** menu sections.

Mobile Dashboards

The **Mobile Dashboards** solution is an app specifically developed to work on the Apple iPad device. The setting to allows users to install the app is automatically enabled for all Salesforce organization. This permits users to access and install the app on their Apple iPads without any admin configuration or support.

Since Summer '2015, the Mobile Dashboards for iPad app is no longer supported. At the time of writing, the app can continue to be used Salesforce no longer provides support or enhancements to the app. Salesforce recommends migrating users' experience and requirements for Mobile Dashboards to the Salesforce1 app.

To enable or disable **The Mobile Dashboards for iPad app**, navigate to **Setup | MobileAdministration | Mobile Dashboards**, as shown in the following screenshot:

Mobile Dashboard Settings	Help for this Page
Salesforce.com's Mobile Dashboards iPad application is available from Apple's App Store. To use it, this option must be enabled.	
☑ Enable the Mobile Dashboards iPad app for all users	
Save Cancel	

Now select or deselect **Enable the Mobile Dashboards iPad app for all users** and then click **Save**.

Salesforce Adoption Manager

The **Salesforce Adoption Manager** is a Salesforce1 training and engagement tool provided by Salesforce that sends mobile users intelligent email notifications. The objective of the tool is to drive adoption of the Salesforce1 mobile app by new Salesforce1 users. It also engages with existing users who have not used Salesforce1 for a while to encourage them to start re-using the app.

 Salesforce Adoption Manager is only available, at the time of writing, in the following countries; USA, UK, and Australia.

To enable **Salesforce Adoption Manager**, navigate to **Setup | Manage Users | Adoption Manager** and select **Enable Salesforce Adoption Manager**, as shown in the following screenshot:

Salesforce Adoption Manager

Help for this Page

Salesforce Adoption Manager guides users with customized suggestions based on how they use Salesforce and the Salesforce1 mobile app. Help your users succeed with tips on actions they can take to accomplish more—faster.

See the FAQ for answers to the most common questions.

> ⓘ Salesforce Adoption Manager is currently for U.S., U.K., and Australia-based organizations only.

☑ Enable Salesforce Adoption Manager

Save   Cancel

Once you activate the feature, a personalized invite email is sent to users to download the Salesforce1 mobile app. Once your users have downloaded Salesforce1, they then receive an email containing a custom link to install the Salesforce1 downloadable app. Subsequent emails are then sent based on users' actual usage of the Salesforce1 mobile app. These emails are optimized for viewing on mobile devices and include tips for viewing a record or other CRM details while mobile, best practices on useful actions like logging calls, or creating tasks etc.

Questions to test your knowledge

The following section is question and answer for related to the topics covered in this chapter.

Questions

We present two questions to verify your understanding of the Salesforce1 app solution.

Question 1 – Salesforce1 App access.

What are the various apps in which Salesforce1 can be accessed? (Select all that apply).

a) Using a mobile browser app

b) Using a desktop browser application

c) Using a downloadable app

d) Using a Salesforce CRM app

Question 2 – Salesforce1 Downloadable Apps.

The Salesforce1 downloadable apps are set up in Salesforce as Connected Apps. When could the Connected Apps be created or amended for the Salesforce1 downloadable apps? (Select all that apply).

a) When a user uninstalls a Salesforce1 downloadable app on their mobile device.

b) When a user installs a Salesforce1 downloadable app on their mobile device and logs in via the mobile app to the Salesforce organization.

c) When an administrator manually installs the Salesforce1 connected apps from the AppExchange to the Salesforce organization.

d) When Salesforce applies a new release to the Salesforce organization.

Answers

Here are the answers to the two questions about the Salesforce AppExchange marketplace.

Answer 1 – Salesforce1 App access.

The answer is **a)** Using a mobile browser app, **b)** Using a desktop browser application, and **c)** Using a downloadable app.

There are three ways to use Salesforce1; either using a mobile browser app that users access by logging into Salesforce from a supported mobile browser, downloadable apps that users install from the App Store or Google Play, or users can navigate to the Salesforce1 app within their desktop browser by appending `/one/one.app` to the end of the Salesforce URL.

Answer 2 – Salesforce1 Downloadable Apps.

The answer is **b)**When a user installs a Salesforce1 downloadable app on their mobile device and logs in via the mobile app to the Salesforce organization, **c)** When an administrator manually installs the Salesforce1 connected apps from the AppExchange to the Salesforce organization, and **d)** When Salesforce applies a new release to the Salesforce organization.

Summary

In this chapter we have looked at ways that mobiles have become the new norm for staying connected in both our personal and professional lives.

Salesforce has recognized that individuals are spending more of their time connected to the cloud and using cloud-based business applications and that these business apps are increasingly being used in a mobile context rather than being used at a desk in an office.

To try and help their customers become successful businesses of this mobile-first world, Salesforce have produced various mobile solutions that can help users get things done, regardless of where they are and what they are doing.

In this chapter we have described the features of **SalesforceA**, a mobile admin app that can help you manage users and monitor the status of Salesforce whilst on the move.

We described the features and benefits of Salesforce1 which is available as a downloadable app and a browser app. Here we detailed the setting up and administration of the solution, and the current capabilities of Salesforce1 at the time of writing.

We also looked at historic Salesforce mobile solutions such as Salesforce Touch which has being replaced by Salesforce1 and Salesforce Classic.

Finally, we posed questions to help clarify some of the key features of the Salesforce1 mobile solution.

In the next chapter, we will look at the Salesforce Certified Administrator exam, provided by Salesforce, which assesses candidate's knowledge of system management and configuration within the Sales Cloud, the Service Cloud, and the Collaboration Cloud and outline resources and strategies to help pass the Certified Administrator exam.

11
Studying for the Certified Administrator Exam

In the previous chapter, we looked at the administration of Salesforce mobile features which can significantly improve productivity and user satisfaction enabling users to access data and application functionality whilst on the move and showed how to configure Salesforce Classic and Salesforce1 mobile solutions.

In this chapter, we will look at the Salesforce Certified Administrator exam, which is the first credential in Salesforce's Certified Administrator program that has been developed by Salesforce for the assessment of individuals who have Salesforce CRM administration knowledge and experience. The Certified Administrator program covers the applications that form the core elements of Salesforce CRM and includes system management and the configuration options that are available to a Salesforce CRM administrator within the Sales Cloud, the Service Cloud, and the Collaboration Cloud.

The Salesforce Certified Administrator exam is used to measure individual's ability to manage and maintain a Salesforce CRM organization. Individuals that pass the exam can be considered proficient in applying the features and functionality for configuration and system management as well as extending their knowledge and accessing advanced learning paths within the Certified Administrator program.

In this chapter, we outline the various resources that are available to study for the Salesforce Certified Administrator exam. Here we review the Salesforce Certified Administrator Study Guide and discuss both, official Salesforce and other third-party resources that will help you understand the features and functionalities that are to be found in the exam. We also look at the process of planning, booking, and sitting the exam, and offer some insight into the types of questions that may appear and offer some suggestions to deal with the questions during the exam.

The following topics will be covered in this chapter:

- Overview of the Salesforce Certified Administrator exam
- Self-assessment of your Salesforce CRM skills and knowledge
- Suggested resources for studying
- Using the Salesforce Certified Administrator study guide
- Registering for the Salesforce Certified Administrator exam
- What to expect during and after the exam

Overview of the Salesforce Certified Administrator exam

The Salesforce Certified Administrator exam consists of 60 multiple-choice (or single-choice) questions and the maximum time allowed is 90 minutes. There is no mandatory prerequisite qualification or experience; however, Salesforce highly recommends that candidates have some real-world experience administering an organization or attend a suitable training course prior to sitting the exam, details of which are covered later in this chapter.

The pass mark for the Salesforce Certified Administrator exam is currently 39 correct answers out of the available 60, which is specified as a percentage passing score of 65%. At the time of writing, the cost of registering for the exam is $200 USD and the cost of registering to re-sit the exam is $100 USD.

During the exam, no written or online resource may be referenced and when you submit the exam you are presented with your exam result immediately. The result is either a pass or fail; there is neither an indication of the number of correct or incorrect answers, nor is there any response that explains the reason for the correct or incorrect answers.

Some people have opined on social networking sites that the questions they were presented with during their Salesforce Certified Administrator exam made for a far more difficult examination than anything they had previously sat and for one individual they felt it was more difficult than their bachelor's degree or their MBA.

People often cite the reason for the difficulty of the exam is that the way in which the multiple-choice questions are worded means that there are one or two word differences between the available choice of answer. This then suggests that the question may be subjective, which presents a challenge when choosing the expected answer.

Later in this chapter, there is an indication of how these potentially subjective questions could be presented and some suggested strategies that may help to derive the correct answer.

Once you have passed the Salesforce Certified Administrator exam, there is a maintenance exam which is a requirement to remain in, Salesforce Certified Administrator program. This is mandatory for all Salesforce Certified individuals to keep their knowledge current as Salesforce releases updates to the Salesforce CRM platform.

 At the time of writing, the cost of registering for the annual maintenance fee for the Salesforce Certified Administrator exam is $100 USD.

Self-assessment

Before considering taking the Salesforce Certified Administrator exam, it is useful to try to gauge just how much knowledge and experience you have in Salesforce CRM administration. Since the exam is part of the Salesforce Certified Administrator program, which exists to assess an individual's ability to implement Salesforce CRM administration, the purpose of the exam is to assess the skills and ensure candidates have the correct level of knowledge in the following features or functions:

- Standard and Custom Objects
- Security and Access
- Analytics, Reports, and Dashboards
- Data Management
- User Setup
- Sales and Marketing Applications
- Workflow Automation
- Service and Support Applications
- Activity Management
- AppExchange
- Desktop and Mobile Administration
- Content and Folder Management
- Chatter

- Global User Interface
- Organization Setup

The features and functions that are listed are taken from the Salesforce Certified Administrator exam Study Guide and will be covered in detail later in this chapter. You should review the features and functions that are listed here and try to give higher or lesser importance accordingly. This means that the number of questions that may be posed will vary in line with the percentages. You should review the features and functions that are listed in this section to help assess what areas your strengths and weaknesses lie in and allow you to plan your studying accordingly.

By going through the list, you can assess how much of the subject area you currently know and which areas you may need to study more. Even seasoned Salesforce professionals may not have experience in all of the areas that are likely to be covered in the exam, so there will generally be some need to study the areas of weakness.

For example, there could be as high as 11 questions, (or 18% exam coverage), in the exam covering standard and custom objects or as few as one question, (or 2% exam coverage) for **Chatter**. Given these numbers, it does seem prudent to focus more of your time available for study on the features and functions of the chapters that carry the largest number of questions.

Resources for studying

There are many resources available to help the process of studying for the Salesforce Certified Administrator exam. The resources that will be outlined in this section include official Salesforce resources and third-party resources that have been provided by the wider Salesforce community. There are resources that require some level of payment and some that are free for both the official and third-party resources.

If you are fortunate to be currently working with the Salesforce CRM platform for a Salesforce customer or partner and have system administrator permission, then you should be able to gain valuable on-the-job experience and will be able to gain much of the knowledge of the features and functionality whilst carrying out your day job.

For individuals that may not currently be full-time system administrators in their company, but work for organizations with a training budget and a desire to train them in the role of Salesforce administrator, these individuals can take advantage of the instructor-led training courses that are produced by Salesforce. Also, individuals who are able to pay for their own training can attend these official instructor-led Salesforce training courses.

Salesforce recommends carrying out on-the-job experience, attending training course(s), and self-study to help improve an individual's chances of passing the Salesforce Certified Administrator exam.

Official Salesforce resources

The official Salesforce resources for training and studying for the Certified Administrator exam are:

- Instructor-led and Online Certified Administrator training courses
- Premier Support Online Courses
- Salesforce Developer Edition
- Trailhead
- Official online and social networking channels
- The Salesforce Certified Administrator Study Guide

Instructor-led and Online Certified Administrator training courses

Some people find it easier to learn in a classroom-based environment where they are guided through an agenda of Salesforce CRM administration.

In this type of class, students are able to carry out practical tasks while under the supervision of a skilled training professional with Salesforce certification skills. Students can ask various questions to help gain better understanding and knowledge of administration and configuration of the Salesforce CRM features and functionality.

The following instructor-led training courses are available from Salesforce or an authorized training center:

- Administration Essentials for New Admins (ADM-201) 5 days course
- Administration Essentials for New Admins plus Certification (ADM-201C) 5 day course
- Administration Essentials for Experienced Admins (ADM211) 4 day course
- Certification Preparation for Administrator (CRT101) 1 day course

Salesforce offers these courses in two delivery formats, namely conventional classroom-based and virtual classroom enabled.

To find out more information about the instructor-led training courses navigate to: https://www.salesforce.com/services/cloud-services/training/

At the time of writing, the cost for the course, Administration Essentials for New Admins (ADM-201), is $4,500 USD.

Premier Support Online Courses

If your company has subscribed to Premier Support you are entitled to various training courses that are included with your subscription. These courses are provided online and are accessed by typing Premier Toolkit in the Salesforce Help and Training search page within the Salesforce CRM application.

The Premier Support online courses can be very useful for learning about the features and functionality of Salesforce CRM in general. There is one course in particular that has been designed by Salesforce to provide certification preparation and guidance toward the Certified Salesforce Administrator exam and is called Preparing for Your Salesforce Administrator Certification.

Salesforce Developer Edition

It can be assumed that if you have read this far into this book, you have already signed up or have access to a Salesforce instance. If you have been using your company's organization either within the production instance or a sandbox, it may be wise to sign up for your own developer organization.

To sign up for a free Developer Edition Salesforce CRM organization navigate to: https://developer.salesforce.com/signup

You may think that having a developer organization is only needed by developers and not system administrators, but the environment is intended for use by both disciplines.

It is particularly beneficial to set up a developer organization by using a personal e-mail address; this allows you to try out changes and switch on or off functionality without affecting others in your company organization, even if you are no longer associated with the company that you were working with, to keep the changes and access the organization.

Trailhead

Trailhead is a free interactive online learning tool developed and supported by Salesforce that provides useful training resources for administrators and developers at various levels of experience.

The Salesforce Administrator training content in Trailhead is arranged into trails, modules, and units, which can be used to help guide you through the features and function of Salesforce administration and configuration.

Trailhead offers the following set of self-paced training courses, which are delivered online and permits a training experience where you can learn on demand. Here, you can select the features and functionality that will assist in preparing for the Salesforce Certified Administrator exam.

 To access the Trailhead interactivive learning and challenges navigate to: h ttps://trailhead.salesforce.com/

Trailhead also allows you to gain award points and badges that show that you have applied the Trailhead modules to the salesforce instance and have been successful in the completion of the Salesforce Administration units and modules. The badges that have been achieved during the course of a trail can be displayed on your user profile, so you are recognized for your experience and achievements.

Official online and social networking channels

Salesforce has a number of official online and social networking channels that provide videos, files, forums, and guidance for individuals looking for resources to help them study for the Salesforce Certified Administrator exam. These online and social networking channels can be found on YouTube, Twitter, LinkedIn, and the Salesforce Success Community.

The Salesforce YouTube channel contains videos of various Salesforce features and functionality that are very useful for training Salesforce professionals at all levels of knowledge and experience.

 To access the Salesforce YouTube channel navigate to the following URL: h ttps://www.youtube.com/user/salesforce

Third-party resources

There are a number of resources that are not endorsed by Salesforce that may be useful. A word of caution though; they are not sanctioned or endorsed by Salesforce and you need to be very careful when using these types of material.

 It is essential that you carry out due diligence to ensure that the information is accurate and that the facts shown are valid for the current version of the Salesforce CRM platform.

The following types of resources are not official Salesforce resources and are not endorsed by Salesforce but may or may not be useful to help identify further information that helps with the studying of the Salesforce Certified Administrator exam:

- Salesforce study groups
- Blogs
- Forums
- Online tests
- Flash cards

Be wary of third-party resources that are presenting questions and answers as they are often outdated, no longer valid, or in some cases, completely incorrect and misleading. For the online tests and flash cards, verify first that they are correct for the current release of Salesforce CRM.

It is suggested not to use them without carrying out some due diligence to ensure the questions that are presented are accurate.

The Salesforce Certified Administrator Study Guide

Salesforce provides a study guide for the Certified Administrator exam and some guidelines on what material to be familiar with.

The study guide is useful as it outlines the features and functions that a candidate with hands-on experience would have demonstrated the application of. It also shows the weighting of the features and functions that are applied to the Salesforce Certified Administrator exam. By looking at the weighting, it is possible to determine the approximate number of questions that appear and help you to study the highest areas.

It is highly likely that even the most seasoned Salesforce professional will not have applied some of the features and functions that are tested, so you will need to appraise yourself in this area to see where you may need to study more.

 At the time of writing, the link to access the details for the Salesforce Certified Administrator exam is located at: `http://certification.sales force.com/administrator`

Using the Salesforce Certified Administrator Study Guide

The following table outlines the features or functions, ordered by weighting, that can be found in the exam, and some chapter reference sources in this book that may be useful:

Number	Feature or Function	Chapter Reference	Exam Weighting %	Approx. calculated number of questions in exam
1	Standard and Custom Objects	Chapter 3 *Configuring Objects and Apps*	18%	11
2	Security and Access	Chapter 4 *Securing Access to Data and Data Validation*	15%	9
3	Analytics, Reports and Dashboards	Chapter 6 *Generating Data Analytics with Reports and Dashboards*	13%	8
4	Data Management	Chapter 5 *Managing Data in Salesforce CRM*	11%	7
5	User Setup	Chapter 2 *Managing Users and Controlling System Access*	9%	5

6	Sales and Marketing Applications	Chapter 8 *Introducing Sales Cloud, Service Cloud, and the Collaborative Features of Salesforce CRM*	9%	5
7	Workflow Automation	Chapter 7 *Implementing Business Processes in Salesforce CRM*	7%	4
8	Service and Support Applications	Chapter 8 *Introducing Sales Cloud, Service Cloud, and the Collaborative Features of Salesforce CRM*	6%	4
9	Activity Management	Chapter 8 *Introducing Sales Cloud, Service Cloud, and the Collaborative Features of Salesforce CRM*	3%	2
10	AppExchange	Chapter 9 *Extending and Enhancing Salesforce CRM*	2%	1
11	Desktop and Mobile Administration	Chapter 10 *Administrating the Mobile Features of Salesforce CRM*	2%	1
12	Content and Folder Management	Chapter 8 *Introducing Sales Cloud, Service Cloud, and the Collaborative Features of Salesforce CRM*	2%	1
13	Chatter	Chapter 8 *Introducing Sales Cloud, Service Cloud, and the Collaborative Features of Salesforce CRM*	1%	1
14	Global User Interface	Chapter 1 *Setting up Salesforce CRM and the Company Profile*	1%	1
15	Organization Setup	Chapter 1 *Setting up Salesforce CRM and the Company Profile*	1%	1

The following set of questions are retrieved from the sample questions that have been presented by Salesforce in the Certified Administrator exam Study Guide.

There are five questions in total with which we review the answers that were provided by Salesforce:

1. What should a system administrator use to disable access to a custom application for a group of users? Choose one answer:

a) Profiles

b) Sharing rules

c) Web tabs

d) Page layouts

2. Universal Containers needs to track the manufacturer and model for specific car companies.How can the system administrator ensure that the manufacturer selected influences the values available for the model? Choose one answer:

a) Create the manufacturer field as a dependent picklist and the model as a controlling picklist.

b) Create a lookup field from the manufacturer object to the model object.

c) Create the manufacturer field as a controlling picklist and the model as a dependent picklist.

d) Create a multi-select picklist field that includes both manufacturers and models.

3. Sales representatives at Universal Containers need assistance from product managers when selling certain products. Product managers do not have access to opportunities, but need to gain access when they are assisting with a specific deal. How can a system administrator accomplish this? Choose one answer:

a) Notify the product manager using opportunity update reminders.

b) Enable opportunity teams and allow users to add the product manager.

c) Use similar opportunities to show opportunities related to the product manager.

d) Enable account teams and allow users to add the product manager.

4. What should a system administrator consider before importing a set of records into Salesforce? Choose two answers:

a) The import file should include a record owner for each record.

b) Currency field values will default to the personal currency of the record owner.

c) Data should be de-duplicated in the import file prior to import.

d) Validation rules are not triggered when importing data using the import wizard.

5. Which statement about custom summary formulas in reports is true? Choose two answers:

a) Reports can be grouped by a custom summary formula result.

b) Custom summary formulas can reference a formula field within a report.

c) Custom summary formulas can reference another custom summary formula.

d) Custom summary formulas can be used in a report built from a custom report type.

Answers to the questions:

1. **a**

2. **c**

3. **b**

4. **a, c**

5. **b, d**

We will now review the first example question that has been provided by Salesforce and look at how we can breakdown and analyze the information that is contained in the question in order to derive the correct answer.

By analyzing the question we can identify what business requirements are covered in the scenario that is presented and then work out which feature or functionality of Salesforce administration could be used to satisfy these requirements.

We can then step through each of the answers and either look further into the details of the answer to see if it is related to the feature of functionality needed to fulfill the requirements or discard it as a possible answer if it is unable to meet the requirements.

Question 1 – Analysis

The sample question that was provided by Salesforce is "What should a system administrator use to disable access to a custom application for a group of users?".

We were asked to choose one answer from the following:

a) Profiles

b) Sharing rules

c) Web tabs

d) Page layouts

Analyzing the question

The requirement is to disable access to a custom application for a group of users, so we can deduce that the following feature or functionality is being tested:

- Custom App
- Grouping of users

Reviewing the answers

Let's look at the choice of answers to see what is relevant to the features above and able to control access to a custom App for a group of users. By stepping through each of the given answers we can identify whether each answer has a feature that is able to meet the requirements.

The following table is used to show the analysis that we can carry out and see which of the answers provide a feature to meet the requirements of the question:

	Answers			
	a) Profiles	**b)** Sharing rules	**c)** Web tabs	**d)** Page layouts
Answer detail	Profiles are a control mechanism used to determine the functions the user can perform	Sharing rules are used to extend access to records	Web Tabs are user-interface elements that when clicked on invoke a URL	Page layouts are used to organize the display of fields, button, custom links etc.
Chapter Reference	Chapter 2: *Managing Users and Controlling System access*	Chapter 4: *Securing Access to Data and Data Validation*	Chapter 3: *Configuring Objects and Apps*	Chapter 3: *Configuring Objects and Apps*
Able to manage a group of users?	Yes	No	No	No.
Able to control custom Apps?	Yes	No	No	No

Conclusion

We can see that a) Profiles is the correct answer.

Profiles are a control mechanism used to determine the functions the user can perform. A group of users can be set with a common profile and within this profile access to a custom application can be disabled therefore this answer contains the correct feature that meets the requirement as outlined in the scenario for the question.

Registering for the Salesforce Certified Administrator exam

Before you can register for the Salesforce Certified Administrator exam, you will need to register your details with Webassessor.

 To access the Salesforce Webassessor exam registration page navigate to: h ttps://www.webassessor.com/salesforce

Once you have registered and created an account, you can register for a new exam with the same link.

 When booking the Salesforce Certified Administrator exam, you will notice that there is a version of the exam, for example, WI18 (winter'18), SP19 (spring'19), SU19 (summer '19).

When you book the exam, you have the choice to take the exam at a testing center or use online proctoring, which allows you to sit the exam remotely from your own computer.

Online proctored exams are delivered through secure software, which allows the exam to be monitored through a webcam.

If you opt for the testing center you will first select a test center and then you will be presented with a calendar showing available dates in which you can select a suitable date and time.

Rescheduling the exam

If you are unable to take the test at the date and time that was scheduled, or you feel that you are not ready to take it, you must reschedule the exam with at least 72 hour's notice or you will be charged a reschedule fee.

You will notice that the booked exam shows a version of the exam, for example, WI18 (winter '18), SP19 (spring '19), SU19 (summer '19). If you book your exam in an earlier period, but take your after rescheduling the exam, the exam will automatically be set to the latest version. For example, you register for the exam during SU17 (summer '17), but reschedule after, say, around November, which takes your exam to fall into the WI18 (winter '18) exam period.

What to expect during and after the exam

You need to arrive 15 minutes prior to the examination and will not be able to sit the exam if you are late. Do not bring too much baggage into the testing center as you only have a small locker in which to store all your personal belongings.

You will need to take two forms of identifying details, which can be your passport and driving license. In addition, you need to either print the e-mail that you received when you registered for the exam, or show the test code to the examination room proctor as they will need the code to start the exam. Alternatively, show the exam proctor the code on your smartphone.

During the exam

You are provided with a couple of sheets of paper or a clean wipe sheet and dry wipe pens, which you can use to make notes. It is worth reading the questions slowly as it is quite easy to make a snap judgement. In certain situations you may find it helpful to write notes on the written materials just to clarify your understanding of the question.

Also, you may find that a question that you are currently answering has provided a clue for a question you encountered earlier in the exam that you did not know and so is currently set as Marked for Review.

Do not panic if you find yourself spending too long on one question and you are unable to proceed either because of the complexity of the exam question or you do not know with total confidence. Mark the question for review and then come back to it later.

Be mindful of the 90-minute time limit. The remaining time is shown in the upper-left hand of the screen.

You can review the questions that have been marked for review by clicking **Review Exam.** The screen shows the questions that have been marked for review marked with an asterisk.

After the exam

As soon as you click the **Finish exam** button, you will be notified on-screen whether you have passed or failed. If you have passed, you will receive an e-mail confirming the pass.

It may take a short time for the confirmation e-mail showing your result to be received. I personally sat the exam at 10:30 in the morning and did not get the result until later that evening. In this scenario, by logging into the Webassessor login after the exam I was able to see my result.

You can show that you have successfully gained the Salesforce Certified Administration credential by agreeing to show your details via the Webassessor site. When this is done, people can navigate to the certification verification page and search and select your name to display the types of certification that you hold.

 To access the certification verification page navigate to: `http://certifica tion.salesforce.com/verification`

Summary

In this, the final chapter of *Salesforce CRM: The Definitive Admin Handbook*, we have looked at the various resources that are available to study for the Salesforce Certified Administrator exam.

We have reviewed the Salesforce Certified Administrator Study Guide and discussed both, official Salesforce and other third-party resources that will help you understand the features and functionalities to be found in the exam.

We have also outlined the process of planning, booking, and sitting the exam and have offered some insight into the types of questions that may appear and offered some suggestions to deal with the questions during the exam.

Finally, we looked at what happens after the exam and the next steps that are available for a Salesforce Certified Administrator.

Index